I0188101

WALTER BYERS AND THE NCAA

WALTER BYERS *and the* NCAA

Power, Amateurism, and Growing Controversy in Big-Time College Sport

RONALD A. SMITH

Sport and Popular Culture
Brian M. Ingrassia, *Series Editor*

The University of Tennessee Press
Knoxville

The Sport and Popular Culture series is designed to promote critical, innovative research in the history of sport through a wide spectrum of works—monographs, edited volumes, biographies, and reprints of classics.

FIRST EDITION.

Library of Congress Cataloging-in-Publication Data
Names: Smith, Ronald A. (Ronald Austin), 1936- author
Title: Walter Byers and the NCAA : power, amateurism, and growing controversy in big-time college sport / Ronald A. Smith.
Description: Knoxville : The University of Tennessee Press, 2025. | Series: Sports and popular culture | Includes bibliographical references and index. | Summary: "Walter Byers long played a role in college athletics, initially with the Big Ten Conference and then as the first executive director of the NCAA. This new study examines Byers's term as executive director, from 1951–1988, a time when collegiate sports, especially football, saw a rise both in popularity and in coaching and administrative salaries. But Byers held fast to the ideals of amateurism upon which the NCAA was originally founded. Historian Ron Smith explores the duality of a rapidly growing NCAA in a collegiate context previously defined by the student-athlete and an ethos of amateurism. Smith focuses on Byers's guidance of major cultural shifts in the NCAA during his tenure, including the long integration of collegiate sports, the passage of Title IX, which saw women's sports placed, at least legislatively, on an equal playing field with men's athletics, and the development of major television deals for NCAA sports, especially football and basketball. All in all, Smith's study of Walter Byers and his leadership of the NCAA sheds light on a tumultuous time in the organization's history and presents arguments against an amateurism that is still present despite recent NIL rights and the reclassification of the student-athlete" —Provided by publisher.
Identifiers: LCCN 2024054312 (print) | LCCN 2024054313 (ebook) | ISBN 9781621909491 hardcover | IISBN 9781621909507 kindle edition | ISBN 9781621909514 adobe pdf
Subjects: LCSH: Byers, Walter, 1922–2015 | National Collegiate Athletic Association—History. | College sports—United States—History. | College athletes—United States—History.
Classification: LCC GV351 .S623 2025 (print) | LCC GV351 (ebook) | DDC 796.04/3092 [B]—dc23/eng/20250326
LC record available at https://lccn.loc.gov/2024054312
LC ebook record available at https://lccn.loc.gov/2024054313

To the scores of archivists who have provided their expertise over the years and particularly Ursula Walsh of the NCAA who opened the Walter Byers Papers for many weeks of research.

— RONALD A. SMITH

CONTENTS

FOREWORD

A new twelve-team college football playoff debuted in December 2024, with traditional powerhouses Notre Dame, Ohio State, Penn State, and Texas making it to the semifinals. In the leadup to the big games, some social media pundits asked whether this new format was primarily about making money off the backs of college athletes. But was there ever any doubt? Of course the games were largely about profits. Big-time intercollegiate sports, especially football and men's basketball, have long been more about making money than about high-minded ideals (or shibboleths) regarding education, amateurism, and morality. American society desires bread and circuses—or at least light beers and kickoff returns—and so we clamor for more games. The pigskin ritual is one way to decide which universities field the best gridiron teams, but it is also a way to profit from spectators' enjoyment of students' athletic performances.

In *Walter Byers and the NCAA*, renowned historian Ronald A. Smith explores the dramatic transformation of the National Collegiate Athletic Association (NCAA) throughout the twentieth century, especially during the years of Walter Byers's leadership. As many readers already know, a group of concerned college leaders founded the earliest incarnation of the NCAA in New York City in late 1905 and early 1906 as a way to address and redress scandals associated with college football. Initially, the association was no regulatory body, just an advisory one. But that changed after World War II. At the same time the NCAA struggled to enforce its so-called Sanity Code, which attempted to ban all but tuition compensation for athletes. It also took control of the vast profits to be made from television. TV was then an innovative technology that promised to beam entertainment, including sporting events, directly into millions of living rooms throughout America and beyond. Soon, the NCAA crafted a media policy that placed itself in charge of televised college sports, and even threatened to expel members who went rogue by signing their own media contracts. Not long after that, it created and disseminated a legal neologism for all college students playing under NCAA auspices: "student-athletes." As Smith rightly points out—and as every fan of American intercollegiate athletics should know—that now-ubiquitous term was created for the primary purpose of denying worker-compensation claims to college students injured or killed while exerting athletic labor on behalf of institutions of higher education.

In this book, we learn just how instrumental Walter Byers was in creating the modern NCAA. Byers was born in Kansas City in 1922 and was hired as the association's first executive director in 1951, at age twenty-nine, after having served for several years as special assistant to Big Ten commissioner Tug Wilson. Byers already had experience with media rights, and by the 1970s he had become ruthless in his quest to demand the best TV deals. Indeed, during that decade the NCAA made millions per year from the men's basketball tournament, a televised, springtime quasi-holiday that we now affectionately refer to as "March Madness." It may seem perverse that an organization loudly proclaiming amateurism for college athletes has made billions from intercollegiate sport—while at the same time enabling big-time coaches and athletic departments to make their own millions. Yet the contradiction makes sense when we understand the paradox that was Walter Byers. The NCAA executive was an enigma: a decent athlete who nevertheless became one of the most influential figures in American sport; a family man who had difficulty sustaining positive relations with his own family members; and a fierce defender of amateurism who changed his tune within just a few years of his 1987 retirement. In his memoir, *Unsportsmanlike Conduct: Exploiting College Athletes*, published by the University of Michigan Press in 1995, Byers criticized the association he had led for so long, calling it a monopoly that unfairly limited college students' athletic earnings.

The NCAA, now based in Indianapolis after many years in Kansas City, is a powerful institution that holds in reserve significant resources to curate its own image as a near-benevolent organization that regulates collegiate sports competition while also promoting the education of thousands of collegiate athletes. But there is a more complex story to be told, and Smith is not afraid to tell it. I have said this before, and I will say it again here: No one knows more about the history of American intercollegiate athletics than Ron Smith. Since his retirement from Penn State, Smith has published more than a half-dozen books on the subject, plus scores of articles and reviews. If a university in the United States has a significant athletic program, there is a good chance that he has researched in its archives. Smith has read and analyzed reams of NCAA annual reports, and in recent years he has served as an expert witness in federal court cases, including *NCAA v. Alston* (2021), for which he wrote an award-winning amicus curiae brief.

When Ron Smith writes about the history of intercollegiate athletics, we listen.

Although this book might seem like a biography of Walter Byers, it is better characterized as an account of the NCAA during the years when Byers served as executive director. This era was a time when the association worked harder than ever to reconcile tensions between amateurism and professionalism at the very moment when intercollegiate football and basketball were growing in popularity and marketability. Byers was successful, to a point, but things started changing in the late twentieth century. One major challenge to the NCAA's seeming ironclad hold over intercollegiate athletics came with the rise of the College Football Association (CFA) in the 1970s, and a resulting US Supreme Court ruling, *NCAA v. Board of Regents of the University of Oklahoma* (1984). The CFA was a group of big-time universities that hoped to circumvent NCAA hegemony, especially in televising the games of well-known programs. Although NCAA attorneys claimed the association did not hold "market power"—the ability to profit by selling a distinctive product—a majority of Supreme Court justices disagreed. College sports were profitable, and therefore the NCAA was not immune from antitrust laws that have regulated marketplace competition since the late nineteenth century. It has now been more than forty years since that 1984 court case, but in recent years observers have begun to witness the vast legal ramifications of the high court's Reagan-era antitrust ruling. Cases regarding the ability of college athletes to profit from NIL (name, image, and likeness) are another step in a long erosion of NCAA power over athletic revenues, a power that dates to the Byers era.

Smith can help us understand Walter Byers's influence while also prompting us to ponder a difficult yet important question: Is our own society in the midst of witnessing a Byers-like about-face? Are we now arriving at the conclusion that it simply does not make sense *not* to pay college athletes for the labor they provide to entertain a sports-obsessed society? Smith's incisive and thought-provoking analysis of Byers's career in relation to the broad sweep of the twentieth-century NCAA helps us understand the quickly changing landscape of intercollegiate athletics. As we see in this book, the NCAA has grown into a de facto governing body for college sports. But with seismic changes shattering ideas about amateurism, will the NCAA remain the powerful force into which Byers transformed it from the 1950s to the 1980s? And if not, who might be the next Walter Byers—the person who takes advantage of new and profitable media in order to shape legal and economic structures in relation to college athletics?

No historian dares predict the future, but with insights from Ronald A. Smith's perceptive and thought-provoking scholarship, we have a tremendous starting point for understanding intercollegiate athletics in the forthcoming years and decades. Let us listen to the story.

BRIAN M. INGRASSIA
West Texas A&M

OVERTURE

As a young kid growing up on a Wisconsin dairy farm, I was given a choice of either getting up at 5:30 each morning to help my two older brothers milk the cows or practicing the piano for an hour. My brothers chose the barn—I chose the piano. When I finished practicing, I could shoot baskets on the plank wood barn floor or pitch off the wall of cement-block milk house. I just didn't want to milk the cows.

In practicing both the piano and sport skills, I was intent on being successful. That intensity followed me throughout a lifetime, or maybe I just did not want to milk cows. Either way, later in life I transferred my focus from piano or ball skills to delving into university archives looking for clues to the history of intercollegiate athletics. I have spent hour after hour in the National Collegiate Athletic Association headquarters searching its Walter Byers papers, along with papers in numerous other university archives. I never met Walter Byers, but I read his insightful book *Unsportsmanlike Conduct: Exploiting College Athletes* in manuscript form just prior to its publication by the University of Michigan Press.

I retained a copy of a letter that I wrote to Walter Byers in early 1995. I quote it to indicate my interest in Byers, his manuscript, and his influence before I retired from Penn State:

> Dear Mr. Byers: It was good to talk with you last night about your manuscript and the place of athletics in higher education. I indicated that I have found an articulate letter from the president of the University of Iowa, Virgil Hancher, on the question of grants-in-aid. I enclose excerpts from that letter. I know little about Hancher, except he was the Iowa

> president when I was attending Northwestern University in the mid-1950s. I majored in history and played baseball on one of NU's few Big 10 championship teams in 1957 and was on the basketball team. The closest I came to greatness in basketball was watching Wilt Chamberlain play in a freshman game at Kansas and thinking that it was fortunate for NU that he was not on the varsity. I did not get a chance to see his convertible or whatever as you note in your manuscript. I did see a great player, even as a freshman. I think that he had a "full ride" and more. Hancher would have agreed with the "full ride" if not the "more."
>
> I look forward to seeing your manuscript in print. I will use it in a course I teach, the history of athletics in higher education. The course includes at the present time, two lengthy books and over 100 articles, mostly primary sources dating back to colonial time. I expect a lengthy term paper based on primary sources also. I guess you would say that it is not a "jock" course. The non-serious students generally drop it after the first day when they get a 6-page list of readings and a 7-page guide to term papers.
>
> I, too, am in favor of raising standards, but I don't think presidents will be the source of real standards raising. Sincerely, Ronald A. Smith, Professor.

I still admire Walter Byers's administrative abilities, but I now better understand his warts and those of the National Collegiate Athletic Association.

PREFACE

Amateur Athletes, Byers, and the NCAA

The role that Walter Byers played in the development of the National Collegiate Athletic Association (NCAA) in his years as executive director (1951–1987) has not been adequately examined. I have collected a vast amount of material on both Byers and the NCAA in my more than a half-century of researching and writing about the history of intercollegiate athletics. My background has been helpful in uncovering the problems the NCAA faced in the period after World War II and the ways its primary leader dealt with those challenges. First, I majored in history while playing both varsity baseball and basketball at Northwestern University in the 1950s. During my undergraduate days, I was paid to play baseball in a summer league, the Basin League, conducted for those who had professional baseball potential. After I completed my undergraduate degree, I and six of my baseball teammates signed professional baseball contracts. Three of us made the Major League. I was not one of them. I noted little difference as an athlete between so-called amateur baseball in college and professional baseball in the Chicago White Sox system. I was paid minimally in both venues. The NCAA and Byers, on the other hand, claimed college sport to be amateur, though nearly all the big-time universities were compensating their athletes to attend school and participate in the major sports. I paid little attention as I went on to get a master's degree in history at the University of Wisconsin, teach history, and coach baseball in a Wisconsin high school.

I had almost forgotten my experience of nearly being denied the opportunity to play football my senior year in high school because I was playing on a town team in a baseball tournament at the end of the season while simultaneously participating in pre-season football practice. That was not allowed by the Wisconsin Interscholastic Athletic Association as part of its amateur rules. That may have tainted my views of amateurism some years later when the Amateur Athletic Union of Wisconsin banned me from participating in the "amateur" AAU basketball tournament in my first year as a teacher and coach. Because I coached a junior high school basketball team, I was considered a professional. I was beginning to see the hypocrisy of amateur sports in America. Amateurism was something that Walter Byers and the NCAA attempted to uphold at the college level. Only after he retired from the NCAA in the 1980s did Byers do an about-face and call amateur sport what it really was: phony and deceitful.

Early on, I did not see that coaches, athletic departments, and universities benefited by calling college athletics "amateur." I benefited from receiving a scholarship to attend Northwestern based on my strong academic record in high school, but the academic scholarship I received was influenced by my recruitment as an athlete by a Northwestern trustee and the athletic department. In my years as an undergraduate history major, I knew almost nothing about the history of intercollegiate athletics and may never have encountered the name Walter Byers. This changed during my doctoral studies at the University of Wisconsin at Madison—I began to investigate the history of intercollegiate athletics, particularly how athletics were administered. My interest persisted when I became a faculty member at Penn State University, and I continued researching at numerous university archives and the NCAA. Since retirement, I have written six books on intercollegiate athletics in addition to this one. The actions of Byers and the NCAA have intrigued me for most of my academic life, and I was one of the first to devote scholarly attention to the subject. Both the NCAA and Byers are worthy of study.

One could argue that the four most important years in the NCAA's history were 1905–1906, 1948–49, 1978–79, and 2021–22. Walter Byers was involved directly in only one of these four periods. He was not born in 1905 and was only an assistant to Kenneth "Tug" Wilson, Big Ten commissioner and secretary-treasurer of the NCAA, in 1948–49. Byers was a generation into his position as executive director of the NCAA in 1978–79. He had been dead for six years by 2021–22. Yet these four eras, spanning more than a century, reveal the inheritance and legacy as well as the dynamics of Walter Byers's thirty-six years as leader of the most important institution in college sports. They also reveal an important trait of the NCAA for its entire history—the promotion of "amateur" sport without the administrative participation of athletes.

The principal purpose of the NCAA before, during, and after Byers's reign was to accommodate and promote the interests of athletics in institutions of higher learning. In practice, this often meant the control of athletes. One can conclude that the NCAA was not created or developed for the benefit of athletes but, rather, for the benefit of the institutions for which they played as well as the organization itself.

This was true well before Walter Byers was born. The year the NCAA was created, 1905–1906, followed decades in which male athletes in America first created intercollegiate athletics. Soon after, the alumni of individual institutions became the dominant force in the direction taken by college athletics. Athletically talented students created a variety of prominent sports: crew, baseball, football, and track and field. Students financially supported their favored teams, with alumni often coming to their aid when they faced debt or losing seasons. Faculty and presidents became concerned when interest in the extra-curriculum, especially football, began to dominate the curriculum. The 1905 crisis of ethics, brutality, and death in football brought about both a regional and a national conference to reform the sport.[1] The NCAA was born in 1905 to challenge athlete and alumni control, and to bring men's athletics under institutional restraints.

A half-century later, with individual institutions and conferences generally managing collegiate athletics on a local or regional level, the NCAA decided to add a mechanism for national control. Beginning in 1948, the NCAA allowed the payment of athletes with tuition waivers through a system called the "Sanity Code."[2] Soon after, the NCAA had discussions about the control of the telecasting of football contests to preserve gate receipts. Thus, when Walter Byers became the first NCAA executive director, his lengthy tenure commenced just as the NCAA began to attract money by controlling the contracts for telecasting football. The other important financial draw for the NCAA was the early success of the NCAA basketball tournament, eventually known as March Madness. Financial support was needed to oversee the enforcement of rules, principally regarding the recruiting and payment of athletes in the NCAA's two primary commercial sports, football and men's basketball. The NCAA implemented this supervision to "level the playing field" for competitive equity and, more importantly, to try to keep college athletes "amateur."

In 1978, a generation after Byers became executive director, the NCAA won a major victory over the Amateur Athletic Union (AAU), the long-dominant amateur sport organization. With the passage of the national Amateur Sports Act of 1978, the NCAA prevailed in its century-long fight against this organization.[3] The AAU lost control of amateur athletics, and the NCAA extended its influence on amateur sport at the national level. However, the NCAA was besieged with legal concerns, particularly after the publication of the *Yale Law Review* article charging the NCAA with price fixing and violations of antitrust laws.[4] At the same time, Congress held hearings on the lack of due process in the NCAA's enforcement policies, including specifically the treatment of Jerry Tarkanian, basketball coach at the University of Nevada-Las Vegas. In addition, two major college organizations, the College Football Association (CFA) and the Association for Intercollegiate Athletics for Women (AIAW), challenged the NCAA over its policies. Made up of about sixty big-time football powers, the CFA contested the NCAA's television policy as monopolistic, while the AIAW railed against the NCAA for its policies regarding championship competition for women.

Legal protections for athletes only became important to the NCAA after the organization's defeat in the 2015 Ed O'Bannon case, which found that the NCAA violated control of athletes' rights to their own images and likenesses in electronic games. The NCAA, with financial reserves approaching a billion dollars, was content to settle out of court, benefiting a few athletes financially but holding the NCAA legally blameless. Only after Byers retired did he conclude that he no longer felt the need to protect the NCAA's interests over the rights of athletes individually and collectively. In 2021, six years after Walter Byers died, the NCAA lost decisively in the US Supreme Court, with a 9-0 decision in the *NCAA v. Shawne Alston* case. This decision effectively destroyed the changing NCAA concept of amateurism. The Supreme Court ruling provided the possibility that athletes, like other college students, could profit from their talents, including those derived from their names, images, and likenesses. Other court cases followed, including the *Robert Geathers v. NCAA* lawsuit in South Carolina, which argued that the health of athletes was never a major concern for the NCAA.[5] Far more important were financial and legal protections for institutions, conferences, and especially the NCAA itself.

Years after Byers's death and decades after he ruled over the NCAA, his influence on college athletics is still felt. The consequences of actions taken during the Byers era are evident well into the twenty-first century. These include the diminished emphasis on amateurism; the lack of academic standards for athletes; the increased role of women in national championships; the dominating role of African Americans in the major sports; the question of playoffs in college football; and the leading role of television in financing institutions, conferences, and the national organization. One important facet of college sport is the increased role of state and federal legislatures and lawsuits confronting the NCAA since Walter Byers first became executive director in 1951. While most of the problems experienced by NCAA officials in the Byers era still exist, an expanded role for athletes in determining NCAA policy has emerged, often forced upon athletic administrators, college presidents, and the NCAA by legislators and the legal system.

ACKNOWLEDGMENTS

Few books have ever been written without the influence of other writers. One of the first to write a scholarly history of college sports was Guy Lewis, a graduate of the University of Maryland, who completed his doctoral dissertation in 1964, "The American Intercollegiate Football Spectacle, 1869–1917." Lewis's research influenced me as a graduate student at the University of Wisconsin, Madison prior to writing my own dissertation on the history of an intercollegiate athletic conference. That was six decades ago when writing about any aspect of sport was generally discouraged by historians in higher education. Neither was it a subject to be studied in a scholarly manner in other departments such as American studies, anthropology, Black studies, classics, economics, geography, journalism, kinesiology, law, literature, philosophy, political science, psychology, religious studies, sociology, or women's studies.

In the last half century, each of the above academic departments have had studies conducted in the history of sport. Specifically, intercollegiate sport history has grown exponentially with the proliferation of master's theses, PhD dissertations, journal articles, and books. There are many examples, but I would specifically note three that have been most helpful in specific ways for my better understanding of college sport. Robin Lester, *Stagg's University: The Rise, Decline, and Fall of Big-Time Football at Chicago* (1995); Susan K. Cahn, *Coming on Strong: Gender and Sexuality in Twentieth-Century Women's Sport* (1994); and Roger R. Tamte, *Walter Camp and the Creation of American Football* (2018). None have emphasized the role of Walter Byers and the development of the NCAA, but these three have placed men's and women's college sport in the larger context of American society.

My research for the Byers and NCAA book comes principally from primary sources found in university archives and most from the Walter Byers Papers in the archives at the National Collegiate Athletic Association. In this volume, the university archives I searched and which provided useful material included: Alabama, Colorado, Eastern College Athletic Conference, Georgia, Georgia Tech, Harvard, Illinois, Maryland, Michigan, Minnesota, Nebraska, Northwestern, Notre Dame, Ohio State, Oklahoma, Pennsylvania, Pennsylvania State, Stanford, Swarthmore, Tennessee, Tulane, Virginia, William & Mary, and Wisconsin.

Archivists are often unrecognized, but they should more often be honored. From the largest intercollegiate athletic archives at Harvard, Illinois, and Michigan to the smallest at Swarthmore and William & Mary, the professional archivists have been universally supportive in bringing source material to my attention. No one was more accommodating and helpful in the writing of the Byers-NCAA book than Dr. Ursula Walsh, Director of Research at the NCAA and head of the NCAA Library-Archives (1985–1999). Not only were her recommendations instrumental in my obtaining five NCAA research grants, but she allowed me to search the Walter Byers Papers soon after the NCAA Archives received them and before they were archived by the staff. Several times, I spent weeks in the NCAA Archives, which allowed me access to the dozens of boxes in the Walter Byers collection before and after they were reorganized. Since then, the NCAA, regrettably, has closed its archives and library to outside researchers. A scholarly researcher could ask: What is contained in the NCAA documents that needs to be concealed?

I only became involved in sport history when I was completing my masters' degree at the University of Wisconsin with a thesis titled "Religion and the Land Ordinance of 1785." Then, I was in a discussion with a young professor in the Physical Education Department, Karl Stoedefalke. He suggested that if I was interested in history and sport, I should develop my own program for a PhD in his department. I was accepted in the program and was fortunate to receive a National Defense Education Act Fellowship for financial support. Fred Jacoby, the commissioner of the Wisconsin State University Conference, suggested to me that a study of his conference from 1967 on would be a worthy research topic. The on-campus Wisconsin State Historical Society gave me space to conduct my dissertation research on the development of Wisconsin normal schools, teachers colleges, state universities, and eventually part of the University of Wisconsin System. This began a lifetime of research on the history of college sport. As I was completing my dissertation in 1968, a position opened at Penn State University, and I began my career teaching and researching the history of physical activity and sport.

My first book on college sport was published in 1988, *Sports and Freedom: The Rise of Big-Time College Athletics* with Oxford University Press. Since then, I have found four other sympathetic university presses to publish another six volumes. Four sabbaticals and a limited teaching load at Penn State allowed me time to devote to archival research in over sixty university archives. I have remained active in my retirement years beginning in the 1990s to continue research and writing. I have been fortunate to have individuals willing to critique parts or whole manuscripts. One who has critiqued all my articles and book manuscripts is my wife, with the hard to remember name, Susan Catherine Bard McFarland Fernald Smith. I am grateful to a few individuals who read and commented on parts of this book. They include Bob Barney, Chad Carlson, Dick Crepeau, Elizabeth Demers, Bob Downs, Frank Deutsch, Sarah Fields, Roger Geiger, Art Glenn, Tom Jable, Bruce Kidd, Donna Lopiano, Dan Nathan, Joan Nessler, John Nichols, Allen Sack, Ellen Staurowsky, John Thelin, and Patricia Vertinsky. I am indebted to two individuals who read and closely critiqued the entire manuscript, David Wiggins and Ying Wushanley.

I was fortunate to have a North American Society for Sport History colleague, Brian Ingrassia, suggest that I publish my manuscript with the University of Tennessee Press in its Sport and Popular Culture Series. At the Tennessee Press, I was initially privileged to work with Thomas Wells, whose area of expertise is history and literature and whose choice of manuscript reviewers was superb. Jonathon Boggs, who is editorial coordinator, made the publishing process enjoyable with his keen eye to details. Most important for this book, the copy editor, Meg Olsen, did an outstanding job of suggesting editorial modifications. She is at the top of the list of copy editors of my dozen books.

Finally, I want to acknowledge the support I received from my parents,

Arthur Wendell Smith and Freda McClellan Smith, college-educated dairy farmers from Wisconsin. They allowed me to develop my musical, athletic, and educational talents and promote a work ethic that has carried me well into my ninth decade. With the help of my parents and an academic scholarship, I was able to attend Northwestern University, major in history while participating on the Northwestern basketball and baseball teams and eventually participating in the Chicago White Sox system following graduation. My short tenure teaching and coaching in the Fort Atkinson High School was followed by study as a graduate student at the University of Wisconsin. I acknowledge my fortunate circumstances arising from my earliest years being raised on a farm as a kid during the Great Depression to eventually pursuing sport history at a fine state university, Penn State. Mothers and fathers, and those who have touched us, cast wide and lengthy shadows.

INTRODUCTION

The NCAA in the Era of Walter Byers, 1951–1987

The media reported the death of a cowboy with a quarter horse, a western hat, and Tony Lama boots.[1] He died on May 26, 2015, at the Seven Cross Ranch, near Emmett, in Pottawatomie County, Kansas, one hundred miles northwest of Kansas City, between Topeka and Manhattan. His death made the obituary page of the *New York Times* and other newspapers across America. Walter Byers, the longtime executive director of the National Collegiate Athletic Association (1951–1987) passed at the age of ninety-three, but a lawsuit against him by his daughter survived. Ellen Byers Bouton claimed she had been verbally promised ranch land worth over a million dollars if she left her tenure-track, $100,000-per-year position on the faculty at the Washburn University School of Law in Topeka. Her family pulled up stakes and moved in 2005 to the family ranch owned by Byers to help her eighty-three-year-old dad run his cattle business.

Seventy-seven years before his death, eighteen-year-old Byers, an undersized Kansas City high school all-city football center, had traveled west to Houston, Texas, to enter Rice University, where he sought a position on the football team. Rice had recently come off a successful Southwest Conference season by winning the Cotton Bowl and being ranked eighteenth. With his team in the national spotlight, football coach Jimmy Kitts told Byers, "You're too small" to play football. In less than a year, Byers transferred to the University of Iowa. The young and disappointed 5'9" hopeful never played college football, but he kept his interest in sport with a persistence that is hard to duplicate. His fighting spirit stayed with him his entire life, even as he moved to his cattle ranch after retiring from his thirty-six-year tenure heading the National Collegiate Athletic Association (NCAA).

The personality traits that helped Byers build a national organization, the NCAA, out of a financially insecure and often powerless association in 1951 were not necessarily the traits needed to build close interpersonal relationships. Byers had a perfectionist personality and an authoritarian mentality.[2] While he helped create a national sport organization that became a financial behemoth, one with exacting rules, he did not succeed in building lasting personal relations with those closest to him, as demonstrated by his three marriages, all of which ended in divorce, his relationship with his eldest son, and especially his conflict with his daughter Ellen Byers Bouton.[3]

Ellen Bouton, youngest of Byers's three children, had an undergraduate degree from Kansas State University, a masters in fine arts from the University of Iowa, and a law degree from Georgetown University. She was teaching criminal law at Kansas's Washburn University School of Law in 2005 when her father asked Ellen to leave her position to help him run his three-thousand-acre Seven Cross Ranch.[4] The Bouton family moved to the ranch with only a verbal agreement that she would manage the cattle business and inherit the ranch upon Byers's death. Three years later, a mid-December cold wave set in, plummeting the average high temperature from the mid-fifties to five degrees above zero. For several days, the low temperature hovered near zero, causing the water pipes to freeze and jeopardizing the entire beef herd.[5] As a consequence, Byers told his daughter that her services on the ranch were no longer needed. She had failed the retired NCAA administrator, and she and her family were soon gone from the ranch. There was no written account of Bouton's inheritance of any of the ranchland.[6]

As with Walter Byers's marriages, there was no reconciliation with his daughter. Bouton sued her father, and the lengthy lawsuit continued for the next decade. She remained discontented; meanwhile, her father sold the ranch.[7] Byers was so used to lawsuits by players, institutions, and commercial concerns that this one by his daughter may not have strongly affected him in the last of his ninety-three years. Upon his death, the *New York Times* wrote that Byers's NCAA was "overly bureaucratic and rules-obsessed, and utterly lacking in empathy or compassion. . . ."[8] That could have described the way Walter Byers dealt with his daughter as well.

The ranch incident reflected Walter Byers's actions over his three-decade history at the NCAA and his reversal in perspective on the NCAA once he retired. Soon after retirement to his ranch, Byers began writing a lengthy book about his years at the NCAA, titled *Unsportsmanlike Conduct: Exploiting College Athletes*.[9] I was fortunate that Byers sent me his manuscript, and I commented upon it twice in its manuscript form.[10] In a turnabout from his years at the NCAA, Byers used the book to seriously criticize the organization that he, more than any other individual, was responsible for building. The association had grown so commercially and professionally powerful that most people had forgotten that the NCAA was formed only to rewrite the football rules in 1906, allowing faculty to take control and try to preserve amateurism at the financial expense of athletes.

Faculty and to some extent presidents of colleges in the early twentieth century wanted to take power away from students, who had created intercollegiate athletics, and from alumni, who had often taken over for financial reasons. The NCAA was not created to support athletes, as can been seen in the four pages of rules in its original constitution placing restrictions on athletes. The original 1906 NCAA constitution asked member institutions to enforce certain measures, nearly all of which began, "No student shall . . . ," followed by some aspect of amateurism.[11] From the outset, the NCAA constrained college athletes rather than making athletics an integral part of education. Its primary mission was to save athletics from commercialism and professionalism and to bring athletics under faculty control. This vision for the NCAA fit neatly into the early twentieth-century Progressive Movement, with its reliance on management by experts. Leaders of the Progressive playground movement, for example, sought to bring children's play under the influence of educated adults, who supposedly knew what was best for the playing habits of children. At the forefront of the playground movement were Luther Gulick, Clark Hetherington, and R. Tait

McKenzie, members of the Playground Association of America, who also attended early NCAA meetings and left their mark on college athletics. In the case of the NCAA, the "experts" were members of the college faculty and educated leaders of colleges and universities, who sought control of athletic practices.[12]

Early NCAA leaders, such as Hetherington, Gulick, and McKenzie, were bent on fostering amateurism, as seen in the aforementioned restrictions included in the original NCAA constitution.[13] Specifically, the rules promoted by the NCAA for students included the following prohibitions:

> No inducements to enter college for athletics
> No participation if the athlete accepts any money
> No playing on teams of those ineligible as amateurs
> No playing if not a bona-fide student
> No participation if the athlete accepts money from gate receipts
> No training table expenses to be paid for the athlete
> No participation until an eligibility card is filled out and signed

The card's final statement read, "On my honor as a gentleman I state that the above answers [to fifteen questions] contain the whole truth, without any mental reservations."[14] These and similar "NOs" for athletes were established nearly two decades before Walter Byers was born. Most of the prohibitions had been in place for a half-century by the time he was placed in charge of the NCAA. They continued throughout his career and well into the twenty-first century.

Byers bought into the moral belief that players should not accept money for athletic participation. The amateur code, made popular by the upper-class British in nineteenth-century England, held that elite social classes were superior to those below them and, thus, that it was not appropriate for them to compete against their social inferiors. In America, the separation of those who competed for money and those who agreed not to was principally a financial consideration. "Thou shall not accept money" in any form was something that American athletes tended to ignore whenever possible. Yet, it was thrust upon them by those who came to dominate the rules fostered by the NCAA, athletic conferences, and faculty and presidents of individual institutions. From the earliest years of the NCAA, "Thou shall not" included no free college tuition, no free food at training tables, and no free tutoring to help athletes remain eligible academically. Although rules changed for pragmatic reasons, the demand for amateurism was the life blood of the NCAA and college athletics for generations after the association's 1906 founding, through the Walter Byers years and into the twenty-first century.

Ironically, the "thou shall nots" were applied only to athletes, not to others who were also involved in athletics, such as coaches, athletic directors, faculty, presidents, boards of trustees, alumni, and anyone who could profit from the performance of amateur athletes. For instance, coaches could forsake contracts and jump from one team to another, as John Heisman and Glenn "Pop" Warner did in the late nineteenth and early twentieth centuries. Future coaches took similar actions, including Knute Rockne, who threatened to leave Notre Dame if his salary was not raised, or "Bear" Bryant, who changed institutions for more money. As revenues burgeoned from gate receipts and television contracts, many coaches, such as Nick Saban and Brian Kelley, followed the money to Alabama and Louisiana State. For a century, athletes could not transfer to another institution and participate in athletics without penalties. This punishment was a questionable standard used against athletes by the NCAA and colleges for nearly the entire history of the organization. Walter Byers did little to change this disparity when he was able to do so; after he retired, he lacked power to bring about change. He then said that the negative treatment of athletes was part of the "neo-plantation mentality" of his amateur-favoring NCAA, "that the rewards belong to the overseers and the supervisors. What trickles down after that can go to the athletes."[15]

By the time Byers became executive director in 1951, the NCAA had been given the onerous task, which had once belonged to institutions and conferences, of controlling athletes' lives. This practice continued throughout Byers's career at the NCAA and into the twenty-first century. The NCAA was created by institutions of higher education to serve the interests of its members, not to benefit individual male athletes. This dynamic intensified in the thirty-six years under Byers's leadership, including eventual control over women's athletics. The story of Walter Byers and the NCAA from 1951 to 1987 clearly reveals that the interests of athletes, especially elite athletes at big-time institutions, had been mostly forgotten in the grasp of the NCAA's desire to promote its member institutions at the expense of the athletes representing those institutions. Forgotten by the NCAA, athletic conferences, and those in power at individual institutions that prospered were these athletes, who lost their freedom as the NCAA attempted to promote and sustain amateurism.

This is in part the saga of Walter Byers, one of the dominating individuals in organized sport in America. Byers's leadership in intercollegiate sport is similar to the governance of other powerful heads of sports organizations, such as Kenesaw Mountain Landis in organized baseball, David Stern in professional basketball, Pete Rozelle in pro football, John Montgomery Ward in the unionization of baseball players, and Roone Arledge in sport telecasting. We can learn a good deal about intercollegiate athletics, both men's and women's, by exploring Walter Byers's influence on a variety of episodes—namely, creating "amateur" athletic scholarships; confronting federal taxation of gate receipts and state workers' compensation for athletes; fearing the impact of professional football on the college game; dealing with the ethics of professional coaches; encountering civil rights campaigns of African Americans; facing Title IX and women's sports; fighting with another "amateur" sport organization, the Amateur Athletic Union; and guiding the NCAA while being punished for a television restraint of trade conspiracy policy that Byers helped to create.

Ellen Byers Bouton's lawsuit against her father may be as significant as any other incident in telling the story of Walter Byers, the central figure in the development of the NCAA in mid-twentieth-century America. That episode, however, has generally been forgotten. Other issues—including paying athletes, protecting their health and safety, and allowing them freedoms that other college students possess—remain major issues decades after Byers was the voice of the National Collegiate Athletic Association. Finally, during his thirty-six years as administrator of the NCAA, I argue that Byers was caught between his desire for amateurism for athletes and the creation of financial success for institutions, conferences, and the NCAA itself. He and his organization were particularly effective in commercializing big-time football and men's basketball. During those same years, the NCAA's effort under Byers to maintain amateur sports should be considered a failure. The legal problem with Byers's daughter and the status of athletes in higher education remained unresolved.

ONE

Byers and Early NCAA Issues for a Rookie Executive Director

"The Greeks made it a cult; the English a spectacle; the Americans have made it a business."
—**ALBERT BUSHNELL HART (1929)**

"Enforcement is the bedrock upon which the NCAA edifice is based."
—**WALTER BYERS (CA. 1953)**

In the generation before Walter Byers became the first executive director of the NCAA, a Harvard professor of history passed his verdict on big-time college sport: "The Greeks made it a cult; the English a spectacle; the Americans have made it a business."[1] Byers came to leadership just as college athletics were becoming nationally prominent as a business under the NCAA, superseding the power of the dominant conferences of the first half of the twentieth century. Byers took charge just as NCAA leaders were trying to pass national legislation to reform many problems that existed in the nineteenth century and that had been reoccurring since the NCAA was formed in the early twentieth century.

HOME RULE COMES TO AN END AS BYERS BEGINS HIS ERA

From the founding of the NCAA in 1905 until after World War II, a belief prevailed that colleges and universities with athletic programs should be governed by the individual institutions themselves and by conferences.[2]

Known from the beginning as Home Rule, this policy served as a kind of "states' rights" for institutions of higher education. There would be no legislation or enforcement of rules by a national organization. Home Rule covered regulations about recruiting or subsidization of athletes, punishment of institutions for any kind of misconduct, and, later, controls over contests broadcast on the radio or television. In fact, Home Rule determined most aspects of athletics except for national playing rules for sports such as football, boxing, or track and field and any national tournaments the NCAA decided to hold. The first NCAA rules for football were developed for the 1906 season, and the first national tourney occurred in 1921 for track athletes. Nothing else. During the first couple years of the NCAA's existence, faculty representatives to the national organization discussed such issues as amateurism, the number of years of eligibility, freshman and graduate student eligibility, summer baseball for pay, entrance requirements, athletic scholarships, faculty control of athletes, and the role of professional coaches.[3] No national legislation, however, was proposed.

Rather than legislating, the NCAA faculty representatives studied the questions around which athletic reform might be addressed by conferences and individual institutions. So, if playing baseball for money by collegians during the summer months was considered a violation of the concept of amateurism by NCAA leaders, institutions or conferences would dictate proposed solutions. The question of amateurism would remain front and center for leaders of intercollegiate athletics from these early years to the time that Walter Byers was appointed administrative leader in 1951. Preserving the British concept of amateurism in American athletic competition was considered morally upright by a clear majority of the college and university faculty members who ran the NCAA for a good portion of the twentieth century. However, those who participated in athletics were not nearly as committed to that concept. Most athletes welcomed being financed because of their athletic abilities. The athletes wanted their coaches to be paid, another action deemed questionable by advocates of amateurism. Members of football or baseball teams, or those on college crews, were nearly always in favor of hiring a professional coach to lead them if it would help them produce victories on playing fields, in arenas, or on bodies of water.

Thus, when Byers assumed his position as the new executive director of the NCAA, amateurism was the de jure position of individual institutions and conferences as written into their bylaws and policies, but the policy was often ignored in practice. Byers, who was a strong believer in amateurism in college sport, had to deal with institutions that allowed professionalism in the way their programs were run. This was most clearly seen in the question of paying athletes to compete, often called athletic scholarships or grants in aid by those who believed these scholarships were pay for athletic participation. When Byers took over the executive directorship, the NCAA had just experienced the agony of passing the first national control of the paying of athletes, a policy called the Sanity Code. The Sanity Code, first known as the "Purity Code," proposed to limit financial aid for athletes to tuition based on financial need. Passage of the 1948 Sanity Code made the 1930s Southeastern Conference full athletic scholarship illegal.[4] Nevertheless, the payment of athletes' tuition in the post–World War II era appeared to go against the new NCAA constitutional change, which stated, "Any college athlete who takes or is promised *pay in any form* for participation in athletics does not meet this definition of an amateur."[5] However, the NCAA did not consider covering an athlete's tuition to be pay. Byers, for his entire thirty-six-year career, had to deal with the payment of athletes while the NCAA constitution technically did not allow it. The hypocrisy of the NCAA in nominally adhering to the concept of amateurism while allowing the paying of players continued well after Byers left office. Despite these discrepancies in its adherence to amateurism, the NCAA's passage of the Sanity Code effectively ended Home Rule.

THE DEATH OF HOME RULE WITH THE ERA OF TV AND AIR TRAVEL

The death of NCAA Home Rule rested on the development of two major changes in American society: the era of television and the impact of air travel. Problems that had existed on a local or regional basis gained greater national attention, something the NCAA would be requested to manage under new leadership. The advent of the railroad in the mid-nineteenth century had made possible the development of intercollegiate athletics, such as the first American intercollegiate contest—a crew meet in New

Hampshire—financed by a railroad magnate. A century later, air travel following World War II provided rapid transport of football and basketball teams across the country.[6] Long-distance intercollegiate play occurred prior to air travel. In fact, it dated back to coach Amos Alonzo Stagg taking his University of Chicago football team on a transcontinental train in 1894 to meet and beat Stanford in California. The 6,200-mile journey was the first between teams on the two sides of the Rocky Mountains, preceding the Pasadena Rose Bowl by more than half a decade.[7] Further, Notre Dame's football contests with the University of Southern California began in 1926 and continued annually well into the twenty-first century. Nevertheless, air travel intensified interregional contests following World War II.

The change in travel can been seen at Notre Dame between 1949 and 1950. Notre Dame's vice president Theodore Hesburgh, in charge of athletics, allowed the team to travel by rail to Seattle to play the University of Washington Huskies in the fall of 1949. The train left South Bend, Indiana, three days prior to its arrival in Seattle on Friday for a Saturday game. The entire trip took seven days, involving player absence from the classroom for a week. The following year, Hesburgh decided his team would fly to away games, including the game against Wake Forest in North Carolina. For that game, the Fighting Irish left on a Friday afternoon, arrived that evening, and played the game the next day.[8] Two years before Notre Dame's venture into flying, the women's basketball team at Wayland Baptist College, in west Texas, became the first college basketball team to fly to games. Airplane enthusiast Clyde Hutcherson of Hutcherson Flying Service offered to fly the Wayland women's team for contests primarily against teams affiliated with the Amateur Athletic Union.[9] Hutcherson's offer occurred at a time when there were few women's intercollegiate athletic teams, two decades before the passage of Title IX of the Educational Amendment Act of 1972 and the push for greater equality for women relative to men's athletics. Other schools that could afford to fly soon began the practice for key men's sports.

The advent of television gave a whole new dimension to the financing of big-time athletics and the nationalizing of college sport. Television had a particular impact upon two sports, football and, later, men's basketball. When World War II ended with the capitulation of Japan following the first atomic bombs dropped on Hiroshima and Nagasaki in August 1945, four TV networks went into overdrive to attempt to dominate the airwaves, sport being a major attraction. The two well-established networks, CBS and NBC, were competing against upstarts ABC (a network emerging from the antitrust breakup of the NBC monopoly) and Du Mont, a TV manufacturer with aspirations to become a dominant TV network. Just before Walter Byers was hired as an assistant to the NCAA's secretary-treasurer and commissioner of the Big Ten, Kenneth "Tug" Wilson, Du Mont aired the New York Yankees home games in 1946, as well as the New York Giants football games and the first Southern sport telecast, Army v. Duke in football. Byers was still in New York City, working as a reporter for United Press, and likely watched the NBC telecast of what was called "the most important event in history of television," the heavyweight boxing match between Joe Louis and Billy Conn in June 1946.[10]

Both Notre Dame and the University of Pennsylvania acquired contracts with the Du Mont Television Network worth hundreds of thousand dollars in the late 1940s, while most big-time college football officials were trying to determine whether TV would be detrimental to their gate receipts.[11] The NCAA and Byers would have to deal with the TV threat to the financial success of college football. Even before Byers became executive director, he was asked to substitute for Tom Hamilton, University of Pittsburgh athletic director and chair of the NCAA Television Committee. Shortly after his twenty-ninth birthday, Byers spoke to the annual convention of the National Association of Radio and Television Broadcasters. He told them that the NCAA was not about to ban football telecasts but wished to experiment by limiting telecasts to one game a week in the fall of 1951.[12] By the time Byers became executive director, the NCAA had already established that 1951 would be an experimental year, with its first national control on football telecasts. If the NCAA had viewed athletics as an integral part of higher education, the organization could have accomplished its experimental year by contracting with educational TV, which was being introduced across the nation. Well over two hundred TV channels had been reserved by the federal government for non-commercial use by the early 1950s, but universities lacked presidents who would suggest that their institutions carry football games on television as part of higher education.[13] Even then, money controlled intercollegiate athletics, as it did from the nineteenth century into the twenty-first. Football would be promoted commercially, not educationally.

MONEY DOMINATES: TV FOOTBALL AND TOURNEY BASKETBALL

Walter Byers was placed in a NCAA leadership role even before he was elected as the first executive director. The experimental year of football telecasting in 1951 was agreed upon while Byers was still an assistant to Big Ten commissioner and NCAA secretary-treasurer Tug Wilson, a position Byers held for four years. That year, the NCAA restricted football telecasts to one per week, dictated that no team would televise more than one home and one away game, and blacked out two Saturdays entirely to see the effect of no telecasting on gate attendance.[14] Byers had already been working with Big Ten television and game highlight films for Tug Wilson prior to the NCAA restrictions on football telecasts.[15] Wilson was likely aware that Byers's success with the NCAA depended on boosting the income from two key sources, football telecasting and the increasingly popular NCAA basketball tournament—what eventually became known as March Madness.

Basketball, not football, became the first significant moneymaker for the NCAA—but not from the first national tourney. The initial NCAA basketball tournament in 1939 took place in the Northwestern University gymnasium and produced a profit of $42.54, with the University of Oregon defeating Ohio State to win the finals.[16] Soon after, however, the tourney was raising more money than NCAA membership fees, even during World War II. For comparison, the NCAA boxing tourney produced $3,476 in profits in 1939, while the NCAA ended that year with a balance of $7,110. Basketball was not thriving financially, nor was the NCAA. The tournament, however, was not suspended during World War II, and when the NCAA decided to go commercial by holding the 1943 tournament in Madison Square Garden (MSG) in New York City, this event became the organization's principal moneymaker. The year before, the NCAA profited just over $1,000. The first year the event was held at MSG, profits exceeded $10,000.[17] By the end of the war, the NCAA was gaining enough wealth from the basketball tournament to begin paying a part-time assistant, Byers, just over $4,000 to aid the NCAA secretary-treasurer (along with his work for the Big Ten).[18]

With additional cash on hand, and because conducting the numerous NCAA tournaments required a great deal of work, shortly after World War

II, NCAA officials decided to create a central national office with a paid official to assist the secretary-treasurer. Not only did the NCAA conduct the increasingly important basketball tourney, but by the time the organization hired Byers to assist Wilson, there were ten other national tournaments managed by the NCAA: track and field (1921), swimming (1924), wrestling (1928), boxing (1937), gymnastics (1938), tennis (1938), golf (1939), fencing (1941), baseball (1947), and ice hockey (1948). Byers was already a valued administrator with four years' experience before he became the first executive director.

A major question confronted Byers and the NCAA at this time: Should the NCAA control the growth of football telecasts and, in doing so, protect gate receipts, the principal financial resource for the vast majority of athletic programs at institutions of higher learning? Even as Byers was completing his last year as foreign correspondent for the United Press in New York City, the NCAA decided to hold a discussion on the impact of television on college football.[19] Chairman of the roundtable discussion T. P. Heard, athletic director at Louisiana State University, began the discussion by stating that "the whole television subject is worrying most of us." He was wrong in his expectation that "there is no intention at this time to set up any regulatory body" to handle television.[20] At the same time, Asa Bushnell, commissioner of the Eastern College Athletic Conference, warned, "If you gentlemen are not worried about television, I think you should be."[21] That was 1947, and the threat of TV to gate receipts was a major concern, even before there were one million TV sets in America. National regulation of football telecasts would arise in several years. Byers, living in the East where TV began but a Midwesterner at heart, soon quit his job in New York and, on August 26, 1947, took up his dual position as Big Ten Service Bureau Director (publicity director) and Executive Assistant of the NCAA, both under Tug Wilson in Chicago.[22]

By then, television had spread quickly. Coaxial cable to carry the TV signals was first laid on the East Coast and then to the Midwest past South Bend, Indiana, the home of reigning football powerhouse Notre Dame. Within two years, Notre Dame had signed a contract with the Du Mont network. At about the same time, the University of Pennsylvania, which had been telecasting football locally since 1940, created a network on the East Coast. Game attendance elsewhere began to drop as free-to-the-public television grew.[23] Byers was cognizant of the arguments for and against football telecasts from his four years as executive assistant. Meanwhile, Notre Dame was gaining financial and advertising profits from its Home Rule football network. In contrast, the Big Ten voted to ban TV for the 1950 season, with Byers in attendance at the meeting.[24] Football attendance did rise momentarily with the Big Ten TV ban, and Byers continued to gain valuable experience with TV.

The next year, the NCAA took a collective action regarding television that radically changed the function of the organization and eventually gave the NCAA additional income. Combined with income from the national basketball tourney, control of TV broadcasts allowed the NCAA to become a national force in enforcement of its own rules. Following its decision to regulate broadcasts, the NCAA could boycott or ban individual institutions and conferences for not upholding the limits on telecasting football games. That power of enforcement began just as Byers became the first executive director of the NCAA on October 1, 1951. From that position, following the first effective defeat of Home Rule in the history of the NCAA, Byers helped build a national organization, taking the NCAA from an impoverished association with one secretary in a rented hotel room in Chicago to a multi-million-dollar enterprise. "No one," according to journalist and historian Keith Dunnavant, immersed himself in the operation of television more than Byers; he "knew more about the medium than anyone else."[25] A national football television policy and control of March Madness in basketball allowed for the NCAA's phenomenal growth. With Byers in control, the NCAA began more effective enforcement of "amateur" college sport. Enforcement began with a basketball scandal at the University of Kentucky.

POWER THROUGH ENFORCEMENT AND THE KENTUCKY DEATH PENALTY

Later in his life, Walter Byers noted the historic and tenuous position of the NCAA in enforcing its rules, attempting to keep athletics from moving closer to being professional—at least for the athletes. The year Byers became the full-time employee of the NCAA at a salary of $11,000, scandals of major proportions broke out in college football and basketball.[26] Nearly the entire US Military Academy football team was dismissed for academic cheating.

At William and Mary College, athletes lacking academic credentials were admitted in an attempt to make the small college into a big-time football and basketball power. A racist attack by an Oklahoma A&M football player on a great Black player for Drake University, Johnny Bright, became national news through a series of photographs in *Life Magazine*. However, most lasting was the basketball scandal at the University of Kentucky. Kentucky's team was led by coach Adolph Rupp, then the most honored basketball coach in the nation. Rupp's players were found guilty of both being paid salaries and shaving points for gamblers in games while winning two straight NCAA national championships and being considered the top basketball team in the nation. Following the Southeastern Conference vote to ban Kentucky from playing basketball, the Walter Byers-led NCAA Subcommittee on Infractions recommended banning all intercollegiate competition with Kentucky's basketball team for one year, thereby boycotting the school.[27] The so-called NCAA "Death Penalty" solidified the effort of Byers and the NCAA to enforce the organization's rules, the first such successful effort in history. Byers called the action by the NCAA "a shaky death penalty," but it was important, according to the executive director, because the decision made the first precarious enforcement by the national office into "the bedrock upon which the NCAA edifice is based."[28]

There is irony in the 122–1 vote to give the "Death Penalty" to Kentucky.[29] The single negative vote was cast by Nathan Dougherty, the University of Tennessee's faculty representative and former star football player. The other two Tennessee members at the conference with Dougherty were the honored military general, football coach, and athletic director Robert Neyland and Cloide Brehm, the university president. Tennessee was the sole vote against punishing Kentucky, and the vote was publicized to demonstrate that none of Kentucky's representatives had cast the dissenting vote themselves. At the same time, Tennessee president Brehm knew that Neyland had a secret and illegal fund used to pay football players. Brehm privately admitted that he did not expose the slush fund because he feared being fired by the Tennessee Board of Trustees, who loved Neyland's winning record. Brehm stated in a transcript of a closed meeting about ridding Neyland of his slush fund that, if the members of the governing board knew of the meeting, "they may cut my throat."[30] President Brehm saved his job, General Neyland continued his position as athletic director until his death, and the trustees never found out about the slush fund. Kentucky accepted the "death penalty" without a protest, and Tennessee continued cheating by paying players, as Kentucky had done. Justice does not always prevail.

Enforcement under Walter Byers was established only a couple of years before the NCAA's 1948 Sanity Code was defeated. The Sanity Code limited the payment of athletes to tuition and fees, but the policy ultimately failed when a two-thirds majority could not be reached to terminate the NCAA membership of the so-called "Seven Sinners." These seven mostly Southern institutions would not accept anything less than a full scholarship for athletes.[31] Penalties for infractions, however, became accepted, initiated by the NCAA's stand against Kentucky. According to Byers, the Kentucky "decision to accept the penalty erased the haunting failure of the Sanity Code. It gave a new and needed legitimacy," he stated after he retired, "to the NCAA's fledgling effort to police big-time college sport."[32] The NCAA established the Committee on Infractions, and this committee eventually became the costliest instrument in the NCAA budget as well as the most dreaded by institutions that violated its many rules. The NCAA's ability to absorb the cost of rule enforcement was only made possible by the increasing revenue from the annual basketball tournament and football telecasts.

BYERS, "FULL RIDES," AND THE CONCEPT OF "AMATEURISM"

Walter Byers never defined the term amateurism, but he was a major force in defending the ever-changing way the NCAA applied it to college athletics. From his initial years with the NCAA until he retired thirty-six years later, Byers stood for amateurism as it applied to the nonpayment of athletes. Nevertheless, he was a fierce competitor in raising money for the NCAA, conferences, and individual institutions; in professionalizing college athletics and paying coaches and administrators; in building NCAA offices and university facilities; and in collecting a cadre of college sport professionals to match those who ran professional sports. He apparently never turned down a salary increase for administering NCAA athletics after he accepted the initial $11,000 offer, advancing from his $4,000 position as an assistant administrator. Neither did he later decline an interest-free loan of nearly half a million dollars from the NCAA to help pay for his additional one thousand or so acres of ranch land in Kansas.[33] When the loan was exposed, Byers said that the loans offered to key administrators served to keep them at the NCAA. A loan to an athlete, however, could lead to ineligibility, not to a ranch. Before TV and tourney revenue, it should be noted, there was no money to loan.

Well before the time of Byers's no-interest loans, the NCAA had loosened its amorphous definition of amateurism and allowed an increase in payments for an athlete's education. In the South particularly, there was a push to allow "free rides," primarily to football players and a few other star athletes. This campaign began officially when the Southeastern Conference voted in 1935 to allow "full" athletic scholarships. Prominent institutions, such as Alabama, Georgia, and Louisiana State, began to triumph in football against Northern institutions in the postseason bowl games that were founded in the South during the Great Depression. There was increasing pressure from institutions that did not offer athletic scholarships, especially in the North, to either increase unofficial athletic scholarships or, on the other hand, advocate for no scholarships for NCAA members. A compromise of sorts came with the Sanity Code in 1948, which allowed for tuition and fee payments for athletes. Yet violations were not punished when a vote came before the NCAA convention. With the abandonment of the Sanity Code's tuition and fee compromise while Byers was still an assistant executive came the push for full athletic scholarships. Byers later called the Sanity Code defeat one of the three or four most important decisions in the history of college sport.[34] To Byers, this decision was not positive. He was a believer in amateurism.

As an Ohio State athletic director stated before the NCAA assembly more than a decade before, the NCAA and football could not survive "half amateur and half professional."[35] Yet this is exactly what the Big Ten Conference attempted to do until after 1960—sponsor big-time sports, especially football and basketball, without full athletic scholarships. By the mid-1950s, NCAA members, without the backing of the Midwestern Big Ten institutions, voted in assembly to allow the paying of athletes up to the cost of education, including tuition, room, board, fees, books, and "laundry money" of $15 per month.[36] The Big Ten, with faculty representatives more in tune with the concept of amateurism, kept voting NO to full scholarships.

One Big Ten president, Virgil Hancher of Iowa, turned his experience as a Rhodes Scholar at England's Oxford University toward drafting a very different approach to amateurism and the payment of athletic scholarships in America. In a cogently written explanation in favor of full athletic scholarships, Hancher explained why need-based scholarships would not work in America. Knowing that the elite Oxford-Cambridge model of amateurism would never be achieved in a more egalitarian America, he made the case for the Big Ten and American institutions of higher learning:[37]

> Both our past and present project us into a quite different social order. Yet in athletics we have consciously or unconsciously attempted to carry into the American way of life much of the British distinction between the gentleman [amateur] and the professional in the field of sport. As a result, we are acting hypocritically and making hypocrites of our athletes all the way from the high schools to the Olympic games.

President Hancher wrote that financial need was not generally used as a criterion for aid to "band men, debaters, actors, members of choruses and orchestras." Intercollegiate athletes, he believed, should be no different. He speculated that the Big Ten, unfortunately, was continuing in athletics on a "path to needs-base scholarships" and subjecting the conference "to the intervening agony." It took the Big Ten four more years of scholarship anguish before the conference voted to join the rest of big-time NCAA programs in allowing full scholarships based principally on physical talent, something prized in America far more than amateurism.

Walter Byers strongly favored amateurism and the Big Ten policy of offering only need-based payments to athletes. As the new executive director of the NCAA, he said little from his office, which had moved to Byers's hometown, Kansas City. Soon, the Big Ten and the rest of the big-time universities in the nation turned to paying their favored athletes to attend college, including a small stipend called "laundry money." Nevertheless, it became clear that Byers only favored pay to athletes based on financial need.[38] Meanwhile, the NCAA continued its hypocrisy by paying athletes while at the same time perpetuating its longtime definition of amateurism. That is, the NCAA moved to pay athletes while at the same time defining an amateur as one who only "engages in athletics for the physical, mental, or social benefits" derived from competing. By the mid-1950s, the NCAA added another restriction to its definition by banning an athlete who has "directly or indirectly used his athletic skill for pay in any form. . . ."[39]

In 1957 the NCAA ruled that any income from employment while on full scholarships would make the athlete ineligible.[40] The next year, the NCAA further declared that an athlete's "picture may not be associated with a commercial product in such a way as to imply endorsement, nor may he receive remuneration."[41] That same year, the NCAA Council and the NCAA approved unanimously the statement that a basic purpose of the NCAA was to "maintain intercollegiate athletics as an integral part of the educational programs and the athlete as an integral part of the student body. . . ." Why was this the case? The simple answer is that the NCAA wanted to "retain a clear line of demarcation between college athletics and professional sports."[42] The noose was tightening on athletes in terms of additional payments, if they received full scholarships.

Walter Byers could argue that preserving that which was uncorrupted and good in college athletics necessitated strongly enforced rules for amateurism. There was, however, a more powerful argument for trying to preserve the amateur status of college athletes and differentiating them from their counterparts in professional sports. Byers became the leader in defining athletes as prioritizing education first and tying athletics intimately to higher education. It took the injury and death of several football players, lawsuits, and major financial issues in the 1950s for the NCAA to constitutionally solidify football and its educational mission in institutions of higher education.

TWO

Workers' Compensation, Taxation, and Byers's "Student-Athlete"

The NCAA uses "an outmoded code of amateurism drawn, quite frankly, with many of the same words that they had drawn in 1956."

—**WALTER BYERS, 2012**

"The label 'student-athlete' is mere window dressing for individuals who, in substance, are employees."

—**ROBERT A. MCCORMICK AND AMY C. MCCORMICK, 2006**

Walter Byers was the originator of the most overused and misleading hyphenated word in intercollegiate athletics: "student-athlete." Before Byers and the 1950s, the term "student-athlete" was almost never used when referring to a college athlete.[1] However, by the twenty-first century, the term was used almost universally, including 253 times in 2014 by a district judge in the ninety-nine-page Ed O'Bannon image and likeness case against the NCAA. When the US Supreme Court decided the Shawne Alston case toppling the NCAA monopoly that placed compensation limits on college athletes in 2021, "student-athlete" was used 48 times in thirty-six pages of Justice Gorsuch's decision and 22 times in a five-page concurring decision by Justice Kavanaugh.

The origins of the now ubiquitous "student-athlete" in the American lexicon demand clarification. Walter Byers concocted the term for the NCAA to convince the public, legislators, and most importantly the courts that athletes are neither workers nor treated as workers under state and federal law. The construction placing "student" first and "athlete" second was deliberate, so rendered to convince individuals and institutions that athletes were students, connected to education, and were playing sports, primarily football, as amateurs. The concept of football players as workers emerged in the 1950s under state workers' compensation laws, but several decades previously college football was the focus of the federal law taxing football gate receipts. Workers' compensation and taxes on gate receipts have one common feature for the NCAA and its institutions—money.

COMMERCIALISM, FOOTBALL GATE RECEIPTS, AND FEDERAL TAXES

Prior to Walter Byers creating the term "student-athlete" as a euphemism for "college athlete" or just plain "athlete," the NCAA was concerned about how governmental legislation and decisions in the courts impacted college athletics financially. Legislation has not always been kind to big-time intercollegiate athletics, including a law creating the first tax on football gate receipts. It was a major tax. As the Great Depression deepened in the early 1930s, President Herbert Hoover advocated increasing taxes on individuals and institutions to balance the national budget. To go along with the largest peacetime income tax increase in American history, Congress passed an excise tax on several items, including football gate receipts. Football was the only collegiate sport program with substantial profits. A 10 percent tax was placed on gate receipts, and the state of Georgia soon challenged the legality of the tax in court.[2] The state argued that the federal government could not tax an integral part of an educational institution, while the federal government argued that "football was a business and the men were hired specifically to play football."[3] The US Supreme Court eventually ruled Hoover's tax constitutional, and the tax was eventually increased to 20 percent during World War II, a rate which stayed in place even after the war.

When Byers became executive director, there was still confusion about whether athletics was educational or commercial. The Federal Revenue Act of 1951 removed the tax on high school gate receipts but not on those at college games. Why high school football was considered educational and exempted from the tax when college programs continued to pay was not clear. Nevertheless, within three years, President Dwight Eisenhower signed a bill exempting colleges from paying the federal admission tax.[4] Yet whether gate receipts or, for that matter, the increasing income generated from radio and television broadcasts of highly commercial and professionalized college football (and eventually men's basketball) should be taxed remained ambiguous.[5]

Were college athletics educational? If college football and basketball were truly educational in nature, surely educational radio and television would have been used to transmit games. That was not common—there was too much money to harvest in commercial radio and TV for colleges to go the educational route. Whether players on athletic scholarships should be taxed was also unclear, though the 1954 federal designation of higher education institutions as 501(c)(3) entities would exempt college athletics. The Internal Revenue Code of 1954 included the important section 117 stating that scholarships in educational institutions for degree candidates were tax free.[6] The NCAA and Byers decided to try to convince legislators and the courts that athletics were educational and that athletes were an integral part of higher education. There was good reason for the NCAA to begin calling athletic scholarships "grants in aid" and athletes "student-athletes." This was especially true when football injury lawsuits with workers' compensation consequences came about in the 1950s.

FOOTBALL INJURIES AND STATE WORKERS' COMPENSATION

Ironically, the made-up term "student-athlete" is tied historically to the concept that workers and their families deserved to be compensated for injuries sustained while working on their jobs. For most of history, including the history of sport, the doctrine of "assumption of risk" held sway, suggesting that workers agreed to work and assumed the risks of the job. This began to change during the Industrial Revolution with the growth of a perceived need for national social welfare rules, which arose first in industrialized Europe and the British Isles.[7] In the late 1800s, governments there came to believe they had a stake in protecting workers who were injured on the job. In America, most governmental actions, such as regulating education, running elections, or setting the drinking age, have historically been left to the states. Similarly, legislating for the rights of workers injured in the course of their employment was a states' rights issue, but state legislation regulating these rights did not emerge until the twentieth century. That occurred well after athletes, such as football players, began to be injured in "workouts" or hurt in games.

There was no thought of claiming compensation for the family of Union College's Harold Moore, killed by a brain hemorrhage in a 1905 football game, though his death led to the eventual forming of the NCAA at the end of the football season.[8] The assumption of risk in football dominated any claim of liability for injury and, thus, any claim for injury-related compensation in 1905. More to the point, workers' compensation laws existed nowhere in America until the next decade, when Wisconsin, Colorado, and several other states passed the first such laws.[9] Even if a person was injured in intercollegiate athletics, there was little thought of recompense for injuries sustained in games or practices. The NCAA constitution stated early on that an athlete participated on his own terms for the "physical, mental, moral, or social benefits he derived therefrom."[10]

Paying the costs resulting from injuries was principally up to the individual athlete. Athletes or their families did not ask for compensation—that is, until a football player from the University of Denver asked for compensation for an injury he suffered in the year before Walter Byers became NCAA executive director. Football player Ernest Nemeth injured his back during spring football practice in 1950 and was no longer able to compete. He had previously been given a job taking care of the Denver campus furnace and cleaning sidewalks in exchange for participating in football. He was the first NCAA player to claim workers' compensation, justifying the claim under the new Colorado law. After a three-year battle with the University of Denver, the Colorado Supreme Court ruled in Nemeth's favor, affirming that "the injuries sustained by Nemeth arose out of and in the course of his employment."[11] He became the first NCAA athlete to win in court and receive workers' compensation payment for his injuries. He would, however, also be one of the last athletes to win a college workers' compensation case, thanks in part to the efforts of Walter Byers, who fought successfully to limit financial losses to colleges. This was another case demonstrating that the NCAA, from its early existence, acted not to benefit athletes but to serve collegiate institutions.

THE HYPHENATED EUPHEMISM: BYERS'S "STUDENT-ATHLETE"

The influence of the NCAA and Walter Byers rose dramatically following a second injury case in Colorado. In this case, the player was not only injured but died. September 24, 1955, is an important date in the history of the NCAA, for on that date Ray Dennison was killed making a tackle during the first play for Colorado's Ft. Lewis A&M in a game against Trinidad Junior College.[12] The death of Dennison alerted the relatively new executive director of the NCAA that the organization must do something to try to prevent college athletes from being considered workers, thereby making the NCAA and individual institutions liable under state workers' compensation laws. Not only was amateurism under threat, but individual institutions would be forced to pay thousands of dollars for workers' compensation insurance if court decisions favorable to athletes and against NCAA institutions continued. Athletes, Byers argued and the leaders of the NCAA insisted, must be perceived primarily as students, participating in athletics for the "physical, mental, and social benefits" of amateur sports. Byers was convinced that the concept of "student" must be emphasized, rather than "athlete." His concept of the "student-athlete" was conceived to convince the public and the legal system that athletes were both amateurs and, fundamentally, students attending college.

In less than a half year after Dennison's death, Byers inserted the term "student-athlete" sixteen times in Article III of the NCAA constitution, "Principles for the Conduct of Intercollegiate Athletics."[13] To Byers, Dennison had been a student first and an athlete second, and he wanted everyone to know this, including officials such as judges. Not only was it written in the NCAA constitution but individuals in the NCAA were instructed that all written and spoken references to athletes would henceforth use the term "student-athletes." Athletes were to be integral parts of the educational system, and the term "student-athlete" would convey the academic meaning. In creating the "student-athlete" myth, Byers acted fully in the tradition of opposing the rights of athletes and favoring the interests of institutions and conferences.

The use of the term "student-athlete" was the most important of the euphemisms developed to highlight amateurism and to convince the public, as well as legislatures and courts, to side with the NCAA and institutions rather than athletes, but it was only part of the word games that Byers and NCAA leaders played after the death of Dennison.[14] Athletic scholarships were often termed "grants-in-aid" to make it appear that athletes were not being paid to be athletes. One-year athletic scholarship contracts were quickly reinterpreted by the NCAA as four-year financial aid packages to "student-athletes," to give the impression that athletes were not contracted year by year but were on the rolls for four years, until an academic degree was earned.[15] Soon, journalists were asked to use the term "college teams" rather than "clubs," which was used to describe professional teams. Those hired to advertise or publicize college athletics were part of "sports information" departments to soften the commercial-professional aspects of college sports. Above all else, as Byers stated about the early workers' compensation cases, the NCAA would make certain "that no employment relationship was created between the institution and the student-athlete involving a duty to participate in athletics." Byers successfully reworded terms related to athletics and athletes to benefit institutions, conferences, and the NCAA. In the NCAA constitution and all written and spoken references, athletes would henceforth be titled "student-athletes."[16]

To prevent lawsuits and legislative action against individual institutions and the NCAA, the organization needed to emphasize athletics being educational and athletes being an integral part of education. Prior to Dennison's death, not once did Byers refer to athletes as "student-athletes," nor would "student-athlete" be written in the NCAA constitution for the half-century between 1906 and 1955.[17] Why the abrupt change in wordage over the course of one year? The Dennison case raised a red flag, showing how successful claims for workers' compensation would negatively impact the perception of football and other college sports being amateur. Amateurism had been a primary tenet, a binding principle for the NCAA from the beginning. Now it was made fundamental to the financial welfare of the NCAA and its member institutions.

Dennison was the second football player to claim workers' compensation. As previously mentioned, the first was Ernest Nemeth, who did so following a disabling injury in 1950, prior to the full-time hiring of Byers.[18] Nemeth claimed, and the court confirmed, that the injuries he sustained "arose out of and in the course of employment."[19] Nemeth won after a lengthy court case against the Colorado State Industrial Commission. Dennison's death, which occurred under Byers's tenure at the NCAA, was handled differently. One must remember that the NCAA was not formed in the early twentieth century to benefit athletes but to save institutional athletics, particularly football, from problems emanating from games that students had created in the nineteenth century. The NCAA fighting workers' compensation was part of the fifty-year tradition of the organization looking out for institutions, not athletes. Walter Byers, in crafting the "student-athlete" myth, was fully in support of this tradition of opposing the rights of athletes and in favor of fostering the interests of institutions and conferences.

Only a couple of years after the emergence of Byers's "student-athlete" euphemism, the NCAA etched the educational component of college athletics into its constitution permanently. Passed in a 150–0 unanimous standing vote, the constitution's "Principle of Educational Objective" read:[20] "A basic purpose of this association is to maintain intercollegiate athletics as an integral part of the educational program and the athlete as an integral part of the student body, and, by so doing, detail a clear line of demarcation between college athletics and professional sports." Over sixty years later, in 2022, when a new NCAA constitution was written and adopted overwhelmingly, the document contained not a word about amateurism but retained similar words connecting athletics to education. The NCAA's Supreme Court loss in the *NCAA v. Shawn Alston* case—in which the justices ruled unanimously that the NCAA's limited "amateur" payment of athletes violated antitrust laws—effectively forced the NCAA to adopt a new constitution. This new document, for legal reasons, avoided the term "amateurism," the dominant theme for the past twelve decades.[21] With amateurism eliminated, the new document's preamble nevertheless opened with a familiar statement declaring that the basic purpose of the association was to maintain athletics as "an integral part of the education program and the student-athlete as an integral part of the student body."[22] Those words had helped the NCAA and Byers's heritage remain steadfast in college athletics for a large portion of two centuries.

WORKERS' COMPENSATION CASES CONTINUE INTO THE TWENTY-FIRST CENTURY

For the benefit of the NCAA and Byers's success in leading it, other workers' compensation cases tended to favor institutions of higher education over athletes as workers. Once the 1957 Ray Dennison decision was rendered by the Colorado Supreme Court, stating that Dennison had no contractual obligation to play football and that no employer-employee relationship existed from which his surviving wife and three children could receive death benefits, rulings continued to oppose athletes as workers. The next important case occurred in the 1960s, when California State Poly football player Edward Gary Van Horn was killed along with his teammates in a plane crash while returning from a football game in Ohio. The original workers' compensation decision denied compensation to Van Horn's family, but the ruling was overturned by an appeals court. The court determined that Van Horn was an employee and that an employee-employers relationship existed between the athlete and the institution. Before the California legislature in 1965 excluded athletes from workers' compensation, the NCAA, led by Byers, the president Robert Ray, and secretary-treasurer Everett Barnes, contacted all athletic directors, faculty representatives, and conferences that all institutions should rewrite the language to change the wording of athletic scholarships so that these "contracts" not suggest employment as workers."[23]

A decade later, a spring football practice injury rendered Indiana State University football player Fred Rensing a quadriplegic. Split decisions sent the case all the way to the Indiana Supreme Court, where the justices concluded that, even though Rensing had a contract with the institution, there was no employer-employee relationship established. The court reasoned that "Rensing and the university did not intend to enter into an employer-employee relations." The court agreed with Walter Byers and the NCAA's wording in its constitution that athletes "are integral parts of the institution's student body [and Rensing was] first and foremost a student."[24] Allen Sack, a leader in campaigning for workers' rights for a half-century, summed up the Rensing case better than anyone else in his book, *Counterfeit Amateurs*. The former University of Notre Dame athlete and later professor of sociology and sport management stated of the attorneys who backed the denial of Rensing's workers' compensation by the NCAA and Byers:[25]

> The attorneys were applauding the clever way the court had spun the facts to defend the interests of big-time college sports. The court, as they saw it, had saved college sports from financial ruin. Recognizing college athletes as employees would have opened a Pandora's box of labor unions, unrelated business income taxes, and athletes demanding a share of the revenue they generate. . . . The clear message was that college athletes are amateurs whose compensation can be capped at room, board, tuition, and fees, regardless of the revenues they generate.

Meanwhile, Rensing spent the rest of his life in a wheelchair.

The question of whether athletes were workers was never satisfactorily settled, and for a quarter-century the case of Alvin Waldrep, an injured Texas Christian University football player, lingered in the courts. In a game against the University of Alabama in 1974, Waldrep crashed helmet first into artificial turf, resulting in a spinal injury that left him paralyzed and rendering him a quadriplegic. Waldrep did not claim workers' compensation for nearly two decades, but when he did, he asked Walter Byers to be an expert witness. By then Byers had done an about-face and believed that athletes were exploited by commercialized college athletics. His book, *Unsportsmanlike Conduct: Exploiting College Athletes*, which was published seven years after his retirement and five years before the 2000 Waldrep decision, demonstrated that Byers no longer backed the NCAA and the insurance industry in the fight against Waldrep's claims for compensation. No longer praising amateurism and no longer defending NCAA policies in the name of amateurism, Byers wrote, "Collegiate amateurism is not a moral issue; it is an economic camouflage for monopoly practice."[26]

Called as an expert witness, Byers gave a deposition in support of Waldrep. When asked, Byers said that the term "student-athlete" was created to better "deal with" workers' compensation claims. He further stated that the concept of the "student-athlete" was "put in place to make clear the colleges' intent that the grant-in-aid was not for-pay contract. . . ." Yet, unfortunately for Waldrep, Byers never said that the term "student-athlete" was created to thwart workers' compensation claims. The judge ultimately threw out Byers's deposition, saying that it would unfairly prejudice the jury for blasting the NCAA's continual effort to make money while constraining athletes' rights.[27] Byers is now dead, but the question of the rights of "college workers" is not. When Waldrep died in 2022, the NCAA had never done what he asked the national organization to do. "I want the N.C.A.A. to admit that they've made a mistake all these years," he noted in 1997, "by not protecting the kids who bring in the millions of dollars and make college athletics possible."[28]

The Waldrep case did move the NCAA into the twenty-first century relative to workers' rights, even as Waldrep lost in court by a 10–2 jury vote. It was quite clear that Waldrep had signed two agreements in his senior year of high school—a "Letter of Intent" to attend and participate in athletics at Texas Christian and a Financial Aid Agreement including payment of $10 a month for "laundry." In other words, he had agreed to a full athletic scholarship. Two decades later, the NCAA no longer used the term "amateur" in its constitution, and players' rights were expanded to include rights to their names, images, and likenesses following the 2021 *NCAA v. Shawne Alston* decision.

Cases arguing that athlete workers should be compensated continued to challenge the NCAA. The most cited case is *Gillian Berger v. NCAA*. Berger was a former member of the University of Pennsylvania track and field team. Competing for an Ivy League university that did not offer athletic scholarships, Berger and her teammates claimed in 2016 that they were workers deserving minimum wages under the federal government's Fair Labor Standards Act. They were not physically injured, as were players in workers' compensation cases, but they argued that they were being deprived of minimum wages as workers for their track team. In a more emphatic ruling than judges had offered in workers' compensation cases, the court ruled that NCAA sports are "extracurricular" and that, therefore, the Fair Labor Standards Act did not apply.[29] However, in a concurring decision, circuit court judge David Hamilton stated that the decision might be different with the big-time sports of men's basketball and football, as the "economic reality and the tradition of amateurism may not point in the same direction."[30] Hamilton might have added that college amateurism was moving in the direction of extinction, while economics and lawsuits continued to dominate.

Even as its use in public discourse and in law persisted, the term "student-athlete" continued to come under attack. These attacks rarely came from officials in the NCAA, though one early leader did so sarcastically. In 1974 the Big Ten commissioner spoke out cryptically following the defeat of the NCAA 1.600 grade point average as the minimum predictive score to receive an athletic scholarship. "I for one," Commissioner Wayne Duke told the NCAA assembly, "would move the elimination of the word *student* from *student-athlete*. . . ." He was applauded by several of the assembled members. Few others would speak out against the words embedded in the NCAA constitution. Decades later, following the University of North Carolina's academic scandal involving courses in Black studies being part of a sham curriculum, the North Carolina school newspaper acted. The *Daily Tar Heel* decided never to use the term "student-athlete" after North Carolina "failed to educate hundreds of 'student-athletes' for nearly 20 years."[31]

In an even more powerful statement, Jennifer Abruzzo, the general counsel of the National Labor Relations Board, declared that the term "student-athletes" had been "created to deprive those individuals of workplace protections." This was a decade after honored writer Taylor Branch simply penned, "It's a sham," when referring to the term "student-athlete."[32] As head of the National Labor Relations Board in 2022, Abruzzo promised to "pursue an independent violation where an employer misclassifies Players at Academic Institutions as student-athletes." Misclassifying college athletic employees "as mere 'student-athletes,'" Abruzzo warned, was a violation of Section 8(a)(1) of the National Labor Relations Act. Whether the NLRA and Abruzzo would have any success in defending athlete worker rights by eliminating the term "student-athlete" was questionable.

The term "student-athlete" is likely to remain, but at the same time, the movement for athletes' worker rights is also likely to persist, unless the term is attacked in the courts. The billion-dollar NCAA is quite capable of financially insuring its athletes without them being cited as workers. The Nebraska state legislature moved in that direction in the 1980s when it contemplated paying college football players, who would then come under the Nebraska workers' compensation law. This proposed change followed on the heels of advice from Ed Garvey, executive director of the National Football League Players Association. Garvey wanted college athletics to recognize four-year athletic scholarships, apply minimum wage laws to college athletes, and require workers' compensation for all college athletes.[33]

Ernie Chambers was a leader in the Nebraska state legislature favoring the compensation of college athletes. He was a far-left legislator from Omaha in a right-wing state who loved Nebraska's historically dominant football teams. Beginning in 1981 and continuing for years, Chambers pressed for legislation to make workers of Nebraska football players. In Chambers's vision, college athletes would then be similar to other state employees, with workers' compensation rights. By writing an op ed in the *New York Times*, Chambers made his cause a national issue, at least in the eyes of Walter Byers and NCAA leadership.[34] Could a Nebraska legislator influence other states to consider football players as workers and ruin the NCAA's long-standing claim that they were amateurs, playing for the intrinsic benefits of participation as an avocation for physical, mental, and social reasons? Chambers wanted the hypocrisy of non-compensation amateur rules to end.

As Chambers kept up his call for pay for players, he even invited All-American Dean Steinkuhler, the Nebraska winner of both the Outland and Lombardi trophies, to dress up in Nebraska football togs and speak before the legislators. This stunt garnered enough attention nationally for Byers to write to the chancellor of the University of Nebraska, Martin Massengale, indicating that Chambers's legislative proposals were not compatible with NCAA legislation. Disability compensation for football players, Byers wrote, would be an "improper benefit to a student-athlete under NCAA legislation." Byers relayed to the chancellor that Chambers's proposals "would be directly contrary to the continuing effort to maintain intercollegiate sports as part of the educational system and distinguishable from a professional sports business."[35] Byers asked if Nebraska legislation favoring workers' compensation might be changed to an insurance package for athletes, to avoid the Nebraska workers' compensation bill. This change could save amateurism and the financial benefits that would accrue to the NCAA and institutions such as the University of Nebraska.[36] Eventually, the Nebraska state legislature passed a bill for mandatory insurance for athletes.[37] Byers had temporarily helped solve the payment riddle, but the debate was not completely forgotten. One who remembered was Keith Haskins, who wrote a law article in the 1990s titled "Pay for Play." Haskins was convinced, as had been stated legally before, that "the cost of the product should bear the blood of the workman."[39] Haskins concluded that most college athletes were in fact employees of their universities and should receive benefits, such as workers' compensation, that attach to such a status.

Walter Byers had been successful for decades in warding off legal judgments by legislators and courts against the myth of amateurism. He had protected "amateur" athletes from becoming workers under the law. Earlier in his career, another major threat from professional sports, particularly professional football and baseball, jeopardized his success as a leading sport administrator. The risk to the NCAA's version of amateurism in these highly competitive, commercialized, and professionalized sports demanded a strong leader. Whether court cases opposing workers' compensation were ultimately beneficial to intercollegiate athletics, defeating athletes as workers had been a clear victory for the head of the NCAA. The effectiveness of Byers's leadership was clearly demonstrated as the fear of professional sports negatively impacting amateur college athletics called for strong NCAA action.

THREE

Fear of the Pros, Especially Football

"Dig in and fight like hell on this one."

—WALTER BYERS, OPPOSING FRIDAY NIGHT AND SATURDAY TV BY PROS, 1964

"[Y]ou are the one person in whom I have confidence enough in to beat Rozelle."

—FOREST EVASHEVSKI, TO WALTER BYERS, 1971

Walter Byers spent his adult life accepting the idea that college athletes should be amateurs. The concept of amateurism might have been augmented by his work for the NCAA in trying to convince state agencies and federal legislators that athletes were amateur and, thus, not subject to workers' compensation laws and taxation. After all, gate receipts from college athletics had been taxed up to 20 percent from the time of the Great Depression until the Korean War in the early 1950s. Nonetheless, the major professional sports, especially football, likely posed as great a threat to the prosperity of big-time college sports as workers' compensation and gate receipt taxation. Byers took a leadership role with athletic directors, coaches, and college presidents in fighting the threat of professional sports as they expanded commercially following World War II. But the fear of professional sports began much earlier, and as with most activities in college sports, the professional threat was centered primarily around football, the dominant college sport since the late nineteenth century.

FEARING THE PROS BEFORE BYERS WAS BORN

A fear of professional sports was not new when Walter Byers became NCAA executive director, but it intensified during his tenure, as professional football, particularly, was considered a major threat to the collegiate game. The collegiate fear of the pros began in the nineteenth century with baseball, but when pro football took root after World War I, and particularly when the National Football League was formed in 1920, this sport became a greater threat to the NCAA.[1] Many towns and cities in America formed football teams in the early 1900s, including two keen Ohio competitors, the Canton Bulldogs and the Massillon Tigers. They were paying some or all of their players when the NFL was born in Canton, with each franchise paying $100 to join the NFL. In Illinois, two small cities with a population of six thousand or less, Carlinville and Taylorville, had teams. Though these two towns, both just south of Springfield, Illinois, did not pay to join the NFL, as did Canton and Massillon, their small-town rivalry was apparent when, in the fall of 1921, each town's football team decided to defeat the other with players hired from the University of Notre Dame and University of Illinois just after the college season concluded. Carlinville's team was composed mostly of Notre Dame players, and Taylorville, the winners 16–0, with players from the University of Illinois. The matchup became national news when an estimated $100,000 was bet on the game, though the victorious Illinois players were paid less than $500 collectively.[2] This type of pro football upset the "amateur" institutions of the NCAA and prompted them to take national action.

The Taylorville-Carlinville headline event hastened the formation of the American Football Coaches Association by college coaches across America, to fight the perceived negative impact of pro football on the "amateur" college game.[3] The Southwest Conference passed a regulation against any student participating in exhibition football games, while the Missouri Valley Conference voted unanimously to refuse recognition to any player or official involved in professional football.[4] Probably more importantly, the Big Ten Conference had been advocating to ban players or officials who took part in professional football since before America's entry into World War I. The Taylorville-Carlinville game spurred the Big Ten into action. The conference passed a resolution to bar any athlete or official involved in professional football from college participation or employment. Among those most vocal against professionalizing college football was the Big Ten's Amos Alonzo Stagg, the prominent football coach and athletic director at the University of Chicago since 1892. "I have noted the danger of the college sport because of the professional game for years," Stagg remarked, "and it is time that we stopped it."[5] Within six months, the Big Ten had hired the first college conference commissioner, Major John L. Griffith, to uphold amateurism—something Walter Byers would be called upon to accomplish three decades later.[6] History, it is worth noting, has not been kind toward their efforts.

Two years after Griffith left the University of Illinois to take the position of commissioner, arguably the most celebrated star in collegiate football history, Harold "Red" Grange, who played for Illinois, agreed to sign the most lucrative contract ever given to a college player to play professional football. The few hundred dollars given to Taylorville-Carlinville collegians just before Grange starred at Illinois seemed like pocket change compared to the $100,000 and more that Grange received from his agent, Charles "Cash and Carry" Pyle, to sign with the professional Chicago Bears. It was the most controversial signing of a football player in intercollegiate history and supported the common belief that professional football contaminated the collegiate game.[7] This belief continued until after World War II, when the growth of television intensified the conflict and led many collegiate leaders to fear that professional football telecasts would ruin college football.

THE PROFESSIONAL CHALLENGE OF TWO-PLATOON FOOTBALL

By the time Walter Byers became executive director of the NCAA, college and professional football were being televised, though this only became a major concern to college officials because of diminishing gate receipts. The advent of sport telecasting elevated pro football, which would eventually overtake the college game in national interest. Part of that popularity came from the pros not needing to accommodate tradition, such as a belief in building character, attached to the college game. One of the collegiate traditions was that players on starting teams should play the entire game, except for in the event of serious injuries. The pros, by contrast, began using specific defensive and offensive teams during World War II and continued the tactic after the war. Fresh teams, the pros believed, produced more interesting games. For example, quarterbacks could concentrate on completing passes rather than on tackling opponents when playing defense.

Yet the collegiate tradition of players playing the entire game persisted, especially among older coaches and administrators. Howard Bingham, Harvard athletic director since the 1920s, chimed in on the side of the retention of restricted substitution as chairman of the Football Rules Committee in the 1940s. "Old players, spectators, radio, and newspaper men," Bingham stated, "are almost unanimous in their condemnation [of liberalized rules] . . . We just cannot disregard the past and consider only what the present generation wants."[8] Later, Robert Neyland, another Football Rules Committee chairman, agreed. He was a famed coach at the University of Tennessee, a West Point athlete and general during World War II, and the most honored Southern college coach from the 1930s into the 1950s. By 1960, Neyland had retired from coaching, but as chairman of the Rules Committee, he was strident when the question of voting for free substitutions came up. The Rules Committee members were by then nearly unanimous in favor of two-platoon football to increase the quality of play and to help combat the rising interest in pro football. Neyland asked the committee how many were opposed to two-platoon football. Only he raised his hand, and while grabbing and raising the hand of David Nelson, who was sitting next to him, Neyland forcefully declared, "There doesn't seem to be any sentiment to return to that chicken-shit football. Meeting is adjourned."[9] It took several more years before the Rules Committee adopted two-platoon football.

Walter Byers did not have an official voice on limiting substitutions, but he expressed strong opinions from early in his tenure with the NCAA. He sided with Bob Neyland and another individual key to crafting NCAA legislation, Fritz Crisler, former football coach and then athletic director at the University of Michigan. Crisler had favored two-platoon football in the 1940s but came to oppose it in the next decade, because he believed the game built less character when players did not participate in both the offense and the defense. In addition, he opposed the increased costs associated with recruiting and subsidizing larger squads and coaching staffs.[10] Early on, Byers hesitated to take sides in the controversial issue, but he let newspaper reporters know that the NCAA Council voted in 1953 to eliminate the NCAA's participation in liberal substitution, which had been initiated during World War II and continued during the Korean War era.[11] Byers and the NCAA Council , however, did not make football rules—the Football Rules Committee did. Byers continued to oppose unlimited substitutions well into the 1960s.

Byers used the controlled substitution argument to demonstrate that he and the NCAA were attempting to help all institutions, small and large, not just the big-time universities, build profitable football programs. Byers and many NCAA leaders wanted to contain the costs of expanded player and coaching personnel that the allowance of unlimited substitutions brought about in 1965. At the end of the 1960s, when two-platoon football was still being discussed, Byers used the *NCAA News* as a vehicle for expressing his views on how big-time football, including free substitutions, was negatively impacting college football, the entire NCAA membership, and all of college sport. Approaching nearly two decades as the head of the NCAA, he likely felt confident that he could take on big-time football.

Byers expressed his fear of increased professionalism in college sport in his unexpected diatribe, "A Personal Viewpoint: Assault on Amateurism," printed in the *NCAA News* that regularly went to every member of the NCAA. Byers condemned what he saw as some of the worst faults of big-time college football programs, including football athletic dorms, bonuses given to coaches for bowl game participation, use of weight training classes for football players to get around out-of-season practice limits, as well as limited substitution. But on the eve of the 100th anniversary of college football, Byers aimed his vitriol at big-time football coaches, saying that "College football does not belong exclusively to . . . a ruling aristocracy of winning coaches who believe championships and national acclaim giving them a godly omniscience as to what should be done with the game." He wrote that "college football does not belong to the coaches and the Football Rules Committee." Specifically, Byers opposed the free substitution and two-platoon system that placed "a premium on more players, more coaches and larger traveling squads. . . ." Athletes, he believed, should know both offense and defense, rather than playing the equivalent of a game of golf that allowed one golfer to drive the ball and another to putt it. He opposed the spiraling costs of college football and the drive toward "aping the stereotyped offensive and defensive patterns of the professionals."[12] He said his piece, but not without retorts.

An immediate response came from the president of the American Football Coaches Association, Paul F. Dietzel. He called Byers's attack on coaches as "pro-oriented thinkers" the "most ridiculous of your charges." Dietzel, the University of South Carolina coach and a strong supporter of unlimited substitution, condemned the executive director's "unsubstantiated public attack" on coaches as "unwarranted and flimsy," below the dignity of the head of the NCAA.[13] Byers, not being one to take a reprisal lightly, responded with a piece called "Assault on Amateurism," singling out "some harried administrators, a few win-conscious coaches and the professionals themselves who have no regard or respect for amateur principles." Sarcastically reacting to Dietzel and "the newly discovered pen pals in the football coaching fraternity," he suggested that they attempt to reduce "football costs instead of repeated oaths of allegiance to two-platoon football. . . ."[14] The ultimate result, however, was the Rules Committee eventually voting to continue the more exciting two-platoon football. As a future coach of Notre Dame, Dan Devine, admitted, this "enabled college football to compete with professional football for fan interest."[15] The score became football coaches—1; Byers—0. Two-platoon football remained a dominant feature of college football, just as it did in the pros.

PROFESSIONAL FOOTBALL TELECASTING AND THE SATURDAY ENCOUNTERS

Two-platoon football had implications for competition between collegiate and professional sports, but the potential of pro football telecasts airing on the day most colleges played their games was a greater threat to the financial viability of collegiate athletics. Though pro football was a Sunday afternoon sport, and their telecasts did not interfere with traditional college football games, the threat to colleges became more apparent after the National Football League's 1958 championship game had a TV audience of thirty million. The New York Giants lost to the Baltimore Colts in overtime, with a one-yard run by the University of Wisconsin's Heisman Trophy winner Alan "The Horse" Ameche. *Sports Illustrated* called it "the best football game ever played," and Roone Arledge, leader of ABC-TV sports, labeled it "the ultimate game."[16] This was an indication that pro football had become a major challenge to the college game.

There was enough interest in pro football for a second league, the American Football League, to invade the space in 1960. The AFL's success was dependent on TV contracts and the possibility of playing on both Friday nights and Saturdays, times historically dominated by high school and college football. The threat of pro football telecast expansion caused Senator Estes Kefauver of Tennessee to introduce a bill to compel the NFL and the new AFL to restrict their games to Sundays only. An important result was the passage of the Sports Broadcasting Act of 1961, which was helpful to both pro football and the college game. The act gave pro football an antitrust exemption allowing it to eliminate TV competition among the competing teams and to divide the media profits equally among NFL teams.[17] At the same time, college football was protected from pro telecasts on Saturdays. Though not written into the original law, the intention was to reserve Saturdays for college football and Friday nights for the feeder group of high school football players to perform without telecast competition from pro teams.

A loophole prompted the NFL to announce, three years after the passage of the 1961 act, that it would legally telecast on Friday nights, at a time when eighteen thousand weekly high school games were played. Byers and the NCAA quickly came to the aid of the high schools that fed their college football programs. As soon as he heard of the NFL's intentions, Byers telegraphed fifteen US senators protesting NFL commissioner Pete Rozelle's decision to move some games to Friday evenings.[18] Paradoxically, the NCAA had strongly considered telecasting football games on Friday evenings in the decade before the Sports Broadcasting Act.[19] However, in 1964, the NCAA claimed this as a major violation by the NFL of the Sports Broadcasting Act. Fridays and Saturdays were considered almost sacrosanct for "amateur" football because they ensured the financial wellbeing of both high school football programs and most sports on big-time college campuses. Because the NFL and the new American Football League were in discussions with congressional leaders to broaden their exemptions from antitrust laws, politically it was not a good time for the NFL to encroach upon what Congress and many Americans saw as nearly sacred ground. Almost immediately, college leaders called upon congressional leaders to reverse the Sports Broadcasting Act monopoly exemptions for pro football television revenues. "Dig in and fight like hell on this one," Byers told commissioner of the Big Ten, William Reed, encouraging him to make sure that high schools got involved in protesting the NFL's actions.[20] Soon, the NFL reevaluated its incursions into Friday night football. The NCAA response to their fear of the pros had been successful, at least temporarily.

THE PROS AND THE SIGNING OF COLLEGE PLAYERS

The pros agreed to not play their games in time slots traditionally reserved for high schools and colleges. While the NCAA was pushing for a law to prevent the NFL and AFL from reneging on their promise, another issue came to the fore—signing collegiate athletes before the end of their eligibility. If it were not already clear that the NCAA was primarily interested in the welfare of institutions playing football at the expense of athletes who might make money from their on-field expertise, the organization's response to the signing of college players before their eligibility was completed proved the point. No one made it a national issue if a collegiate debater or musician left college for personal reasons before they graduated. Even in sports, a collegiate golfer, swimmer, or soccer player leaving school with eligibility remaining resulted in hardly a murmur. But if a football player at a big-time institution considered dropping out of school to join the pro football ranks, it was considered nearly a criminal act.

Major figures began to criticize pro football leaders for signing collegians to pro contracts. Harold Keith, a University of Oklahoma supporter and president of the College Sports Information Directors of America, stated pointedly that Oklahoma players could hardly keep their minds on football when "some professional representative would be wining and dining them at some café and talking contract." To Keith, it wasn't that leaving school interfered with their education but that professional recruiters interfered with the focus of the football team.[21] Walter Byers and the NCAA leadership had to decide what to do to protect institutional football but not the players. Was it legally wrong for University of Georgia star tackle James Wilson to sign a contract with the professional Boston [New England] Patriots before the start of his senior season? Was it criminal for the Patriots to ask Wilson to drop out of Georgia so that he could play pro football in the fall? Or did it simply run counter to the NCAA's eventually failed effort to preserve "amateurism" and money in college sports? What would the NCAA do to prevent pro teams from signing the already written but unsigned contracts at the end of the Gator Bowl contest, such as transpired with Florida State's star quarterback Steve Tensi, end Fred Biletnekoff, and two others? Four Oklahoma players earlier had been dropped from the same Gator Bowl for signing contracts. These contracts brought criticism from university officials, including Clemson University president Robert Edwards, for a college becoming "a farm club for the professional football leagues."[22] Byers would only comment that the signings were a "disgrace," but were they disgraceful to the athletes who could have benefitted financially in America's free enterprise system?[23] These athletes had no say except in the "underground" system in effect with the pros.

Byers and the NCAA went to Congress for help in protecting college football from the pros. Byers wrote to the NCAA Legislative Committee that, because pro football was "dependent upon the college product," the NCAA would ask Congress to prevent both the early signing of football players and the airing of pro football games during Friday night high school football.[24] While the NFL and the new American Football League did not stop airing games on Friday nights and Saturdays, there was an eventual joint NFL-AFL agreement not to sign college athletes who had remaining eligibility. Then, in 1983, an upstart league, the United States Football League, and its New York City member, the New York Generals, offered Herschel Walker, then finishing his junior year at Georgia, a reported $5 million contract.[25] As when Red Grange signed and participated with the Chicago Bears in the 1920s, Walker's jump to the pros when he was arguably the greatest college football player in history caused the NCAA to condemn the action in the name of amateurism. In the month before Byers retired, early professional contracts for college football players had not been successfully terminated. In his last days with the NCAA, Byers condemned the NFL supplemental draft allowing Ohio State's Cris Carter and Pittsburgh's Charles Gladman to join the pro league.[26] The fear of the pros evident when Byers began his tenure as a twenty-nine-year-old was still present over three and a half decades later.

BYERS TV NEGOTIATIONS WITH THE EASTERN ELITE

We may never know how much Walter Byers's distrust of people from the East Coast played into his attitude and actions as head of the NCAA. Byers's birth, rearing, and schooling in the Midwest likely tainted his image of Easterners, especially New Yorkers who worked in the communications center of the world. According to ABC's Roone Arledge, an Easterner, Byers had a strong bias against Eastern "city slickers" involved in pro football.[27] A fear of the pros and of New York City's media dominance appeared to influence Byers's approach to dealing with Easterners and the haughty Ivy League. "I was reared in the Midwest," Byers once wrote, "where it was common to poke fun at the intellectual elitism and athletic hypocrisy of the eight private Ivy institutions."[28] Byers had many ways to combat Eastern elitism, but negotiating NCAA television contracts was likely his most powerful tactic. The financial strength of the NCAA in Byers's years came from the successful negotiations with the feared Eastern establishment.

From the early onset of commercial television, New York City networks came to dominate big-time football telecasts. Walter Byers, who became the chief negotiator of the NCAA's television committee, had to navigate the power and influence of the chief networks, well-established NBC and CBS as well as upstart ABC. His ability to negotiate effectively with networks was legendary and became central to the commercial success of the NCAA and its institutions. Byers was not a newcomer to media rights when he became executive director in 1951, since he had worked for the Big Ten for four years and had previously worked for United Press in New York City for several years. The NCAA created the first television committee just before Byers became executive director. Two Ivy League Easterners, Robert Hall of Yale and Ralph Furey of Columbia, led the committee as co-chairs. This Eastern control continued the next year with the TV steering committee consisting of three Easterners, Hall, Asa Bushnell of the Eastern College Athletic Conference, and Shober Barr of Franklin and Marshall College in Pennsylvania, along with Byers.[29] Byers's tenure lasted decades, becoming more important as the years went by due to his superb negotiating skills.

While Byers became the chief negotiator for the NCAA, an even younger Roone Arledge proved to be the mastermind of ABC Sports, using NCAA football telecasts as a major vehicle to success. The relationship began in

1960 when the twenty-nine-year-old Arledge was hired away from NBC to produce college football after ABC shrewdly outmaneuvered NBC to gain the NCAA contract.[30] ABC would win nearly all of the NCAA football contracts for the next two decades, until the US Supreme Court ruled in 1984 that the NCAA violated the Sherman Antitrust Act of 1890 by fixing prices and limiting telecast production.[31] In that time, ABC, with the addition of Arledge, moved from a relatively unimportant network to a world class organization. The network's rise included creating *Monday Night Football* and possibly the greatest regular sports show in history, *Wide World of Sports*.[32] ABC soon became the NCAA's favored network, in part because of such Arledge innovations as numerous and isolated camera angles, slow-motion shorts and instant replays, split-screen views, and titillating shots of female cheerleaders.

Arledge's negotiations with the NCAA were constantly accompanied by documents showing how much ABC was losing on NCAA football telecasts. Byers was not moved by Arledge's claims. Byers always did his homework, coming to negotiations with solid facts. He knew the Nielson ratings, advertising rates and the average cost of ads, the rights fees of other sport packages, the number and acceptable types of commercials, and who he wanted for game announcers.[33] Byers was much more skeptical than were members of his NCAA television committee, demanding answers from the New York-dominated networks. He specifically favored ABC in the 1960s because the network then had no relationship to professional football.[34] However, he rejected ABC's economic tears of penury, knowing that ABC needed NCAA telecasts to keep its affiliated stations happy, thereby keeping ABC profitable. Byers used all his skills to wring out every dollar he could for the NCAA and its institutions.

Problems arose when ABC and Arledge decided to get into professional football with prime time *Monday Night Football* (*MNF*) in 1970. Although Byers began by thinking that a "good movie will do better" than a pro football game on Monday evening, he soon found out that *MNF* was a rare TV phenomenon.[35] Byers became even more testy and fearful when dealing with the network that produced pro football's biggest draw. Within a year of the first *MNF* telecast, Byers wrote Arledge that ABC would not be allowed to promote *MNF* on any Saturday college football telecast from the pregame show to the end of the postgame show.[36]

One negotiation that became legendary among the NCAA leadership happened a decade later, when the NCAA was in a heated battle with the new College Football Association (CFA) over who controlled the rights to telecast college games. Was it individual institutions, such as the University of Oklahoma or Georgia, or was it the NCAA? The NCAA wanted to squeeze out the last dollar in negotiations with ABC. Attempting to out-profit the CFA as it was negotiating TV rights, Byers got into a verbal battle that nearly became a physical confrontation with the negotiating team for ABC, Charlie Lavery and his superior Jim Spence, longtime assistant to Roone Arledge.

In a series of negotiations with ABC beginning in Denver, Byers and the NCAA needed to reach an agreement with ABC prior to a two-network deal that would include CBS. The two-network proposal would counter NBC's proposal with the CFA to telecast big-time football. In the negotiations, ABC's Charlie Lavery made a false statement about a previously agreed upon item, Byers got up, stuck his finger in Lavery's face, and, as Byers remembered, blurted out, "You're lying, you sonofabitch, and you know it!"[37] Byers, short of stature like Napoleon Bonaparte but strong in determination, then walked out of the meeting as the two sides were close to a deal worth either $131,500,000 or $131,750,000. Leaving the deal unsigned at the Denver meeting, the parties met again in Newport, Rhode Island. In those discussions, Jim Spence wanted a small by TV standards $250,000 concession that he could take back to Arledge. He asked, "Walter, if ABC Sports will commit one hundred and thirty-one and a half million dollars, do we have a deal?" Byers replied sharply, "The number is one thirty-one seven fifty!" As Jim Spence wrote in his *Up Close and Personal*, "There would not be one single crumb for me to take back to New York. Strike one for the cowboy from Kansas City. . . . He had once again stuck it to the television hotshots from New York."[38] The unrefined Midwesterner with cowboy boots who had once worked for the United Press in New York City had extracted what he wanted from the sophisticated Easterners.[39] Byers–1, ABC–0.

THE MANY FACES OF PRO FOOTBALL FEAR

Even as the NCAA and its college football and men's basketball grew in wealth in the Byers era, the lingering fear that pro football would damage colleges financially and cause great harm to all "amateur" college sport remained. The pro impact was felt in more than TV negotiations, Saturday games, competing with two-platoon football, or pros signing college players. Beginning in the 1950s, the NCAA asked broadcasters to ban discussions of professional events when broadcasting college games. When networks began showing commercials starring professionals in various sports, Walter Byers and the rest of the NCAA television committee voted unanimously to oppose Coca Cola's request to feature star pro athletes such as Arnold Palmer in golf, Willie Mays in baseball, Barbara Ann Scott in figure skating, Parnelli Jones in auto racing, and Jim Taylor, the featured Green Bay Packer, in football.[40] Why? To protect its amateur image from the contamination of professionals. Five years later, in 1969, the television committee voted 11–0 to "bar pro football mentions in station break commercials," including one featuring O. J. Simpson in his pro football uniform that, along with other ads, would "publicize or promote professional football either directly or indirectly."[41] Byers, in his negotiating stance with Roone Arledge, asked that there be no commercial that is "derogatory to college football."[42] Ads with professional athletes were considered derogatory to the college game, and this ban on pro athletes continued well into the future. In the NCAA's last football contract before the US Supreme Court ruled that the organization violated antitrust laws, ABC was still prohibited from using pro athletes in advertising during college football games. Byers wrote in the margins of a negotiation letter, "No pro FB players," reinforcing his belief in amateurism and fear of the pros.[43]

Barring pro athletes from advertising during college games was similar to efforts by Byers and other NCAA leaders to exclude television announcers from working college games if they had been closely associated with professional athletics. In the 1960s, the NCAA continued to negotiate the elimination of most chief announcers and color commentators who were involved in professional football. The NCAA loved Lindsey Nelson not only for his broadcasting insights and voice but because he had done minimal announcing of professional football games. At the same time, former professional players suggested as color commentators, including Frank Albert (San Francisco 49ers), Paul Hornung (Green Bay Packers), and John Lujack (Chicago Bears), were all rejected for being closely identified with professional football.[44] A major exception to this rule was the acceptance of Red

Grange as the color man to team up with the favored Lindsay Nelson. It would be difficult to reject the most famous player in college football. In addition, the NCAA television committee argued that "it is important in the football telecasts to maintain the college image with which Lindsey Nelson has come to be closely identified."[45] Forest Evashevski, who had been a successful coach and later athletic director at the University of Iowa, told Byers in the early 1970s that, to better compete against the pros, he must focus on "First, the insistence of play by play and color men who are college oriented [giving] continuity to the promotion of the college game."[46] Byers did not need to be told, and announcers were particularly cognizant that they must emphasize only positive aspects of college football during their broadcasts.

While announcers associated with the pros were condemned by the NCAA, so too were college bands who were invited to participate at professional games. By the time Walter Byers became executive director, marching bands had existed at colleges for over half a century. Bands, led first by cornets and then by trumpets, were warlike instruments from antiquity used to fire up military troops before engagement with the enemy. They were used similarly with competitors on the athletic field.[47] As football became the dominant college sport by the end of the nineteenth century, it was natural for bands to play at home games to fire up not only the competitors but the fans, similar to the use of cheerleaders. If bands were successful at home games, money was often raised to send them on the road. Gate receipts were sometimes used to fund this travel. When television became more prominent following World War II, bands were used to keep the attention of fans at games and in front of the TVs, especially during halftimes. Since most professional football teams did not have their own bands, they would often invite bands from local colleges to entertain during Sunday afternoon games.[48] This use of college bands offended the NCAA. The NCAA television committee, consumed by its fear of professional football, even voted nearly unanimously to ask the NCAA Council to restrict college bands from appearing at pro games.[49] Image mattered.

Allowing professional teams to compete in college stadiums was almost as abhorrent to the NCAA as pro football announcers. Most big-time college stadiums in the second half of the twentieth century were larger than the professional team stadiums, and they were often eyed by the pros as possible venues for their games. Before Byers was hired, the NCAA exerted little leverage in any important decisions, except in establishing rules for football and other sports. Under Home Rule, the NCAA was never involved in negotiating for the use of college stadiums. Early on, professional teams negotiated with colleges for facilities without pressure from NCAA officials. The Detroit Lions played in the University of Detroit stadium in the mid-1930s, and the Green Bay Packers competed in the Marquette University stadium in Milwaukee in the early 1950s. Little notice was paid to the pros renting college stadiums until television made pro football attractive later in the1950s and into the 1960s.

The threat of professional teams using college stadiums prompted conferences and the NCAA to act. When the Pittsburgh Steelers rented the University of Pittsburgh stadium in the 1950s, Byers commented that "professional athletes and college athletes must be separated," while former Big Ten commissioner Tug Wilson remarked that "we must draw a firm line of demarcation" between the pros and the amateurs.[50] In the early 1970s, the Chicago Bears needed an alternative venue to Wrigley Field, where the Chicago Cubs baseball team resided. They looked at a site only a few miles away, Northwestern University's Dyche Stadium. After a court fight with the town of Evanston, a judge allowed one game in 1970 to avoid a possible baseball playoff game in Wrigley Field, then the home of the Bears. This Bears game was played in Evanston, but the following year a five-year Northwestern agreement with George Halas of the Bears was nullified by the Big Ten. Following a letter to each conference athletic director containing a *Chicago Tribune* article titled "Byers' Letter Put Pressure on Big 10," the Big Ten voted "no" to the $2.2 million agreement. Despite Northwestern athletic director Tippy Die acknowledging that "we needed that money badly," Michigan's AD, Don Canham, stated plainly that "If the pros come in, the college game is dead."[51] Canham and Byers agreed.

Contrary to the Big Ten, from the 1950s to the 1970s, the Ivy League did not prevent the University of Pennsylvania from subletting its stadium to a professional team. Another Ivy school, Princeton University, allowed its Palmer Stadium to be used for a professional football charity event in the year the Bears played their one game at Northwestern's venue.[52] The Philadelphia Eagles moved into the University of Pennsylvania's massive Franklin Field at about the same time that the Big Ten voted the Chicago

Bears out of one of its facilities—and the Eagles stayed on the Penn campus for a dozen years.[53] The NCAA may not have given much thought to Penn's Franklin Field, since Ivy League football was no longer considered big-time and the Eastern Ivies were an afterthought. Michigan's Don Canham did use a questionable argument that Penn's football average game attendance was 50,000 before the Philadelphia Eagles began to compete on Franklin Field and dropped to 10,000 following the stadium's use by professionals.[54] Canham, however, took the Penn figures two decades apart, the second figure emerging after Penn and the Ivy League no longer played big-time football. He nevertheless made his point with the other Big Ten voters on the issue. The leading conference in America would not open its facilities for professional use because of the belief that pro football would diminish the college game. The fear factor had been made manifest.

NO HALL OF FAME—NO FEARS?

Professional football's influence on college football may seem distant from discussions on building a college football hall of fame, but one should consider the relationship. Fear of professional teams influenced even these decisions, and Walter Byers was in the middle of the debate. Canton, Ohio, the birthplace of the National Football League in 1920, was the logical place for a professional hall of fame. Less than a year after 1958's "Greatest Game Ever Played" between the Baltimore Colts and the New York Giants, a Canton newspaper published a piece titled, "PRO FOOTBALL NEEDS A HALL OF FAME AND THE LOGICAL SITE IS HERE." Within four years, Canton raised the money, received donated land, broke ground, and opened the Pro Football Hall of Fame.[55] Why hadn't the football schools of the NCAA already made a similar effort, particularly since intercollegiate football existed more than half a century before the NFL was born? Not only that, but national halls of fame had been present in America since 1936, when the Baseball Hall of Fame in Cooperstown, New York, was established. Before the Pro Football Hall of Fame was opened in 1963, many other major sports had halls of fame, including PGA golf (1940), women's golf (1951), tennis (1954), softball (1957), and basketball (1959).

The construction of a college football hall of fame seemed logical because of the long history and prominence of football at the intercollegiate level of competition. Rutgers and Princeton initiated intercollegiate play shortly after the Civil War. NCAA institutions preceded the professional game by decades, with crowds in the tens of thousands prior to the first pro game. College also boasted much larger stadiums and greater TV revenue, season-ending bowl games, and strong alumni support before professional football made its move after World War II. Maybe college football fans were content with their superior position in the world of sports without displaying their collective history in a singular location. Maybe there was public arrogance that the college "amateur" game was far superior to the professional model and did not need a symbol of its superiority. Maybe individual universities had their own halls of fame, such as Louisiana State, Nebraska, and Texas, or were considering it, like Michigan and Ohio State. Maybe the concept of a hall of fame was negatively influenced by Easterners, who wanted the world to know that the Eastern Ivy League should be celebrated for the origin of football. Maybe the Eastern emphasis on a potential hall of fame irritated some individuals who were from the Midwest, where football dominated for decades after World War I. Might Walter Byers, a Midwesterner from birth who spent most of his college years at Iowa, be brought into the discussion?

Byers was working for the United Press in New York City when a football fan in Syracuse, New York, Arthur Evans, suggested the idea of a college football hall of fame. A national football foundation was soon created and a hall of fame proposed. With the help of sportswriter Grantland Rice and West Point football coach Earl "Red" Blaik, Rutgers University, the birthplace of intercollegiate football, was chosen as the site for a college football hall of fame, prior to Byers becoming NCAA executive director. The founders began fundraising efforts by contacting football schools in the NCAA and soon decided to choose the first hall of fame class in 1951. They chose well: Walter Camp of Yale, Harold "Red" Grange of Illinois, Bronko Nagurski of Minnesota, Knute Rockne of Notre Dame, Jim Thorpe of the Carlisle Indian School, and Glenn "Pop" Warner, coach of Cornell, the Carlisle Indians, Pittsburgh, and Stanford. While no Southern hall of famers were chosen, these individuals did represent a number of successful football-playing schools. Yet the original eleven schools subscribing to the hall of fame were principally Eastern universities, with six from the Ivy League and only two—Michigan and Notre Dame—from outside the East. Chester LaRoche, a former Yale quarterback and wealthy New

Yorker, became the first chairman of the National Football Foundation, which always held its black tie annual awards dinner in New York City's elite Hotel Astor.[56] Led by individuals from what were often considered the inferior football schools of the East, the NCAA paid little attention to Eastern control of the construction of a hall of fame.

Chester LaRoche and the National Football Foundation stayed at arm's length from the NCAA when the NCAA was flexing its muscles over college athletics in the decades following the hiring of an executive director. If the idea of a National Football Foundation and Hall of Fame had grown out of the NCAA with Walter Byers's backing, its chance of early success would have brightened. However, the idea of a Hall of Fame came from an individual from Syracuse, New York, not closely associated with the NCAA. Soon, a wealthy New York City advertising magnate and autocrat, Chester LaRoche, came to dominate the National Football Foundation (1956–71) and its policies. That did not please Byers or other NCAA leaders as they were quickly expanding their own institution, including the construction of a multi-million-dollar NCAA headquarters in the Kansas City area in the early 1970s. Funding a college football hall of fame to counter the professional hall of fame in Canton, Ohio, by taking a small percentage of each football television contract would have been relatively easy. This did not happen.

In the meantime, the National Football Foundation was fumbling football's college hall of fame. The foundation first obtained a site in 1967 at Rutgers University, held a groundbreaking ceremony at Rutgers, and then backtracked to place the hall of fame in a New York City mansion owned by Chester LaRoche.[57] Meanwhile, Tom Hamilton, former naval admiral and commissioner of the Pacific Athletic Conference, wrote to the NCAA television committee in the early 1970s and strongly suggested that the NCAA combat the growth of professional football. "The 'pros' have outstripped us in press, broadcasting, and political relations," his proposal read, "and are rapidly supplanting the 'hero worship' image of the college athlete." What to do? Should they compete with the pros by establishing a collegiate hall of fame like the one built in Canton, where the pros played an exhibition game each year for the institution's benefit? "I believe we are all blind and foolish," Hamilton wrote, "if we don't build it as rapidly as possible." He wanted one-half of 1 percent of the football TV revenue for six years be set aside to build the National Football Foundation's Hall of Fame.[58] Despite his plea, there was not enough support for Hamilton's envisioned hall of fame to garner NCAA patronage. Lacking NCAA backing, an unsuccessful hall was built on Kings Island, near Cincinnati, in 1978.[59] The efforts to establish a successful hall of fame continued.

By the early 1980s, with the backing of the National Association of College Athletic Directors and the American Football Coaches Association, the National Football Foundation began a successful fundraising effort with the Kickoff Classic Benefit Game, a contest featuring highly ranked teams playing just outside of New York City at the Meadowlands Stadium.[60] When Nebraska crushed the previous national champs, Penn State, in the first Kickoff Classic, 44–6, each team received considerably more than the guaranteed $550,000, while the National Football Foundation was guaranteed $350,000, the American Football Coaches Association $100,000, and the National Association of Collegiate Directors of Athletics $75,000. The "amateur" football players agreed to play for no remuneration. Jim Tarman, athletic director at Penn State, responded, "You're asking kids to play a game to benefit athletic directors and coaches. That's wrong."[61] Wrong or not, that is what the NCAA under Byers agreed to do. It was another case of the NCAA agreeing to help institutions while promoting its favored game with little or no thought about the athletes who were the visual feature of that game. As for the National Football Foundation, nearly two decades after Byers retired, the foundation elected Steve Hatchel as CEO in 2005. A Westerner and graduate of the University of Colorado, he was the first commissioner of the Big 12 Conference in the West. When elected to lead the National Football Foundation, Hatchel moved the headquarters from the East Coast to Irving, Texas, "to change the national perception of the National Football Foundation as an East Coast organization."[62] Walter Byers, then well into his eighties and living on his Kansas ranch, must have been pleased.

College football, despite its dominance since 1869, when the first intercollegiate soccer-like football game took place between Princeton and Rutgers, was challenged financially and in popular culture by professional football following World War II and during the Walter Byers era at the NCAA. Byers and the NCAA fought to keep the "amateur" college game with moderate success. When he resigned in 1987, Byers began writing his memoir about his involvement in the development of the NCAA. It was eventually published under the title *Unsportsmanlike Conduct: Exploiting College Athletes*. Nowhere in the index or the narrative are found the words "professional athletics," "fear of the pros," "National Football League," "Monday Night Football," or "Pete Rozelle." It was as if professional football was akin to victims of the disease of ancient and medieval society, leprosy—shunned and avoided. Or, as ABC's Roone Arledge believed, Byers may have considered pro football a "plague upon the land."[63] The impact of "fear of the pros," nonetheless, was immense on college sport and especially on football, and this fear strongly influenced the direction taken by Byers and the NCAA. So too, at about the same time, did the athletic struggle emanating from the larger American societal problems, namely the Cold War, the war in Vietnam, and the civil rights movement.

FOUR

The Cold War, Vietnam, and the Civil Rights Struggle

> "[We need to] assure academic integrity for the races and maintain athletic equality for the races."
>
> **—WALTER BYERS, 1968**

> "Those unconstructive dissenters are likely to come home to roost sooner than we expect."
>
> **—WALTER BYERS, 1969**

Walter Byers and the NCAA's "fear of the pros" primarily resulted from internal affairs of the NCAA and the growth of professional sport in America. Yet, major societal changes, including the decades-long Cold War with the Russian-dominated Union of Soviet Socialist Republics (USSR) had a profound impact upon the growth of the NCAA and Walter Byers's place in the organization. Byers, a political conservative, was a Cold War warrior against communism. Along with most individuals within the NCAA, he waved the flag for America in its lengthy Cold War battles with the USSR. His conservative views aligned with the views of those who backed America's involvement in the Vietnam War. A Cold War conservative, Byers was not in the forefront of a movement to bring African Americans and Historically Black Colleges and Universities (HBCUs) into full membership in the NCAA. His conservatism, as we shall later see, also led him to oppose bringing women in as equals in intercollegiate athletic competition.

WALTER BYERS JOINS THE COLD WAR

The Cold War relationship between the United States and the Soviet Union emerged soon after World War II, when the USSR and the United States were strained allies in defeating Nazi Germany. However, America's relationship with Russia had never been amicable from the time of the communist revolution during World War I and the creation of the USSR. The United States condemned the socialists of the USSR from the beginning, and this criticism intensified following the conclusion of the Second World War in 1945. Many Americans were concerned that "Russian Communists" planned to use Marxist ideology to control the world.[1] Government officials in the United States came to believe in a strategy of containment. That is, in territories where the Soviet Union attempted to expand its empire, the United States would resist. Containment took many forms, including the creation of a North Atlantic Treaty Organization of primarily European nations to prevent communist expansion into Western Europe. The Cold War saw the Soviets creating nuclear weapons to match America's in an arms race, as well as contests to see who could first send a satellite into space (the USSR) and who could first send an individual to the moon (the United States). In a less spectacular but memorable way, the Cold War inaugurated nuclear drills in American schools, where children covered their heads with backpacks and hid under their desks and encouraged some of their parents to build bomb shelters in their homes.

Sports, including those under NCAA control, played an important part in the Cold War relations between the Soviet Union and the United States. Just a few months prior to the building of the Berlin Wall separating Communist-held East Berlin from West Berlin, under western democratic control, a NCAA leader asked what American universities were doing to "defeat the Russians and the Communists in this important battle area of the Cold War."[2] Shortly before the symbolic and actual wall was constructed, and two years after the Soviet Union launched the first satellite, Sputnik, NCAA's Thomas Hamilton called for American colleges to promote Olympic development programs because in the "Cold War, the Olympic games have a great effect. . . ." For example, the Soviet Union hired fifty field hockey coaches from India, where the sport was popular, so that the USSR could medal in the 1960 Rome Olympics; they were unsuccessful.[3]

The Soviets, who first participated in the Olympics in 1952, made medaling in international sport a high priority.[4] In its initial entry, Russia led in medals won until the last day, when the Americans pulled ahead. They consistently outperformed America and its many collegiate athletes in international sport competition in the 1950s, 1960s, and 1970s. The best-known competitions were the track and field contests between the Soviet Union and the United States from 1958 well into the 1980s. The Soviets generally won by combining men's and women's scores. The US men won most of their meets, while Soviet women overwhelmed American women, who bested the Russians in only one of nineteen competitions. The Soviet–USA meets continued even as the Soviets kept up their Cold War expansion plans. The Soviet Union invaded Hungary in 1958 to snuff out a rebellion. A decade later, the USSR and its Eastern Europe allies invaded Czechoslovakia to put down a revolutionary threat to communist rulers. The Cold War had not abated even a dozen years later, when the Soviet Union invaded Afghanistan in another Olympic year. Many athletic officials opposed President Jimmy Carter's threat and America's eventual withdrawal from the Moscow Olympic Games of 1980. However, American patriot Walter Byers stated that he would "support a decision to boycott the Games as a national response to an unacceptable aggression by the host country." The interests of the United States as leaders of the free world, Byers remarked, "far surpasses the interests of amateur athletics. . . ."[5] That was very different from President Franklin Roosevelt's refusal to endorse the strong movement in America to boycott the 1936 Berlin Olympics in Nazi Germany.[6]

Byers may have learned a lesson in international relations from an incident only three years before the boycott of the Moscow Olympics. In 1977 ABC angered Byers by preempting the telecast of a touchdown in a Michigan-Ohio State game to show Egyptian leader Anwar Sadat's airplane touching down in Israel to conclude peace between the two nations, which had been at war for the previous three decades. The interruption of the telecast eliminated a few commercials and impacted the Nielsen TV ratings. Byers believed the interruption was a "breach of our contract."[7] Roone Arledge, head of ABC Sports, rejected Byers's complaint about the television stoppage of the game in favor of what Arledge claimed was an "event of overwhelming public importance." Arledge condemned the "NCAA and those prestigious institutions of higher learning it represents" for believing a football game to be more important than a historic event.[8] In this case, Byers let a few missed game commercials get in the way of acknowledging an important event on the global stage. Three years later, Byers was more circumspect in supporting America's Cold War attempt to punish the USSR for its invasion of Afghanistan by withdrawing from the Moscow Olympic Games.

BYERS DURING THE AGE OF MID-CENTURY AMERICAN WARS

The Cold War was not the only, nor the first, war that Walter Byers lived through and that affected the way he administered the NCAA. Born in 1922, Byers was nineteen as the United States entered World War II. He joined the war effort in his senior year at the University of Iowa but was released due to his poor eyesight, eliminating his participation. Nine years later, the Korean War was at its height when he was hired to lead the NCAA. In about a decade, the Cold War almost became a hot war during the Berlin Wall emergency and, a year later, when the Soviets attempted to construct missile bases in communist Cuba. Later in the 1960s and into the next decade, the controversial war in Vietnam brought Byers into conflict with much of America as his conservative views conflicted with anti-war sentiment. Many Americans questioned competitive and combative athletics as collegians across the nation protested US involvement in the unpopular war.

Vietnam created turmoil within college athletics more than any other military conflict in American history. Byers supported stopping communist expansion and condemned those who opposed the war on the college campuses.[9] Across America, campus riots broke out from the mid-1960s to the early 1970s. For instance, students at the University of Wisconsin, Madison, protested the maker of napalm, Dow Chemical Company. Napalm was used in America's fiery bombing of North Vietnamese positions and resulted in the killing of many civilians. One conservative student opposed these student protests, stating that the 1967 demonstrators against the war "were using the Vietnam War as a proxy to spread their views on socialism and Communism."[10] This was likely close to the views of Walter Byers, who believed that the radical university Students for a Democratic Society (SDS) were not only creating havoc by rioting across American campuses but also conspiring to undermine college football. Sometime later, Byers praised President Richard Nixon for opposing the SDS as "unconstructive dissenters [who] are likely to come home to roost—sooner than we expect." Byers emphasized that "athletics is a likely target." In a piece in the widely distributed *NCAA News* titled "A Personal Viewpoint," Byers complained of "the New Left," a group that should "face up to the American people who believe so strongly in competitive athletics. . . ."[11] He certainly appreciated Nixon's vice president, Spiro Agnew, who condemned the anti-Vietnam media as "nattering nabobs of negativism" and student protesters as a "cacophony of seditious drivel."[12] Byers remained on the side of those who protested the protesters, praising Agnew as someone who "planted his feet, hit his opponent as hard as he could."[13]

Television negotiations reflected the cultural conflict over involvement in Vietnam as the nation entered the 1970s. Only five months after the spring 1970 anti-war riots at Kent State and Jackson State Universities, which resulted in several student deaths, the NCAA asked ABC-TV to refrain from interfering with its telecasting of football games and to avoid focusing its cameras on any disturbances. Byers believed that ABC's request to televise disruptions "is much too broad and tends to assist the very type of activity we are trying to discourage."[14] Byers did not want Vietnam dissenters to interrupt the fall football games, and especially the telecasts by ABC, asking that the network turn its cameras away from any anti-Vietnam demonstrations.[15] This position not only favored American participation in the Vietnam War but also prioritized financial concerns, as a disrupted telecast could cause the NCAA license fee to be canceled.[16]

Byers's protest of the protesters had an effect. When the 1970 University of Buffalo-Holy Cross football game halftime show was about to be telecast, ABC turned away, panning traffic, elm trees, and cloudy skies to avoid showing the band's performance called "Give Peace a Chance." ABC declined to show the band because their performance was viewed as a "political demonstration."[17] Yet, a couple of months later at pro football's Super Bowl halftime show in New Orleans, a performance of the glorified military defeat of the British in the American Revolutionary War's Battle of New Orleans was shown to completion, after which US Air Force planes buzzed the field and arch-conservative Anita Bryant sang the "Battle Hymn of the Republic." This, strangely, was not considered political.[18]

Byers allowed his political views to taint his administration of NCAA affairs. He was quite sure that the leadership of the NCAA agreed with him and his conservative views on the negative impact of the liberal media and student unrest. The number of times a university band of this era played "God Bless America" or "America the Beautiful" at football games as opposed to anti-Vietnam refrains of Bob Dylan's "Blowing in the Wind" or Pete Seeger's "Bring 'Em Home" does suggest that athletic departments across America did not appreciate anti-war symbols. Walter Byers was well supported in his leadership of college athletics.[19] The Vietnam War had its impact upon college sport, but it was entangled with civil rights struggles at the same time.

THE NCAA, WALTER BYERS, AND THE JOHNNY BRIGHT INCIDENT

Walter Byers was actively involved in the conflict over American intervention in the Vietnam War, but he was much less visible in the fight for equality for all citizens during the civil rights movement of the 1950s and 1960s. Byers's background does not suggest that he would be strongly involved in pressuring for the rights of African Americans in collegiate sports in the 1950s. Byers was born and raised in a former slave state, Missouri, brought into the Union via congressional compromise 102 years before to keep free and slave states equal in number. He went to segregated schools and participated in segregated sports in Kansas City, and began college at Houston's segregated Rice University, one of the last schools in the South to desegregate. Prior to being named NCAA executive director, he was working part-time with the NCAA and Big Ten Conference when President Harry Truman desegregated the armed forces in 1948. He had been in the position of executive director for three years when the US Supreme Court ruled 9–0 in *Brown v. Board of Education* that segregation by race in education was unconstitutional, violating the equal protection clause of the Fourteenth Amendment to the Constitution.

These early events did not foretell much positive action by Byers to bring about racial equity in college athletics. Byers does not appear to have noted the iconic Rosa Park's refusal to give up her seat on a Montgomery, Alabama, bus in 1955, nor did he comment on Martin Luther King's movement for nonviolent protests against racial segregation. There is no strong evidence that Byers worked to end the NCAA's opposition to Black colleges entering the NCAA basketball tournament in the 1950s and 1960s. He later suggested that he "tried during the 1950s to arrange integrated accommodations for the teams in my own segregated hometown, Kansas City, Missouri."[20] At minimum, Byers was unsuccessful. And he did not suggest that the NCAA should eliminate segregated Kansas City either as the site to house the NCAA or as a major site for the NCAA basketball tourney. Both the small college-focused National Association of Intercollegiate Athletics and the NCAA used Kansas City as a venue for their annual basketball tournaments, and both the NAIA and the NCAA continued segregationist policies early in the 1950s. The NCAA could have selected a team from one of five Black conferences to play in the NCAA tourney but chose not to. Basketball coaches in Black colleges began remarking that the NCAA stood for "No Colored Athletes Allowed."[21]

The month Byers officially became executive director in 1951, an incident of national significance took place in a Midwestern football game between Iowa's Drake University and a segregationist institution, Oklahoma A&M (now Oklahoma State). Drake University's fine football team was led by its Black quarterback, Johnny Bright, the nation's leading ground gainer. There were rumors of betting pools on when the Missouri Valley Conference Oklahoma A&M Aggies would injure and remove Bright from the game. On the first play of the game, following a handoff by Bright, the A&M defensive tackle caught Bright with a forearm uppercut, breaking Bright's jaw. A cameraman caught the racist sequence on film, and the image was duly printed in the nationally popular *Life Magazine*.[22] The impact upon the NCAA was negligible, as the organization took little notice of the racist attack on an all-American football player. The NCAA Fifth District, which included Oklahoma A&M, reported two months later that Johnny Bright set a new all-time rushing record "before being forced out for the season by injuries."[23] The incident received national media exposure but no other comments in over 250 pages of *NCAA Proceedings*. Meanwhile, Drake withdrew from the Missouri Valley Conference over the racist event. "I feel very good that Drake stood behind me," commented Johnny Bright, "rather than drop the whole thing like the [Missouri] Valley [Conference] did."[24] Walter Byers and other NCAA leaders had no apparent comment about the Johnny Bright incident or racism on the part of institutions in the NCAA. The Bright incident occurred three years before the *Brown v. Board of Education* decision banning segregation in schools such as Oklahoma A&M.

Unlike the NCAA, the prominent Black newspaper the *Chicago Defender* would not stay silent and editorialized:[25]

> We know and every other American who is familiar with racism knows why Johnny Bright was attacked. The boys who have been brought up on white supremacy propaganda simply cannot stand to see their illusions threatened. The Negro quarterback struck fear into them, fear that this presumably 'inferior' should make monkeys out of them. Too many whites are afraid that in a true test of individual merit, their racist convictions will be shattered.

Not only did the NCAA ignore Johnny Bright but the national organization basically ignored Black colleges and their athletes as a whole, just as most of American society ignored Blacks in sport and more broadly. Walter Byers was part of that society, though he might be excused for not taking up the plight of Blacks in college sport as the new twenty-nine-year-old executive who had been NCAA administrator for less than a month at the time of the Bright incident.

In 1951, that same year as the Bright attack, the great basketball coach and Black civil rights leader John McLendon helped organize a National Athletic Steering Committee to challenge the segregation in both the NCAA and the National Association of Intercollegiate Athletics. The purpose of the National Athletic Steering Committee was to oppose the two national organizations that prevented Black college teams from entering their post-season tournaments. McLendon, who broke North Carolina's Jim Crow law when, during World War II, his Black North Carolina College team played and soundly defeated the white team from Duke's Medical School in a secluded contest deep in Durham's Black community.[26] A basketball hall of famer, McLendon won several NAIA championships with his Tennessee Agricultural and Industrial State College Negro team before becoming the first Black coach of a team from a dominant white university (Cleveland State) and of a professional basketball team (the Cleveland Pipers). He even refused to have his team participate in Kansas City, Byers's hometown and place of residence as head of the NCAA, if his players were not allowed to stay at the hotel accommodating white teams.[27] Byers and the NCAA, fierce defenders of amateurism in college sport, continued to support Jim Crow America in the early 1950s.

In the year before the *Brown v. Board of Education* ruling, Byers attended a meeting of the NCAA Executive Committee in Kansas City where Mack Greene, athletic director at the Central State College of Wilberforce, spoke of the NCAA's "Negro problem." Speaking for Black colleges regarding NCAA tournaments, Greene appealed to NCAA leaders to allow Black institutions into NCAA championships and for Black colleges to have a representative on the NCAA Council.[28] There is no indication that Byers contributed to any discussion, nor was any concern expressed by the native Kansas Citian. His background may have been of consequence in this moment since, as mentioned previously, Byers was brought up in a former slave and segregated state, the state that initiated the case resulting in the 1857 Dred Scott decision by the US Supreme Court, which stated that a slave brought to a free state was neither free nor a citizen. Byers's Kansas City was still a racially segregated city a century later, when the NCAA met in 1953.[29] There is no sign that the NCAA agreed with Mack Greene that the practice of racial discrimination was, as Greene noted, both "undemocratic and un-American."[30] His call for a NCAA investigation of discriminatory practices, while not rejected outright, was channeled to the NCAA Committee on Small College Relations. This left the handling of the "undemocratic and un-American" action of the NCAA in the hands of a new and peripheral committee, and the proposal was not acted upon.[31] There is no question that Byers was not in the forefront of Black civil rights in the early years of his leadership of the NCAA.

LOUISIANA AND THE CHARGE OF NCAA RACISM

A charge of racism was brought following the NCAA's probation and "death penalty" actions against the University of Southwestern Louisiana (now the University of Louisiana at Lafayette). This important story about race in the segregated state of Louisiana and the NCAA is not mentioned in Walter Byers's memoir, *Unsportsmanlike Conduct*.[32] Byers did not note that Southwestern Louisiana was given the second "death penalty" doled out by the NCAA in 1973 (the first was given to the University of Kentucky in

1952, when the traditional white Southern basketball power had no Black athletes). In the Southwestern Louisiana case, a white coach, Beryl Shipley, got the permission of his university president to recruit some Black players at a time when the state of Louisiana did not allow integrated teams or teams with African Americans to play against white teams. At the same time, the segregationist commissioner of the Gulf States Conference, Stanley Galloway, forbade Coach Shipley from offering athletic scholarships to non-white players. Shipley was asked by the commissioner to arrange some activities with the recruited Black athletes, violating NCAA rules.[33] For instance, Galloway asked Shipley to hold practice before the official opening date so that he could dismiss Black athletes from the team. Shipley held the illegal practices but did not dismiss the Black players. In addition, Shipley organized an outside group to fundraise to support his athletes, some of whom were in violation of the 1.600 grade point average legislation on the academic admittance of athletes.[34] Ultimately, a judge's restraining order allowed Black players to participate, while an investigation by the NCAA, which lacked common due process procedures, eventually turned up numerous violations, some involving racism.[35]

Coach Beryl Shipley claimed that Walter Byers did not respond to a lengthy letter from him explaining the situation surrounding the NCAA's actions against his university. Shipley believed that SLU had not been treated fairly and that racism was involved in the drastic two-year probation that prevented Shipley's top-ten basketball team from participating in the NCAA tournament.[36] Neither the charge of racism nor the eventual "death penalty" was addressed by Byers in his book, while he wrote pages about the Kentucky "death penalty" that had nothing to do with race. This suggests that Byers was never as concerned about the race issue as he was about the Kentucky basketball scandal and the bribing and payment of his all-white athletes violating amateur rules.

To Byers's credit, his book did address the race situation in a section titled "Racial Barriers Crumble." In this section, he noted the outstanding African American athlete and scholar at Rutgers in the early twentieth century, Paul Robeson. However, Byers ignored Robeson's greatness as a Shakespearean actor, singer, and activist for civil rights following his Phi Beta Kappa academic performance as an undergraduate at Rutgers, as well as his law degree from Columbia. Robeson, a strong anti-fascist, tried to end

Jim Crowism in America, but Byers ends by commenting that "this great college football player supported communism." Byers does not reveal that Robeson was contrasting how well he was treated as a star performer in the Soviet Union in the 1930s and 1940s with how he was discriminated against in segregationist America when he returned to his home country.[37] Byers instead contrasted the character of Robeson with that of Jerome "Brud" Holland, the Black all-American football player at Cornell who became a college president and ambassador to Sweden. Byers dismissed Robeson as a radical while praising Holland, far more conservative, as a "good friend of mine [who] contributed mightily in trying to make the NCAA a better organization." Byers's conservativism likely influenced how he viewed the University of Southeastern Louisiana "death penalty" as well as his views on civil rights in America.

THE HIRING OF A BLACK INVESTIGATOR, RON STRATTON

While Walter Byers denied the charges of racism, there were no African Americans in positions of leadership in the NCAA under Byers until Ron Stratton was employed, two years after the Southwestern Louisiana "death penalty" decision and twenty-one years after Byers became executive director. Stratton played football at the University of Oregon and coached at Portland State University in the early 1970s. In 1975 he became the first African American investigator hired by the NCAA, nearly a quarter century after Byers became executive director and at a time when the number of African Americans involved in leadership roles in the NCAA was limited. Throughout the civil rights movement of the 1960s and early 1970s, the lack of Blacks in the NCAA was noticeable, though there were two "Negroes" (Byers's term) in non-leadership roles.[38] At the same time, a higher percentage of Black troops fought in the Vietnam War than Caucasians.[39] And while there were no African Americans working at Walter Byers's NCAA in leadership positions, there were three Black Heisman Trophy winners in the 1960s, including the first, Ernie Davis of Syracuse University (1961); Mike Garrett of the University of Southern California (1965); and O. J. Simpson of the University of Southern California (1968).

As African Americans began to dominate football and men's basketball teams, South and North, the lack of representation in leadership roles in the NCAA became apparent and impacted the area favored by Byers—the enforcement of amateur rules for college athletes. The head of NCAA enforcement, Warren Brown, felt that it was difficult for white investigators to talk to Black athletes, such as those at Southwestern Louisiana, about the recruitment and payment of athletes in their investigations of violations of the NCAA's amateur code. Attempting to improve the NCAA's enforcement efforts, Byers hired Ron Stratton only a short time after the NCAA desegregated the officers of the national organization. In 1971, just before Stratton became the first significant minority hire by the NCAA, the NCAA elected its first Black officer, Samuel Barnes from Howard University, as secretary-treasurer.[40] It may have been the Southwestern Louisiana infraction that triggered the hiring of Stratton, who had just completed his third year as an unsuccessful football coach at Portland State University. At the time, Byers was also strongly involved in the Jerry Tarkanian basketball coaching infraction case involving the eligibility of several Black players at the University of Nevada, Las Vegas—a case that went on for several decades.

Stratton was eventually placed as head of NCAA enforcement by Byers, but earlier in his career, Stratton was charged with using a questionable technique in an NCAA investigation. While investigating a case of improper recruiting at Oklahoma State University in the fall of 1975, Stratton was accused of representing himself as a federal agent. He was alleged to have illegally boarded a private airplane employed in transporting a recruited athlete free of charge. While in the plane, he obtained the pilot's logbook verifying the illegal recruiting action.[41] The owner of the plane, Clarence Wright, a former OSU athlete and then the president of Oklahoma National Bank, sued the NCAA for invasion of privacy and defamation. Wright was eventually prohibited from recruiting for Oklahoma State, but the questionable violations of due process by the NCAA caught the attention of the US House of Representatives.

Representative John Moss (D-CA) held a lengthy investigation of the NCAA, not only for questionable NCAA due process procedures at Oklahoma State but for those at the University of Alabama, University of Nevada, Las Vegas, and the University of Minnesota. Moss, a reforming liberal congressman who initiated the Freedom of Information Act and Consumer Product Safety legislation in the 1960s and 1970s, wanted the NCAA to reform questionable due process rules.[42] He was prominently supported by a representative from Nevada, James Santini, who backed University of Nevada, Las Vegas basketball coach Jerry Tarkanian in his two-decade battle with the NCAA over violations of the NCAA amateur laws and the questionable due process procedures of Walter Byers's NCAA infractions and enforcement office. As the congressional investigation came to an end in 1978, Representative Santini condemned the NCAA for its lack of due process. "Every one of those persons in prisons," Santini stated, "had a heck of a lot more rights than anybody that ever went before the NCAA ever got." Chairman John Moss agreed, stating that there was "an amazing lack of due process available for those who became involved in the NCAA."[43] Byers and the NCAA stood firm, as they had the year before when they handed Southern Methodist University the NCAA's third "death penalty" for football violations.

Though no federal legislation resulted from the congressional condemnation of the NCAA, later charges resulted in the NCAA finally acting in 1991, four years after Byers retired, to establish a commission to study due process and to adopt some of its findings. Then, a dozen years later, in the early twenty-first century, Congress held another hearing about lack of due process in the NCAA enforcement of infractions. What began as an effort under Byers's hands to preserve amateurism and punish athletes and institutions for violations of amateur regulations began to move slowly toward generally accepted due process procedures. In general, decency and fairness are goals of the flexible doctrine of due process. The NCAA under Byers believed that what was fair to his group of investigators and the unpaid judges of the committee on infractions differed from what was fair for those charged with a major problem associated with recruiting and paying athletes. According to generally accepted due process rules, the enforcement staff should not assist the judges of the wrongdoing (separate prosecutor and judge); the accused should be allowed to introduce witnesses; hearsay evidence should not be accepted; cross-examinations should be allowed; open hearings should exist; testimony should be sworn and recorded; and athletes should receive due process. The NCAA's handling of infractions under Walter Byers was lacking in these generally accepted due process policies.[44]

In short, some believed the NCAA was "some kind of powerful, heavy-handed, arbitrary and vaguely sinister Politburo of college sports," a statement that could only come about during the Cold War period. To these kinds of charges, Byers responded that he and the NCAA were not a "Czarist regime held secure by an awesome authority that wrecks revenge upon informers."[45] But that is how individuals and institutions punished by the NCAA—including President Peter Magrath of the University of Minnesota, coach Jerry Tarkanian of the University of Nevada Las Vegas, coach Beryl Shipley of the Southwest Louisiana University, and Canadian junior hockey players, who were rendered ineligible as professionals at the University of Denver by the NCAA in the mid-1970s—felt about the NCAA's handling of their cases.[46] The NCAA was no Czarist regime during the Cold War, but its strict treatment of individuals and institutions may have appeared this way under the administration of Walter Byers. The NCAA leader took the side of America in fighting the Soviet regime in athletics, but he was slow to reject American racism as the USSR expanded its empire and charged the United States with systemic racism. Meanwhile, the Cold War dragged on for close to four decades, and Byers and the NCAA had to deal with a new minority challenge. This challenge was the 1.600 GPA.

FIVE

Losing

Academics, Race, and the 1.600 GPA

> "Byers is not 'national commissioner.'"
>
> —**HUGH C. WILLETT AND K. L. WILSON, 1951**

> "Losing the 1.600 rule was one of the most painful experiences . . . as executive director."
>
> —**WALTER BYERS, 1995**

As Walter Byers grew up in the former slave state of Missouri, strong segregationist sentiment and policies prevailed in Kansas City during and well after his childhood. How Byers dealt with the question of race would become more apparent as he struggled with a major divisive issue within the NCAA in the 1960s and 1970s: academics and what was considered by many to be the racist 1.600 grade point average rule. The issue of what academic requirements should be mandatory for men to enter and participate in college athletics had never been far from the minds of those who administered the NCAA. The "dumb jock" image had a long history and was never more pronounced than in the image created by famed cartoonist, Thomas Nast, in the 1870s, when he pictured a large-brained and frail college scholar reading from ancient Greek and Etruscan books next to a large-muscled athlete with an undersized brain ready for a contest. The caption read: "EDUCATION: IS THERE NO MIDDLE COURSE?"[1] Since Nast's caricature, there were concerted efforts to restrict colleges from admitting athletes who were underprepared academically. When Byers was in college, this was not an issue faced by African American athletes, for there were none at Rice University and nearly none when he transferred to the University of Iowa. This was true in white-majority institutions throughout America.

As a youth, Byers attended an all-white segregated elementary school and Westport High School. In his early life in the 1920s, Kansas City experienced the Great Migration of Black people from the Deep South northward to urban centers. The partitioning of Kansas City education along racial lines became official in 1905 when the Kansas City School Board mandated separate schools for Black and white students. It was highly noticeable to the Byers family following World War I, when Troost Avenue became "Troost Wall," an "endless dividing line between black and white schools."[2] Black activist Roy Wilkins came to Kansas City as a reporter-editor for the *Kansas City Call* the year Byers was born. The future longtime executive director of the National Association for the Advancement of Colored People (NAACP) described Kansas City as "a Jim Crow town right down to its bootstraps [where] stopping race mixing is a more sacred duty than stopping any bank robbery."[3] Byers's upbringing as a white man in segregated Kansas City likely tainted his later attitude toward racial academic policy and the 1.600 grade point average legislation of the NCAA.

ACADEMIC ACHIEVEMENT AND THE SANITY CODE FAILURE

A half-dozen years before the NCAA was formed, President Charles Eliot of Harvard University became concerned about the academic performance of freshmen football players at his institution. Late nineteenth-century statistics from the renowned head of America's leading institution showed that football-playing freshmen at Harvard had more failing grades than the total of "A's" and "B's."[4] This suggested to President Eliot that a rule should be adopted prohibiting athletic participation by freshmen and that academics, not athletics, should be the emphasis at universities. When the NCAA was formed following the 1905 ethical and injury crisis in football, the focus of the new organization was on creating acceptable football rules and a code of eligibility based on the principles of amateurism. Institutions in conferences reported the need for academic standards, and the NCAA bylaws called for athletes to be "bona-fide students in good and regular standing."[5] However, faculty leaders of the NCAA, which Harvard had not yet joined, were far more interested in preserving amateurism than in upholding athletes' grades for participation. Two pages of the original bylaws were devoted to preventing any athlete from participating "who is paid or receives, directly or indirectly, any money, or financial concession, or emolument as past or present compensation. . . ." To emphasize the case, the bylaws disqualified an athlete "who receives from any source whatever, gain, or emolument, or position of profit, direct or indirect, in order to render it possible for him to participate in college or university athletics." In addition, seemingly as an afterthought, the bylaws required the athlete to take a "full schedule of [academic] work."[6] Because the NCAA was founded on the principle of Home Rule, it was up to individual institutions and conferences to determine eligibility rules, academic and otherwise. The NCAA, early on and for the next half-century, did not prescribe any academic requirements for athletes entering college or during their course of studies.

Home Rule reigned until the NCAA passed the Sanity Code, three years before Byers became the first executive director in 1951. For the first time, the NCAA was given the power to make national rules with the authority to punish those who did not follow them. The Sanity Code, nevertheless, paid little attention to academics, except to state that athletes should be admitted into college on the same basis as non-athletes. It merely allowed an athlete in the upper 25 percent of his high school graduating class to receive a scholarship more than tuition. The Sanity Code allowed financial aid based on financial need, not on athletic ability. Though the code passed nearly unanimously, the policies were never enforced and died following a failed vote to punish transgressors.[7] Byers, who came into office as the Sanity Code was voted out, called the defeat of the Sanity Code one of the worst decisions in the history of intercollegiate athletics.[8] Byers was always a strong advocate of amateurism in college sport during his working lifetime, and the defeat of the Sanity Code was the beginning of his disappointment in the direction amateurism was moving.

Although the failed Sanity Code attempted to provide a more level playing field in the recruitment and payment of athletes, the 1950s saw an increase in the number of schools and conferences offering full athletic scholarships with little regard for the academic preparation of those receiving these scholarships. The Sanity Code, which advocated that athletes must meet the academic profile of the institution they were attending, "died aborning of hypocrisy," according to sportswriter Tim Cohane.[9] The NCAA,

Cohane stated, allowed limited scholarships to athletes under the Sanity Code, but many athletes would need to work to pay for their schooling.

With the defeat of the Sanity Code and eligibility standards, there was a period of deteriorating academic standards for athletes in the 1950s and into the 1960s. This occurred while air travel and the burgeoning of network sport television brought an increased need for national rules, especially in the two dominant college sports of football and men's basketball. No national standard for the payment of players was reached until the NCAA voted to make full scholarships available in 1956. The NCAA believed payment of tuition, room, board, fees, and "laundry" money were commonly accepted educational expenses. The NCAA rationalized this payment to athletes to participate in athletics and continued to call paid "scholarship" athletes amateurs. Providing "[a]bove-board provisions for room, board, tuition, books . . . and incidental expenses," the president of the University of Iowa stated, would level the playing field for all schools in recruiting and the payment of players.[10] Byers asserted that the 1956 decision to allow full athletic scholarships would render cheating obsolete.[11] He was wrong.

THE BEGINNING OF NATIONAL MINIMUM ACADEMIC STANDARDS

Once the NCAA believed they had achieved a level playing field with full athletic scholarships, the organization became more concerned about the academic quality of athletes entering universities principally to participate in football and men's basketball. There were no national academic standards for admittance of athletes nor were there uniform academic standards across institutions or conferences. The lack of academic standards for athletic performance was brought to the attention of the NCAA when Walter Byers invited a Stanford University professor to speak on the subject at the 1959 NCAA conference. Rixford Snyder, Stanford historian, director of admissions, and faculty athletic representative to the NCAA, led a roundtable discussion of college admission tests and requirements.[12] He maintained that there must be a minimum standard for athletes to enter college. Snyder's 1950s study showed that the best predictor of academic success in college was a combination of national academic achievement tests and high school grade point averages. Snyder argued that America's Cold War interests demanded greater academic standards to adequately confront the Soviet challenge. Snyder emphasized: "The age of rockets and of satellites will not accept the free ride for an athlete of limited academic potential while the physicist with only moderate physical prowess goes unaided financially." Pointing to the Soviet and American space programs, Snyder added that "Sputnik and Atlas may turn out to be the two forces which will return intercollegiate athletics to the truly amateur stage. . . ."[13] His caveat may have influenced action to bring about minimal academic standards for athletic participation, but it did not stall the athletic scholarship payment to athletes or the intense desire to put winning teams into the arena.

The Atlantic Coast Conference, which contained some highly ranked educational institutions, including Duke and Virginia, was the first major conference to adopt minimal academic standards for the awarding of athletic scholarships in the 1960s.[14] As minimal academic standards were increasingly viewed as racially biased, it should be noted that this was not the case in the early 1960s, when the ACC segregation policy was in place in Jim Crow America and no Blacks participated in ACC conference play. Minimum academic standards were originally a white problem, not a Black problem. The ACC adopted a minimum 750 Standardized Academic Test (SAT) score to be eligible in 1960, and this score was raised to an 800 SAT score four years later.[15] The argument that the ACC developed minimum standards to keep African Americans from playing sports is specious, for not until after the passage of the national Civil Rights Act of 1964 did Blacks become prominent athletes in Southern institutions.

THE 1.600 GPA FOR FRESHMAN ELIGIBILITY IS APPROVED

On the national level, the NCAA set up a committee to determine a formula for predicting academic success for those receiving athletic scholarships. Not surprisingly, the committee included Stanford's Rixford Snyder and ACC commissioner James Weaver. In 1963 the NCAA determined that a college-predicted 1.600 grade point average was necessary for athletic participation. The 1.600 GPA was a C- average on a 4.000 scale. This high school grade point average and an athlete's Scholastic Aptitude Test (SAT) or American College Testing (ACT) score served as the minimum requirement to receive a scholarship and to participate in athletics. In addition, the NCAA required athletes to maintain a 1.600 GPA to continue athletic participation in college.[16] Surprisingly, the Ivy League and other elite educational institutions were most opposed to the new standard. They argued that, because they had more demanding standards, athletes might have a more difficult task maintaining the minimal 1.600 GPA.[17] Byers, on the other hand, contended that "the solid majority of the colleges believe this rule in the long run will do as much as any rule the NCAA has ever passed to improve intercollegiate athletics." To Byers, a predicted "C minus is low enough."[18] Besides, it could easily be argued that the ACC, with its established 800 minimum SAT score, was at a recruiting and competitive disadvantage with other conferences that had no minimal academic standards to allow athletic participation.[19]

The NCAA passed the national 1.600 GPA rule in 1965, and the regulation took effect before most Southern schools desegregated athletics, but the race issue soon surfaced. From Moses Fleetwood Walker at Oberlin College in 1881 and William H. Lewis at Amherst College in 1888 to Wilbur Jackson and John Mitchell at the University of Alabama in 1971, very few African Americans participated in college athletics anywhere except at the Historically Black Colleges and Universities (HBCUs) and a few Northern universities.[20] With a US Supreme Court decision and federal legislation in the 1950s and 1960s, as well as changes in societal norms away from Jim Crow policies nationally, the NCAA under Walter Byers moved toward greater rights for African American athletes. Northern teams with Black players began to dominate. One example of this phenomenon was Michigan State football under Coach Duffy Daugherty, who recruited forty African Americans from the South to turn out winning teams and win a national championship. Michigan State's quarterback in 1966, Jimmy Raye, was recruited northward from Fayetteville, North Carolina, to East Lansing. To Raye, this move offered "a chance to leave segregated water fountains and restrooms and other indignities of the Jim Crow South."[21] In basketball, the University of California Los Angeles built an outstanding team with numerous Black players, and the 1966 team from Texas Western in El Paso had five Black starters who beat the all-white Kentucky team for the national championship. In the 1960s and early 1970s, UCLA won ten championships under coach John Wooden, with African American players such as Lew Alcindor (soon to become Kareem Abdul-Jabbar) and Lucius Allen.

The Ivy League protested the 1.600 NCAA rule and was given a reprieve for 1966 as the legislation came into being. Byers responded that "the solid majority of the colleges believe this rule in the long run will do as much as any rule the NCAA has ever passed to improve intercollegiate athletics." He stated that "it has been more thoroughly considered than any NCAA legislation ever enacted" and that most members have agreed "upon a minimum level of academic attainment for athletes."[22] It wasn't people demanding racial equality but the elite Eastern academic institutions opposing the 1.600 GPA rule that filled Byers's and the NCAA's mailbox against the legislation. To his friends, Byers referred to the regulation as the "G! D! Weaver rule," since it was introduced by Commissioner James Weaver of the ACC.[23] Early on, institutions such as Harvard and Columbia and smaller colleges, including Amherst, Grinnell, Haverford, Oberlin, Swarthmore, and Tufts, were reluctant to play by the 1.600 GPA rule.[24] There was so much early opposition by the supposed educational elite that the commissioner of the Southeastern Conference, A. M. "Tonto" Coleman, saw the split among NCAA institutions as a threat to its existence. "The dissolution of the NCAA," Coleman told the Football Writers of America in the summer of 1966, "would lead to chaos."[25] And it was not then a question of the purported racial bias of the academic achievement scores contributing to low scores of Black students, but it soon would be.

BLACK STUDENTS AND THE CHARGE OF RACISM

Within a year, as the recruitment of Black students into both Northern and Southern institutions increased, the question of the impact upon the recruiting and retention of African American athletes began to dominate the arguments of those who questioned the 1.600 GPA rule. During the 1960s, the civil rights movement in America combined with opposition to the war in Vietnam to cause educational turmoil. This was in concert with a movement for affirmative action and an Educational Opportunity Program (EOP) for underprivileged students to help break down existing segregation of the races in American institutions of higher education. The 1.600 GPA rule came to symbolize the racism of American culture.[26] Standardized tests were shown to be culturally biased against African Americans. Increasingly, the NCAA 1.600 GPA legislation came to represent not a minimum standard for academic performance for athletes but rather a racist barrier to Black students entering college.

With the passage of Title VI of the Civil Rights Act of 1964, there was pressure to desegregate Southern colleges to meet the standards of the new law, which prohibited discrimination based on race and national origin in programs receiving federal financial assistance. The 1.600 rule restricting who could come to college and compete athletically created an obvious conflict for those who believed that there should be open admissions, providing college access for minority students. Louisiana State University offers a clear example of a Jim Crow institution opposing the recruitment of racial minorities to meet the new civil rights legislation in the mid-1960s. On LSU's football roster of over one hundred men, there was not one African American. This reflected the situation at other segregated institutions in former slave states.[27] In the seven-year existence of the 1.600 GPA rule, the argument that the rule was racist came up several times for a vote at annual NCAA conventions. Finally, in 1973, after the NCAA voted to allow freshman athletes to compete on varsity teams and after several lawsuits against the 1.600 rule had been brought before the courts, the NCAA voted 204–187 to kill the controversial rule.[28]

Walter Byers, who consistently fought for the survival of the 1.600 rule, claimed the year it passed that athletes would enter competition who "are representative of the student-body . . . on an academic basis." Further, Byers believed that the minimum academic performance requirement for athletic participation would improve the tarnished image of intercollegiate athletics and was "one of the most constructive pieces of legislation in the history of intercollegiate athletics."[29] Byers did not believe in open admissions, double admission standards, or special financial aid programs for "disadvantaged students," and he wrote editorials expressing his opposition to the NCAA membership. Byers, in his campaign for amateur athletics, called for no "backdoor admissions, tutors, special courses, friendly professors, and modified quantitative-qualitative requirements," believing that the NCAA's 1.600 GPA legislation would help produce his more perfect amateur world.[30] He would again be disappointed with the path of intercollegiate athletics.

DEATH OF THE 1.600 RULE: SEPARATING ATHLETICS FROM ACADEMICS

"The tyranny of the lowest common denominator would control" college athlete admissions, wrote Byers two decades after the 1.600 defeat. Losing the academic rule was one of the "most painful experiences" in his years at the NCAA, Byers recorded in *Unsportsmanlike Conduct*[31] The NCAA head would not admit, however, that control over athletes' academic performance related to any racism in the construction of academic achievement tests. In an unrecorded count, the NCAA membership voted that men's collegiate athletic eligibility would in the future be based on a mostly meaningless high school grade point average of 2.0 that could be established using subjects other than English, history, math, or science.[32] In other words, as the football coach at the University of Georgia, Vince Dooley, commented, there was "little or no standard at all."[33] The lack of academic accountability for college athletes lasted almost to the end of Byers's NCAA tenure, when lack of any meaningful academic standards embarrassed the NCAA into again taking action.

The 1970s and early 1980s saw a drastic increase in big-time college athletic coffers resulting from the millions earned by the televised March Madness basketball tournament, burgeoning TV contracts from Saturday afternoon football games, and profitable bowl contests. Successful national recruiting brought increased athletic wealth to big-time institutions, regardless of academic talent, in the quest to win conference titles, be invited to the NCAA basketball tourney, or included in major bowl games. In 1979, for instance, the Rose Bowl between two perennial powers, University of Southern California and Michigan, garnered attendance of over 105,000, while the great March Madness matchup between Michigan State's Magic Johnson and Indiana State's Larry Bird drew forty million TV viewers and the highest ever Nielson basketball rating of 24.1.[34] At the same time, colleges recruited football and basketball players who lacked academic credentials, including even the ability to read at an elementary grade school level. When an Oklahoma State football player carried around a *Wall Street Journal* to make it look like he could read and a basketball player admitted that he was illiterate but played four years with the Wichita State team, the NCAA suffered serious hits to its credibility.[35]

Chris Washburn, a star basketball player at North Carolina State University in the mid-1980s, seriously lacked academic credentials. Peter Golenbock tells Washburn's depressing story in his book *Personal Fouls*. He writes that, with 470 SAT score—just above the minimum score of 400—and after going to three different high schools to reach a 2.0 GPA, Washburn was admitted to North Carolina State University as a 6'11" center to play for coach Jimmy Valvano. With the 1.600 GPA rule thrown out several years before due to charges of racism and essentially no NCAA academic requirements, Golenbock did not exaggerate when he charged that too many big-time athletes concluded their collegiate years with "no education, no degree, no skills, no money, no pro career, and no hope."[36] For Washburn, it was only no education and no degree, but his short career in the National Basketball Association ended with several million dollars wasted on drug addiction before he was rehabilitated.[37]

With the minimum 1.600 GPA rule gone, many universities attempting to turn out athletic victories made a mockery of college athletics. Walter Byers's "tyranny of the lowest common denominator" was lampooned when it became known that a star player at Oklahoma State University and all-pro lineman with the Washington Redskins (now Commanders), Dexter Manley, could not read a Dr. Seuss book and that his ACT score hardly registered.[38] Similarly, Kevin Ross, a star basketball player at Omaha's Creighton University, whose ACT test was far from acceptable at Creighton, remained athletically eligible only after the athletic department hired a secretary to do his school work.[39] Even at what was often considered an exemplary academic-athletic school during the so-called "decade of academic-athletic darkness," Penn State's football coach and athletic director, Joe Paterno, asked his president, John Oswald, for nine presidential admits for football players who could not meet Penn State's academic requirements for admittance.[40] President Oswald admitted all nine academically deficient athletes, and two years later, in 1982, these athletes helped Paterno win his first national championship. How many of the nine graduated from Penn State? One. Similar stories of a lack of academic standards reverberated across America until another racially biased NCAA piece of legislation came into being in the late 1980s.

During the late 1960s and early 1970s, there was a significant increase in the number of African American men participating in intercollegiate athletics, while at the same time academic standards in universities were dropping precipitously. Relative to students who scored a perfect 1600 score on the SAT, Black male athletes with scholarships appeared painfully unprepared for academic study, based on standardized test scores. The lower quartile averaged a score of 650, while white high school athletes averaged an SAT score of 820. In terms of grade point averages, African American males averaged a 2.39 GPA, while comparable white athletes averaged a GPA of 2.90. The grade point averages rose only after the influence of the civil rights movement and the Vietnam War led to rapid grade inflation. Thus, as academic achievement standards for athletic participation fell, it became easier for athletes, Black and white, to remain academically eligible. This discrepancy was not lost on college administrators and leaders of the presidentially led American Council of Education. These groups began to press once again for combining high school grade point averages and standardized test scores to set a minimum standard for athletic participation.

PRESIDENTS AND PROPOSITION 48

Without any involvement of African American educators, the American Council on Education (ACE) joined forces with leaders of the NCAA and created an Ad Hoc Committee on Intercollegiate Athletics to come up with another standard for athletic participation. In so doing, the American Council on Education made strategic mistakes by disregarding the voices of African Americans and ignoring issues of representation and racism in determining athletic eligibility. The ACE proposal, which became known as Proposition 48, came before the NCAA membership in 1983, at the first NCAA meeting dominated by college presidents. Proposition 48 stipulated that a college athlete must have minimum grades and test scores to be eligible for athletic participation. President Joseph Johnson of Grambling State University, an HBCU, condemned the proposal, arguing that the racially biased Proposition 48 discriminated against athletes "from low income and minority-group families by introducing arbitrary SAT and ACT cutoff scores as academic criteria for eligibility."[41] Another HBCU college president, Luna Mishoe from Delaware State College, told the NCAA membership that the "SAT is a restraint which penalizes low-economic students [particularly African Americans] and is an unnecessary restraint pertaining to whether or not a student can do college work."[42] As in the 1.600 GPA legislation of the previous decade, concern about racial bias in standardized test scores was expressed but failed to convince. Rhetoric highlighting racial bias was drowned out by those who saw the need to raise academic standards. One strong proponent of Proposition 48 was Notre Dame's representative to the NCAA, Edmund P. Joyce, vice president in charge of Notre Dame athletics. "We must guard against using the test-score argument," he told the NCAA delegates, "as an excuse to prevent a much-needed reform from being initiated."[43] Academic reformers, including successful football coach Joe Paterno, who presented a strong statement, won the day over civil rights advocates.[44] Proposition 48 became the law of the NCAA with no recorded vote.[45] Byers was satisfied in his long-held belief that all should be treated equally, "the same for athlete and non-athlete, for black and white" alike.[46]

A longtime advocate of academic standards, Byers strongly supported Proposition 48, even though NCAA standards were minimal. The NCAA allotted four years for the implementation of Proposition 48, but it was never a satisfactory solution to needed academic requirements for athletes. Even American Council for Education vice president Robert Atwell confirmed the controversy over standardized test and their impact upon African American athletes soon after passage of the NCAA law.[47] For the next decade, and after the retirement of Byers, the NCAA passed several amendments attempting to make Proposition 48 more palatable but never settled on satisfactory solutions to concerns about either academic or racial equity. Neither the 1.600 legislation nor Proposition 48 and its successors would satisfy Byers's desire to have college athletes be representative of the academic standard of each institution's student body. If Byers was to be judged on this standard, he would be considered a failure. So would all the other leaders of intercollegiate athletics, including nearly all college presidents. As research has conclusively shown, male athletes in all divisions of the NCAA—I, II, and III—have underperformed academically relative to the general student body. To a lesser extent, this was also true with women athletes after the passage of Title IX legislation in 1972.[48]

After three decades of leading the NCAA, Walter Byers may not have been as influential dealing with race, academics, and athletics as many have asserted. In these areas of leadership, Byers claimed he was carrying out NCAA policy and not forming the athletic policy. Byers stated more than once that "The director's office simply would implement the will of the organization," with the supreme authority being the voting membership at the annual conventions. When Byers became executive director in 1951, the president of the NCAA, Hugh Willett, and the secretary-treasurer, Tug Wilson, made it clear that "Byers is not 'national commissioner.'" Wilson emphasized that Byers was not to be like baseball commissioner Kenesaw Mountain Landis, hired to clean up baseball following the Chicago White Sox "Black Sox" World Series scandal of 1919.[49] Byers was lauded by the leaders of the NCAA for years, not for setting policy but for carrying it out. He was at the same time criticized by those who opposed NCAA policy, for being an authoritarian or a despot. This was true with the academic-athletic requirements passed by the NCAA under the 1.600 GPA rules and in the early years of the Proposition 48 rulings. As we shall see, the way Byers carried out the NCAA's wishes regarding women's involvement in intercollegiate athletics and the NCAA reaction to it in the period of the 1970s and 1980s followed a similar pattern.

SIX

Admitting Women

Title IX and an All-Male NCAA

> "We are gratified that the NCAA Council has decided to study developments in women's intercollegiate athletics. . . ."
>
> **—CLIFFORD B. FAGAN, 1967**

> "[Title IX] regulations are a major assault upon the revenue producing potential of men's intercollegiate athletics."
>
> **—WALTER BYERS, 1975**

If Walter Byers lost his battle to maintain academic eligibility standards for what he and the NCAA considered "amateur" sports, he would receive another stinging defeat in defending men's athletics from the financial encroachment of women's intercollegiate athletics. Byers had problems with women from a young age until he was in his nineties, and this issue may have carried over to his feelings about women's athletics. He had three failed marriages as well as a falling out with his attorney daughter when she ran his ranch, and he could not reconcile women's intercollegiate athletics and a federal law. He had been in power at the NCAA for over two decades when the second wave feminism movement caught up with the all-male domination of sports in America, including intercollegiate athletics, in the 1970s.

Byers was one decade into running the NCAA when President John F. Kennedy established the President's Commission on the Status of Women in 1961.[1] A couple of years later, Betty Freidan's *The Feminine Mystique* was published and sold about three million copies in the first three years. In 1966 the National Organization for Women (NOW) was founded. Two years later, NOW launched its campaign to place the Equal Rights Amendment in the US Constitution. The ERA was supported by a spin-off of NOW, the Women's Equity Action League. In 1970 the first women's studies department was created in a university, and in another two years the first issue of *Ms. Magazine* was published.

That was the same year Title IX of the Educational Amendments of 1972 became law. There was plenty of notice to Walter Byers and the NCAA that women were moving rapidly into many areas of American society, including sports on college campuses. One had only to read the thirty-seven words in Title IX to know that a statement of the place of women in education was the law of the land:[2] "No person in the United States, shall, on the basis of sex, be excluded from participation in, be denied the benefits of, or be subjected to discrimination under any education program or activities receiving federal financial assistance." It was equally clear, however, that male-dominated competitive sports would have difficulty accepting women into their domain—and would especially struggle with some particular types of equality.

BYERS AND THE NCAA BECOME INTERESTED IN WOMEN'S SPORTS

One might suspect that the NCAA and Byers had little or nothing to do with women's sports prior to Title IX, but that is not true. Byers often saw problem areas, especially legal obstacles, well before most college presidents, athletic administrators, and coaches. He was aware of the women's movement and the need to address women's place in college sports in the 1960s. Yet, prior to that there is no evidence that he had either knowledge of or interest in women's sports. When he entered Rice University in 1939, women in charge of women's collegiate athletics were only beginning to challenge the concept that women should not participate in competitive college athletics. Many leading women physical educators for the previous half-century had been united in their opposition to intercollegiate athletics, but the opposition was not unanimous.

It was rare in the 1930s for any woman physical educator to challenge the prevailing philosophy that competing athletically would bring problems similar to those found in men's sports.[3] Ina Gittings, however, was one. "There is nothing wrong with games, competition, the girls, or travel," wrote Ina Gittings, a physical education advocate for competitive women's sports, in a 1931 article titled "Why Cramp Competition."[4] She eventually had a major sports building named after her at the University of Arizona, the first building at the university to be named after a woman. Even more remarkable, as an undergraduate at the University of Nebraska, she had a photo taken of her pole vaulting the very year the NCAA was born. She later said that the return of intercollegiate competition for women was "inevitable." Gittings was one of the rare women physical educators to speak out for collegiate competition.

Gittings was one of a minority of college women physical educators who fought for the rights of talented women athletes to participate. The first national championship for college women in any sport occurred soon after Byers transferred from Rice to the University of Iowa. While Byers wrote for the *Daily Iowan* school newspaper, neither he nor any other student reporter in the Big Ten Conference would report on the Ohio State University sponsorship of the first national championship in women's collegiate sport, a golf tournament. This was five months before the US entry into World War II. Men's football at Iowa, not women's golf, dominated Byers's thoughts. Within a decade, before he was thirty years old, Byers would be the new executive director of the NCAA, and women's athletics were far from the concern of either Byers or the NCAA. Following World War II, the Cold War between the Russian-dominated Soviet Union and the United States brought women's sports to the attention of Americans. Athletic competitions for men and women were contested on an international level to the detriment of Americans. College women athletes fared poorly in competition on the international level, except for some African American women from "Negro" colleges.

While a push for women to excel for the good of the nation emerged in the 1950s and 1960s, the women's movement exploded in North America. A year before the Soviets placed Sputnik into orbit in 1957 and left America in an inferior position in the Cold War space race, the United States was swamped by the Soviet Union in the 1956 Melbourne Olympics. Four years later, the United States again lost the medal count at the 1960 Rome Olympics. In track and field in Rome, while the American men's track team won twenty-two medals, American women won only four.[5] All four were captured by African Americans from one of the HBCUs, Tennessee State

University, under the famed Black coach Ed Temple. Only months after this stinging defeat by the Soviets, the NCAA's Thomas Hamilton campaigned for women's competitive sport in colleges. "What are we colleges going to do to defeat the Russians and the Communists in this important battle area of the Cold War," he asked members of the NCAA convention. "The United States needs women's intercollegiate competition in sports," stated the former naval officer, athletic director, and then conference commissioner.[6]

A special NCAA report came out in 1962, only months after the Soviets built the Berlin Wall to keep those under communist control from fleeing to democratic Western Europe. It was clear that America had lost its leadership in the Olympics, and the lack of women athletes in college was contributing to the United States losing the Cold War.[7] The NCAA report concluded that "competitive sports have become a vital factor in international relationships and the 'cold war propaganda.'"[8] Even if there had been no strong women's movement, there was reason for the nationalistic patriots in the NCAA, like Byers, to push for greater women's participation. The NCAA began helping financially in early 1963, when the NCAA Council voted a significant $9,500 to underwrite the costs of a National Institute for Girls' Sport. The institute was jointly sponsored by the Division of Girls and Women's Sport of the American Association for Health, Physical Education and Recreation (AAHPER) and the Women's Board of Olympic Development Committee.[9] The NCAA contributed to the first Institute for Girls and Women's Sport held at the University of Oklahoma later that year.

There was, however, another reason—a self-serving one—that the NCAA and Byers wanted to be involved in college women's athletic participation. The NCAA had been in a battle for control of amateur sport for much of the twentieth century, a clash principally with the dominating amateur organization, the Amateur Athletic Union.[10] NCAA control of women's athletics would bolster the NCAA's influence in international athletics. Nearly all successful male Olympians were collegiate athletes, but NCAA officials had little influence on US representation in international competitions. The Amateur Athletic Union dominated amateur sport, and the NCAA under Walter Byers's assertive hand sought to contest AAU control. This generations-old power struggle helped fuel NCAA involvement on the women's side of athletics.[11]

WOMEN PHYSICAL EDUCATION LEADERS PRIOR TO TITLE IX

In the mid-1960s, even before women physical educators decided to form a committee to conduct collegiate championships, the NCAA was discussing possible sponsorship of women's sports. Byers, the man who administered the NCAA, would eventually be considered the chief antagonist of women's sport. But not at first. Eight years before the passage of Title IX in 1972, Byers and the NCAA were considering supervising the development of college women's athletic competition. Byers followed the elected leaders of the NCAA in offering administrative and financial help for women physical educators, many of whom were reluctant to fully move into competitive athletics. In early 1964 two women physical education leaders spoke at the annual NCAA convention about competitive athletics for women. Marguerite Clifton, from the University of California, Los Angeles, the more conservative of the two, warned against awarding conference championships in women's sports. She believed it would be "foolish for men to take on the responsibility." More importantly, she emphasized that for men to superimpose their programs "is undoubtedly the greatest fear that many women leaders have as they move cautiously ahead with this latest development in competition."[12] Men were forewarned.

Sara Staff Jernigan of Stetson University in Florida was far more aggressive in calling for women's competition. She was one of two or three very outspoken college women physical educators supporting high level competition for women. She called for providing "more instruction, more coaching, and more practice." Jernigan specifically praised Tom Hamilton, the commissioner of the Athletic Association of Western Universities, and Dick Larkins, athletic director at Ohio State University, as being most helpful in moving women's athletics forward. Most NCAA attendees seemed little interested in women's sports, for the lengthy discussions by Clifton and Jernigan received not one question or comment from the all-male assembly.[13]

While women physical educators made cautious preliminary inroads into the administration of competitive women's sports, they made it clear that they did not want men to be involved. This was especially true when the NCAA Council created a Special Committee on Women's Sport soon after Clifton and Jernigan spoke. The two leaders had asked that the NCAA no longer allow women to participate in individual NCAA championships, such as tennis, swimming, and diving. The NCAA quickly legislated to that effect.[14] Women of the Division for Girls and Women's Sport (DGWS) knew that sports in high schools and colleges were moving rapidly to higher level competition. They also recognized that if they did not do something soon, the control of athletics would come from outside male groups. The threat to women's control of female athletes pressured the DGWS to form its own association for college women's athletics. Or as Katherine Ley, a women's sport leader from the University of Michigan stated, there was a need to set up a body for skilled girls and women "whether or not women physical educators were ready."[15]

The DGWS and the National Association for Physical Education of College Women (NAPECW) met in early 1966 and established the Commission on Intercollegiate Sports for Women (CISW), soon to be renamed the Commission on Intercollegiate Athletics for Women (CIAW).[16] According to one woman who attended the meeting, a major goal was to "keep control of women's intercollegiate athletics and forestall NCAA invasion."[17] On this front, women leaders were too late, for Walter Byers was already looking for women leaders who could foster intercollegiate competition on the national level "when the time comes for the NCAA to organize development activities involving women."[18] A few months later, a vice president under Byers, Chuck Neinas, wrote to the AAHPER, the organization under which the DGWS and CIAW operated. Neinas questioned whether women physical educators and the CIAW were ready for national championships, such as the NCAA could offer. He wanted to know "if the DGWS has made any definite plans to increase its national championship schedule of events."[19]

Whether Byers and the NCAA were interested in promoting women's athletics for the good of women athletes can certainly be questioned. In 1966, the year the CIAW was founded, Byers knew so little about college women's sports that, as he wrote to an inquirer, "we don't know who runs the intercollegiate golf tournament for women"—the competition begun at Ohio State University in 1941. The sole women's tourney was still operating—barely—and was then run by the DGWS, NAPECW, and the Athletic and Recreation Federation for College Women.[20] The NCAA inquiry about women's sport had far more to do with Byers's and the NCAA's need to wrest control of amateur sport from the Amateur Athletic Union than with any desire to promote equality with men on college campuses for women athletes.

For the next few years, at the close of the 1960s, it was not clear how the administration of women's sports would be conducted. Byers was particularly uncertain, and a NCAA committee was formed to "study the feasibility of the NCAA establishing appropriate machinery to provide for the development and supervision of women's intercollegiate athletics."[21] Byers was concerned well before the creation of Title IX that, if women of the CIAW (which was part of the DGWS and under AAHPER control) were to supervise women's athletics, these athletics would not then be under the control of institutions of higher education but would be managed by individual educators, specifically women physical educators. The NCAA, by contrast, had institutional membership, and NCAA athletes were not supervised by individuals in an outside educational organization such as the CIAW.[22]

CREATING THE AIAW AND THE NCAA REACTION

The conflict between the NCAA and women physical educators heated up in 1967, following the creation of a NCAA committee to study women's sport. Katherine Ley, new chair of the CIAW, wrote Byers that there should be a "hands off" NCAA policy toward women's sports. Byers replied, "I don't know precisely what you mean by a 'hands off' policy." He did not reassure Ley when he wrote, "the NCAA committee is only a 'study committee.'" He did question whether the CIAW, DGWS, and AAHPER organizations were appropriate for running women's sports, as they "were not institutional members." Byers suggested that governing boards and university administrators would not likely be satisfied with anything other than institutional membership governing women's athletics. "The appropriate organization to supervise and control women's intercollegiate sports," the NCAA head stated, "has not been determined."[23]

It was only natural that women physical educators claimed control. They had been in control of women's physical education programs from the 1800s, including intramural sports and any "extramural competition," something they refused to call "intercollegiate" because that term was associated with men's athletics. Women had been in control of their own athletic domain for a century and had generally been left alone to run their own programs.

As Joan Hult, a historian of women's sports, states, "Although women lost much of their power base in the public domain, within the sacred wall of the school gymnasium the women physical educators reigned supreme." Or as Susan K. Cahn documents, women were in control of "the insular world of women's physical education."[24] Agnes Wayman said it best when the Women's Division of the National Amateur Athletic Federation was formed in 1923. To Wayman, women physical educators were sailing forth "with women at the helm and women manning the whole craft."[25]

Little changed until the 1960s with the exception that young women athletes in the women's movement of the 1960s began calling for a rightful place for talented women in sports.[26] By then, the anti-competition old guard of women physical educators were being replaced by those who desired more competition for young athletes. Nevertheless, this new cohort of women physical educators did not want to lose any of their power to men, who had dominated competitive sports on the campuses. In almost no other American activity did women control their own destiny. Even in nursing, dominated by women, male administrators and male doctors generally had control of their lives. Not so in women's physical education. Women were determined not to lose this domain of power in the one area in American society they appeared to control. But would they?

When Byers told AIAW's Katherine Ley it was not clear what organization would direct college women's athletes, he emphasized that it should be one connected to institutions of higher education. The threat from the NCAA pushed the CIAW to approve national championships for women. Traditionally, the women of the CIAW controlled their own organization and believed that, by assuming institutional rather than individual membership, they would likely be under male domination. The chief advocate for institutional membership for several years was Walter Byers of the all-male NCAA, and the institutions of the NCAA were nearly always run by male college presidents, something women knew and feared.

For the CIAW and its successor, the Association for Intercollegiate Athletics for Women (AIAW), to be successful, the organizations needed money. Income from individual members was never sufficient to run national tournaments. In addition, women's opposition to commercialized athletics, like those under NCAA control, was problematic from the beginning. The challenge faced by the CIAW, and later the AIAW, in running national championships on limited membership resources was exacerbated by the lack of public support for these championships, as evidenced by a dearth of gate receipts and very limited television revenues. This eventually doomed the organization, but the CIAW and AIAW lacked pragmatic foresight as they proceeded with their emphasis on what they considered the educational model for athletics. Lack of money and lack of institutional membership contributed to the organization's decline as the NCAA made incursions into women's sport to combat the AAU and claim control of amateur athletics.

From a legal standpoint, Byers knew that the NCAA would need to provide competitive opportunities for women as well as men, even if women preferred their go-it-alone "separate but equal" policy. The women did not believe that the 1954 US Supreme Court decision banning "separate but equal" race policy in education applied to them. Byers asked the NCAA's counsel for legal advice prior to the CIAW becoming the AIAW and a year before the passage of Title IX in 1972.[27] NCAA counsel George Gangwere answered that the NCAA would likely be in violation of the Federal Constitution's Fourteenth Amendment equal protection clause if it did not provide for women's athletics. Byers then wrote to the DGWS and CIAW that barriers to participation by women athletes in NCAA-sponsored meets and tournaments were probably illegal and that the NCAA needed to consider providing "competitive opportunities for women as well as men."[28] While it took nearly a decade before the NCAA offered championships for women, the issue of equal protection did not go away.

THE AIAW, KELLMEYER, AND ATHLETIC SCHOLARSHIPS

The Association for Intercollegiate Athletics for Women was created out of the CIAW in 1971 to be the national organization running national championships for women. The group was founded a year before the federal government passed Title IX. The AIAW was intended to be a student-centered and education-oriented model, attempting to avoid the negatives of the commercial and professional model of the NCAA.[29] The AIAW grew rapidly but was unsuccessful philosophically and financially in its one decade of existence trying to be educational, amateur, and non-commercial.

Before the death of the AIAW in the early 1980s, the group moved from its educational and amateur model toward the commercial-professional standard that prevailed in men's athletics. In only a few years, the AIAW voted to allow athletic scholarships, began recruiting athletes (the group called it "talent assessment"), and accepted the hiring of professional coaches, all of which it initially opposed. The AIAW also contracted with commercial television rather than telecasting contests through public educational TV. The group accepted alcohol advertising for sport events and sought commercial sponsors to recognize their athletic stars through all-American honors and all-star contests. The AIAW even hired male officials for its games. Further, leaders of the AIAW voted to separate from affiliated educational organizations, including the DGWS and the AAHPER. Significantly, the AIAW spent far more on legal advice than on its main goal of providing national championships for the elite women's intercollegiate teams.[30] While Walter Byers and the NCAA may have been a significant component of the demise of the AIAW, the organization had already given up many of the original policies intended to keep athletics educational, amateur, and non-commercial.

AIAW women's steadfast opposition to recruiting and, more importantly, to paying athletes through athletic scholarships were the first major and crucial failures for the group. As soon as the AIAW was created, a few women coaches and administrators recognized that the women leaders of the AIAW were violating the equal protection clause of the Fourteenth Amendment by prohibiting what men had achieved a generation before, when athletes were paid to compete in athletics with "full scholarships." The Fourteenth Amendment demanded "equal protection." As with African Americans and whites in the civil rights cases of the 1960s, female athletes needed to be treated in the same way as male athletes. If men were allowed to receive athletic scholarships, women should have the same opportunity. Most AIAW leaders steadfastly opposed athletic scholarships, but not Linda Estes, women's athletic director at the University of New Mexico and a member of organization. Estes was opposed to "women who insist on discriminating against other women" when they disallowed both athletic scholarships and the recruiting of high school athletes.[31]

The scholarship issue resulted in a lawsuit early in the tenure of the AIAW and just after Congress passed Title IX. The case began at little Marymount

College in Florida. One of coach Fern Lee 'Peachy' Kellmeyer's tennis players, Kathy Kemper, was on an athletic scholarship. The AIAW denied Kemper an opportunity to participate in the women's AIAW tennis championship because she was ruled, as a scholarship recipient, not to be an amateur. Kemper and Kellmeyer used the Fourteenth Amendment, passed to protect the rights of newly freed Black Americans following the Civil War, to free women from another kind of oppression. They charged the AIAW with discriminating against its own athletes when it denied them equal opportunity to receive athletic scholarships. The AIAW was then under the auspices of the DGWS and the AAHPER and affiliated with the National Education Association (NEA), so Kellmeyer, the lead plaintiff, and her athletes sued the NEA under the Fourteenth Amendment's equal protection clause.

NEA lawyers realized that the AIAW scholarship rule was illegal and told the AIAW that they would not defend the group's unconstitutional restrictions on scholarships. The lawsuit was withdrawn, but Kellmeyer would likely have won. This was an important action that moved the AIAW closer to what Byers and the NCAA believed were needed, common policies in the two national organizations. AIAW antagonist, Linda Estes, wrote at the time: "While the AIAW is going bankrupt fighting a case that they cannot possibly win, the NCAA can take over women's athletics." She continued in a letter to the AIAW president-elect, "At this point, that doesn't sound like a bad idea to me."[32]

THE AIAW DILEMMA: LEGAL RIGHTS OR CONTROL

As important as the Kellmeyer lawsuit was for women's sports, the case has largely been forgotten. However, the passage, interpretations, and impact of Title IX of the Educational Amendments of 1972 have survived for more than a half-century. Title IX has affected Walter Byers's legacy, the NCAA, and the growth of women's athletics. Byers has been highly criticized for opposing how Title IX was interpreted by officials from the Department of Health, Education, and Welfare, who were charged with interpreting and administering the unspecific thirty-seven-word law. Byers and the NCAA first opposed Title IX being applied to college sports since college sports did not receive federal aid. Then, when that failed, they wanted revenue-producing or profit-making sports, mostly football and men's basketball, to be eliminated from Title IX mandates. Byers asked for help from representatives to the NCAA to combat "a major assault upon the revenue producing potential" of football and men's basketball.[33] Byers wrote Texas Senator John Tower praising him for his proposed amendment to Title IX. "We thank you for your leadership," he told Senator Tower, "in protecting the intercollegiate athletic programs of the colleges of this nation."[34] But Tower's amendment favoring revenue-producing sports never became law, and the protection never occurred. Byers failed in his attempt to limit how Title IX was applied to men's basketball and football. He asked NCAA members "to create a volume of mail and political pressure," as he stated in a memo, "to offset the militancy of the women representatives."[35] But Byers's pressure failed.

Since Title IX decisions favored accommodating women's athletics, the NCAA moved more strongly toward taking control of women's sports. To the NCAA, application of rules about athletic participation for both men and women should be men's rules. But why? NCAA legal counsel George Gangwere advised that NCAA rules must "equally apply to all athletes, male and female." Gangwere counseled that the most effective way to avoid discrimination was "to have the same basic rules for all students," including athletic scholarships, recruitment, academic requirements, and transfer of athletes. The same held for national championship competition. Head of the NCAA Committee on Women's Athletics, Edward Betz, agreed that the NCAA was "obligated to offer national championships."[36] Besides, the NCAA argued, the AIAW had few resources to support national championships at a high level, in part because its counsel, Margo Polivy, received far more money for defending the AIAW than did all of the women's championships.

By the mid-1970s, the NCAA had enough money to construct its own building in Mission, Kansas, and to guarantee payments for travel to all national championships. The NCAA established a championship transportation reserve of $100,000 in 1975 from the profits of March Madness basketball championship receipts. The NCAA would pay up to 80 percent of tournament travel expenses for all sports in 1976, then 100 percent in 1977, and all travel expenses and per diems in 1978.[37] The AIAW could not come close to these championship payments, as the income from AIAW tournaments by 1978 was less than $25,000, and the legal expenses of counsel Margo Polivy were over twice the cost of running all AIAW championships.[38]

The AIAW faced a dilemma. As with any institution caught on the horns of a dilemma, both choices were disagreeable. If the AIAW chose to run its own tournaments against those operated by the NCAA, individual schools would likely opt for the less costly and better financed NCAA tourneys. If AIAW leaders chose to strike a deal with the NCAA, they would lose their power position in women's athletics. After being in charge of women's sport for nearly a century, most AIAW leaders refused to bend to the wishes of men. These women chose maintaining control over the more pragmatic approach of joining and likely losing control to the NCAA. After about four years of meetings, the women leaders of the AIAW still would not agree to the major changes desired by Byers and the NCAA. Ed Betz of the University of the Pacific, a major negotiator, concluded, "It may be that the only way we can reach a common set of rules is by offering national championships."[39] The NCAA began offering paid-for championships, first to the AIAW teams in Division II and III NCAA institutions. A year later, the NCAA decided to offer championships to women in Division I schools. With a clear majority, nearly all Division I institutions chose the free NCAA tourneys over those of the AIAW, and the AIAW was doomed.[40] Almost.

When the NCAA Division II and III championships for women were announced in early January 1980, to begin in 1981, AIAW president-elect Christine Grant responded, "This is an outrage. . . . The preservation of our organization is at stake." AIAW members discussed possible responses, such as lobbying college presidents, alumni, and Congress, conducting an economic boycott of NCAA advertisers, effecting lawsuits based on Title IX violations, and bringing an antitrust case based on the NCAA monopoly.[41] Walter Byers privately referred to the women's opposition to the NCAA as the "AIAW war dance in Washington." Publicly, Byers stated that he personally hoped the "A.I.A.W. continues to exist," avowing that there was room for both the AIAW and NCAA.[42] However, if the AIAW opposition was a war dance, it was being directed to a great extent by the AIAW legal counsel Margo Polivy, who some AIAW members criticized as a major decision maker rather than just a legal adviser, for which she was being paid a large percentage of AIAW revenue.[43]

A final meeting between representatives of the AIAW and NCAA occurred in the spring of 1981. After the April 30 meeting, the NCAA's president, James Frank—the first African American to head the NCAA and a strong opponent of "separate but equal"—concluded that "a unified governance structure for both men's and women's athletics is not feasible within the foreseeable future." The University of Iowa's Christine Grant, past president of the AIAW, was adamant that the AIAW was "absolutely" only interested in being "committed on a joint, equal basis" with the NCAA. Lawyer Margo Polivy conceded that the AIAW "does not acknowledge the legitimacy of NCAA's involvement in women's athletics." And these were the polite words uttered by the angered women leaders. The meeting broke up soon after it began that morning.[44]

With the organization nearly bankrupt, the leaders of the AIAW, on the advice of legal counsel Margo Polivy, decided to go to court.[45] Unfortunately, the lawsuit drawn up by the AIAW began with false information. "The history of men's intercollegiate athletics as a unified national commercial activity is essentially the history of the NCAA," the lawsuit read. The text stated that the NCAA was created "in response to President Theodore Roosevelt's threat to ban football if institutions themselves did not act to curb pandemic financial and physical abuses in men's college sport."[46] The beginning of the NCAA had nothing to do with curbing "pandemic financial" abuses in men's intercollegiate sport. It was far from being a "unified commercial activity" in 1906, with a balance of $28.82 in its treasury.[47] Nor did Theodore Roosevelt say one word about the possibility of banning football, as he was strongly in favor of football for not only for the nation but for his freshman son attending Harvard.[48] Misleading statements by Polivy did not help the AIAW case.

The AIAW first moved to procure an injunction to prevent the NCAA from conducting national championships for women. This quickly failed. The judge, Thomas Jackson, then asked for mediation efforts. When the AIAW proposed sex-separate autonomous divisions in the NCAA, the NCAA rejected the idea. Judge Jackson also rejected the idea of sex separation. In the trial, the AIAW did not prove that the NCAA had violated antitrust laws by conspiring to destroy the AIAW through offering national championships. The purpose of antitrust laws, the judge pointed out, "has always been the protection of competition, not competitors."[49] The AIAW, already bankrupt, closed its doors, and the NCAA became the dominant force in college women's sports. The NCAA used its vast resources to conduct national championships and to fight future lawsuits, which were increasing in number.

Walter Byers and the NCAA would not always be on the winning side of legal arguments. At the time of the AIAW litigation, a more important issue to the future of the NCAA and Byers's legacy was emerging. A lawsuit, *Board of Regents of the University of Oklahoma v. NCAA*, was brought against the NCAA over football television rights one month after the AIAW-NCAA suit was settled at the appeals court level, with Judge Ruth Bader Ginsburg, later a giant in the US Supreme Court, and two others unanimously agreeing with the NCAA.[50] The Oklahoma case against the NCAA was financially backed by a group of about sixty big-time football institutions, the College Football Association. The CFA vigorously opposed Title IX and women's sport, and the financial challenges to football income that they posed. The two most impactful court cases for Walter Byers and the NCAA occurred in the early 1980s, resulting in one win and one loss. They have had lasting impacts ever since.

SEVEN

A Win for Byers

The NCAA Defeats the AAU

> "We believe the proposed federations are the soundest means of advancing amateur sports in America."
>
> **—WALTER BYERS, 1962**

> "I was as competitive and combative as a football coach."
>
> **—WALTER BYERS, 1995**

If Walter Byers carried out the will of the NCAA membership in women's athletics, he was also head of the line in athletic administrators' long-standing war on the Amateur Athletic Union (AAU) for control of amateur sport. Nowhere was he as confrontational as in his efforts to defeat the AAU, except perhaps in his efforts to crush Eastern broadcasters in football telecast negotiations. Byers was not the first NCAA official to lead the fight against the AAU, but during his tenure he spearheaded the movement of the NCAA-backed sport federations by advocating and supporting them with NCAA money. The NCAA spent several decades contesting the AAU over the rights to sanction amateur sports, to select leaders of international sports, and to be recognized for producing most world-class athletes in collegiate competition. In the end, the executive director would be the NCAA's prime mover in wresting control of amateur sport away from the AAU as the federal government passed the Amateur Sports Act of 1978. Walter Byers's tenacious attacks could hardly be denied. Byers later summed up his actions against the AAU, stating, "I was as competitive and combative as a football coach."[1]

THE NCAA'S HISTORIC FIGHT FOR CONTROL OF AMATEUR ATHLETICS

Colleges challenged the AAU before the NCAA was established. The AAU was born in 1888 among New York City athletic clubs, during a fight to control the growth of amateur sport. At that time, college sports, particularly track and field, began certifying the status of amateur athletes in meets open to collegians. The collegiate and student-run Intercollegiate Amateur Athletic Association of America (IC4A), formed in 1875, aligned itself with the New York City-centered National Association of Amateur Athletes of America (NAAAA) after it was founded in 1879. Prior to the creation of the AAU, the National Association of Amateur Athletes of America, designed for athletic clubs, was the most powerful amateur governing body in sports.

In the late 1880s, however, internal squabbles over who was considered an amateur led to the prominent New York Athletic Club's (NYAC) withdrawal from the NAAAA. With a number of other prestigious athletic clubs, the NYAC formed a new governing body to oversee amateur athletics: the Amateur Athletic Union.[2] To help destroy the NAAAA, the AAU decreed that any amateur competing in "open" contests must do so under AAU rules or be debarred from meets sponsored by the AAU.[3] This power play backed by the influential and wealthy NYAC caused the collapse of the NAAAA, which was forced to close its doors. Its members, including the IC4A colleges, then joined the AAU.[4] When the AAU began to charge a fee to sanction track and field meets, the colleges were forced to pay this fee to the AAU, even if they were conducting their own meets.[5] The fees supported the AAU financially, but colleges were not satisfied with being required to pay for their own events to prevent their athletes from being banned from AAU and other "open" competitions. Prior to the formation of the NCAA in 1905, payment of registration fees to the AAU by colleges for holding their own meets caused resentment toward the AAU. As early as 1893, the founder of the modern Olympic Games, Pierre de Coubertin, observed, "I am disillusioned with the secret war going on between the universities of America and the AAU."[6] Antagonism between colleges and the AAU lasted for nearly a century.

Sanctioning of meets and registration of individual competitors continued until the demise of AAU's power with the passage of the Amateur Sports

Act of 1978. Two years after the NCAA was formed, James E. Sullivan, longtime secretary and then president of the AAU, addressed members of the AAU and boasted that registration "is the backbone of this organization. It is centralization, it means control, . . . absolute control over the individual athlete who competes under our protection."[7] (In another half-century it was Walter Byers and the NCAA that had "absolute control over the individual athlete.") Soon, Harvard athletic leader and NCAA district representative William Garcelon took exception to the iron hand of the AAU. Speaking to the NCAA membership, he remarked that "the line of demarcation between the authority of the Union, and the exclusive authority of the colleges, is very indistinct." Garcelon opposed the AAU's "foolish restrictions upon competition by college men."[8] Yet, by the early 1900s, the AAU (through its majority control of the American Olympic Committee) chose and funded the American Olympic team, though many athletes were collegians.[9]

Antipathy between the colleges and the AAU continued into the 1920s, especially over the question of how athletes and coaches should be chosen for the Olympic Games. The AAU controlled the American Olympic Committee.[10] Since most of the American participants in the Antwerp, Paris, and Amsterdam Olympic Games in the 1920s were, or had been, collegiate athletes, NCAA members continually complained about AAU dominance in choosing Olympians. The NCAA's prominence grew when it sponsored its first national track and field meet in 1921. That year, the AAU-dominated American Olympic Committee was reorganized because of the botched management of the US Olympic team in Antwerp, Belgium. In the process, the NCAA was slighted and given only three seats in the new American Olympic Association (AOA), while the dominant AAU held thirty-three seats.[11] One writer called the AAU a "self-appointed and self-perpetuating hierarchy of bosses" who controlled the American Olympic Committee.[12] At one meeting with the AAU, both the president of the NCAA, General Palmer Pierce, and Big Ten commissioner Major John L. Griffith walked out in opposition to what they considered the "dictatorial powers" of the AAU.[13] The NCAA then withdrew from the AOA until some changes were made in representation.

An uneasy truce existed from the end of the 1920s until after World War II. Then, in 1946, the AAU and the NCAA signed an Articles of Alliance agreement that was a cover for the "uneasy truce." For international meets, especially in Olympic sports such as track and field, the AAU often bypassed competent NCAA coaches to choose traditional favorites. One journalist stated that the mismanagement of AAU events was shown by "the arrogances, the hypocrisy, the stupidity, and the incompetence" of AAU officials. As historian of the AAU conflict Joseph Turrini has stated, the AAU was guilty of ignoring "athlete complaints, managing meets poorly, neglecting research, disregarding coaches, and behaving in an unresponsive and dictatorial manner."[14] Quoted in journalist Red Smith's article, "The Amateurs Are All Upstairs," an AAU cynic concluded that "The trouble in many ways with amateur athletics in this country is that the athletes have been professionals and the administrators have been amateurs."[15] An egregious example of AAU arrogance and lack of justice in its fight with the NCAA occurred after a world record 880-yard run by Jim Ryun in the 1966 United States Track and Field Federation (USTFF) championship. The USTFF was a relatively new organization backed by the NCAA in the early 1960s. Ryun, a freshman at the University of Kansas, set the world record, but because the AAU had not sanctioned the meet, the organization refused to certify the record.[16] As a result of a host of similar actions over many decades, college coaches decided to organize their own sport organizations, like the USTFF, in opposition to AAU control.

INTERCOLLEGIATE FEDERATIONS UNDER BYERS AND NCAA FINANCING

By the early 1960s, with Walter Byers in the role as executive director for about a decade, coaches in sports with Olympic connections were ready to officially challenge the AAU's control of those sports. The five American Olympic sports that became prominent were collegiately run federations in basketball, gymnastics, swimming, track and field, and wrestling. Each, with NCAA backing, organized in the early 1960s to challenge the AAU's dominance in the US Olympic involvement. In track and field, University of Michigan track coach Don Canham and Penn State's Chick Werner led the formalization in June 1962 of the USTFF, with Werner serving as executive director.[17] Byers and the NCAA executive committee assured the new federations of their support, including financial backing.

The NCAA Executive Committee, with Byers in attendance, first disbanded a committee that had been appointed to deal with the NCAA-AAU conflict. The NCAA suspended the decade-long NCAA-AAU working agreement in 1960, when the NCAA decided it would no longer back autocratic suspensions imposed by the AAU.[18] "We have exhausted all avenues of discussion," Byers stated for the executive committee. To be successful against the powerful AAU and its international backing, Byers believed that "the first thing you measure is loyalty. We have it."[19] When formed, the federations had the financial backing of the NCAA, ensuring that each sport federation would succeed. The financially stable NCAA would back the federations to prevent the AAU from using the threat of suspension of athletes under NCAA control. Under Byers's direction, the NCAA budgeted the same amount of money on the new sport federations as it spent on the NCAA TV Committee. The money for the federations came directly from the TV network football contract in the early 1960s. The federations were supported by a percentage of the $3 million TV contract, which went directly to the NCAA rather than the football teams on the telecasts.[20]

The AAU was invited but refused to join the new college federations. Under the NCAA-sponsored federations, colleges could begin to run their own amateur programs and coaches could negotiate meetings with other international sports teams. As an example, the new US Gymnastic Federation (USGF) could invite a team from Sweden to participate in a Penn State- sponsored meet and not worry about the AAU deciding whether it was legal or not.[21] The United States had not won an Olympic gold medal in gymnastics since 1932, but college coaches believed that they could help develop champion Olympians under USGF control. Byers was a strong supporter because he believed the USGF could improve both high school and college gymnastics. According to Byers, "We're the only one to do it," because the AAU was not helpful, despite the organization's control of gymnastics and seven other Olympic sports.[22]

The fight between the AAU and the NCAA continued even as US Attorney General Robert Kennedy and retired General Douglas MacArthur tried to bring the two sides together.[23] When Byers was asked whether his fourteen-year-old son, Ward, had an eligibility card for an AAU track meet in which he cleared five feet, the clenched-teeth father replied, "He had no A.A.U. card."[24] The inflexible Byers was asked to offer the AAU a peace plan, but the first two planks of the peace offering stated that any qualified organization, such as a NCAA institution, could conduct contests "without interference from the AAU" and that any athlete from a qualified organization could compete "without ineligibility rules from the AAU."[25] No peace plan was that.

The NCAA-AAU feud resulted in congressional action by the US Senate. After unsuccessful mediation and arbitration efforts of Kennedy and MacArthur in the early 1960s, the US Senate Committee on Commerce held lengthy hearings to get at the root of the trouble, specifically in track and field administration. By this time, the conflict had become a standoff between the two organizations, with highly charged accusations and little room for mutual action. The AAU's executive director, Colonel Donald Hull, called the NCAA and its funded USTFF "puppet organizations" with "power-mad executives" and accused them of being "undemocratic and unpatriotic." The NCAA's response was no less antagonistic. The conflict was exacerbated by the Cold War competition between the United States and the Russian-led Soviet Union, and particularly by a loss to Russia in a dual track and field event.[26] By most counts, Byers led those who provided evidence against the AAU when testifying before the Senate committee. He criticized the AAU for its "self-perpetuation and dictatorship" as well as its use of "outdated methods" and an "indefensible 'lockout' against the NCAA." The AAU failed, Byers stated, with shortcomings in "equipment, facilities, training of the athletes, diet, medical care, coaching supervision, or management of meets and related travel and facilities arrangements."[27] All of that was true, but neither Byers nor the NCAA had a perfect record.

THE JACK LANGER MACCABIAH GAMES DISPUTE

The NCAA's steely stance against the AAU was never clearer than in the Jack Langer case in 1969.[28] Langer attended Yale and, at 6'8" tall, was a second-string basketball center. He was invited to participate with other Jewish athletes in the Maccabiah Games in Israel.[29] He asked his athletic director, DeLaney Kiphuth, if, as a Yale athlete, he could compete in Israel. Kiphuth said yes without contacting the Eastern College Athletic Conference, of which Yale was a member, or the NCAA. At the time, the NCAA was only sanctioning AAU-sponsored basketball teams for international competition in the Olympics, not in the Maccabiah Games. The NCAA put this rule in place, according to Byers, to support the NCAA-backed Basketball Federation USA (BFUSA).[30] While the NCAA allowed soccer players, swimmers, and track participants to compete in the Maccabiah Games, the BFUSA banned all AAU-sponsored basketball team tours. Though the NCAA backed the BFUSA ban, Langer nevertheless went to Israel. When Langer returned and again played for Yale, the NCAA made Langer ineligible for NCAA action, and the Eastern College Athletic Conference punished Yale with two-year probation for violating NCAA rules.[31] There was no question that Langer had been the victim of the NCAA-AAU struggle for control of amateur sport. Langer knew it, and athletic director Kiphuth later noted that the NCAA was "using students as pawns in the endless NCAA struggle with the AAU."[32]

Congressional action followed. By 1973 the House of Representatives called a hearing on the "Protection of College Athlete," in which two bills were discussed to give athletes greater rights and the government some control over international athletic competition. US congressmen were mostly concerned that American athletes, such as UCLA's great basketball player Bill Walton, should be able to compete in international contests against the Soviet Union. Seven days of hearings were conducted in which Jack Langer gave testimony along with representatives of the AAU, NCAA, NAIA, Junior College Association, conferences, coaches and athletic directors, the High School Federation, and the YMCA, among others.[33]

The Langer controversy lingered as part of the AAU-NCAA fight over amateur sport control. With only a shaky truce effected just before each Olympics, the battle continued until the disastrous 1972 Munich Games. With the weakest medal showing in American track and field history, the Soviets again won the Olympic medal contest, outpacing the United States in total gold medals fifty to thirty-three. Administrative failures plagued the American team in part because only one-third of the coaches and managers of the Munich delegation had previous Olympic experience. There were many faux pas. Two of the world's best American track athletes missed starting times because of administrative failures. World record holder in the pole vault, Bob Seagren, was not allowed to use his fiberglass pole at the last moment. Rick DeMont, a world record holder in swimming, lost his gold medal following a ruling that an asthma medicine he required was not considered a legal drug.[34] During this same Olympics, officials gave the Soviet team competing against the United States in the basketball finals several chances to win the game. Byers called it "the Olympic debacle at Munich" and blamed the AAU-dominated US Olympic Committee (USOC). He stated that "the situation is worse now than in the '60s." "The only external force that has the clout to bring about reorganization," Byers believed, was "Congress."[35] Charges against inept AAU-dominated Olympic administrators triggered the involvement of the US federal government once again.

BACKGROUND FOR THE AMATEUR SPORTS ACT OF 1978

The one-hundred-year war between colleges and the AAU finally ended in the decade following the Munich Olympics. While the radical Palestinian militant attack on Israeli Olympians in Munich caused immediate worldwide outrage, the involvement of two presidents and the US Congress in reforming amateur sport in America after these games had a more significant long-term impact on the NCAA and Byers's central role. Soon after the 1972 Olympics concluded, the NCAA withdrew from involvement in the USOC, and the contest for the control of amateur sport continued. The sting of the Langer case lingered when Jack Langer himself, then completing a graduate degree at Harvard University, testified that a government Amateur Sports Commission was needed to solve the bickering between the Byers-led NCAA and the traditional AAU controllers of international amateur sports and especially participation in the Olympic movement.

Rep. James O'Hara of Michigan, chair of the special House subcommittee, spoke prior to receiving testimony in the 1973 "Protection of College Athletes" hearing. "The participants in the dispute are associations," O'Hara began, "the pawns in the dispute are college athletes."[36] Supporting the two bills before Congress, Langer advised, "these bills are the only way to effectively deal with a continually deteriorating showing of U.S. athletics abroad."[37] It appeared, however, that athletes would remain pawns. While the AAU sponsored a series of basketball games in America, Byers was adamant about not using college athletes against the Russians. Byers was unyielding, declaring, "No student of any NCAA institution may participate in the games." Additionally, he asserted, "No coach of a member NCAA institution may be attached" in any way to the AAU-sponsored basketball tour.[38]

Despite the continued conflict, there was plenty of opposition in the numerous amateur organizations and in Congress itself to having the government form a federal commission to control amateur sport. Fear of government control was not new in America nor in intercollegiate athletics, for America was originally formed in part due to fear of British control of the American colonies. Fear of federal control continued for the next two centuries, especially after World War II, when the USSR attempted to conquer the world for its form of communism. The federal control alarm began before that war was concluded, during debates over a possible GI Bill of Rights. Providing millions of dollars to returning veterans for education, technical training, and home ownership, the GI Bill, to some, approached government control and a welfare state. "Republicans," historian Meredith Hindley writes, "worried the bill would lead to further expansion of the federal government," taking a step toward the United States becoming a "social-welfare state."[39] In spite of the threat of "big government" following the massive expansion of federal control during the Great Depression, Congress narrowly passed the GI Bill of Rights. It was signed into law by President Franklin Roosevelt one month after the D-Day attack against the Nazis in France and less than a year before Germany capitulated, ending the war in Europe.

When the war concluded with the surrender of Japan in 1945, the risk of Soviet expansion in Europe emerged. During congressional debate of the GI Bill, Mississippi representative John Rankin's had cautioned, "I would rather send my child to a red schoolhouse, than to a red school."[40] Was America turning to government control? To some, the threat of the socialist-communist "reds" was reflected in American federal control of athletics. National athletic scholarships and national control of college football telecasts were believed to reflect a move toward "big brother" governmental control in American institutions of higher education. This peril also impacted intercollegiate athletics. The NCAA became especially suspect after the organization allowed national control of paying athletes through scholarships soon after World War II and, within a couple of years, the nationwide command of telecasting football games. The charge of socialism was common then and decades later. Even college presidents spoke out. The president of the University of Tennessee, Cloide Brehm, complained about the "socialistic and un-American" trend "toward socialism."[41] President John

Cavanaugh of Notre Dame and President Theodore Hesburgh, who followed him at that institution, both opposed the equal sharing of football television receipts by the NCAA, viewing this policy as "socialistic in nature."[42]

Two decades later, in the midst of the lingering AAU-NCAA fight over the Maccabiah and Olympic Games, there was continued talk of a federal commission with authority to arbitrate disputes between the warring organizations. Walter Byers spoke out in opposition to federal control: "It seems to be going against the traditions of our country," he stated. "You may be turning away from the old concept and going to a socialistic kind of central board."[43] Again, Byers used the long-standing socialistic language of the Cold War era to defend the NCAA and advocate for less governmental control of sport. Byers was attempting to defeat the AAU without the federal government coming in to control amateur sport and to tell the NCAA what to do.

THE AMATEUR SPORTS ACT OF 1978 RUINS THE AAU

No NCAA member had a greater impact on eliminating the AAU power hold on amateur sport than Walter Byers. Shortly after the AAU's and USOC's bungled 1972 Munich Olympics, he told Senator Mike Gravel of Alaska, who had proposed a bill establishing governmental supervision of amateur athletics, that the NCAA was opposed to another "quasi-government agency" attempting to solve amateur athletic differences. Byers believed governmental officials could help break up the amateur athletic monopoly of the AAU and restructure the USOC to make it a "more democratic body." Nevertheless, Byers did not want the government to impose "another layer of bureaucracy upon amateur athletics."[44] Despite Byers's opposition, Senator Gravel introduced the National Amateur Sports Foundation bill to fund the amateur governing bodies and provide a forum for voluntary settlement of amateur sport conflicts. History had shown that voluntary settlement of conflicts would only occur just prior to each Olympics as Cold War pressure developed to provide the American Olympic team with superior athletes to defeat the Soviet team.[45] In addition, Byers did not want federal money to go to the AAU or the USOC, both of whom wanted to restrict NCAA influence in international sport.[46] One former Eastern College Athletic Conference (ECAC) athletic director thought Byers was a major problem in resolving America's amateur athletics conflicts. He told a *New York Times* reporter that he feared the "predatory ambitions" of Byers. "Byers will kill any compromise," he remarked, "to reach his own ends."[47] The ECAC did not back Byers in his stance against the AAU and the USOC, but many NCAA members did.

Presidents Richard Nixon and Gerald Ford were concerned about America's athletic success and prestige in international affairs during the Cold War. President Nixon proposed a commission to study amateur sports but this proposal in July 1974 was completely derailed the next month with Nixon's resignation arising out of his impeachment proceedings following the Watergate scandal. Less than a year after assuming office, President Ford created the President's Commission on Olympic Sports in response to "declining performance by the United Sates in international competition such as the Olympic Games."[48] After a two-year intensive investigation, the final report of the commission created to solve conflicts among the AAU, the NCAA, and the USOC became the basis for Congress's passage of the Amateur Sports Act of 1978.

Nearly 100,000 pages of testimony and documents were devoted to the debate over the bill. Congress accepted most of the findings of the President's Commission on Olympic Sports, as detailed in its report, and created the Amateur Sports Act of 1978, which was eventually signed by President Jimmy Carter. Byers may not have favored all its measures, but he was overjoyed that the act stated that single organizations, such as the AAU, could control only one international sport, not eight as in the past. The AAU had been outmaneuvered and outvoted in Congress. In the future, the USOC would be in charge of international sport policy, with the AAU controlling only one sport.[49] This essentially removed the AAU dominance of international sport, including the Olympic Games and the Pan-American Games. Although Byers campaigned against federal intervention in amateur sport, he did not condemn the $16 million in federal money to bolster sports that received little attention from privately run amateur organizations. The legislation also eliminated any athletes' bill of rights, which had been discussed a few years earlier.[50]

Walter Byers came out the winner in the NCAA's long-term fight to eviscerate the AAU and eliminate its century-long control of amateur sport, but he eventually changed his mind about the place of the athlete as an amateur. Ironically, once Byers retired from the NCAA in 1987, his views on the NCAA in the AAU battle changed drastically. Whereas Byers had portrayed the AAU as a dictator over athletes' rights, he later found that the NCAA played that role. "The liberator of the past," Byers wrote of the NCAA in his *Unsportsmanlike Conduct*, "has become today's oppressor."[51] Byers and the NCAA eliminated the AAU as the major player in determining the amateur status of athletes and replaced it with an oppressive National Collegiate Athletic Association. Meanwhile, a battle was brewing within the NCAA among smaller colleges and big-time institutions over legislative control.

EIGHT

Small Colleges, NCAA Divisions, and the CFA Schism

> "How many people are going to want to attend a small college game if they can sit home and watch Notre Dame instead?"
>
> **—ASA BUSHNELL, 1949**

> "The CFA was going for the jugular. . . ."
>
> **—WALTER BYERS, 1995**

While the NCAA and Walter Byers were challenging the AAU and winning a major victory in the campaign to control amateur athletics, another battle was being fought over internal control among small and large institutions within the NCAA. There was always tension between the athletic "haves" and "have nots," even before the NCAA was formed. Tension existed over the value of football between the big-time schools and the lesser athletic institutions following the 1905 death of a small college football player from Union College, who sustained a brain injury playing against another non-elite football team, New York University. In the next century of athletic competition, while the colleges or universities that were considered leading athletic powers changed, those in the power positions continued to have different priorities relating to how contests should be played and who would benefit the most from the rules they made. By the 1890s, when football became the favored intercollegiate sport in most American institutions of higher learning, a pecking order had been created, often determined by the size of the college or university. Splits between small and large institutions took place, especially three-quarters of a century later in the 1970s, when television began to dominate financially and a big-time NCAA basketball tournament brought in millions of dollars to college athletics. Byers, as head of the NCAA, was at the center of the controversy building toward a schism tied to how this money was divided.

SMALL VERSUS LARGE COLLEGE ATHLETICS OCCURS EARLY

Early on, the dominant educational institutions of Harvard, Yale, and Princeton led in college athletics. They controlled college sport from 1876, when the Intercollegiate Football Association was created of the Big Three and Columbia, until the NCAA was created in 1905. The schools in what later became the Ivy League ruled the collegiate sport scene. From the Harvard and Yale crew meet in 1852 until the first soccer match in 1905, future Ivy League schools won thirteen of twenty-three of the first American men's intercollegiate matchups.[1] Schools from the future Eastern Ivy League were the big-time institutions until after the NCAA was formed and state universities and a few large private institutions became the leaders.

Ironically, the NCAA was formed in 1905 primarily of small colleges following the football death of Harold Moore of Union College in a game against New York University. Then, Chancellor Henry MacCracken of New York University called a meeting of the nineteen schools NYU had recently competed against in football to see if football might be banned. Of the thirteen schools attending, only Columbia and West Point could be considered big-time, while the likes of Haverford, Lafayette, Rochester, and Stevens Institute were not in that class.[2] The MacCracken group of mostly small colleges voted 8–5 not to ban football but to reform it. They decided to call for a national meeting of institutions of higher education to discuss football rule changes. The meeting that launched the NCAA took place on December 28, 1905, in New York City and was sparsely attended by the larger institutions; thirty-two small colleges and six larger institutions (Colorado, Minnesota, Nebraska, North Carolina, Pennsylvania, and West Point) were present. At this gathering, they agreed to write reformed football rules, and this became the principal business of the new NCAA. The elected officers of the original national organization were from West Point, Williams, Rutgers, Vanderbilt, Kansas, and Oberlin, reflecting the early influence of smaller institutions.[3]

The small colleges, though, knew that the NCAA and faculty control could only survive and prosper if they could get the larger and more prestigious institutions to join them. Thus, after the first annual meeting following football rule changes intended to make the sport safer, the NCAA appealed to the big-time sport schools to join the organization by changing the bylaws to state that the NCAA would discuss but not make national policy.[4] Each school or conference would be free to make its own rules about such elements as defining amateurism or allowing freshmen or graduate students to participate; this policy was called Home Rule. The dominant small colleges of the NCAA agreed collectively to act individually, thus creating greater motivation for the dominant Ivy schools and leading Midwestern Big Ten Conference members to join. The appeal of Home Rule enticed big-time schools by ensuring that they did not have to accept rules adopted by the lesser institutions or conferences. Home Rule remained in place from 1906 until after World War II. Within a decade of the creation of the NCAA, representatives of large schools were serving as president, vice president, and district representatives of all eight NCAA districts. Only the secretary-treasurer, Frank Nicolson of Wesleyan, could be considered a small college representative.[5] Home Rule, as an appeal for the larger school support, remained for the next half-century.

There was one exception to Home Rule—football rules. If institutions wanted to play football against most colleges, they would have to follow the national rules of the newly formed NCAA Football Rules Committee. The NCAA Rules Committee was an amalgamation of the pre-1906 "old" rules committee, led by Walter Camp of Yale and other big-time Eastern schools, and the "new" football committee, formed from the MacCracken group of mostly small colleges. Joining the two rules committees was not smooth, but the two groups eventually agreed to such rule changes as legalizing the forward pass, separating the two teams at the line of scrimmage, and a ten-yard rule to replace a five-yard rule to retain the ball.[6] These changes attempted to lessen the impact of mass line plays, which resulted in the numerous injuries including the cerebral hemorrhage death of Union College's Harold Moore six months before.

While football continued to grow as the national sport for colleges, tensions persisted among small and large institutions. The construction of football stadiums, especially in the 1920s, reflected the differences plaguing these two cohorts. Following World War I, the popularity of football and other sports grew rapidly. Harvard, Yale, and Princeton built stadiums before the war, but following the conflict, universities in the Midwest—including Michigan, Notre Dame and Ohio State—and on the West Coast—including California, Stanford, and Washington—constructed stadiums for tens of thousands of spectators.[7] To pay for the debt-ridden stadiums, these institutions needed to continually recruit athletes and subsidize them, to satisfy fans and to keep the stadiums filled.

The recruitment of subsidized athletes by the big-time universities had a negative impact upon the enrollment of both athletes and regular students at many smaller schools. In the Midwest, many small colleges even appealed to the North Central Association (NCA), formed in 1895 to accredit schools and colleges. The publicity, prestige, and payment of football players at big-time institutions tended to draw students away from the smaller colleges, threatening their prosperity. In response, smaller schools sought to maintain their enrollments by appealing to the NCA to take away accreditation from the big-time institutions because they were recruiting and paying athletes in violation of amateur policy and creating a distraction from education. As the North Central Association was dominated by smaller institutions, some larger institutions such as Northwestern and Purdue in the Big Ten feared that the NCA might indeed take away their accreditation.[8] The NCA became involved in athletic accreditation shortly after the famed Carnegie Foundation for the Advancement of Teaching report, *American College Athletics*, was published in 1929. This three-year study of athletics in higher education condemned violations of amateurism in college athletics and questioned the relationship of athletics to the educational process.[9]

SMALL COLLEGES AND THE SUBSIDIZATION OF ATHLETES

The NCA eventually ended its threat to take accreditation away from prestigious Big Ten institutions for violating the principles of amateurism, but small colleges continued to fight for stronger NCAA legislation on recruiting and subsidization of athletes. Shortly before America's entrance into World War II, the NCAA Executive Committee, recognizing the concerns of the small colleges, created a Small College Committee. This Eastern-controlled committee met and voted to support a revised NCAA constitution containing strong provisions, favorable to small colleges, for national restrictions on recruiting and subsidizing athletes.[10] Although the NCAA was moving toward the creation of a national governing body for intercollegiate athletics and away from the principle of Home Rule, the president of the NCAA, W. B. Owens of Stanford University, was not so inclined. Rather, Owens believed that each individual institution should decide for itself if it would remain in the NCAA by following the newly implemented NCAA policy prohibiting the recruiting and subsidization of athletes. Speaking at the annual convention, Owens summed up a quandary for the NCAA when he asked whether the NCAA "shall continue solely as an educational body or establish definite standards to which its members must conform."[11] Small colleges, as well as big-time institutions, had to consider whether they wanted national recruiting and payments to athletes or remain under Home Rule. The 1939 convention went halfway toward national control. The revised constitution passed at this meeting allowed the termination of a member institution by a two-thirds vote for failure to meet acceptable scholastic or athletic standards.[12] The standards were not defined, nor did the constitution state how they would be implemented.

At this time, Walter Byers had transferred as an undergraduate from one big-time athletic institution, Rice, to another, the University of Iowa. He was almost certainly not aware of the conflict between small and large athletic programs being discussed at the 1939 NCAA meeting. As a nineteen-year-old, Byers was probably not particularly concerned that large institutions dominated such activities as football bowl games, which had been regularly played since 1916, or the new NCAA basketball tournament first conducted the previous spring. A competent athlete but not big enough for big-time college football, Byers was not likely cognizant of conflicts among small colleges and large institutions over recruiting and paying athletes.[13] Yet, in less than a decade, he would be at the center of a major decision when the NCAA, with small college support, passed the Sanity Code and tried to enforce recruiting and financial aid legislation.

A half-year after World War II ended, the NCAA small college group met to discuss changes they wanted the NCAA to institute. One proposal by the big-time–controlled American Football Coaches Association (AFCA) exemplifies the kind of efforts they sought to resist. The AFCA had been working to create a publicity and statistics bureau that would promote big-time football to more successfully compete with the increasingly popular professional football. The Small College Committee unanimously opposed the large-school coaches' proposal for greater commercialization.[14] The big schools, however, prevailed. What was far more important to the small schools was the NCAA's passage of the Sanity Code, which eventually destroyed Home Rule.

THE DIVISIVE SANITY CODE AND BYERS'S FIRST MAJOR DISAPPOINTMENT

When the Sanity Code was passed in 1948, Byers was in his first year as an assistant to Kenneth "Tug" Wilson, commissioner of the Big Ten and secretary-treasurer of the NCAA. The Sanity Code, first called the "Purity Code," was intended to restrict athletic recruiting and prohibit athletic scholarships at the national level. At the time of its passage, most schools, large and small, recruited athletes, and three Southern conferences—the Southeastern, Southwest, and Missouri Valley conferences—allowed full athletic scholarships. Many of the NCAA faculty representatives, however, were reformers at heart and knew that national policies were needed as increased commercialization would likely occur following the war, especially after the passage of the GI Bill of Rights brought masses of war veterans to American colleges. The Sanity Code, or "Principles for the Conduct of Intercollegiate Athletics," adopted in the NCAA constitution, had six provisions: (1) a definition of amateurism; (2) a demand for institutional faculty control; (3) a requirement that athletes be admitted into college on the same basis as other students; (4) a prohibition on off-campus recruiting; (5) a requirement that financial aid to athletes be based on financial need; and (6) a restriction of athletic competition to only those players who conformed to the first five principles.[15]

At first glance, there looked to be general agreement among small and large colleges, as only the recruiting principle did not receive unanimous agreement when passed in early January 1948. Yet, many probably knew that the near unanimous vote was tempered by a half-century of "states' rights" Home Rule in which institutions and, more importantly, conferences passed their own rules. Besides, all institutions were free to do what they wanted until the next meeting in 1948, when the Sanity Code was added to the constitution. In that year, the three Southern big-time conferences with full athletic scholarships met to discuss whether they should withdraw from the NCAA or just refuse to conform to the NCAA recruiting and scholarship rules.[16]

The 1948 NCAA conference to ratify the Sanity Code within the NCAA constitution could be considered the most important meeting since the formation of the NCAA after the 1905 football crisis. Out of the Sanity Code compliance convention, the NCAA created a Constitutional Compliance Committee of three faculty representatives to ensure compliance.[17] Undermanned, under-funded, and under-respected, the Compliance Committee had only one option to deal with those it believed were violating recruiting and athletic payment regulations. It could recommend to the NCAA convention that the violators be banished from NCAA membership. The Compliance Committee chose seven "sinners" to lose NCAA membership. Byers, as a firm believer in amateurism, was at the meeting as a part-time assistant to the secretary-treasurer of the NCAA, Tug Wilson.

Prior to the vote to include the Sanity Code in the NCAA constitution, a discussion took place. The small college group met in early 1950 and heard a talk by Oberlin president William Stevenson, a Rhodes Scholar with a law degree. Stevenson advocated upholding the concept of amateurism and "the real amateur approach to sports in English universities," particularly at Oxford and Cambridge.[18] Two other small college representatives, on the other hand, were curious about whether large intercollegiate athletic programs "do an inferior academic job" in the "overemphasized athletics" programs and "whether the academic life of the institution suffers because of the intercollegiate program." No one could answer the query scientifically, including Rhodes Scholar Stevenson, because no academic research had been carried out on the subject.[19] Academic institutions conducted little research on athletics, which were often considered peripheral to educational goals.

The convention majority vote on sustaining the Sanity Code failed to meet the two-thirds constitutional requirement to remove the seven "sinning" universities, which included five Southern schools—Virginia, Virginia Military Institute, Virginia Polytechnic Institute, Citadel, and Maryland—and two Roman Catholic institutions—Boston College and Villanova. Byers was depressed, he later stated, over the loss of the amateur-promoting Sanity Code.[20] With the Sanity Code broken, the NCAA removed its provision limiting need-based scholarships from the constitution in 1951. By then, nine months before he was made executive director of the NCAA, twenty-eight-year-old Byers was asked to testify on the role of athletics in higher education before the American Council on Education, an organization run by college presidents.[21] He was, obviously, positive in his testimony about the educational value of amateur athletics, even as commercialism grew in big-time football programs. So, while Home Rule returned momentarily relative to the legality of athletic scholarships, another issue of national control—television—came to the fore.

SMALL COLLEGES AND THE INTRODUCTION OF TELEVISION

As the Sanity Code's national control of recruiting and paying athletes went down to defeat, the NCAA membership ironically voted to place football telecasts under nationwide control. Incongruously, the two votes took place on the same day. Small colleges, not wanting to be overwhelmed by the impact of big-time television coverage, voted to create a steering committee to set priorities for the NCAA TV Committee, a group dominated by large colleges. The steering committee of four had three members committed to strict control of football telecasting so that small college football wouldn't be wiped out by the attraction of a series of big-time football telecasts on Saturday afternoons. These three were Easterners—Asa Bushnell, ECAC commissioner; Robert Hall of Yale; and J. Shober Barr of Pennsylvania's Franklin and Marshall College. The fourth member was Walter Byers, who, early in the effort to control television, was a staunch defender of amateurism and the needs of smaller colleges. The steering committee was committed to the "widest possible participation" in telecasting games and opposed to a few top football teams, such as Notre Dame, monopolizing the television networks.[22] Or, as Asa Bushnell of the ECAC indicated, the committee proposed that when TV networks or local stations were reluctant to telecast small college games, the NCAA could distribute some of the TV income, acting as a "Robin Hood," to untelevised colleges.[23]

The NCAA TV Committee, on the other hand, was formed by the dominant football institutions, including four big-time conference commissioners and faculty representatives from the University of Alabama and the University of Southern California.[24] Following the NCAA's experimental plan in 1951 to restrict game telecasts each Saturday, the NCAA could have tied football telecasts to education rather than going the commercial route. The TV Committee could have chosen to sign contracts with the new educational television stations being created across the nation. Whether Byers favored the commercial direction is not clear, though both large and small institutions were always looking for additional money. Obviously, greater revenue could come from commercial television, as opposed to educational TV. Since he was a firm believer in the amateur ideal and college athletics fitting into an educational model, however, it seems logical that Byers would have chosen the educational television route. Whether Byers, at such a relatively young age, expressed an opinion on this matter is not known. At this stage of his career, he would not likely be inclined to do anything other than what the established leaders of the TV Committee and other leaders of the NCAA chose to do. The NCAA went the commercial television network route but with limited telecasts, principally of the big-time powers, to attract the profit-seeking networks while limiting the loss of gate receipts. Both the small and large NCAA institutions voted overwhelmingly 163–8 to continue a restricted but commercial television policy.[25]

The small college desire to spread TV wealth more widely was in the original proposal. The plan was for 60 percent of TV revenues from football to go to the NCAA, while the dominating football powers would get the remainder. When the big schools complained about the amount going to the NCAA, the NCAA portion was sliced to 18 percent, and shortly thereafter to around 5 percent, where it remained until the NCAA-TV network contracts were deemed in violation of antitrust law in 1984. The big-time schools profited more than the smaller institutions, especially when the TV Committee moved to provide for the more popular regional games, such as Michigan-Ohio State, Oklahoma-Texas, or California-Stanford. The popularity of regional games was considered detrimental to small college game receipts, or, as J. Shober Barr, a small college member of the TV Committee, remarked, "Regional television would mean electric chair death to our kind of football."[26] More regional games being telecast might detract from attendance at football games such as Hardin Simmons University or Sul Ross State in Texas, or Olivet College or Ferris State in Michigan.

Attendance at college football games dropped for four straight years from 1950 to 1954. It was not likely that the Korean War during those years had a negative impact on stadium attendance, but rather that the novelty of television and increased pressure by big-time schools for additional money from the telecasting of conference or regional games contributed to the declining crowds. Regional games were in high demand in the two parts of the country where big-time football ruled. This was true in television's fastest growing regions, home of the Midwest's Big Ten and the Pacific Coast, where TV ratings were the highest, garnering the greatest advertising revenues.[27] There was even some movement for the regional conferences to leave the NCAA contract and form their own to include lucrative regional telecasts, something that some state legislators in those areas were also demanding. In the South, where television was late in arriving, big-time schools did not want Big Ten regional games to be telecast in their area. "We in the South," wrote a faculty representative from the Southeast Conference, "are very anxious to keep the control of television under a national agency rather than to make it a regional activity."[28] Ironic yes, since the South traditionally favored states' rights from the time of the Confederacy and before and generally opposed national control. Walter Byers's position is not known, but as a political conservative, born in the South, and as an individual who wanted television money to be used by the NCAA in a variety of ways, it would have been logical for him to oppose more regional television for the big-time institutions while favoring protection of small institutions from the loss of gate receipts.

Small colleges had a strong incentive to lobby for spreading the increasing wealth from television and the basketball tournament as widely as possible. Football money could be used to support national championships for small colleges, including travel and per diem expenses; to provide injury insurance for all athletes; and, later, to pay for women's championships following passage of Title IX. As NCAA income was increasingly magnified by big-time basketball tournaments and football television revenue, smaller institutions saw the opportunity to profit from the accumulating revenue. It became clearer, especially to the football powers, that separating the NCAA into divisions might allow the dominant institutions to make their own policies while keeping most of the revenues produced through television. Splitting the NCAA into divisions was a long time coming, and the change came principally through the strength of big-time football.

THE NCAA SPLITS INTO THREE DIVISIONS

When football telecasts came under NCAA control in 1951, Byers's first year as executive director, the majority of NCAA income came from the NCAA basketball tournament, not from football revenue. Money earned from televised football was accounted for outside the general NCAA budget. Not until 1972 was football TV income channeled into the general budget.[29] The TV revenues to the NCAA accumulated after paying the cost of the TV committee. Various interests within the NCAA that had little to do with big-time football targeted this excess revenue. For instance, there were calls for the NCAA to use TV income to fund the creation of single-sport federations, for sports such as track and field and gymnastics, to combat control of amateur sports by the Amateur Athletic Union; to initiate post-graduate fellowships for athletes to make the NCAA look more supportive of education; to provide injury insurance for all athletes; to finance a new NCAA headquarters; to pay for travel/per diem expenses to all NCAA championships; and by the 1970s, to support women's sports. To those who wanted the excess TV money to be divided up among those schools not involved in big-time football, Walter Byers was circumspect enough not to outright favor direct grants to smaller institutions. Byers, as executive director, was moderately supportive of small colleges benefiting from big-time football revenues. He suggested that the large colleges should find a "respectable means of repaying their debt to college football."[30] Sharing the wealth was widely popular among the smaller colleges.

Byers had another reason for supporting the smaller colleges, and it had to do with the prosperity of the NCAA. The growth of the National Association of Intercollegiate Athletics (NAIA) was challenging the NCAA. The NAIA was first created by college basketball coaches in 1937 as the National Association for Intercollegiate Basketball, to establish a national championship in college basketball.[31] The following year, a group of newspaper writers in New York City organized the National Invitational Tournament (NIT) to begin what it called the national basketball championship.

The NAIA championship became known as the championship for small colleges, while the NCAA (beginning in 1939) and NIT battled it out for the national championship of the larger universities. The NAIA was attractive to the smaller colleges, and some smaller institutions left the NCAA to join the NAIA. Competition among the NAIA, NCAA, and NIT existed through the 1940s and continued after the NCAA created the position of executive director.

When Byers was selected as executive director, he became concerned about the NCAA losing members to competing organizations. In the early 1950s, NAIA members actually outnumbered members in the NCAA, 465 to 395.[32] Byers recognized the disaffiliation and helped create a NCAA committee in 1953 to address the problems caused for the organization by the loss of smaller institutions. Father Wilfred Crowley of Santa Clara College in California chaired this committee, which was charged with examining concerns of small colleges within the NCAA. The primary goal was not to recommend creating divisions within the NCAA but to deal with small college concerns as they impacted NCAA membership. The committee's recommendations pleased Byers, who hoped that more could be done for small colleges but did not wish to split the NCAA into divisions. One of the first actions of the NCAA was to a create a vice president for small colleges. More importantly, the NCAA created a separate College Division for smaller institutions in a national basketball tourney held in 1956, while the national tourney dominated by larger schools would be called the University Division.[33] The practical reason for divisional sports was the negative impact the NAIA was having on NCAA membership. Conserving the voting within the NCAA as one organization while creating a College Division and a University Division for NCAA-run tournaments was an example of Byers's "genius of organizational management," according to historian Ying Wushanley.[34] The NCAA preserved its lack of strict divisions for more than a decade, while the Crowley committee's recommendations and Byers's successful battle against the NAIA thwarted wholesale small college withdrawal from the organization. Commented adversary Al Duer, executive director of the NAIA, in testimony during a US Senate hearing, "our organization was viewed with no little resentment by its executive director," Walter Byers.[35]

Byers and the NCAA fought the NAIA and eventually funded travel expenses for all NCAA championships, the costs of which were offset by increased revenues from football TV rights, March Madness, and NCAA merchandizing.[36] Small colleges recognized the financial value of staying in the NCAA. For example, Jim Borcherding, coach at Augustana College in Illinois, stated, "We dropped out of the NAIA because of money reasons." Borcherding and others recognized early on that "the NCAA has picked up the complete tab" for the various sponsored championships.[37] (This is what the women's basketball teams of the AIAW similarly realized around 1980, when they abandoned the AIAW tourney and joined the NCAA.) In the meantime, there were discussions of two divisions, "A" and "B," within the NCAA, in an effort to satisfy the needs of small colleges. The NCAA created the Wilfred Crowley Committee in 1953 to counter the NAIA by examining small college concerns.[38] Not until the 1960s, however, when the NCAA Long Range Planning Committee recommended a reorganization study, did the NCAA consider dividing institutions into divisions. Appointed in the summer of 1971, a seven-member reorganization committee recommended to the NCAA Council that three divisions be created.[39] It is not known how much influence Byers had with the council in opposing the three divisions, but it is likely he did not favor the splintering of the NCAA into divisions, each with a degree of autonomy. The reorganization was defeated by a narrow margin, 224–218.[40]

Less than a month after the close defeat of reorganization, the NCAA Council created another Special Committee on Reorganization. Committee member J. Neils Thompson, longtime faculty representative of the University of Texas at Austin and vice president for NCAA District 6, spoke for the committee on its new plan to divide the NCAA into three divisions. Thompson warned the voting membership at its first special convention,[41] "Our institutions can retain control of intercollegiate athletics only if we can organize [the] NCAA into an effective body to serve a broad spectrum of programs we have in our institutions." In the proposal, large basketball and especially football institutions would have a major say in council decisions. Division I would be represented by eight members, while Divisions II and III would have three members each. However, the NCAA would retain the requirement that two-thirds of members must vote in favor for any change in the organization's Constitution to succeed. Thus, Divisions II and III would be guaranteed protection against big-time institutions increasing their power. This time, the reorganization by divisions succeeded, not by a counted vote but by an unrecorded numerical vote by show of hands and voice vote.[42]

THE COLLEGE FOOTBALL ASSOCIATION BIG-TIME SCHISM

Divisional happiness, if it ever existed, did not last for long. Most of the conflicts centered on the telecasting policy for Division I football. Byers and the NCAA TV Committee, a committee for which Byers became known as a most effective contract negotiator, had to answer questions from programs in Divisions II and III who felt slighted because most of the TV money went to big-time football programs. Byers tried to justify the distribution of television money. "While the NCAA program does indeed benefit the largest football programs," the Byers defense read, "it provides many benefits as well for the institution which does not expect its games to be shown from Coast to Coast." Over the previous dozen years, the TV assessments going to the NCAA approached $6 million, a tidy sum of which the smaller institutions were clearly aware.[43] But more importantly, under the new $16 million football TV contract in 1974, every time an institution got on the Game of the Week telecast, it was worth nearly a half-million dollars to that university for a national game and about $350,000 for a regional game. As most telecast games involved schools in Division I, moving to Division I was an attractive proposition for lesser football institutions. Many of the "Robin Hoods" among the small institutions wanted to cash in on NCAA money. The TV Committee was pressured to allot a certain number of television appearances to Division II and III programs to discourage lesser football institutions from seeking Division I status.[44] Don Canham, influential athletic director from the University of Michigan, warned early on that "any reductions in money to the traditional football powers would break up the Association."[45]

Enemy number one of the big-time football schools was the president of California State University, Long Beach, Stephen Horn. President Horn was a scholar with degrees from Stanford and Harvard and political ambitions, but his verbal exchanges with NCAA members left much to be desired. In his first NCAA conference meeting, he insulted the other representatives by suggesting that college presidents "appoint intelligent delegates next year" and that anyone who did not favor reform was "either naïve, a fool or stupid . . . maybe all three."[46] In 1975 the Long Beach president had a football team at his institution that brought in little money and few spectators. The Long Beach football program had less than $18,000 in total gate receipts; only $576 came from student attendance at games.[47] Byers could see that Horn wanted some of the Division I television money because Horn's institution was hurting financially as it tried to run a Division I football program with little institutional and public support. Byers warned Horn of the "unacceptability of your approach" to divide up all football TV money among the three divisions of the NCAA.[48] In addition, Horn wanted all the revenue from football bowls and the NCAA basketball tournament distributed throughout the three divisions. Horn's "Robin Hood" proposals were slated for a vote at the 1976 annual convention. In the meantime, these proposals set off alarm bells, bringing together the commissioners of six big-time conferences—the Atlantic Coast, Big Eight, Big Ten, Pacific-8, Southeastern, Southwest, and Western Athletic. Hearing of the big-time football meeting, Horn reported to Byers that representatives from the conferences were "secretly planning a 'super' division either within or without the framework of the [NCAA]."[49] That turned out to be true.

Pressure by big-time institutions to restructure the NCAA continued. Walter Byers knew that, if the major conferences joined together and withdrew from the NCAA, the NCAA would be ruined financially because well over 90 percent of the NCAA budget came from the major athletic institutions' televised football and the basketball tourney. Byers joined the influential universities in fighting President Horn's proposals and worked hard to prevent them from passing at the 1976 convention. Byers also conceded that the reorganization of the NCAA into three divisions "did not decide the issue of television controls."[50] Byers took the middle course in opposing Horn's "socialistic" distribution of TV money while not favoring the new big-time CFA desire to separate the power football schools from the NCAA, thereby ruining the organization. Horn's share-the-wealth proposal to give 50 percent of the television earnings to Division I and the other half to Division II and III was voted down at the 1976 convention by a voice vote.[51]

The CFA wanted to divide the NCAA's Division I into two tiers, Division I (big-time) and IA (the others), and eliminate the Ivy League Division I members, limiting the power institutions to about eighty members. About sixty members joined the original CFA, with the Big Ten and Pac-8 as reluctant holdouts. To control the number of institutions entering Division I, the CFA proposed limits on Division I status in football, such as requiring a 30,000-seat stadium and an average game attendance of 20,000. Big-time CFA institutions were upset that several of the smaller institutions wanted cost-cutting measures due to the high inflation that came with the Vietnam War. These cost-cutting measures included limiting athletic scholarships to financial need only; cutting the number of athletic scholarships, especially for football; limiting the number of football coaches; and cutting the number of players traveling to away games. Yet the principal CFA complaint was that its schools were not being treated fairly by the NCAA's television committee, based on the number of football television appearances.[52] In the years between the 1976 NCAA rejection of the CFA's proposal to limit the number of Division I football institutions and 1979, the number of CFA football appearances had dropped 17 percent. The Big Ten and Pac-8 [10] appearances had grown. Not only that, but the Nielsen TV ratings for football had dropped significantly in those years.[53] The result was a new call for reorganization of the NCAA to give the football powers more autonomy.

Father Edmund Joyce, the Notre Dame vice president in control of athletics, spoke for those CFA members who wanted an effective reorganization. Father Joyce, who had favored TV rights remaining with individual institutions since the early 1950s, stated that effective reorganization had failed. It posed a "severe economic threat to CFA schools, and the major schools lacked voting power in the NCAA."[54] At about the same time, Walter Byers's handwritten notes about TV negotiations show a lack of support for Joyce's desires. "Limit appearances on TV to restrain TV aristocracy," Byers wrote, and "reduce TV hurt to other games" that are not on television.[55] Byers did not want to give in entirely to the big-time powers. The NCAA executive director was caught between what the smaller institution were willing to support and what the College Football Association might do.

At the end of the 1970s, the CFA continued to work with the NCAA and its TV Committee for a more favorable contract with a network or multiple networks. Byers and the NCAA knew from a 1975 US Supreme Court decision, *Goldfarb v. Virginia State Bar*, that educational institutions, including those with NCAA TV contracts, were not entitled to a blanket immunity from antitrust laws. Previously, NCAA officials acted as if they were immune from antitrust laws. "After Goldfarb," an important *Yale Law Review* article noted, "the NCAA anticompetitive practices are susceptible to antitrust attack."[56] The CFA increasingly claimed that the NCAA was vulnerable legally. By 1980 the CFA's TV Committee met with several television networks to discuss a two-network plan that would bring in additional revenue. The CFA membership was supportive, but not overwhelmingly, of a two-network plan within or outside the NCAA plan. When a 1981 NCAA multiple-network TV plan was submitted to the organization's members, support was overwhelming favorable, 220–6, but CFA members had withheld their 60 votes.

The CFA had its own TV proposal with NBC, but when the proposal came up for a preliminary vote, twenty of its members voted to reject it. Before the proposal came to a final vote, the CFA leadership decided to support legal action against the NCAA for threatening to punish NCAA members who did not accept the NCAA TV contract with ABC, CBS, and Turner Broadcasting. The University of Oklahoma and the University of Georgia, with financial support from the CFA and many of its members, filed a suit against the NCAA as a monopoly.[57] In response, the NCAA quickly held a special convention to discuss the long controversial question of divisions and especially the question of how many universities should be in Division I football. However, the TV monopoly lawsuit against the NCAA by the University of Oklahoma and Georgia would be fought over the next three years.

NINE

Television and the NCAA Antitrust Defeat

"[Restructuring] is a separate and more important issue than television."
—WALTER BYERS, 1981

"I still don't understand what we did for football television that was so bad."
—WALTER BYERS, 1985

"The CFA was going for the jugular," Walter Byers stated some years after the College Football Association fought for and won the right to negotiate TV contracts for its Division I members.[1] That was true in the early 1980s, but Byers himself earlier warned the membership not of an internal attack but of what ended as an external one, a legal challenge resulting in a US Supreme Court decision to eliminate the NCAA's monopolistic control of college football telecasting.[2] Byers, who had the strongest impact upon negotiations and the outcome of NCAA riches from television, warned his own legal counsel in 1977 that he foresaw the NCAA being "blind-sided with antitrust charges" in the future.[3] What transpired in a few years destroyed three decades of NCAA telecasting of American colleges' most important sport.

THE NCAA-CFA DIVISION VERSUS TV CONTROVERSY

The longtime conflict between the smaller colleges and the athletically dominant larger institutions led to the need for competitive divisions within the NCAA. First, College and University classifications were created, then Divisions I and II, and finally Divisions, I, II, and III. Most divisional problems revolved around money. These conflicts might be about the cost of need-based versus full scholarships, or about the expense of recruiting, or about the number of coaches allowed for each team. They might even be about the financial savings gained by making freshmen eligible for varsity competition. They certainly centered on the divisional distribution of TV riches. In September 1981 the Big Eight Conference (touching Kansas and Nebraska) threatened to leave the NCAA over differing TV contracts proposed by the CFA and NCAA. Byers attended the Big Eight meeting supportive of reorganization but also with the threat of Big Eight withdrawal hanging over the welfare of the NCAA.[4]

Byers, in response, conceded that previous reorganization efforts had failed but stated that he was still working for a restructuring of divisions. He proposed that "football television policies should be determined by the institutions who conducted intercollegiate football programs."[5] In the same month, the Universities of Oklahoma and Georgia went to court challenging the NCAA's football TV contract as a monopoly that violated the Sherman Antitrust Act of 1890. Byers and the NCAA indicated that a special meeting of the NCAA would address restructuring NCAA divisions but not the conflicting TV contracts. Divisional restructuring, wrote Byers, "is a separate and more important issue than television."[6] NCAA President James Frank and the organization's secretary-treasurer, John Toner, agreed, believing that the 1978 football reorganization of Divisions IA and IAA "has not accomplished its intended goals, and the growth of Division I is uncontrollable."[7] The issue of TV control, however, would be dealt with by the NCAA after the restructuring conference.

Whether members of Division I believed that television was less important than restructuring, or even that television and restructuring were two different issues, is questionable. The NCAA Council, however, turned down the CFA's request to discuss who owned TV property rights, individual institutions or the NCAA, at the NCAA's special meeting to discuss division reorganization. Nevertheless, the president of the University of Oklahoma, William Banowsky, brought up the question of TV property rights at the special convention. Banowsky, who was a leader in the lawsuit against the NCAA over television rights, stated that property rights were not "extraneous to the issues of restructuring. . . ."[8] The Oklahoma president was correct, despite what Byers and the NCAA leadership claimed.

When TV property rights were brought up, however, the issue was ruled out of order by President James Frank, and the membership sustained this ruling. That decision came after the defeat of the CFA's proposal to create a Division IV in the NCAA, to better control big-time football.[9] The restructuring convention did little for restructuring. One could argue that eliminating the Ivy League and a few other schools from Division I football because they did not meet the stadium size or average attendance requirements was an important change, but television was of greater concern.[10] Walter Byers believed that limiting the number of football-playing institutions in Division I would satisfy the big-time powers. He later conceded his hope that, if the NCAA "gave the football powerhouses more control, perhaps they would reject the lure and illusions of the CFA."[11] It didn't work out that way, as a lawsuit under the name of Oklahoma erupted.

TOWARD A TV COURT CASE CONFRONTATION: *OKLAHOMA V. NCAA*

In early 1982, a month after the restructuring meeting, the annual NCAA conference was held. The NCAA television contract was the major consideration. Most NCAA members favored the NCAA's lucrative television plan rather than the one proposed by the College Football Association.[12] The question of the CFA's four-year TV proposal was settled previously when a third of CFA members refused to vote for it, leaving that proposal more or less "dead in the water."[13] At the 1982 conference, what stood in the way of the NCAA continuing to rule college football telecasting was the lawsuit by two members of the CFA, the Universities of Oklahoma and Georgia, which declared in 1981 that the NCAA football contracts violated the Sherman Antitrust Act of 1890.[14] The NCAA, up to the 1980s, had seldom lost any lawsuits to institutions or individuals, athletes, or administrators of institutions. Oklahoma had lost a couple of court antitrust cases against the NCAA prior to the 1981 suit against the NCAA over TV rights. Oklahoma's president, William Banowsky, was likely buoyed by a 1975 US Supreme Court ruling in *Goldfarb v. Virginia State Bar*, which stated that educational institutions were not entitled to the blanket immunity from antitrust laws they had previously enjoyed. Further, Walter Byers and NCAA officials were quite aware of an important *Yale Law Review* article in 1978 indicating that the NCAA's anticompetitive practices were "susceptible to antitrust attack."[15] George Gangwere, the NCAA's chief legal counsel, warned Byers that the NCAA's protections against antitrust actions had been "somewhat eroded."[16]

Eroded they were. When the Oklahoma case against the NCAA came before Federal judge Juan Burciaga of the Western District in Oklahoma, he ruled that universities, not the NCAA, were entitled to their television property rights and condemned the NCAA for its TV contracts, which he argued were conspiracies in restraint of trade under the 1890 Sherman Antitrust Act.[17] The NCAA challenged Judge Burciaga's decision at the US Court of Appeals, where only one judge of the panel of three believed that the NCAA TV monopoly was a reasonable restraint of trade to prevent telecasting from hurting game attendance while maintaining intercollegiate football as an amateur sport.[18] The NCAA then appealed to the US Supreme Court, where the most important NCAA court case was finally decided in 1984.

Of major significance in the Oklahoma case was whether it would be tried on a "per se" as opposed to a "rule of reason" basis. If the US Supreme Court ruled on a "rule of reason" analysis, the antitrust violations of the NCAA television contract might be found to be a reasonable restraint of trade—that is, if, for instance, the reasonable violation of antitrust laws helped protect college football from loss of gate receipts or helped maintain the amateur status of college athletics. On the other hand, if the case were tried on a "per se" basis, the NCAA could be found guilty of violating antitrust laws regardless of any asserted justification or alleged reasonableness of the TV contract. The US Supreme Court tried the antitrust case under a "rule of reason." Notably, the lobbying group of college presidents, the American Council on Education, asked the highest court to try the case under the "rule of reason," for the ACE did not want a "per se" ruling to set a precedent that any higher education case could come under the harsh "per se" restraint of trade. Officials in higher education were concerned because colleges and universities engaged in several commercial activities that might be considered "per se" violations of the Sherman Antitrust Act of 1890.[19] Further, the ACE believed that "uninhibited 'big-time' football" was "on a collision course with broader educational goals."[20]

While the various court maneuverings took place, Byers and the NCAA considered whether they should persuade the US Congress to grant an antitrust exemption for rights to telecast. The National Football League accomplished this in the early 1960s so that its TV policy would divide up television proceeds evenly. Thus, a small market team such as the Green Bay Packers could receive the same TV income that the New York Giants might attract from its millions of TV viewers. The American Council on Education again asked the NCAA not to pursue an antitrust exemption.[21] "College presidents," as executive director Chuck Neinas of the CFA was aware, "believe that they need to save their ammunition to secure favorable consideration of other proposals that may be more import to higher education than football." Byers and the NCAA ended their pursuit of an antitrust exemption action that could have saved the NCAA television plan from defeat in court.[22]

After the NCAA had controlled televised football for a third of a century, the US Supreme Court took up the Oklahoma case in early 1984 on a "rule of reason" basis. The court found in a 7–2 decision that the NCAA TV plan was purely a commercial venture and had little to do in the 1980s with protecting gate receipts. According to the ruling, the NCAA monopoly had illegally fixed the prices of football telecasts while threatening to boycott NCAA institutions that diverged from the television contract. "It is manifest," the Supreme Court ruled, "that the new plan for football television does not limit televised football in order to protect gate attendance."[23] Two justices, Byron White and William Rehnquist, dissented, and their dissenting opinions were often quoted by the NCAA in future cases.[24] Byron "Whizzer" White was an all-American football player in the 1930s at the University of Colorado, a runner-up Heisman Trophy candidate, and a Rhodes Scholar at Oxford University. Significantly, Justice White won the NCAA's most prestigious Theodore Roosevelt Award in 1969. William Rehnquist was a future chief justice of the Supreme Court. Both were defenders of amateur sports. While the decision against the NCAA was the first time that the Supreme Court ruled amateur sport to be in violation of antitrust laws, it was Rehnquist and White's dissenting opinions that were quoted consistently by the NCAA well into the twenty-first century. The NCAA has "attempted to maintain intercollegiate athletics as an integral part of the education program, and the athletes as an integral part of the student body," White and Rehnquist wrote, "and, by so doing, retain a clear line of demarcation between college athletics and professional sports."[25] While the NCAA used that specific line regularly into the 2020s, in 1984 the Supreme Court decision brought about a free market for NCAA television. Byers's three-decade tenure as chief negotiator for televised NCAA football was over. He conceded to his friend Donald Canham at the University of Michigan, "I still don't understand what we did for football television that was so bad."[26]

THE US SUPREME COURT IMPACT

An insightful newspaper journalist, Joe Nocera, commented that Byers and the loss in the 1984 Supreme Court case led to near anarchy in telecasting college football. Byers, he stated, "stubbornly refused to negotiate a compromise" with the College Football Association.[27]

This refusal to bend by the NCAA and Byers brought about the Oklahoma lawsuit and the destruction of the NCAA TV monopoly. While the NCAA lost, there were no immediate financial winners for the colleges in the Supreme Court decision. There was a mad scramble for conferences and individual institutions to negotiate TV contracts. The CFA, with five major conferences and independents Notre Dame and Penn State, achieved the largest TV contract, though less than what was expected. Individual conferences, however, negotiated their own contracts. Thus, the Big Ten-PAC-10 had their own deal, as did the conferences aligned with the CFA, the ACC, the Big 8, the SEC, and the Southwest Conference. Smaller conferences negotiated their own specific agreements, including the Eastern Independents, Missouri Valley, and Mid-American. Even the Ivy League hooked up with the Public Broadcasting System. Individual institutions including Notre Dame, Penn State, Army, Navy, Boston College, and Miami joined the televised cavalcade. Home Rule had indeed returned to college telecasting policy. There would be far more than double the number of football games televised in 1984 than in the previous year, but for far less money, as the law of supply and demand turned in favor of the networks and syndicators.

College administrators, such as chancellor of UCLA, Charles Young, asked, "How do we get out of this mess we are in?"[28] Ivy League executive director Jim Litvack, a former professor of economics at Princeton, had the sharpest critique of the situation. "Some colleges learned what we teach in Econ I," Litvack told a reporter, "Members of a monopoly form that monopoly to make lots and lots of money. You break that monopoly and they no longer make as much money." The CFA's Chuck Neinas, who did not go to Princeton and major in economics, learned his economics by practical experience. Under the new Neinas-CFA contract with ABC, institutions televising games would experience a cut of about 50 percent from what they would have received under the abandoned NCAA contract.[29] Don Canham of Michigan and the Big Ten bemoaned the situation in football. He stated that universities would "suffer severely next year and beyond."[30]

While there was chaos among the football-playing institutions, the spectators received much of what they wanted—more football games on television—that is, except for Ivy League football fans. There wasn't enough interest in Ivy League football to sustain the 1984 contract with the Public Broadcasting System.[31] If athletics were educational, the Ivy League contract with PBS should have led the way, but commercial television would make clear that athletics were not educational. Nevertheless, even a non-profit corporation such as PBS did not want to lose money on Ivy League football. Television viewership of the games on PBS was so low that it did not register on the Nielson ratings. Other than the failure of PBS to attract Ivy League spectators, would the new free market lead to the collapse of the major moneymaker in college sport? At first, it appeared that the plethora of games being telecast would severely limit the dominating collegiate sport. Football, though, was too ingrained in American society for that to happen.

Congress was asked to intervene, but politically this was an era of deregulation of American business in the period after the Vietnam War. Members of Congress declined. The decision to deregulate college football telecasting was compatible with the deregulation of other businesses such as the airline, rail, trucking, and telephone industries. College football, like other businesses, would have to learn how to be successful in a free-market television field. The shrinking dollars from telecasts during the 1984 season prompted Byers and NCAA leaders to meet to see if they could once again control TV contracts. This effort proved unsuccessful. Chuck Neinas, head of the CFA, blamed the NCAA for not negotiating a better NCAA contract.[32] Byers blamed the CFA and stated that progress could only be made if the two parties could put the past behind them. Byers believed that those who "supported the original lawsuit don't want to consider . . . legally permissible answers."[33] Byers was right, for Neinas was willing to let Byers and the NCAA, as well as Wayne Duke, commissioner of the Big Ten, suffer from the lack of TV money.

The one institution that held the television trump card was Notre Dame. The dominant football program, which had a national audience, was offered a multi-million-dollar network contract when the Supreme Court decision was made in 1984. As the only "national university" in intercollegiate football, Notre Dame, led by President Father Theodore Hesburgh, had wanted its own TV network since 1951, when the NCAA voted to control college football. Now, Hesburgh had the opportunity. A decade before the Supreme Court decision, Roone Arledge of ABC noted that Notre Dame "could do infinitely better selling [its] own schedule to one of the networks and would be a very attractive package."[34] Soon after the US Supreme Court decision, Notre Dame was offered a $20 million TV proposal but turned it down to remain in the CFA TV deal.[35] Individual institutions such as Georgia, Nebraska, Oklahoma, and Southern California put their games up for sale, but the offers were disappointing. Only Notre Dame had a national audience, but the Catholic institution, surprisingly, stayed with the CFA. It would not be long, however, before Notre Dame would go the route that it would have taken in 1951, before the NCAA controlled all football telecasts. Ultimately, Notre Dame would get its own TV network for football, as it had in the late 1940s.

The Supreme Court impact was immediate and favorable to the TV networks, who offered institutions and big-time conferences such as the Big-Ten/Pac-10 and the CFA much less than they could have received under a NCAA plan. Had the Big Ten and Pac-10 joined the CFA, their bargaining power would have increased dramatically. They did not unite. The CFA made overtures to the Big Ten and Pac-10, but they were rejected. Chuck Neinas of the CFA lost the prestige and money that the Big Ten and Pac-10 would have given the CFA. Neinas then complained that it was the NCAA's fault from the beginning, that had Walter Byers and the NCAA "responded in a statesmanlike manner, the situation could be entirely different today."[36]

Byers, in turn, said the CFA had caused the situation in the first place. He did not think the "two sides could get together."[37] What Byers wanted was a congressional antitrust exemption to return football television contracts to the NCAA. That was not to be as a recalcitrant Congress favored free enterprise, not support for a commercial business that excluded competition.

THE DEMISE OF THE COLLEGE FOOTBALL ASSOCIATION

The position of Notre Dame is significant to understanding football telecasting, and the Catholic institution was crucial to the existence of the CFA. Two major independents, Notre Dame and Penn State, along with five major conferences made up the CFA for the half-dozen years after the Supreme Court decision, lasting until three years after Byers retired to his ranch in Kansas. Significantly, in early 1990, even as a member of the Notre Dame administration was actively negotiating with the CFA for a new five-year TV contract with ABC, Notre Dame ignored its CFA negotiations and signed a five-year $38 million deal with NBC. This made Notre Dame the first institution with an independent television contract since 1950, when Notre Dame and the University of Pennsylvania had their own deals.

Notre Dame was highly criticized for abandoning the CFA. The Catholic school claimed that it did so because the CFA was giving Notre Dame only regional telecasts while the Irish wanted national exposure. Father Hesburgh, involved in television negotiations since the 1950s, responded to the criticism by stating, "Some might call it greed; some might call it free enterprise."[38] Hesburgh considered money helpful in his quest for a greater University of Notre Dame. With the Notre Dame withdrawal, greed and free enterprise soon motivated the other sixty-some CFA institutions and five major conferences as they began to splinter off. *Sports Illustrated* fittingly headlined its article on the importance of Notre Dame's withdrawal from the CFA, "We're Notre Dame and You're Not."[39] This was the beginning of the end of the CFA, as other institutions and conferences abandoned the organization. Byers may have been thinking, as he rounded up cattle on his ranch, that the CFA deserved what it got. The CFA never should have broken away from the NCAA, Byers must have mused, nor should they have supported the Oklahoma-Georgia 1984 NCAA antitrust lawsuit, which broke up the lucrative NCAA football television pact.

Notre Dame's desertion came about just as football telecasting money was becoming a major force in the realignment or structure of conferences. First, Penn State, a major independent football power, was about to become a member of the Big Ten and bring an Eastern television market into the century-old Midwestern conference. With Penn State withdrawing from competition with most Eastern schools, a basketball conference, the Big East, decided that it needed to include football. Along with Eastern universities, such as Syracuse and Pittsburgh, the Big East brought Virginia Tech, West Virginia, and particularly Miami into its fold to form a power football conference with TV potential. Other conferences soon expanded, with the dominant Southeastern Conference adding Arkansas, the Atlantic Coast Conference bringing in Florida State, and the Big 8 conference becoming the Big 12 with four additional teams. The CFA kept losing members to strengthened conferences and the possibility of negotiating larger regional TV packages.

By the 1990s, the CFA was no longer a factor in television or in college sport administration. The CFA's Chuck Neinas vanished from the limelight, and Byers lived on but with little to say after he put on his Tony Lama boots at his home on the range. What Byers once said came true: the "pyrrhic victory" of the CFA "worked against the financial interests of their clients."[40] It took half a decade from 1984 for CFA members to realize it. The CFA lost its television market, abandoned in the mine of history, while Neinas was relegated to the post of adviser to the similarly named College Football Coaches Association.

What appeared to be a calamity for big-time football when television money dropped lasted only a few years. Instead, the new system became a disaster for the CFA. While the NCAA could easily survive financially on its ever-growing national basketball championship, the CFA could not last as its members broke away. College football gate receipts remained steady throughout the 1980s in the wake of the 1984 Supreme Court decision. Yet, it did not take long for conferences, such as the Big Ten and the Southeastern conferences, to learn that regional television contracts, not the CFA contract, were most profitable. These conferences would eventually set up their own networks that would produce millions for conference teams. The free enterprise system had defeated the monopolistic NCAA and Byers in the world of commercialized and professionalized college football. The Supreme Court decision against the NCAA TV football monopoly was a great disappointment to Byers, but it did not diminish his historic success in directing the NCAA's contracts. That success included the dominant, moneymaking NCAA basketball tournament, March Madness.

TEN

Byers at His Best

The Great TV Basketball/ Football Negotiator

> "[Byers] you are the one person to whom I have confidence enough to beat Rozelle."
>
> —**FOREST EVASHEVSKI, 1971**

> "The NCAA has apparently come to be more interested in revenues produced from television receipts, postseason bowl games, basketball tournaments, etc. than the welfare of student athletes who participate."
>
> —**ROBERT EDWARDS, 1978**

Walter Byers may have been the big-time NCAA football telecasting loser after the 1984 US Supreme Court decision, but he was also the great negotiator who brought TV wealth to the NCAA in both football and men's basketball. As soon as he became executive director of the NCAA, he was placed on the TV Committee, the group negotiating football contracts. There was no thought of telecasting basketball in 1951 when Byers became administrative head of the NCAA, but his talents as a hard-headed negotiator for football soon became apparent. Byers should get credit as an iconic sport leader because of his successful negotiations with the Eastern television network leaders he disliked, negotiations that made the NCAA wealthy.

THE DELAYED TELECASTING OF COLLEGE BASKETBALL

Walter Byers came from a sports-writing position for United Press in New York City to the NCAA in 1947, hired as an assistant to Big Ten commissioner and secretary-treasurer of the NCAA, Kenneth "Tug" Wilson. Television was in its football infancy, and basketball telecasting was a NCAA non-entity. However, prior to becoming executive director of the NCAA, Byers was involved with television, as he transported Big Ten football game movies to a film lab and then wrote scripts and helped make half-hour highlight films for distribution to Midwestern stations.[1] It was therefore natural for Byers to be intimately involved in NCAA telecasting of football when he was hired full-time by the NCAA. The fact that basketball was growing rapidly as the second most important college sport would naturally get Byers involved.

Next to the NCAA's original involvement in writing football rules and trying to uphold the concept of amateurism, running the national championships in a variety of sports was high on the organization's agenda. By the time of the first national basketball championship in 1939, the NCAA had conducted tourneys in several sports: track and field (1921), swimming (1924), wrestling (1928), boxing (1937), gymnastics (1938), tennis (1938), and cross country (1938). Basketball was next. The growing popularity of basketball in the 1920s and 1930s expanded when a young journalist with the *New York World-Telegram*, Ned Irish, scheduled games in New York City's Madison Square Garden. Amid the Great Depression, Irish scheduled eight doubleheader basketball games in the largest arena in America in 1934–35. The next year, he invited Stanford University's team, with the great shooter Hank Luisetti, to play before a sold-out Madison Square Garden, ending a forty-three-game winning streak by Long Island University.[2] This set the stage for Ned Irish and the Metropolitan Basketball Writers Association to create the National Invitational Tournament (NIT) in 1938.

The NIT tournament began by inviting six teams and sparking additional national interest in basketball, generated in New York City as the communications capital of the world. With over 14,000 spectators watching Temple beat Colorado 60–36, the NIT became the preeminent basketball tournament in America.[3] It is true that the first so-called "national championship" had been contested prior to the NIT, in Kansas City the previous year. This championship was sponsored by the Intercollegiate Basketball Association (IBA), a group of mostly Midwestern college basketball coaches. (Kansas City-born Walter Byers would not likely have seen the first tourney since he was a freshman that year at Rice University.) The IBA conducted this basketball tourney under the IBA seal, in what was eventually called the National Association of Intercollegiate Athletics (NAIA). Most of the teams, however, were regional and composed of smaller institutions, such as the first four winners, Central Missouri State, Southwestern (Kansas), Tarkio (Missouri), and Hamline (Minnesota). The NIT, on the other hand, had major influence because of its New York City location, while Ohio State University's Harold Olsen proposed a national NCAA basketball tournament for 1939. At first, the NCAA's tournament was not a strong challenger to the NIT's Madison Square Garden tourney. The University of Oregon won the first NCAA championship, defeating Ohio State University in Northwestern University's undersized Patten Gymnasium, which seated one thousand spectators. The tournament netted a meager $42.54 in revenue.[4] Yet, this tournament was the beginning of a billion-dollar March Madness business when television came to play a large role.

Telecasting the NCAA basketball tourney as "March Madness" eventually became the fiscal engine that financed over 90 percent of the NCAA's annual revenue, but not early in Walter Byers's tenure at the NCAA. The money that resulted was almost entirely from gate receipts from four regionals and the finals. A dozen years later, in Byers's first year as executive director, net receipts from the regionals and finals were $132,000, far more than any source of NCAA income and four times more than membership dues, the next highest income producer. The local TV income for the NCAA finals in basketball was a meager $2,500, while radio income was a little more than $1,000.[5] In comparison, the NCAA income from the first football network telecasts grossed $159,000, all of which was spent on the cost of running the program. Any profits from the football telecasts were kept out of the regular NCAA budget.

Television networks, strongly drawn to football, were little interested early on in broadcasting basketball. Outside America, basketball was first televised when the Berlin Olympic Committee telecast the first Olympic basketball games to three different locations (Berlin, Leipzig, and Potsdam) during the 1936 Olympics.[6] What interested American networks were the more popular professional sports of baseball, boxing, and college football. The first college games were telecast in 1939—a New York City baseball game featuring Columbia University and Princeton and a football contest in New York City between Fordham University and a small Pennsylvania institution, Waynesburg College. Even the telecasting of the Rose Bowl parade prior to the 1940 Rose Bowl game won by the University of Southern

California over Tennessee occurred much earlier than the first telecast of the NCAA basketball tourney in New York City in 1946. The Rose Parade, incidentally, not the Rose Bowl game, was first telecast in Los Angeles a half-decade before. The first Rose Bowl game was telecast in 1947.

The NCAA national basketball tourney telecast did not occur until 1954, when the La Salle University team with Tom Gola easily beat Bradley University 92–76 in Kansas City. The national finals were not regularly telecast until the 1960s, and then not by a major network. In the years that the Sports Network Incorporated (SNI) carried the national finals, the NCAA received less than 1 percent of its income, while football telecasting was far more important. Not until 1968 and the basketball "Game of the Century" featuring Lew Alcindor (Kareem Abdul-Jabbar) of UCLA and Elvin Hayes of Houston did a regular season game get a national telecast. The defeat of UCLA and its forty-seven-game winning streak under John Wooden was contested before a record crowd of 52,693 spectators in the Houston Astrodome. According to UCLA announcer Dick Enberg, a national TV audience was "unheard of then. . . . [It was] the launching pad for the incredible popularity of college basketball on television."[7] The specially telecast UCLA-Houston game, with two African American stars, attracted far more short-term attention than the NCAA championship final two years before, when the all-Black starting five of Texas Western University beat the segregationist University of Kentucky team led by the famed coach Adolph Rupp. The Texas Western victory with Black players may have hastened the desegregation of collegiate basketball, but the UCLA-Houston game contributed greatly to the popularization of televised college basketball. By the 1970s the NCAA basketball tourney would become a television moneymaker. Nevertheless, basketball had been a financial boon for the NCAA since World War II. Filled arenas, rather than television, first brought the wealth.

The year Texas Western beat Kentucky, 1966, the NCAA basketball TV package brought in $180,000.[8] In Byers's last full year as executive director, two decades later, that income had risen to $32 million. No other income was needed to efficiently run the NCAA two years after the US Supreme Court stripped the organization of all football income and allowed the CFA, other conferences, and individual institutions to profit from football telecasting. The coaches of college basketball knew Walter Byers's importance to the expansion of their game. In 1969 the National Association of Basketball Coaches honored Byers at their annual conference during "March Madness" for his "outstanding contribution to the game of basketball," making him the first non-coach to be so honored. A significant part of the honor was for his negotiating skill with television networks, which brought wealth to big-time basketball schools and to the NCAA.[9]

FOOTBALL TELECASTING AS WALTER BYERS BECOMES EXECUTIVE DIRECTOR

Football, early on, was a different story. The same year, 1939, that the NCAA introduced its national championship in basketball, the first college football game was telecast by NBC in New York. The next year, a Philadelphia-based network telecast all the home contests of the University of Pennsylvania's football team and continued to do so for a decade, until the NCAA began its football policy prohibiting telecasts by individual institution. In addition, other Ivy League schools threatened Penn with a boycott of Penn football if it continued playing big-time institutions such as Notre Dame, with its policy of telecasting its games.[10] Football game telecasts at Penn and Notre Dame came in conflict with NCAA policy. The Catholic institution in South Bend, Indiana, began charging a broadcasting fee in 1948. Within two years, the institution had contracted with a network to televise its home games for an impressive sum (at that time) of $185,000.[11] Penn, with its Eastern network, received a three-year offer to telecast its games for $850,000 just before the NCAA decided to control its national football game of the week.[12] Four months before Walter Byers became executive director of the NCAA, the NCAA Council labeled Penn a "member not in good standing," for signing an individual TV contract. The NCAA planned to vote on the termination of Penn from the NCAA at its annual meeting if the program did not end the TV contract.[13] Penn reluctantly did so. As an assistant to the NCAA secretary-treasurer Tug Wilson, Byers was on the ground floor of the NCAA's entry into its control of national telecasts of Saturday football.

The NCAA's foray into jurisdiction over football telecasting was the first successful national control effort in its nearly half-century of existence. The NCAA, for instance, had never voted to control radio broadcasting in the 1930s when several conferences had done so. Home Rule no longer existed with the passage of the national TV contract. The NCAA could not only use its power to control television but, within a year, would hand out its first enforcement penalty, a one-year "death penalty" to the University of Kentucky basketball team. The players under Kentucky's Adolph Rupp were being paid even as they were involved in a betting scandal and shaving points for gamblers in 1951, the year Kentucky won the NCAA championship.[14] Byers, chair of the enforcement committee, used the NCAA decision to increase his and the NCAA's power to punish rule violators. "It provides a force to be used by honest administrations," Byers stated, "to convince legal zealots of the necessity of living within the rules and regulations agreed to."[15] Rule enforcement and TV control were the two most important powers of the NCAA from the 1950s until the 1984 Oklahoma lawsuit stripped football TV control from the NCAA. By then Byers had become the major figure in both television and enforcement.

In 1951, the first experimental year of NCAA football television control, televised games brought in less than $700,000, amounting to about $34,000 per game, with 18 percent going directly to the NCAA. Attendance at college football games was still dropping. The numbers of football gate attendance at its height in 1949, before football telecasts were influential, were not again reached for a decade. NCAA TV revenues, however, continued to rise, from $1.4 million in 1952 with NBC to over $5 million with CBS a decade later, and $74 million in the last contract that Byers negotiated.[16] Byers, like other NCAA sport leaders, successfully limited the number of games telecast while consistently raising network income. At the same time, Byers and the NCAA needed to mollify big-time football powers and state legislators, who wanted more of their games to be on TV, especially on regional telecasts.[17] Byers was at the center of the controversial TV negotiations that proved profitable to a small group of elite football institutions even as the "have nots" were seldom featured on either regional or national telecasts.

From the beginning, the TV contracts achieved by Byers and the NCAA TV Committee were consistently receiving well over 90 percent acceptance in yearly NCAA institutional votes, with a few institutions such as Notre Dame continuing to call for individual institutional control.[18] Small colleges voted for national control primarily because the limited number of games telecast each Saturday would have a smaller impact on attendance at small college games. For instance, a televised contest between Texas Christian and Kansas would not likely have a negative effect on game attendance at an Ithaca College versus Mansfield University contest in Pennsylvania. However, contests featuring better known teams, such as a Texas-Oklahoma or a Penn State-Pittsburgh telecast, might well impact Mansfield. Small colleges favored one game-of-the-week telecast and a limit to the number of times fashionable Notre Dame was on TV. Byers tried to make sure that NCAA members felt an obligation to protect small colleges as well as large universities, who would profit most from the telecasting of their games. Every year, there were discussions about how many games would be on television, how many times an individual team might be shown, how often small colleges might be able to locally broadcast their games, and how teams that had never been televised might be telecast. All the while, the NCAA attempted to protect gate receipts by limiting television exposure.[19] Byers did not dominate these discussions nearly as much as he dominated contract negotiations with the networks.

WALTER BYERS AS CHIEF TV NEGOTIATOR

It was known early on that Byers could hold his own and even dominate television network executives when negotiating contracts. Byers, who was as competitive as any coach, used the TV contract negotiations as a major focus of his competitive drive. He, more than any member of the NCAA TV Committee, became an expert on all the elements that went into negotiations with the major networks. His dislike and distrust of the major New York City networks worked to his advantage. As a bright network executive, Neil Pilson, once said of Byers, he was "resolute and yes, stubborn."[20] Going into million-dollar negotiations, Byers made sure that he had statistics on such items as previous Nielson ratings; the potential audience; interest of key sponsors; commercial minutes available to networks; desired content of commercials; TV network advertising rates; pregame and postgame potentials; individuals who might be chosen as TV game announcers; which networks had affiliated stations demanding football telecasts; the competition between the networks; and potential cable deals. It could be argued that, because Byers worked harder and was smarter than most of the network executives he dealt with, he was able to increase the offers of network football telecasts.

According to Michigan's athletic director and one of the power brokers of the NCAA, Don Canham, Byers negotiated more than forty television contracts with the major networks. In Canham's book *From the Inside*, he noted that ABC, CBS, and NBC "were on the short end of negotiations with Walt."[21] Canham, the insider, knew. In the 1960s and 1970s, ABC was the network of choice for Byers and the NCAA. ABC was favored because, at first, it had no association with professional football, which had contracts with NBC and CBS. But in the late 1960s, ABC's Roone Arledge began looking to bring pro football to prime time during the week. Any cordial working relationship between Arledge and Byers soon evaporated when pro football's Monday Night Football was announced by ABC for the fall of 1970.[22] Then, contract negotiations between ABC and the NCAA, and particularly between Arledge and Byers, became encounters upon which legends are built.

ABC would always bring the crying towel to negotiations, claiming after their previous contract that they were losing money on telecasting college football. Imaginative accountants could generally produce profit and loss statements favorable to the networks, but if football telecasting were not favorable to the network's bottom line, they would no longer sign contracts with leagues or the NCAA. Byers knew that networks must satisfy their affiliated stations, or the affiliates would move to another network to carry their signals. Affiliates demand sports, which attracts local advertising, their main source of revenue. Byers and the TV committee knew this going into the 1969 negotiations for the 1970 TV contract. Byers believed there was enough pressure on ABC from affiliates to demand a $12 million contract, nearly 10 percent more than the previous year. Arledge claimed ABC would again lose money for a contract over $10 million. "The negotiations are so damned sensitive, so damned bitter," according to Arledge, "it seems everybody's out for the jugular vein."[23] Beano Cook, who worked for ABC, called the talks the "Roone and Walt duel."[24] Byers was the one with the fanged teeth. He successfully negotiated the contract at $12 million.

For the most part, NCAA committee members let Byers conduct the negotiations as they looked on, often in wonderment. For instance, in the 1977 negotiations, which took place during a period of high inflation following the Vietnam War, Byers was determined that a cost-of-living adjustment (COLA) be agreed to. As the negotiations for a $29 million contract were concluding, Byers asked, "And the cost-of-living clause?" Byers wanted an inflation figure of $1 million for each of the last two years of the four-year contract. Apparently only Byers of the TV Committee was asking for the COLA. After a standoff, Arledge paused and then yielded to Byers's demand.[25]

The last Byers negotiation for an NCAA football contract took place in 1981, before the US Supreme Court ruled that NCAA football contracts were a violation of the Sherman Antitrust Act of 1890. Byers knew that he must drain every dollar out of the three networks (ABC, CBS, and Turner Broadcasting) who were asked to televise many more games for the next four years. Why? Because the College Football Association of sixty-three big-time football schools, including Notre Dame and the Southeastern Conference, was challenging the NCAA to gain the rights to telecast with NBC. The lengthy NCAA negotiations led by Byers began in Columbus, Ohio, then continued in San Francisco, Kansas City, and Denver before an agreement was reached in Newport, Rhode Island. In Denver, the negotiating period's midnight deadline was running out as Byers argued with ABC's Charlie Lavery over one of Lavery's statements about a previous verbal agreement. Byers jumped up, yelling, "You're lying, you sonofabitch, and you know it!"[26] Byers stuck a finger in Lavery's face, and an apparent brawl almost began. Lavery, a former Virginia Military Institute running back, would certainly have overmatched Byers. If a physical battle had occurred, Byers's toupee may have flown off his 5'9" frame and his nearly sixty-year-old body would have succumbed to Lavery, who was a dozen years younger. The fight did not ensue. The clock struck midnight, and the two sides departed without a contract. The nearly signed $131,750,000 deal awaited the Newport meeting, when the chief negotiator for ABC asked Byers if he would knock off $250,000 from the multi-million-dollar contract so he could take something back to the network bosses in New York. Jim Spence, ABC vice president, recalled that the "hard-ass" Byers would not give an inch. Byers had, according to Spence, "once again stuck it to the television hotshots from New York."[27] The total, $131,750,000, was the final figure.

ALCOHOL AND TOBACCO: A BYERS LOSS AND AN NCAA GAIN

Critics of Walter Byers, and there were many, could either praise or condemn him for his views on two television contract features—the advertisement of alcohol and tobacco. Byers helped make millions for the NCAA and its members, but he lost in a morals battle over what ads the networks could use in their football telecasts. Concerns over the morality of commercialized intercollegiate sport was not new. Questions about advertising and commercialization began at the first intercollegiate contest. There was always money to be made on intercollegiate contests from the very first contest in America, a crew meet between Harvard and Yale nine years before the American Civil War. That year, 1852, a railroad magnate paid the Harvard and Yale crews to ride comfortably on his new railroad train to Lake Winnipesaukee, New Hampshire, for an all-expenses-paid "vacation" to row a couple of times. On the trip, athletes could lounge in the lake hotel, smoke cigars, and sip their alcoholic drinks before and after rowing.[28]

Tobacco and alcohol advertisements existed well before the NCAA was founded in 1905. Possibly the best example in athletics is Yale's James Hogan, a three-time all-American football player in the early years of the twentieth century. The many payments to Hogan included free room and board, tuition, a scholarship, and profits from the sale of baseball programs. In addition, Hogan was contracted by the American Tobacco Company and received a commission on every pack of cigarettes sold in New Haven.[29] The sale of "Hogan Cigarettes" was an early form of twenty-first-century name, image, and likeness (NIL) payments to college athletes. By the 1920s and 1930s, cigarette advertising in football game programs was common and continued through the Great Depression and until after World War II. Alcohol advertising followed the abandonment of Prohibition in the early 1930 but was not part of college football telecasting until the mid-1970s.[30]

When television viewership grew following the Second World War, critics began to question whether tobacco and alcohol advertising associated with college football telecasting should be allowed. Byers was in the center of this television discussion, since it was a moral question that could have a possible negative impact on the prestige of institutions. Television contracts would be written banning objectionable advertisements. Objectionable content included such items as habit-forming drugs, patent medicines, laxatives, feminine hygiene products, and controversial organizations or political themes. Alcohol and tobacco were two of the most controversial. The first two institutions to regularly telecast all their home games in the 1940s, Notre Dame and the University of Pennsylvania, banned advertisements of alcohol, which they described as "not in good taste" or "detrimental to American youth."[31] When the NCAA took over all football telecasting, a uniform policy was necessary.

Alcohol advertisements were not shown during NCAA football telecasts until well into the 1960s. The NCAA argued that ads should conform to the "high standards [for] dignified presentations" and, in doing so, make college football "an integral part of the educational program."[32] ABC, the dominant college football network of the 1960s and 1970s, strongly advocated for including beer ads, which were an important source of revenue in other areas of television. ABC argued in their negotiations with the NCAA that both organizations were losing significant income from their no-beer-ads policy. The network asked for a one-year test to see what reactions might result. Most of the NCAA TV Committee agreed with the proposal to allow beer ads so long as an on-air statement clarified that the ads "originate away from the campus and stadium" and so long as they were displayed on-screen away from the NCAA seal. However, the NCAA Council, and especially Walter Byers, opposed beer ads, as they believed that these ads would hurt the reputation of the NCAA and all institutions of higher education.[33] Beer advertising was delayed for a year, but ABC claimed that it was losing money on college games and that this loss would impact the next contract. In addition, the NCAA knew that the National Football League, which allowed beer advertising, was becoming more popular than the college game and that the network telecasting NFL games received about 25 percent more ad revenue than came from college football. Monday Night Football was also about to begin, and the NCAA feared that it was losing its place in the world of televised football. Moreover, the lost revenue hurt college football.

The first TV contract incorporating beer commercials restricted these ads to one a game, preceded by the message, "We return to the studio for this message." One dignified promotional tagline of this era was the popular "Hamm's Beer: From the Land of Sky-Blue Waters."[34] The NCAA thus voted initially to distance itself from the smell of hops. Not for long, however. Soon

Miller Brewing paid for a special halftime feature. Half a decade later, the NCAA permitted ABC to show three sixty-second beer ads. By the time that the NCAA lost its television monopoly lawsuit, the number of beer ads had expanded to four and a half minutes per game. Money overrode concern about higher education selling alcohol to the younger generation who often occupied the seats in front of television sets. Byers lost his initial opposition to alcohol advertising on television. He came to accept beer sales as part of the "economic realities" of pairing televised athletics and higher education.

Similarly, Byers also lost his battle with the TV Committee to do away with cigarette advertising on television. In 1967 the TV Committee voted 8–2 to allow cigarette advertising in the football contract.[35] The desire for money by the NCAA and ABC outweighed concerns presented by the American Cancer Society and the influence of Senator Robert Kennedy, who asked the NCAA to ban tobacco advertising.[36] Shortly thereafter, however, the US Congress banned cigarette advertising on television beginning January 2, 1971, one day after the major football bowls, which could still be played with cigarettes onscreen. To add to the hypocrisy of the NCAA, even though Congress had set the date for banning cigarettes ads before the 1970 football season, the NCAA TV Committee voted 6–4 to allow the advertisements to be shown during that fall's games.[37]

In the last NCAA football television contract prior to the NCAA's conviction for illegal price fixing in its television contracts, the NCAA TV Committee allowed an increase in beer and wine advertising. The "economic realities" that Byers had previously used to justify more alcohol advertising were still in play. Byers needed a contract that would be equal to or better than the one that the CFA was seeking through NBC. The NCAA was clearly driven by financial concerns and had dismissed any moral trepidation over telecasting drugs such as alcohol and (previously) tobacco to all members of society, from youths to adults.

NCAA administrators in the Byers era continued their efforts to do for individual institutions and conferences what they had been doing since the NCAA's formation after the 1905 football crisis—that is, look out for the welfare of the institutions with little thought about the impact on young people and athletes. NCAA administrators might have taken the *in loco parentis* route and made decisions they believed were in the best interests of athletes, as they often did in the early twentieth century. Instead, they prioritized what was best for individual institutions, conferences, and the NCAA itself by acquiring as much money as they could from television contracts. The use of tobacco and alcohol sales symbolizes the way the NCAA operated for those other than athletes throughout the twentieth century. That method of operation would continue well after Byers retired. Because Byers was successful at raising money for the NCAA and institutions of higher learning, he was generally considered a highly successful administrator, receiving accolades for his long tenure at the NCAA. Most NCAA members did not agree with the president of Clemson University, Robert Edwards, who addressed this issue in 1978. In a letter to his athletic director, Bill McLellan, Edwards wrote that the NCAA was "more interested in revenues produced from television receipts, postseason bowl games, basketball tournaments, etc., than the welfare of student athletes who participate."[38] Byers pondered this question, but not until he concluded his career did he write on the need for athletes' rights.[39] Until then, he was doing what the NCAA expected of him: looking out for the well-being of institutions, conferences, and the NCAA.

ELEVEN

Jerry Tarkanian, Enforcement, and Byers's Due Process Quandary

> "It appears that [NCAA officials] are far more interested in punishment than justice."
>
> **—REP. JOHN MOSS, 1977**

> "[Byers] played favorites, conducted vendettas, and meted out punishment for the pettiest of violations, . . . ruled by fear, not consensus."
>
> **—JOE NOCERA, 2015**

While Walter Byers's successful television negotiations became legendary in intercollegiate athletics, his career concluded with the toughest enforcement case in his thirty-six years as executive director. If he received numerous accolades for negotiating television contracts and making the NCAA rich, he likely lost more hair and some of his grittiness in twenty-six years of legal cases with basketball coach Jerry Tarkanian. The Tarkanian lawsuits were so ingrained in Byers's being that he spent more pages on Tarkanian in his NCAA memoir, *Unsportsmanlike Conduct*, than on amateurism, academic standards, and athletic scholarships combined. It is difficult to know which of two events had a greater impact on Byers. Was it his involvement in the Kentucky and Southern Methodist University death penalties, or was it his decades-long conflict with Coach Tarkanian? The answer is likely Tarkanian. Enforcement of NCAA rules was the focus of both the Kentucky and SMU death penalty cases and Tarkanian's lawsuits. Byers's apparent lack of concern for legal due process exposed the deficit of fairness in NCAA's rule enforcement. While the NCAA had seldom shown concern for athletes' rights, in the Tarkanian case, the organization had to deal with the rights of a well-paid and successful basketball coach, his institution, and politics of the state of Nevada.

ENFORCEMENT BEGINS UNDER WALTER BYERS

The NCAA confronted its first enforcement of rules case well before Tarkanian was charged with violations. Enforcement was a priority for the NCAA and for Byers from the beginning of the Byers administration. A quarter-century before the Tarkanian case, the NCAA was involved in a major basketball gambling scandal in which basketball players from several schools were paid by gamblers to shave points and fix games.[1] The NCAA had set up a Committee on Gambling in 1944, well before Byers became executive director. This World War II–era committee looked at rumored gambling concerns such as tip sheets, betting odds, and point-shaving a half-dozen years before a major scandal broke in 1951. Instead of betting on who would win a contest, individuals would bet on whether the favored team would win by less than the number of points of the predicted betting odds. If gamblers paid basketball players to keep the score under a certain number of points, called point shaving (or exceeding the point spread), big money could be made by the fixers while the players might still win games and collect hundreds or thousands of dollars. While several New York City teams, including Long Island University, City College of New York, and St. John's University, participated in this scheme, the NCAA focused on the great basketball teams at the University of Kentucky with corrupted star athletes playing under coach Adolph Rupp at the end of the 1940s and early 1950s. The NCAA only got involved after it decided to do away with Home Rule and begin enforcing rules at the national level. NCAA attention centered on recruiting and athletic scholarships under the Sanity Code, first passed in 1948.

The first successful enforcement of NCAA rules came after the betting scandal broke in 1951, when New York City district attorney Frank Hogan exposed the scheme. However, the NCAA only became involved in Kentucky enforcement after the Southeastern Conference (SEC) first punished the University of Kentucky by suspending its basketball team from conference play for one year.[2] The NCAA, using the decisions of the SEC and Judge Saul Streit's findings in the New York criminal point-shaving case, decided to punish Kentucky by giving what became known as the "death penalty." Kentucky was banned from competing with other NCAA teams for a year. Kentucky chose not to challenge the ruling. The "shaky death penalty," as Byers later called it, held. This was important to both Byers and the NCAA because the first successful enforcement case, according to Byers, "erased the haunting failure of the Sanity Code just a couple years before." Byers acknowledged that the Kentucky penalty "gave a new and needed legitimacy to the NCAA's fledgling effort to police big-time college sports."[3]

The NCAA Infractions Committee Case Report No. 1 against Kentucky in 1952 gave Walter Byers confidence that other enforcement cases would be successful in controlling malfeasance at institutions and among athletes. Indeed, the NCAA was successful in nearly every case up to and including Case No. 915, which resulted in the NCAA death penalty for Southern Methodist University in 1987, Byers's last year at the NCAA. The early Kentucky decision came on the heels of the NCAA failure to uphold the Sanity Code and the punishment of the "seven sinners." Successfully punishing Kentucky was important to Byers and to the NCAA's ability to uphold sanctions in the future. Or, as English professor and athletic director at Dartmouth University Bill McCarter (who could turn a phrase) stated in the early 1950s, "We are in the enforcement business, apparently to stay."[4]

THE NCAA, DUE PROCESS, AND THE FOURTEENTH AMENDMENT

Not until the 1970s did the NCAA and Byers become involved in several lawsuits questioning the legality of NCAA enforcement and due process for athletes and other individuals in intercollegiate athletics. Cases appeared more frequently during the Vietnam War, civil rights movement, and President Richard Nixon's Watergate break-in, when it became popular to question both institutional authority and faith in government. For instance, the prominent PEW Research Center noted a significant decline in trust in the government, from 77 percent in 1964 to 35 percent by 1976.[5] These same dozen years saw a decided increase in suing the NCAA for its national policing of college athletics, even as the organization was winning twenty-nine of thirty cases in which it was involved.[6]

A 1975 case out of the University of Minnesota, *Regents of University of Minnesota v. NCAA*, demonstrates the emerging distrust of the national administration of NCAA rules at this time. Three Minnesota basketball players were cited for NCAA violations without an opportunity for the athletes to attend a hearing before the NCAA Committee on Infractions.[7] This was not the first case in which the NCAA failed to provide due process as found in the US Constitution, specifically Article V of the original Bill of Rights ("nor be deprived of life, liberty, or property, without due process") and the Fourteenth Amendment ("nor shall any State deprive any person of life, liberty, or property, without due process"), but the Minnesota case was significant for the future of the NCAA. NCAA enforcement came with a price—multiple lawsuits. When setting up the Committee on Infractions, the NCAA could have followed Article V of the original Bill of Rights but chose not to. Thus, the NCAA did not fully inform accused institutions or individuals of the nature and cause of the accusation; did not allow them to call witnesses, nor permit them to confront opposition witnesses; did not try them by an impartial jury; and did not allow them counsel for the accused. Concisely, the rights afforded accused criminals nationally by the US Constitution were not available to institutions and individuals under the NCAA constitution. Byers and other NCAA officials did not call for what was generally considered in American society to be basic fairness or principles for due process. At the time of the Minnesota case, and before the Jerry Tarkanian case was tried, members of the NCAA Special Convention Proceedings knew that due process was lacking.[8]

Historically, due process was an important priority in America. Over seven decades after the writing of the US Constitution's Bill of Rights, the Fourteenth Amendment to the Constitution gave citizenship to newly freed Black people. The amendment demanded due process by the states, but the NCAA and universities did not feel the need to adhere to commonly accepted due process practices. Among the many unrecognized customs designed to provide impartiality and fairness were the following: (1) the right to a preliminary notice of impending investigation; (2) the right of an unbiased hearing; (3) the right to a neutral appeal or appellate body; (4) the right to present evidence and to call witnesses; (4) the right to cross-examine witnesses; (5) the right to obtain opposing evidence; (6) the right to open hearings of the NCAA Infractions Committee; (7) the right to a public trial; and importantly, (8) the right to be represented by legal counsel.

In short, commonly accepted due process practices were lacking from the beginning. This did not change under the Byers administration until lawsuits, law articles, government hearings, and a few NCAA members demanded due process changes.[9] Byers and NCAA officials were much less concerned about the due process rights of the accused than that violations of amateur rules and other NCAA infringements be punished. The chairman of a congressional subcommittee investigating the NCAA enforcement program, Representative John Moss, commented with some justification that it appeared that the NCAA was "far more interested in punishment than in justice."[10]

Byers also appeared to be more concerned about the number and cost of lawsuits in the 1970s than about the outcome of these lawsuits, which the NCAA nearly always won.[11] He indicated that the NCAA had to defend itself thirty-nine times in the five years before the Jerry Tarkanian lawsuit. Thirty-two of the thirty-nine cases came from either member NCAA institutions or individual members.[12] One of the most troubling cases for Byers involved the aforementioned group of three University of Minnesota basketball players who violated amateur rules. The NCAA told the university to rule them ineligible for participation, but the athletes had no due process. Minnesota officials highlighted this problem, noting that the state institution was required to provide due process according to the Fourteenth Amendment to the US Constitution—that is, the university "had a constitutional duty to afford minimum due process to the student-athletes before declaring them ineligible." Due process had been denied, according to the lawsuit, and the NCAA Committee on Infractions had violated the players' rights to "life, liberty, and property."[13]

TARKANIAN AND DUE PROCESS

There were similarities between the Minnesota case and the case of Jerry Tarkanian, coach at the University of Nevada, Las Vegas. Byers opposed arguments about property rights and about due process for both coaches and players, calling them "legal obfuscations."[14] Both were ripe for legal action when Jerry Tarkanian was accused of NCAA violations as basketball coach at two universities, California State University at Long Beach State and the University of Nevada Las Vegas (UNLV). The NCAA began investigating Tarkanian while he was coaching at Long Beach State (1968–1973) for alleged recruiting violations as his team won nearly 90 percent of its games. Tarkanian took a new coaching position at UNLV (1973–1992) just as the NCAA gave Long Beach three years' probation for various recruiting breaches.[15] While at UNLV, Tarkanian was charged with providing extra benefits for his basketball players. Of thirty-eight violations of NCAA rules, Tarkanian was involved in ten. The NCAA Committee on Infractions called for the suspension of Tarkanian as UNLV coach. Tarkanian appealed the decision. The NCAA Council then rebuffed Tarkanian. Tarkanian next challenged the ruling for lack of due process. UNLV, however, suspended Tarkanian, because the president of UNLV believed the NCAA would hand down a stiffer penalty if he did not do so. Tarkanian immediately challenged the decision in the Nevada state court. In a confusing array of court maneuvers, Tarkanian's coaching suspension was overruled, and he continued to coach for more than a decade. The case ended up at the US Supreme Court.

For two decades, Byers and the NCAA were embroiled in the Tarkanian fight. The final judgment was made by the US Supreme Court in a close 5–4 decision favoring the NCAA over Tarkanian. Until this decision in 1988, the prevailing belief was that due process and property rights under the Fourteenth Amendment applied when states, such as the state of Nevada, were involved in the governance of universities. As such, until Tarkanian, these rights were constitutionally protected, and there was good evidence that Tarkanian had a property interest as a coach employed by UNLV. Both the UNLV and the NCAA had denied these rights, according to Tarkanian, and due process under the Constitution had been disregarded. The US Supreme Court, however, ruled that the Tarkanian case was not a "state action" and therefore did not come under the protections of the Fourteenth Amendment. The NCAA and Byers won a major decision that would impact the future.

The US Supreme Court ruled that the NCAA, as a private actor and not a state actor, did not need to meet the constitutional requirement of due process for Tarkanian, nor did the organization need to protect his property rights. Ultimately, however, eliminating due process was not so simple. The Supreme Court decision meant that, as a private entity, the NCAA could discipline individuals such as Tarkanian without due process—for example, they were not required to allow Tarkanian to present his side of the case. The federal government and state governments, conversely, were emphatic that the NCAA must ascribe to due process, whether the organization fell under the authority of the Fourteenth Amendment or not. The federal government first looked at what was lacking in the NCAA's due process in the 1970s. To counter the NCAA's lack of a commitment to what was generally considered due process, many states, including Nevada, considered or passed laws about due process that the NCAA and others would have to follow.[16] Even the NCAA decided that it must do something about due process for individuals and institutions alike.

One might ask of the NCAA, what was lacking from its minimal due process procedures? Besides the due process rights already enumerated, there was no real separation between the NCAA prosecutors (the investigative staff) and the judges (the infractions committee), and the accused had no opportunity to present evidence or to cross-examine the prosecution if they presented hearsay evidence, which was a general practice of NCAA investigators.[17] In addition, tape recordings of testimony or verbatim transcripts of proceedings were forbidden. The NCAA bylaws read: "It shall not be permissible for any individuals involved in interviews conducted by the enforcement staff to record such interviews."[18] The NCAA argued that, because it lacked subpoena power, witnesses would not appear to testify, especially if cross-examinations were allowed. Besides, if the NCAA consistently won its cases against institutions and individuals, such as Tarkanian, why should the organization be overly concerned with what was missing in its due process procedures. Not until after Byers retired in 1987 and after the Supreme Court decision regarding due process did the NCAA finally decide that it should study the issue and recommend changes. Byers did not receive passing grades for his influence on due process in enforcement cases.

THE REX LEE INVESTIGATION OF NCAA DUE PROCESS

Walter Byers was gone but certainly not forgotten in the years shortly after his retirement. New NCAA executive director Richard Schultz, a former athlete, coach, and university athletic director, decided that the NCAA needed a study of due process under Byers's administration.[19] Not surprisingly, a conservative individual, similar to Byers, was chosen to lead the inquiry. The NCAA selected Rex Lee, president and former dean of the Brigham Young University law school. Lee had been the chief counsel for the NCAA in the Tarkanian lawsuit and was likely the individual most responsible for the NCAA's victory in that case. Because Lee was on the NCAA's side in its most important previous antitrust case, *NCAA v. Oklahoma* in 1984, and because he had won about 70 percent of his fifty-one oral presentations before the Supreme Court, the suspicion of bias could have hung over Rex Lee's NCAA legal study. Lee had also been the prestigious US solicitor general under President Ronald Reagan, and serving along with him on the "blue ribbon" NCAA committee was a former chief justice of the US Supreme Court, Warren Burger. Working quickly, the committee recommended a list of a dozen due process actions that would give greater credibility to NCAA actions against individuals and institutions.

The Lee Committee recognized that the NCAA lacked many generally accepted due process protections. For instance, the due process committee recommended the right to an unbiased tribunal, the right to call and cross-examine witnesses, the right to a written record of evidence presented and findings of facts, the right to an open hearing, and the right to be represented by counsel.[20] All had previously been absent, giving NCAA victims, including Jerry Tarkanian, good reason to question NCAA's actions. Countering several of the recommendations, the NCAA argued that the absence of subpoena power hampered its investigations and that, therefore, it could not afford to give everyone due process protections. This was a specious argument, bordering on hypocrisy, for the NCAA had never asked for subpoena power from the government.

One intercollegiate athletic reform group, the Knight Foundation Commission on Intercollegiate Athletics, could have helped the NCAA increase due process. The commission, founded in 1988, was weighted with former college presidents. Two well-known presidents-emeriti, William C. Friday of the University of North Carolina and Theodore M. Hesburgh of the University of Notre Dame, presided over the eighteen-person committee. In 1991 the committee circulated a prestigious publication titled *Keeping Faith with the Student-Athlete: A New Model for Intercollegiate Athletics,* which advocated for change. However, as much as due process was in the news and the subject of lawsuits, the text of the Friday-Hesburgh document was silent on the issue as a possible NCAA reform. Nonetheless, one dissenting member of the Knight Report, Congressman Tom McMillen, who had not been a college president, referenced due process in a footnote. McMillen was a former all-American basketball player at Maryland, a Rhodes Scholar, and an NBA player for eleven years before he went into politics. He commented, without commission support, that there should be "appropriate consideration of the due process rights of individuals and institutions [reflecting] the larger imperative for fairness in a democratic society."[21] The Knight Commission, however, did not think due process was important enough as a reform to be included in its final report. This demonstrates once again that presidents and ex-presidents lacked the backbone or intestinal fortitude to deal with either justice or the full breadth of reforms needed in college athletics. The ex-university presidents of the Knight Commission refused to act as major reformers when they were in positions of power. Because the NCAA was increasingly run by college presidents, the organization refused to demand some of the pillars of due process. As history would show, it was left up to legislatures and courts to deal with problems that presidents, individual institutions, conferences, the NCAA, and Walter Byers failed to adequately address.

TARKANIAN'S REVENGE ON BYERS AND THE NCAA

Tarkanian lost his lawsuit in the US Supreme Court in 1988, but he did not withdraw from his fight with Byers and the NCAA. All along, Tarkanian had claimed that the NCAA was after him while refusing to investigate the real moneymakers in basketball, certain violators who were recruiting and paying players. These included the University of California, Los Angeles, and the University of Kentucky, which were bringing millions of dollars into the NCAA treasury. Tarkanian's famous quote that "the NCAA was so mad at Kentucky they're going to give Cleveland State another probation" won him no favor with Walter Byers or with officials in the enforcement department. Tarkanian's comments were in direct opposition to Byers's beliefs. Byers stated, "Big or small, black or white—treat them the same."[22] Tarkanian disagreed, and he continued to fight the NCAA throughout his career. In 1992 he sued the NCAA in the Nevada state court for manufacturing evidence against him, causing emotional distress and financial injury.

After a half-decade in the courts, jury trial in this specific lawsuit was about to begin. The NCAA smartly agreed to mediation when it could not move the case out of Nevada, where significant bias against Byers and the NCAA existed.[23] The NCAA capitulated only after several mock trials showed that Tarkanian was likely to win. The organization agreed to settle by paying Tarkanian $2.5 million but not admitting liability.[24] For the next several decades, the NCAA continued the policy of paying off potential court victors without admitting any liability in out-of-court settlements.[25] Tarkanian's counsel called the victory "the NCAA's 2.5 million apologies." The NCAA's executive director, Cedric Dempsey, merely stated that the NCAA "looks forward to putting this [due process] matter to rest."[26] Rest it did, but likely not in the mind of Byers, who had spent the previous few years in retirement at his ranch. For Byers, it was difficult to forget negative events or to put them out his mind, something well documented in his memoir.[27] Byers's U*nsportsmanlike Conduct was* published just three years after NCAA executive director Cedric Dempsey "apologized" for the continual harassment of Tarkanian during the Byers years.[28]

Walter Byers had his own take on the twenty-six years of action against Tarkanian, and this perspective came up often in his 1995 book. It was as if failing to remove Tarkanian from coaching college basketball for his many transgressions against amateurism was the single most negative event in Byers's thirty-six years as executive director. Byers began his 1995 memoir by highlighting Tarkanian's "greased admissions, suspect grades, under the table payments" and concluding that Tarkanian "beat the system" and left the NCAA in distraught circumstances. In response, Byers wrote, the "NCAA abandoned its penalty of suspending coach violators, while maintaining its awesome power over the eligibility of young athletes."[29]

It is true that Byers and the enforcement wing of the NCAA had "awesome" power over the lives of athletes, who had almost no due process relative to their eligibility. Unlike successful coach Jerry Tarkanian, star athlete and Olympic gold medalist in skiing Jeremy Bloom was prohibited from participating in collegiate athletics and playing football for the University of Colorado after he starred in mogul skiing. Why? Because he was not considered an amateur. Bloom came to the scene well after Byers had retired and at about the same time that Tarkanian left college coaching, but Byers would have been one of the first to condemn Bloom for not being an amateur. Byers, probably more than anyone else at the NCAA, fought for amateurism and against financially tainted athletes from the time he became executive director until he left the organization. Bloom was considered a professional because he accepted money so that he could afford to continue skiing. If Bloom had had the money of a wealthy coach with a prominent legal counsel, he too might have taken on the NCAA and been allowed to compete in another sport.

Tarkanian likely took more liberties in recruiting and stretching NCAA rules than any other individual. He successfully beat the system, whereas Bloom was denied the opportunity to compete because of an outmoded definition of amateurism.[30] Jeremy Bloom got some revenge when he later testified before a US House of Representative committee. He compared his rejection by the NCAA to the experience of Tim Dwight, who was allowed by the NCAA to return to the University of Iowa to run track after signing a professional football endorsement deal. Bloom testified to the hypocrisy of the NCAA:[31] "I'm a professional skier on the Olympic level. I must have endorsements to travel the country. I filed the identical reinstatement request as the University of Iowa [Tim Dwight] did. It was denied, he was allowed. I have no explanation. They didn't talk to me. I have no paperwork, nothing." Due process was denied to athletes such as Bloom, but Tarkanian used the legal system to coach for twenty-six years. Questionable NCAA due process policies never kept the star basketball coach from continuing his profession. Byers later confessed that "Jerry Tarkanian beat the system," but he never said that Jeremy Bloom was denied due process.[32]

Ironically, it was college basketball, though not Tarkanian, that gave Walter Byers his greatest legacy and brought the greatest wealth to the NCAA. Byers will likely be remembered foremost for promoting basketball and March Madness. The Tarkanian conflict with Byers and the NCAA will likely be forgotten by most except for the occasional historian.

TWELVE

March Madness and TV Save the NCAA and Byers's Legacy

> "Arrogantly ambitious, the NCAA people [are] loaded with TV money."
>
> **—JOE WILLIAMS, 1964**

> "An anti-trust exemption would have to be obtained before regular season controls were tied to a championship events package" in basketball.
>
> **—WALTER BYERS, 1973**

If there was one aspect of his career for which Walter Byers was often acclaimed, it was his work on television contracts. But this wasn't always true. When Byers began his three-plus decades with the NCAA, the national organization controlled only the telecasting of football and no other sport. Radio was different, for it was never under NCAA control. The commercial broadcasting of football games began in the 1920s, with individual institutions in control of the destiny of broadcasting. The NCAA had little to do with radio broadcasting, and only sparingly did conferences become involved. While football was the dominant sport, even among televised sports, basketball and its national tournament brought far more money to the NCAA than football, and with that revenue came the power that Byers wielded. Football's season-ending bowl games were principally run by individual bowl committees and schools, and not by the NCAA. The basketball tournament was dominated by the NCAA from the beginning, as were most other tournaments.

BEGINNINGS OF NCAA TOURNAMENTS AND NCAA WELL-BEING

College students, who solely organized intercollegiate athletics in the nineteenth century, formed the first tournaments at the regional level. This was accomplished first in rowing (crew) when the College Union Regatta was held in the East just before the American Civil War. By the 1870s, the largest intercollegiate tournaments were rowing events, with as many as 25,000 spectators, sponsored by the College Rowing Association, a student-run athletic organization. By that time, track and field tourneys were sponsored as part of the regattas.[1] Track and field athletes, desiring a bigger profile, formed the Intercollegiate Association of Amateur Athletics of America (IC4A) in 1875. The student-controlled IC4A held "national" meets in the East well into the twentieth century as teams competed from as far away as Stanford University and the University of California. The IC4A meets were held after the NCAA was formed in 1905 and were considered the important "national" meets until the NCAA decided to hold its first tournament, a track and field competition, in 1921. This was organized, unlike the IC4A meets, by a university athletic director and coach, Amos Alonzo Stagg of the University of Chicago. A major difference between the NCAA and IC4A tournaments was that the IC4A was always student-run while the NCAA meets eliminated student administration. This reflected the NCAA desire to keep athletes out of athletic decision-making from the start.

The first NCAA-sponsored track and field tournament was both a competitive and financial success. Forty-five colleges participated, and 113 individuals competed with athletes from 31 colleges winning points. An income of over $4,000 was collected with enough money to pay about two-thirds of all traveling expenses. The NCAA netted $146.[2] This was good news for the NCAA since the organization's bank balance at the start of 1921 was under $2,000 and could hardly cover any tournament losses. NCAA income then came primarily from two sources, membership fees and royalties from the sale of football and basketball rules booklets. When the second track and field meet brought in receipts of $9,000, the NCAA could feel more comfortable in sponsoring other national tournaments.[3]

With the rapid growth of sports in America during the Roaring Twenties, the NCAA sponsored other tournaments emphasizing individuals, but not popular team sports such as baseball, basketball, and football. Swimming followed track and field with its first NCAA tourney in 1924, held in conjunction with the 1924 Olympic tryouts, appropriately, at the Naval Academy in Annapolis. Not surprisingly, the Intercollegiate Swimming Association soon changed its constitution and bylaws so that students, as in track and field, no longer controlled the administration of swimming.[4] The other 1920s collegiate tournament sponsored by the NCAA, boxing, never had student control since the NCAA became involved following World War I. Leaders of college boxing included the well-known Dr. R. Tait McKenzie, medical doctor, sculptor, and physical educator from the University of Pennsylvania, and Penn State's Hugo Bezdek, who boxed as an undergraduate at the University of Chicago. The Intercollegiate Boxing Association was formed in 1920, holding its first tournament in 1924 at Penn State. Hypocritically, NCAA rules required that a medical doctor be present at its boxing events, and students required medical attendance at track and field contests, but the sport with the most concussions and head injuries, football, did not require doctors to be at contests for the rest of the century.[5] Walter Byers's NCAA would face controversy for the lack of action to combat head injuries by the NCAA Football Rules Committee in his administration.[6] By this time, boxing had been banned as a NCAA sponsored sport because of a head injury death during a national tournament in 1960.[7]

The Great Depression put a damper on NCAA national tournaments, but toward the end of the 1930s the NCAA added gymnastics, tennis, and golf to its list of national championships. These three sports, in addition to track and field, swimming, wrestling, and boxing, were individual rather than team sports, but could also turn out team championships. Notably, the first team sport honored by having a national tournament was basketball, next to football the most dominant college sport. The longtime basketball coach at the University of Kansas, Forrest "Phog" Allen, tried to have basketball included in the 1932 Olympics in Los Angeles but failed. However, he was successful at the 1936 Berlin Olympics. Playing outdoors on a clay tennis court, the US team won all its games, including defeating Canada in the finals of the first international tourney. The finals were played in the "mud" during a rainstorm when dribbling was nearly impossible because of the water on the court.[8] The next year, college basketball coaches organized the National Association of Intercollegiate Basketball and held a national tournament in Kansas City, a tourney that ultimately would be administered by the NAIA, not the NCAA. The following year, sports writers in New York City, including promoter Ned Irish, began the very successful NIT at Madison Square Garden. Not to be outdone, William Owens of Stanford, NCAA president, challenged NCAA membership: "The prestige of college basketball should be supported and demonstrated to the nation by the colleges themselves, rather than being left to private promotion and enterprise" such as the NIT.[9] Soon thereafter, in 1939, the NCAA organized its first team sport tournament, for basketball. In basketball, there were no individual player winners such as were found in boxing, fencing, golf, gymnastics, swimming, track and field, and wrestling.

The Olympic Games were telecast in Berlin in 1936, but sports were not telecast in America until just after the opening of the New York City World's Fair in 1939, where thousands of visitors first experienced television. This was two months after the first NCAA basketball tourney championship was held at Northwestern University. Byers was an eighteen-year-old completing his freshman year at Rice University when the first televised basketball game occurred in New York City. The young, all-Kansas City high school football center and linebacker had tried out for the Rice team the previous fall. He was cut by the Cotton Bowl–winning coach Jimmy Kitts, who told him he was too small to play football at a big-time school. Byers was about 5'9" and weighed 170 pounds but was a fighter, as he showed during his lengthy career at the NCAA.[10] He played little basketball among his youth sports. However, in just over a decade, he would be leading the NCAA as executive director and would soon be involved in the NCAA control not of basketball but of football telecasting.

Basketball, not football, however, would become the dominant moneymaker for the NCAA. That would be true well into the next century. This dominance emerged early, not from selling basketball television rights but from America's interest in attending the NCAA basketball tournament in person. The NCAA broke even financially in the first tournament in 1939, but the next year the NCAA finals were contested in Kansas City, where a crowd of 10,000 watched the University of Oregon beat Ohio State.[11] That the Eastern regional contest was held in New York's Madison Square Garden, which had fifteen thousand seats, contributed to the NCAA's greatest financial success of any of its other tournaments, by far. This second

NCAA basketball tourney championship, held before a capacity crowd in the Kansas City Municipal Auditorium, netted over $9,000. From 1940 forward, no NCAA income would compare favorably to that derived from the basketball tournament, and this continued well into the twenty-first century. Basketball tournament revenue accounted for about half of NCAA income for 1940, two-thirds of its income toward the end of World War II, and later accounted for about 90 percent of the NCAA's finances.[12]

By the end of World War II, one NCAA Council member noted the importance of the NCAA basketball tourney to the financial stability of the NCAA. Beyond stability, the income from basketball supported the hiring of an assistant to the secretary-treasurer of the NCAA, Kenneth "Tug" Wilson. One can conclude that Walter Byers's first position in the NCAA resulted from successful basketball tourneys. The national organization could count on the increasing gate receipts and profits from basketball to fund needed staff and projects, such as operating tournaments and enforcing its amateur rules.[13] The March basketball tournament brought in considerably more money than the other nine sponsored tourneys combined, and this was true well before the telecasting of basketball.[14]

TELEVISION'S SLOW BEGINNING IN NCAA BASKETBALL

There was little interest in telecasting basketball in the early 1950s when the NCAA began controlling football telecasts. In 1951, the experimental year for telecasting football contests under NCAA control, the NCAA received $680,000 in TV fees from the sponsor Westinghouse Corporation. That same year, in basketball, the NCAA received $11,000 for combined radio and television income, primarily derived from radio fees. Gate receipts from the basketball tourney the same year, however, netted the NCAA $105,000, income that was divided evenly among the competing teams and the NCAA treasury.[15] Despite the increased spectator interest in college basketball, networks were reluctant to telecast regular season or tournament games. In Byers's first year as executive director, net receipts from the basketball tournament were $132,000 while TV income was $2,500, and radio income was $1,025.[16]

Early in his career, Byers contributed to the work of Tug Wilson, a javelin-throwing Olympian in the 1920s, who in the 1940s had a dual-role as secretary-treasurer of the NCAA and commissioner of the Big Ten. For his work, the NCAA paid Byers a good "school teacher's salary" of $4,281.[17] As early as the 1949 football season, Byers was asked to prepare Big Ten game film highlights for movie theaters and TV stations such as a major station in Chicago, WGN-TV.[18] He continued to be involved in television for four decades, first with the Big Ten and then with the NCAA. While the NCAA evidently gave Byers few tasks in running the NCAA basketball tourney before he became executive director in 1951, but he was directly involved in conducting a successful NCAA baseball championship. He became publicity chairman for the Omaha, Nebraska, tourney in 1949 and provided weekly material about baseball in the eight NCAA districts prior to the national competition. Because he contributed to doubling receipts over expenses, Byers was lauded for his efforts in making the baseball tourney a financial success.[19] Only the basketball tourney made more money. It was a sign of the abilities of the young administrator.

Basketball, not baseball, was the NCAA's financial success story. It was not television, however, that brought wealth to the NCAA in the early years of the NCAA basketball tourney, for the NCAA's "March Madness" made a large profit with no telecasting. Football was different, however, and far more important to the financial health of individual college and conference sport, then as generations later. Members of the NCAA were therefore principally concerned with this dominating sport and the impact that television might have on the financial welfare of football, and on the other sports that relied on football profits. Radio, once thought in the 1920s and early 1930s to harm gate receipts, had been shown to promote the popularity of football and of universities in general. Nevertheless, most of the administrators of college football believed that viewing instead of listening to football games would reduce the desire to see the game in person.

When Walter Byers was chosen to be the first executive director of the NCAA in the fall of 1951, there was overwhelming opposition to allowing open telecasting of football games at individual institutions. Byers was fully behind the will of NCAA members regarding television, and on several other issues. He accepted the NCAA position before he was thirty years old with the understanding that he would "simply implement the will of the organization." Byers later told a US congressional committee that "the Executive Director and staff exist to execute policy, not to formulate it."[20]

He did this for television policy, and his efforts made the NCAA rich. With that financial gain, a great deal of power came to Byers himself. Because Byers increasingly understood that television would be the lifeblood of both the NCAA and the institutions within the NCAA, he became central to determining the NCAA's relationship to the medium.

Byers, and more importantly the NCAA, had to deal with two recalcitrant institutions before an NCAA TV policy for football could be successful. Both Notre Dame University and the University of Pennsylvania were determined to follow the Home Rule tradition in college sports and control their own football television operations. While Penn began telecasting first among all institutions of higher learning, the Philadelphia institution was less important to any question of telecasting football than Notre Dame, the dominant football power at the close of the 1940s. Theodore Hesburgh, who would become Notre Dame's longtime president in 1952, was vice president in charge of athletics at the Roman Catholic university when he contended that "television can link sports and education together better than anything else."[21] Basketball telecasting, by contrast, had a very different impact upon institutions of higher education, Byers, and the NCAA.

By the time Byers became executive director, the NCAA basketball tourney had grown from an eight-team tournament, including one team from each of eight NCAA districts and composed primarily of conference champions, to an event hosting sixteen teams.[22] Byers asked the head of the NCAA basketball committee, Dutch Lonborg, if he believed that each of the four regional sites for the 1952 basketball tournament could achieve $30,000 in profit. When each district met that goal, turning a cumulative $132,000 profit, the sixteen-team tourney showed that the NCAA could profit by expanding the number of teams. Byers's administrative skill in expanding the tourney made him integral to the financial success of the event. Importantly, this financial success allowed Byers to hire individuals to investigate infractions in recruiting and subsidization violations under the Committee on Infractions, which he chaired. Early in his long career in NCAA leadership, Byers came to dominate the administration of the NCAA basketball tourney, television contract negotiations in football and then basketball, and rules enforcement—the three most important areas under NCAA control. As Byers later noted, the three pillars of the NCAA are (1) enforcement, (2) football telecasting, and (3) basketball final four.[23]

TELEVISION COMES TO THE NCAA TOURNAMENT

The first telecast of NCAA basketball teams came about when New York's Fordham University met the University of Pittsburgh in a Madison Square Garden contest on February 28, 1940. This game took place shortly after the more popular sports of baseball, boxing, and football had experimental telecasts the previous year. The preceding spring and fall, NBC's experimental station, W2XBS, had telecast baseball games between the University of Columbia and Princeton University and the Fordham University-Waynesburg College football game to a few hundred New York City homes with televisions.[24] Yet, networks were reluctant to carry basketball games and suffer financial losses in the 1940s and 1950s. They were doing well financially telecasting football.

In 1954 the national final of the NCAA basketball tourney between La Salle University and Bradley University was telecast, but this did not occur again for another nine years. La Salle defeated Bradley in this first contest, and the basketball television revenue amounted to $7,500, less than 1 percent of the riches from the NCAA TV football plan. Radio receipts were $1,750 for the La Salle victory in the finals in Kansas City, and the NCAA netted $130,000 from the tourney as a whole.[25] This same year, 1954, the US Supreme Court ruled in the historic desegregation case *Brown v. Board of Education* that schools could not be segregated. Not until 1963 were the NCAA finals again telecast, this time with a few Black players included in the sixteen-team tournament. The finals featured the eventual champion, Loyola University from Chicago, a team with four Black starters in the Mid-East Regionals, teamed up against Mississippi State University, from a state with strict segregationist laws. The team had to sneak out of Mississippi, avoiding segregationist state officials, to get to the game.[26] Although that important desegregation game was not telecast, five years later a more important game was. This game pitted two undefeated teams, the University of Houston and the University of California, Los Angeles, in a non-tournament game. The two Black stars from these teams, Elvin Hayes of Houston and Lou Alcindor (Kareem Abdul-Jabbar) of UCLA, participated in the first nationally televised regular season game. It was a made-for-TV spectacle seen on about 120 stations nationally before a gate crowd of over 52,000 spectators, each of whom paid around $3.00 a ticket. Houston won in the Houston Astrodome.[27] UCLA got revenge in the semi-finals of the NCAA tourney, 101–69, before winning its fourth title in a row under coach John Wooden.

The success of the televised Houston-UCLA game likely encouraged major networks to bid on college basketball as a profit-making enterprise. The 1969 NCAA tourney TV rights were purchased by NBC, ending Sports Network Incorporated's (SNI) six-year run. NBC paid a half-million dollars when the rights fees to SNI the previous year had been $200,000.[28] Once a major network took over the March Madness contests, the popularity of the tournament began to grow exponentially. By 1972 NBC paid $2 million for a two-year contract, and the first Monday night NCAA basketball final attracted an estimated thirty-nine million viewers. The NCAA then expanded the tournament to include thirty-two teams, a decision favored by Walter Byers and the chairman of the NCAA Basketball Committee, athletic director from Davidson Tom Scott, who had campaigned for the expansion several years earlier.[29]

The NCAA tournament in the early 1970s, which featured both Black and white athletes, including Bill Walton of UCLA, David Thompson of North Carolina State, and Kevin Grevey of Kentucky, more than quintupled its TV revenues, while college basketball was more popular on television than pro basketball. By the latter 1970s, basketball greats Larry Bird and Earvin "Magic" Johnson helped triple the commercial value of March Madness. The value tripled again in the next five years, with players such as Isaiah Thomas of Indiana, Patrick Ewing of Georgetown, and Michael Jordan of North Carolina, as Byers's term as executive director came to a close.[30] While all of this was happening, the NCAA had to decide whether it would take over the telecasting of seasonal basketball as it had done in football in the early 1950s.

SHOULD THE NCAA HAVE A NATIONAL IN-SEASON TV POLICY?

The growth of the NCAA March Madness tourney obviously led colleges and universities as well as the NCAA to consider making even more money from the regular television season. Iowa's athletic director, Forest

Evashevski, suggested to Byers in the early 1970s that a NCAA network should be formed. He envisioned a national regular season basketball package tied in with the football contract that had been in existence since 1951. Evashevski, a successful football coach at Iowa in the 1950s, was head of the NCAA Television Committee in the early 1970s when he suggested pursuing a combined football and basketball television package. He told Byers that the NCAA chief was "the one person in whom I have confidence enough to beat [Pete Rozelle]" the national football commissioner who, at that time, was completing a three-network package that included ABC's *Monday Night Football*.[31] During this time, the inflationary period of the Vietnam War was affecting athletic budgets, and Evashevski believed that a half-year series of football and basketball games airing from September through February would benefit big-time athletics financially and challenge the NFL's increasing penetration on the entertainment dollar. Though Byers later changed his mind, he initially told Evashevski that "a national basketball package . . . would indeed be a good tie-in to the football series."[32]

In the 1970s athletic conferences were already exploiting the basketball television market. Therefore, whatever the NCAA did to control the TV market would come in conflict with what conferences were already doing. The three major networks—ABC, CBS, and NBC—did not envision basketball being successful in prime time programming. ABC, for instance, believed that college basketball might fill in after its Monday Night Football was completed each fall. NBC suggested airing college basketball on Sunday afternoons. All three networks were wary, according to NCAA officials.[33] The NCAA Television Committee was strongly interested in a basketball-football series that would televise some national games and some regional contests. Yet, individual institutions with their own TV contracts were not as eager as they had been for national control of football in the early 1950s. "National basketball television," officials at Indiana University pointed out, "will have a devastating effect on institutional television."[34] Rather than protecting gate receipts, which was the primary concern for 1950s football programs, big-time basketball schools in the 1970s prioritized their existing television revenue in opposing a national television policy for basketball.

A more important issue arose after a 1975 lawsuit, *Goldfarb v. Virginia State Bar*, came before the US Supreme Court. The court ruled in this suit that educational institutions were no longer immune from violations of antitrust laws where activities of a business nature, such as televised basketball, might violate the Sherman Antitrust Act of 1890. Byers's close legal adviser, George Gangwere, NCAA chief counsel, was aware of the Goldfarb case, in which the Supreme Court's 8–0 decision stated that "Congress did not intend any 'learned profession' exclusion from the Sherman Act."[35] Gangwere forcefully addressed the NCAA Television Committee, warning them that any joint NCAA football and basketball plan, if taken to court under antitrust law, would likely be declared a violation of antitrust legislation. After this threat to joint football and basketball control by the NCAA, the NCAA Television Committee voted to "abandon any further thought of coordinating a combined tournament and in-season basketball package."[36]

BYERS AND TELEVISION CONTROLS

Football was different, though not at first. Football telecasting began in New York City two years before America's entry into World War II. There, NBC produced the first televised game at Triboro Stadium on Randall's Island in New York's East River, an unimportant contest in many ways between Fordham College and a little-known college in Western Pennsylvania, Waynesburg. That was five months after the first US commercial telecast featuring President Franklin D. Roosevelt opening the New York World's Fair in April 1939.[37] There were no televised Iowa games while Byers was attending the University of Iowa during these years. On the other hand, the University of Pennsylvania began its first decade of televising Penn games in 1940. After the very first experimental Penn televised game, a writer for the *Daily Pennsylvanian* commented that "watching the game by television was almost as good as being there."[38]

Teenaged Byers, having transferred from Rice, would not likely have had a clue about television but wrote for the University of Iowa student newspaper at this time. He appeared oblivious to the US troops invading North Africa to fight the Nazis in 1942 as he reveled in his story about the victory of Iowa over Wisconsin in a Big Ten football game. Byers showed that he could clearly describe games in picturesque terms when he wrote for the *Daily Iowan* that fall. Describing the Wisconsin loss to Iowa, he depicted losing coach Harry Stuhldreher, one of the former Notre Dame "Four Horsemen" under Knute Rockne in the 1920s: "All alone among yelling fans and tired football players," Byers wrote, "lonely Harry Stuhldreher, Wisconsin coach, walked unbelievingly toward the Iowa bench to congratulate Dr. Eddie Anderson."[39] If he couldn't play sports at the college level, Byers could effectively write about them, something he did throughout his long life, both as a reporter and later as an administrator.

Byers not only failed to play collegiate football, but he failed to see a television set for many years, unlike the University of Pennsylvania student who commented on the role of TV in 1940. Byers, however, retained his love of college athletics well past his first concentrated viewing of sports on television in New York City, where he was working as a journalist for United Press after World War II. In the Big Apple, Byers hung around the famed "Toots Shor" restaurant and bar, "where the 'crumb bums' who played sports and the 'crumb bums' who wrote about them got together," and where the young reporter could, as he stated, "listen and learn."[40] Byers likely saw the June 1946 heavyweight title fight between Joe Louis and Billy Conn, the first high profile New York City sport telecast, which was, incidentally, the highest rated radio program in history. The previous year, only days before the Allied victory over Hitler, Byers interviewed A. B. "Happy" Chandler, the commissioner of baseball, who told segregationist America that "Negroes should have a chance like everyone else" to play Major League baseball.[41] Televised sport and the desegregation of sport came at about the same time, and Byers was there to experience it all.

In 1947 Byers was happily out of New York and back to the Midwest after accepting an assistant position as director of the Big Ten Service Bureau in Chicago, under Big Ten commissioner "Tug" Wilson. In addition to his Big Ten work, Wilson was also working as secretary-treasurer of the NCAA, and Byers became his executive assistant. By then, the twenty-five-year-old had been exposed to television, which was coming to Midwestern institutions of higher learning. Though telecasts existed of college football and basketball as well as pro football, baseball, ice hockey, and boxing, the Big Ten and the NCAA had a hands-off policy prior to 1950.[42] Young Byers, nevertheless, would soon become involved in the nationalization of college football through television.

While Byers was assisting Tug Wilson, television was making strong inroads into sports. The baseball World Series between the Brooklyn Dodgers and the New York Yankees was telecast in 1947. That was the same year

Notre Dame telecast its first football game in Chicago, and the Eastern College Athletic Conference first discussed the financial impact telecasting football might have on gate attendance. In a year and a half, coaxial cable connected Chicago with the East Coast, making Notre Dame's dominating football accessible to a major part of the nation's population. Most institutions within the NCAA were quite aware that television needed to be dealt with. In early 1948 the NCAA held a lengthy roundtable meeting on whether the new medium would negatively impact attendance at college football games. One television executive told the NCAA convention that TV "will increase your gate," while the Northwestern athletic director warned to "go slowly . . . we are not sure exactly what part television will play in the future."[43] Byers was there, listening, in his role as assistant to Tug Wilson, NCAA secretary-treasurer.[44]

Theodore Hesburgh believed telecasting would have a positive impact on the growth of football and on Notre Dame. Previously under legendary football coach Knute Rockne in the 1920s, Notre Dame's football program brought fame and money to the university. Winning football games meant large crowds and significant revenue, which allowed Notre Dame administrators to build dormitories and additional classrooms.[45] Prior to television, football publicized Notre Dame as the leading Catholic institution in America and raising the student enrollment. Two decades later, television could do the same, especially if Notre Dame televised all its home games in a stadium built at the end of Rockne's career, which was shortened by his unexpected death in an airplane accident in 1931. Hesburgh campaigned for Home Rule in televising and objected to the NCAA policy of national control of television to prevent the loss of gate receipts. The soon-to-be-president of Notre Dame understood by 1950 that within a few years most Americans would own televisions and that home box office TV in each of 35 or 40 million domiciles could bring in millions of dollars through a Notre Dame television network.[46] No wonder that Hesburgh believed that the most prominent football institution in America could profit immensely and build a greater Notre Dame from its own major network contract.

While the vast majority of NCAA institutions supported controlled telecasts of football to protect gate receipts, Notre Dame was moving rapidly by talking with all four major networks—ABC, CBS, NBC, and DuMont. They discussed pregame, postgame, and movie rights, along with the game itself.[47] Only Notre Dame, with its national following, and Penn in the East, where television prospered, could benefit initially from their own television contracts. Walter Byers and other NCAA officials questioned the sincerity of President Hesburgh, who spoke at the NCAA convention early in 1950. "We want to benefit the whole of sports," Hesburgh declared, "because what is good for sports is good for the country at large."[48] Television, he knew, would be good for Notre Dame. When the Big Ten voted to ban live football telecasts in 1950, Notre Dame, with its extraordinarily high bid of $185,000 from DuMont, telecast its games for the third straight year.[49] The following year, the NCAA decided by a 161–7 vote to conduct a limited experimental telecasting program, something both Penn and Notre Dame challenged.

In 1951, the University of Pennsylvania had the largest local and network programming for football, continuing a decade of telecasting all home football games. DuMont, a dominating sport telecasting network, offered $850,000 to televise three years of Penn football and challenged the NCAA's experimental year of limited telecasting. Penn, under new leadership of President Harold Stassen, former governor of Minnesota, hoped to become a leader in big-time football, playing a schedule that included Notre Dame, the University of California, Berkeley, and both powerful military academies, Navy and Army. Only after four Ivy League schools stated they would boycott Penn football and the NCAA threatened to sanction Penn for not following the NCAA telecasting controls did Penn withdraw its plans.

Though a group boycott of Penn was highly illegal under the Sherman Antitrust Act of 1890, amounting to a conspiracy in restraint of trade, Penn did not pursue court action. Going the legal route would come three decades later when Oklahoma and Georgia challenged the NCAA over antitrust issues—and won. Penn lost the battle for unlimited TV in the early 1950s but remained in the Ivy League, something very important to its academic image. Penn's leader, Harold Stassen, soon resigned to join President Dwight D. Eisenhower's administration. Walter Byers would continue to protect gate receipts from the invasion of television. "A control program for the TV audience," commented Byers, "will insure its own vital athletic programs remaining intact."[50] When both Penn and Notre Dame backed out of a confrontation over the property rights of institutions to televise their own sports, the NCAA sustained its national control over a major facet of intercollegiate athletics. Combining control of football telecasts with the successful use of the so-called "Death Penalty" against the University of Kentucky basketball team a year later gave the NCAA legitimate national control, eliminating Home Rule by institutions and conferences.

Within a year of Byers becoming NCAA executive director, he gained additional power when he was placed on the eight-man NCAA TV Committee, formed a couple of years before. More importantly, as previously noted, he was one of four on the television steering committee, along with three Easterners associated with what would be considered less than prominent athletic institutions.[51] The will of the big-time college powers would not be enacted by this crew, dominated as it was by the Eastern establishment—a group with which Byers would seldom identify because of his antipathy to Easterners.

THIRTEEN

Byers, Bowls, and a National Football Championship

> "I don't see any reason why college football cannot follow the same national collegiate playoff pattern as all other intercollegiate sports enjoy."
>
> **—WALTER BYERS, 1966**

> "It's hard on the ego of a president to be less admired than his football coach."
>
> **—WALTER BYERS, 1995**

Walter Byers concluded his more than forty years at the NCAA having presided over seventy-four national championships in the three NCAA divisions. A big-time football championship was not one of them. Football was the only NCAA sport that did not have a championship—that is, except for poll championships. There were, however, on-field football championships thirty years before the NCAA was formed in the early twentieth century. The first was a contest in 1876 between Yale and Princeton, two of the Big Three big-time football institutions in the late 1800s. At the St. George's Cricket Grounds in Hoboken, New Jersey, Yale beat Princeton two "touch-downs" to nothing. It was the first Thanksgiving Day football game in America. Going forward, the two best teams in the country as determined by the student-run Intercollegiate Football Association competed in the Thanksgiving Day championship, generally held in New York City.[1] These on-field championships lasted until the mid-1890s, when questions of brutality, such as the short-lived "flying wedge," and other concerns about violence and eligibility took their toll on the games in New York.

FOOTBALL CHAMPIONSHIPS: POLLS AND BOWLS, NOT PLAY-OFF GAMES

By the time that Byers was a toddler, football held no on-field national championships, unlike the NCAA championships for track and field and swimming. Rather, after World War I, several individuals began ranking college football teams. Frank G. Dickinson, an economics professor at the University of Illinois, may have been the first. Dickinson began the Rissman National Trophy based on rankings. Notre Dame won the Rissman in 1924, followed by Dartmouth (1925), Stanford (1926), Illinois (1927), Southern California (1928), Notre Dame (1929), and Notre Dame (1930). It was not surprising following the untimely airplane death of Notre Dame coach Knute Rockne in 1931 that the tradition continued with the Knute K. Rockne National Intercollegiate Memorial Trophy, given each year to the football champion in rankings. These champions included Southern California (1931), Michigan (1932), Michigan (1933), Minnesota (1934), Southern Methodist (1935), Minnesota (1936), Pittsburgh (1937), Notre Dame (1938), Southern California (1939), and Minnesota (1940).[2] By 1940 the Associated Press had published football rankings for several years but did not call for actual contests to determine a NCAA winner, in contrast to track and field, swimming, boxing, wrestling, gymnastics, tennis, golf, and basketball.

Because football became the dominant college sport by the 1880s and 1890s, it was logical for people to want to know which college team was considered the best. Some individuals, generally sportswriters, would speculate on the dominant team or teams. Individuals such as *Outing* editor Caspar Whitney; Yale's former star and then athletic adviser, Walter Camp; or former football player from Princeton and football historian, Parke Davis, would offer their opinions. While the Thanksgiving Day games no longer were played for the national championship by the twentieth century, Thanksgiving Day games or Thanksgiving weekend games would continue for generations.

After football seasons, "bowl" games, once introduced, became prominent. The first two "bowl" games were played in the new year following the football seasons of 1893 and 1894. Both were organized by University of Chicago football coach Amos Alonzo Stagg. The first was played indoors on January 1, 1894, on a tanbark floor at Tattersall's Riding Academy in

Chicago before two thousand spectators, with Chicago shutting out Notre Dame.[3] The second was contested as part of a six-thousand-mile trip for the Chicago team when, on New Year's weekend 1895, the University of Chicago lost a game against Stanford in Los Angeles.[4] Junkets to make money and give publicity to institutions were beginning. Only a few years later, the Pasadena, California, Tournament of Roses invited the University of Michigan's football team to contest Stanford in what became the Rose Bowl. Michigan defeated Stanford 49–0 on January 1, 1902, in Tournament Park. Beginning in the 1890s, a few years before the first "bowl" game, the Tournament of Roses featured a parade of horse-drawn floats of flowers followed by foot races, tugs-of-war, and polo matches.[5] The Rose Bowl game was discontinued temporarily after this first contest, and chariot racing, put on by the elite Pasadena Hunt Club and based on ancient Roman racing in the hippodrome, took place in Pasadena instead, before football returned in 1916 with a Washington State victory over Brown University.

After the NCAA was formed in the early 1900s, the college faculty representatives who dominated the organization were not receptive to the idea of trips following the football season. The first major controversy over traveling distances for bowl games emerged in 1920, when Harvard was invited to compete in the Rose Bowl. The Harvard faculty voted 37–16 in opposition to its athletes playing in a frivolous game and missing one day of classes in the new year.[6] The Harvard Athletic Committee, however, voted unanimously to go. The tide turned and the trip went forward when it became obvious to President Lawrence Lowell that the Rose Bowl game helped promote Harvard and would likely attract West Coast money for the Harvard Endowment Fund. Harvard participated with the understanding by the faculty that "there would be no time wasted after returning in getting back to the serious work of the class room."[7]

Being asked in the 1920s to participate in the Rose Bowl was considered an honor. Two years after Harvard beat Oregon, 7–6, Stanford and the University of Pittsburgh were invited to the Rose Bowl. Pitt coach Glenn "Pop" Warner had just signed to coach the Stanford team, thus making "Warner's Pitt vs. Warner's Stanford" a possibility.[8] When Pitt demanded $50,000 to go West, the Rose Bowl committee balked and instead invited Penn State and Southern California. Warner's Stanford contract called for an additional $2,500 for taking his team to a Rose Bowl game in addition to his $10,000 salary.[9] Evidently, the Stanford faculty remained out of the discussion of bowl game attendance in the new Rose Bowl, which seated 57,000. Why? The game had the blessing of Stanford president Ray Lyman Wilbur. However, Penn State went West instead, losing to Southern California but taking home $35,000.[10]

By the 1920s, being invited to the Rose Bowl was a prestigious event that most college presidents, though not necessarily college faculties, were anxious to promote. This was especially true for Southern universities, which received little notice from the Northern-dominated press prior to the 1925 Rose Bowl. Southern institutions began to compete effectively with Northern teams around the time of World War I and into the 1920s. Since the faculty-controlled Big Ten banned postseason football games in the 1920s, the Rose Bowl Association looked to others to compete against Western institutions. Alabama was the first Southern institution invited to the Rose Bowl. The 1926 contest between successful Alabama and the University of Washington resulted in what was considered a major upset, 20–19.[11] If "Remember the Alamo" was the cry of Texans who lost the battle to Mexican forces in 1836, "Remember the Rose Bowl" was the cry of Southerners a century later, as if the South had finally won the "lost cause" Civil War in a football game. President George Denny of Alabama said that going to the Pasadena game "means more widespread and sustained publicity for Alabama than any recent event in the history of the state."[12] In these early years, several Southern institutions played in the Rose Bowl, the only annual bowl game until the Great Depression. The 1926 Rose Bowl victory may not have been for the national championship, but the game seemed like it to many Southerners. Still, there were few calls for a tournament to decide an on-field football champion. Most faculty controlling the NCAA were opposed to the commercialism affiliated with bowl games and the strong interest students took in the games at the expense of their studies.

At the professional level, the National Football League was organized in 1920, but the NFL did not have a championship playoff until 1932. Then, the Chicago Bears and the Portsmouth [Ohio] Spartans decided to have a playoff after ending the regular season with identical records. The Bears won. The next year, in the midst of the Great Depression, a championship game between the Eastern Division champions, the New York Giants, and the champions of the Western Division, the Chicago Bears, was scheduled.

The Bears won again. Colleges paid attention but not closely. The college games of the NCAA were still far more popular than the professional game, which was dominated by the New York Giants, Chicago Bears, and Green Bay Packers in the 1930s. The NCAA kept an eye on the popularity of the pro game as it grew more widespread, especially after World War II.

Fear of the growing popularity of the National Football League and its on-field championship game was a major factor in the NCAA finally discussing the need for a playoff to determine a NCAA champion. Yet, the popularity of postseason college football bowl games had become ingrained in the American mind, making the desire for a real NCAA champion more complicated. Opposition remained. By the 1930s the National Association of State Universities recommended that there be "no post-season intercollegiate athletic contests."[13] The president of the University of Colorado, George Norlin, argued that "post-season prolonged the season unnecessarily and further exploited the athletes."[14] Harvard's athletic director, Bill Bingham, called the numerous bowl games "a nuisance."[15] Many in the academy felt the same way, including faculty representatives in the Big Ten, who continued to ban bowl games.

THE ROSE BOWL SURVIVES PEARL HARBOR, BUT NO PLAYOFF CHAMPIONSHIP

By the time of the Japanese attack on Pearl Harbor on December 7, 1941, end-of-season bowl games—Rose, Cotton, Sugar, and Orange—were part of the national consciousness. This was so despite a number of college faculty members and presidents who claimed these games were a waste of students' time and a furtherance of commercialism at the expense of amateurism. Nevertheless, more football coaches received bonuses for taking their teams to bowl games. As an example, head coach Wallace Wade at Alabama in the 1920s and early 1930s received a bonus of about 10 percent of his salary for taking his team to a Rose Bowl game. His successor, Frank Thomas, received a $1,500 bowl bonus in 1935 to go along with his $8,000 base salary. That was more than double the salary of full professors and about the average income of college presidents.[16] NCAA faculty representatives from the Big Ten voted unanimously to oppose both their athletic directors' desire to play in the Rose Bowl and a proposed pact with the Pacific

Coast Conference to compete annually in the Pasadena game. But Big Ten faculty representatives were out of the mainstream.

Bowl games remained popular with regular national radio broadcasts even after Pearl Harbor. A representative of the Orange Bowl, the day after the United States declared war on Japan, offered his perspective on Pearl Harbor and the war effort on the Miami contest. "I think the public will raise hell this New Year's Day," he commented, "and then get down to Business."[17] Instead of canceling the Rose Bowl game of 1942, the two teams and the Rose Bowl Association decided to move it to Durham, North Carolina, home of the Duke Blue Devils, who squared off against Oregon State. There was fear that West Coast sites might be the target of the Japanese navy and air force if the game were held in Pasadena. The Rose Bowl returned to the West Coast the next year and continued in Pasadena through the rest of the war effort and beyond. Many applauded continuing the bowl games during the war, including a British observer of American culture. Denis Brogan, writer of the popular *American Character*, concluded that "the Rose Bowl, the Cotton Bowl, the other intersectional games—these are instruments of national unity."[18] But not for everyone.

The Big Ten and Ivy League rejected bowl bids through the war years, but the Big Ten changed its "no" to "yes" when the war concluded.[19] The year before Walter Byers joined the administrations of both the Big Ten and NCAA, the Big Ten changed its policy on bowl participation and once again participated in the Pasadena contest. Five years later, when Byers was appointed executive director, the Big Ten and the Pacific Coast Conference agreed to an annual bowl game schedule that lasted almost a half-century. The money and prestige of bowl compensation won out over concerns about commercialism in football among the big-time universities. The fact that Southern universities were using participation in bowl games as a recruiting device to attract Northern high school football players to their schools at the expense of Big Ten football powers should not be forgotten. "We scream to the high heavens," wrote Michigan's Fritz Crisler, when Southern institutions such as Alabama, Duke, Tennessee, and Tulane used money earned in the Rose Bowl to "come up in our territory and take away boys who otherwise would remain in the Conference."[20]

When Byers became executive director, there were eight bowl games following the regular season, the four originals, established by the mid-

1930s—Rose, Orange, Sugar, and Cotton Bowls—followed by the Sun, Gator, Tangerine, and Salad Bowls. The Big Ten decided to cement its relationship in 1951 with the Rose Bowl by making an alliance with the Pacific Coast Conference to play each year in that contest.[21] This had been suggested by Stanford professor William Owens in the late 1930s. Owens, the next NCAA president, proposed in 1938 that the Pacific Coast Conference and the Big Ten, "standing for the best in athletics," sign an agreement to play yearly in the Rose Bowl. More than a decade later, the two conferences agreed, four months before Byers became the first NCAA executive director. This contract began with a three-year agreement but lasted to the end of the century.[22] At least one Big Ten individual believed that two conferences controlling the Rose Bowl competition would eliminate the need for the possibility of a national championship game.[23] The success of bowl games was a deterrent, but not the only one, to a playoff among the prominent football powers.

TELEVISION AND THE ARLEDGE INFLUENCE FOR A FOOTBALL PLAYOFF

The emergence of television, more than any other source, created financial pressure that pulled big-time college football into more bowl games and toward the possibility of a football playoff. Between the 1960s and the 1980s, bowl games doubled in number. It was the dollars coming from TV advertising and the accompanying publicity that most affected institutions of higher learning. As has been noted for generations, college presidents seldom turn away money, regardless of the source.[24] This generalization was not sound with reference to a football playoff, for several reasons. First, some college presidents had long experienced, and opposed, football dominating university policy. Woodrow Wilson, Princeton's president in the early twentieth century, made a wry comment about football shortly before becoming president of the United States. "The side-shows have swallowed up the circus," noted Wilson, "and we don't know what is going on in the main tent."[25] In Wilson's analogy, the sideshow was football, which made successful coaches far more popular than college presidents throughout the twentieth century. At the end of the century, Byers echoed Wilson when he concluded that "it's hard on the ego of a president to be less admired than his football coach."[26] It was also probably hard on presidents' egos to have the star football coaches paid as much as or more than they were through most of the twentieth century.[27] Presidents and the lesser-paid faculty generally voted "no" to both bowl games and a football playoff. That idea continued until the money from television made additional bowl games more profitable.

Twentieth-century football playoffs occurred first for the smaller colleges of the NCAA's College Division. The NCAA Extra Events Committee, which was most concerned with bowl games, believed that small colleges should get some favored legislation to make up for the lack of invitations to bowl games and television exposure. Smaller colleges were left out of bowl games and television income because television networks were disinterested in anything but big-time football telecasts. The Extra Events Committee politely stated that "the establishment of such games for our College Division members will be a worthwhile and significant addition."[28] A proposal was eventually passed in 1963 for a four-team playoff beginning the following year in December that included East Carolina, Middle Tennessee, Northern Iowa, and Montana State. These contests were called bowl games, probably to keep the name "playoff" out of official documents and to offer something comparable to the contests played by big-time institutions. The NCAA hoped this would placate small institutions and gain their support to vote annually for the NCAA television plan, which supported big-time football schools.[29]

The playoff scheme continued for the non-profitable football schools. When the NCAA divided itself into three divisions, the organization created a Division III football championship in 1969, with Wittenberg College defeating Juniata College, 41–0, in the first game. A Division II football playoff started in 1973, and Louisiana Tech defeated Western Kentucky. When the large Division I schools booted out the Ivy League and some other small football programs merged into a new Division IAA, the Division IAA championship began in 1978.[30] This left the big-time schools with no playoff. Instead, the number of bowl games increased significantly when the ESPN cable network was founded in 1979 and, shortly after, entered the bidding to air the various bowl games. But all of this came about after ABC's Roone Arledge campaigned for a NCAA playoff.

Arledge, the master of college football telecasting, knew that a big-time football playoff would produce "tremendous audiences and big financial returns." In the mid-1960s, Arledge asked the NCAA TV Committee, on which Byers served, to explore the possibility of "a bona fide playoff" of eight teams over three weekends "to determine a legitimate champion." If the NCAA did not do this, Arledge said "the colleges will waste an opportunity . . . for big financial returns."[31] Arledge's speaking out at the meeting of the NCAA's TV Committee may have encouraged some football coaches to advocate for a playoff. Among others, three highly successful football coaches—Duffy Daugherty of Michigan State, Ara Parseghian of Notre Dame, and Bud Wilkinson of Oklahoma—were favorable to holding a playoff. Earle Edwards, North Carolina State's football coach, suggested a sixteen-team playoff using bowl game sites for the contests. Edwards wrote to Byers, telling him and the NCAA that a football playoff was needed to counter "the constant advances of pro football."[32]

The National Football League agreed in 1966 to a playoff with the upstart American Football League, formed in 1960, in the first Super Bowl. At the time, only the Rose Bowl game challenged the NFL divisional playoff, with about 25 million television viewers. Soon, the Super Bowl would outdo all televised sporting events for viewership, including baseball's World Series, which dominated until the late 1960s.[33] To counter the rise of pro football, the NCAA Executive Committee authorized a committee to study the feasibility of a national collegiate football championship. Included on the committee of nine were conference commissioners, athletic directors, and football coaches.[34] One committee member who opposed a playoff was Paul "Bear" Bryant of Alabama, who more than likely opposed a championship because it might eliminate bowl games, which were often loaded with Southern teams.

Opposition to a big-time championship existed despite pro football outpacing the college game in popularity and the rapid increase in revenue from the annual NCAA basketball tournament relative to the less profitable football bowl games. The proposal by the NCAA TV Committee that "A NCAA play-off could be helpful to college football" was buried by those who opposed a national championship.[35] Stricken from the final 1967 report of the committee was the statement that "an eight team NCAA championship series at season's end in order to lend meaning to each year's competition, . . . adding magnetism and excitement."[36] Byers, who favored a playoff, was always concerned about professional football overcoming the once-dominant collegiate game. He believed that the NFL's four divisions with a televised playoff in December would add luster to the pro game, making it more attractive than college football. "Since college football has no championship games with which to counter the pro championship contests," Byers argued in the NCAA TV Committee meeting, "some wild card arrangement might be helpful." Arledge kept campaigning for a playoff, and the TV Committee's straw vote of 9–2 supported holding a championship playoff to "increase greatly the strength of college football."[37] The playoff idea was not dead, but it was corralled like the beef on Byers's Kansas ranch.

In the early 1970s, a closed-circuit television network, Management Television Systems (MTS), proposed a $15 million closed circuit two-team contest, based upon MTS's successful Joe Frazier-Jimmy Ellis heavyweight title fight. The football title game would be played prior to the regular bowl games to preserve that tradition.[38] The MTS offer raised interest. Among those interested was the NCAA TV consultant Asa S. Bushnell of the Eastern College Athletic Conference (ECAC), who claimed, "we must make more money," some of which should be shared with the smaller colleges of the ECAC.[39] At the same time, Roone Arledge advocated for a "poll bowl," to answer the objections of the numerous bowl committees who feared a playoff system. Among those who opposed Arledge's scheme was Charles Neinas, assistant to Byers, who asserted that "the players probably would not care for such a game"—a suspect observation for athletes who would be playing for a national championship in a potential poll bowl.[40] This was just another case of athletes never being asked by the NCAA for their opinion on a decision that affected them. To Arledge, rejecting a championship to be broadcast on TV was essentially "relinquishing the stage totally to the pros."[41] Yet, there was too much opposition among institutions of higher learning and the numerous bowl committees to vote for a Division I football championship.

THE DIVISION I FOOTBALL PLAYOFF AT THE TIME OF BYERS'S RETIREMENT

By the mid-1970s, Byers continued his advocacy for a playoff system, knowing that a substantial majority of NCAA members were opposed to the plan.[42] Once the College Football Association (CFA) was founded by about sixty big-time football powers in 1975, the chances of a playoff in football were greatly lessened. The coach-dominated CFA favored going to bowls regularly, where 50 percent of teams would win, rather than holding a championship with only one winner. As the chairman of the NCAA Post-season Bowl Committee later explained, with a possible bowl system of sixteen games, there are sixteen winners, while with a playoff system all but one are losers.[43] Being fired for not winning in colleges' most important sport was a reality that could not be dismissed. Coach Vince Dooley, long-time coach at the University of Georgia, said that, of the coaches attending the CFA meeting in 1979, only he favored a football playoff.[44] The next year, the Bowl Association, dedicated to preserving and promoting bowl games, considered offering 1 percent of gross bowl revenues to the CFA to ensure that the "CFA would not promote a national football playoff."[45] By that time, the various bowl committees had been working to prevent any playoff system for two decades and continued to be successful through the tenure of Byers in the late 1980s and into the 1990s.

The fight between the CFA and the NCAA over television policy in the early 1980s eventually led to a major lawsuit over the legality of the NCAA monopoly in the telecasting of NCAA football. The US Supreme Court confirmed in *NCAA v. Oklahoma* the lower court's decision that the NCAA was indeed a monopoly in televised college football. The breakup of the NCAA TV monopoly allowed the CFA to gain control of big-time football telecasts. Byers, opposed to the power of Division I winning basketball and football coaches, wanted presidents, faculty athletic representatives to the NCAA, and athletic directors to assert control over intercollegiate athletics, not the CFA. Prior to retirement, Byers informed the NCAA membership that faculty reps, ADs, and presidents were frequently "by-passed in the 'power coach' structure."[46] The Supreme Court's 1984 decision gave executive director Charles Neinas and the coach-driven CFA immediate power.

Neinas, who had worked for Byers and the NCAA for a decade, became CFA executive director, and his ideas about a playoff changed. When the CFA was created in the mid-1970s, the organization was opposed to any playoff system. However, when it became "king of the hill" in big-time football telecasting following the Supreme Court decision, Neinas changed his tune about the possibility of a playoff and the millions of dollars that it would create for the CFA. Noting the diminishing importance of bowl games, Neinas outlined a plan for a postseason championship. He proposed an eight-team playoff for big-five conference champions, independents, and a couple of additional teams to be chosen by a CFA committee. The revenue generated by this multi-million-dollar playoff would be apportioned among CFA members.[47] Many of the coaches in control of the CFA questioned Neinas's plan. One was Bob Devaney, former Nebraska coach and then athletic director. Devaney was correct that there would be opposition by football coaches but also strong resistance from college presidents and from the bowl committees.[48] Again, as it was throughout the NCAA's history, no athletes were consulted about a possible playoff for a national championship.

Presidents spoke up against a playoff following number two poll-ranked Penn State's upset victory over the University of Miami, ranked number one, in January 1987. Opposition arose quickly after the game, despite the highest ever bowl game payout and the highest Nielson television rating for a college football game (a record that held even decades later). Days after the event the chancellor of the University of California, Berkeley, Michael Heyman, stated there was consensus against a playoff among the forty-four chief executive officers who composed the NCAA's Presidents' Commission.[49] Byers, only months from retirement, was silent. Two months after Dick Schultz replaced Byers as head of the NCAA, the NCAA rejected a proposed national championship playoff in an overwhelming 98–13 vote. Resolution No. 72 at the 1988 NCAA convention stated that "the concept of a Division IA football championship should be given no further consideration unless and until 'compelling evidence' was provided."[50] Many believed there was continual "compelling evidence," namely, money.

Nevertheless, complaints about polling to determine a Division IA championship continued. The coach-dominated College Football Association, now a major player in telecasting big-time football, decided not to vote on a sixteen-team playoff at its January 1989 meeting. This decision came after it was clear that most college presidents were opposed and after athletic directors had voted unanimously not to present a playoff vote.[51] The major arguments against a playoff were that a playoff might destroy the current bowl structure and that it would interfere with athletes' academic progress. At the same time, one heard little about how the sixteen-game

Division II and Division III football playoffs were negatively affecting the players' academics. In the early 1990s, five big-time conferences and Notre Dame formed a bowl coalition and chose to use the polls and the bowls to determine a two-team matchup. The No. 1 and No. 2 teams in the polls would play, and the winner would be crowned national champion.

This Bowl Alliance was created in 1995, without involving the Big Ten and Pac-10, both of which felt comfortable with their financially enriching Rose Bowl agreement. Six years after Byers's retirement, the major football powers created something that would take the place of a true playoff. This Bowl Alliance emerged despite a three-hundred-page "Report to the NCAA Special Committee to Study a Division IA Football Championship," released in 1994, just before its findings were basically rejected.[52] Surprisingly, the authors of the report asked athletes from Division I football teams for their opinions. The report indicated that these athletes liked the system whereby many teams went to bowl games.[53] The report detailed five playoff options, though their examples used an eight-team system. The playoff possibilities included: a two-team, one-game national championship; a four-team, three-game tournament; an eight-team, seven-game tournament; a twelve-team, eleven-game tournament with four teams receiving a first-round bye; a sixteen-team, fifteen-game tournament beginning in early December and concluding in early January.[54] (Sixteen-team Division II and Division III football championships began in the 1980s.) Notably, while the report was the most thorough study of bowls and playoffs ever completed, it contained a major error when it stated that "the first postseason college football game was held on January 1, 1902, in Pasadena, California as part of a winter holiday festival called 'The Tournament of Roses'."[55] Actually, the first big-time college football championship was the student-run postseason game begun in 1876 and dominated by "Big Three," Harvard, Yale, and Princeton. Yale beat Princeton in the first of these championship contests. True, these games were not held on the sunny field in Pasadena, nor in any Southern city, but rather took place traditionally near, or in, New York City on Thanksgiving Day.

The questionable Bowl Alliance arrangement for a national champion lasted only three years. The alliance was controlled not by the NCAA but by the conferences associated with the College Football Association and its TV contract. The absence of the Big Ten and Pac-10 in the alliance eliminated the possibility of calling the alliance champion a national champion. For instance, in 1997 Michigan of the Big Ten had as much right to be called national champion as did Nebraska of the alliance. By 1998 the Bowl Alliance had morphed into what became known as the Bowl Championship Series (BCS). This occurred when the two conferences, reluctant to join the CFA, agreed to participate in what could be considered a cartel run by the leading conferences through a series of bowl games. Having the Big Ten and Pac-10 in the fold increased the chances that the two best teams would play in a championship contest. While using the major bowl sites, teams were chosen by a coaches' poll and a media poll, supplemented by computer models from the five "power" conferences and excluding some outside but strong teams such as Utah and Boise State. For over a decade and a half, the BCS conducted what the leading critic of the BCS games, Dan Wetzel, called in his popular book *Death to the BCS* the "brain-dead Bowl Championship Series."[56]

The BCS, beginning at the end of the 1998 season, found No. 1 ranked Tennessee beating No. 2 Florida State to become the first BCS national champion. Governed by conferences, the BCS used polls, computer rankings, strength of schedule, and team records in selecting its four-team competition. This system lasted through sixteen seasons, some of which were highly controversial. For instance, after the 2003 season, No. 1 ranked and undefeated Oklahoma lost to Kansas State, 35–7, in the Big 12 championship game. Oklahoma dropped to No. 3 in the human polls (the Associated Press's media poll and the USA Today/CNN coaches' poll) but continued to be No. 1 in the computer-driven BCS rankings. Thus, Oklahoma became the opponent of No. 2 Louisiana State, leaving out Southern California, which led in the human polls. LSU went on to beat Oklahoma, 21–14, while USC was relegated to the Rose Bowl, where they dominated Big Ten champion, Michigan, 28–14. USC remained No. 1 in the human polls and claimed the national championship despite not being in the championship game.[57] Other controversies plagued the BCS over the years until a truer scheme emerged (though not without controversy) when the first Division I College Football Playoff was held after the 2014 season.

Walter Byers's early vision for an eight-team playoff was not chosen. Rather, in Byers's last year on earth, a four-team playoff was selected, in part as an attempt to save the bowl system. As it turned out, this four-team system was unsatisfactory. The former executive director could see from his "home on the range" the result of the January 2015 Ohio State victory over the University of Oregon, 42–20. The new College Football Playoff was directed by a committee of thirteen, mostly athletic directors, who met regularly and halfway through the season and provided weekly ratings based on several criteria including the important strength of schedule. There were no polls or computer rankings as had previously been used. This system lasted only a decade. Like the NCAA-run Division I basketball tourney, the new college football playoff started with only a few schools chosen to complete, but because of controversies and the desire for more money, the tournament would be expanded as the years went by. One could have predicted that the choice of the third and fourth teams to fill the tourney would be nearly as controversial as the discarded BCS system. One might also predict that the tourney would go to eight or sixteen teams in the future. That prediction, however, was not to be. Rather, a twelve-team tourney was chosen in 2023, to be instituted in 2024. This tournament will likely be expanded in the future to sixteen teams, as Division II and III have done successfully for years.

Byers would live to see the beginning of the College Football Playoff, but five months after the Ohio State playoff victory in 2015, he died on his ranch in Kansas. This was a decade after the publication of his significant book *Unsportsmanlike Conduct: Exploiting College Athletes*. In his book, Byers still favored an eight-team playoff but suggested that the big-time conferences would never allow the NCAA to run a financially lucrative tournament, like the basketball tourney, and "skim millions for NCAA projects and Division IAA, II, and III colleges."[58] Byers knew a great deal about how big-time athletics operated and about the influence of money on everything, including bowls and playoffs. He would, by 2015, have no direct influence on football or NCAA policy, but his 1995 book would. Byers's change of heart in support of giving athletes some power to determine their own destiny was generally ignored. However, through *Unsportsmanlike Conduct*, Byers would deal with many of the controversies in college sports and continue to be in the conversation.

FOURTEEN

Unsportsmanlike Conduct

> "Enforcement is the bedrock upon which the NCAA's edifice is based."
>
> —**WALTER BYERS, 1995**

> "[Byers] was revered by many and not trusted by others."
>
> —**JUDITH SWEET, 2015**

In the early 1990s, I phoned Walter Byers to see when his manuscript on the NCAA was going to be published, because I knew that he had been working on it for several years. He said he hoped to have it published by one of the New York City commercial publishers. However, they wanted Byers to name more names and make the book more sensational, something Byers refused to do. He was his own man, as he had been for decades with the NCAA. Byers asked me if I would read the manuscript, something that I was glad to do. Later, the University of Michigan Press sent me a copy of the manuscript, and after making editorial comments, I told the press that it was a "wonderful manuscript" and that Michigan was "fortunate to be publishing" it. I concluded with a prediction that the book, *Unsportsmanlike Conduct: Exploiting College Athletes*, "will be read well into the 21st century."[1] I still agree with what I wrote, but a number of individuals have differed with that opinion over the years, especially when the book was first published as a critique of the NCAA and intercollegiate athletics.

My intent in this chapter is to discuss how Byers was perceived externally and within the NCAA before and after *Unsportsmanlike Conduct* was published. Second, I have chosen several issues brought up in the book that particularly interest me to discuss how Byers and the NCAA dealt with these issues. These include the question of athletes' rights; amateurism and the Sanity Code; enforcement and the troublesome Coach Jerry Tarkanian; the College Football Association and television antitrust case; and the treatment of women and minorities.

WAS *UNSPORTSMANLIKE CONDUCT* A LIGHTNING ROD OR A CURRENT ASSESSMENT?

Why was *Unsportsmanlike Conduct* a lightning rod that attracted such negative comments from those who were knowledgeable or had led college athletics over the years? For one thing, journalists and other writers saw the hypocrisy of college athletics acting as if they were amateur while knowing that they were not, and hadn't been during Byers's tenure. The media took apart Byers's efforts, when he was executive director, to keep college athletics amateur through enforcement and his reversal after retirement to favor athletes receiving some of the enormous profits from college athletics. Sportswriter Joe Nocera may have been Byers's harshest critic. Nocera stated that the longtime NCAA head was "secretive, despotic, stubborn and ruthless" while acting with "callous impunity." In addition, Nocera maintained that Byers led an institution that punished colleges while ignoring due process and, questionably, acting as "investigator, prosecutor and judge." There was no "more vindictive institution," claimed Nocera, than Byers's NCAA.[2] Another sportswriter, Tim Sullivan, criticized Byers for "selling a book about selling his soul." Sullivan criticized the former NCAA head, writing that college athletics were like the plantation system in slavery. "If universities perpetuated the plantation system," Sullivan wrote, "Byers was the overseer."[3] Rick Telander, another denigrating sportswriter, had a long history of condemning college football. Before the publication of *Unsportsmanlike Conduct,* Telander had written his 1989 censure of college football, *The Hundred Yard Lie.* Soon after Byers's death, Telander declared his opposition for those who turned the free labor of athletes into profits for others, stating that "Byers knew of the lie, but he waited until he was out of office to admit it publicly."[4] Sportswriters were not kind to Byers during his administration, after he wrote his book, and upon his death two decades later.

A significant number of college officials disliked Byers's involvement in punishing institutions for violations of amateur rules, knowing that many other institutions not being cited for the same abuses. Others disliked Byers for not effectively communicating with officials or the public. On college campuses, faculty, whether interested in athletics or not, often criticized both Byers and big-time college athletics in general because that part of the extra-curriculum tended to overwhelm student attention to the curriculum. Besides, when Byers spearheaded the negotiations for a new athletic TV contract, faculty members knew that some of the TV largesse would go to salaries for coaches and athletic directors. Likely, however, most faculty did not know Walter Byers himself, since he was generally hidden away in his Kansas City office placing his stamp on the official actions of the NCAA.

Byers dealt with the heady issues of TV contracts, rule enforcement, and government legislation and with the continual flow of lawsuits. He was kept busy with much more, such as mediating divisional disputes among the membership; grappling with the football bowl situation; coping with conflicts with athletic conferences; contending with demands of college presidents and their control of the American Council on Education; conducting NCAA roundtables on various matters; dealing with athletic eligibility and the freshman rule; and struggling with medical insurance and workers' compensation.[5] As an administrator of all NCAA problems, he was constantly given accolades by the NCAA's elected officers for effective management of NCAA business.

Byers's administrative leadership was apparent even before he became executive director and while he was as an assistant to "Tug" Wilson. Soon after joining the NCAA in 1947, Byers was praised by Wilson for making "great contributions . . . in aid of the officers" of the association.[6] He was lauded for running an early NCAA baseball tournament and making money at it.[7] When the NCAA experimented with football telecasting, he was asked to take the place of NCAA president Tom Hamilton in discussing the NCAA's telecasting before the National Association of Radio and Television Broadcasters.[8] He was commended by NCAA president Hugh Willett of the University of Southern California for his "wonderful work" in organizing the 1951 NCAA Conference.[9] All of this transpired before he became executive director.

As an administrator, he was applauded consistently. It is little wonder that the officers of the NCAA appreciated his work and chose Byers to be the first executive director of the NCAA before he was thirty years of age. He was doing very well what he was asked to do—that is, to "implement the will of the organization."[10] Throughout his thirty-six years, he continually emphasized that he was executing the NCAA's wishes, whether he was enforcing rules, negotiating television contracts, or accomplishing the many other tasks brought before him. Byers was closest to the thunder and lighting and received the brunt of criticism before and after he wrote his memoir. Or, as Judy Sweet, the first woman president of the NCAA, stated of Byers, "He was revered by many and not trusted by others."[11]

UNSPORTSMANLIKE CONDUCT AND THE RIGHTS OF ATHLETES

Byers knew that he was going to write a memoir about the NCAA before he had retired in 1987.[12] The 1980s had not been kind to Byers and his beliefs about the conduct of intercollegiate athletics. He lost battles early in his career, including the fight for the Sanity Code in the early 1950s. Byers also saw his favored 1.600 GPA eligibility legislation die in the early 1970s. Yet, the NCAA won nearly every legal case brought against it in his first several decades at the helm.[13] By the 1980s, however, Byers failed more often. He was unsuccessful, along with most of the NCAA leadership, in keeping athletics out of Title IX legislation for the equality of women in education. More important to Byers than the question of women in sports, however, was the rise of the College Football Association. The CFA, with support from some sixty big-time football schools, defeated the NCAA's control of college football telecasting in the Oklahoma lawsuit. By then, Byers had failed in his expanded efforts to use TV revenues to help all NCAA institutions, large and small. The number of lawsuits against the NCAA kept piling up, and investigations of NCAA enforcement policies by the US Congress took their toll. When Byres retired, he was in the second year of his four-year contract extension; it was clear that NCAA members still believed in him. NCAA leaders gave him a special NCAA award. They suspended the highest NCAA honor, the Teddy [Roosevelt] Award, for one year to honor

Byers alone.[14] Nevertheless, even before retirement he was becoming an embittered executive who was beginning to speak out against the system.

Before he wrote his memoir, Byers began suggesting that an "open division" be created without amateur rules, like the Olympics, to separate the big-time commercial institutions and their "amateur" cheating from other NCAA programs.[15] "We cannot live with the proposition that adults make a deal with a youngster," Byers told readers of the *NCAA News*, "who then has to lie for four or five years to maintain his eligibility."[16] Byers realized that colleges and the NCAA exploited and controlled the lives of college athletes, who he thought should be amateur in the English tradition. It took Byers a lifetime following the blighted and false concept of amateurism to realize the harm he and the NCAA had been doing to athletes for years—that is, taking away the freedoms that other college students had achieved since the departure of the collegiate control policy of "in loco parentis," taking the place of parents. Several centuries of "in loco parentis" practices had been eliminated from institutions of higher learning by the twentieth century. The remaining exceptions were policies around intercollegiate athletics and possibly women's dorms and dorm hours.

Beginning in 1905, the NCAA acted in the place of the athletes' parents for its entire existence and promoted these policies throughout the intercollegiate scene through athletic conferences and individual institutions. Athletes could not earn their own money, endorse products, consult agents or lawyers, or transfer without loss of eligibility from one school to another. They were unprotected when injured due to the lack of workers' compensation coverage.[17] Furthermore, athletes could have their supposed "four-year" scholarships stripped away if they did not perform to the standards set by exploitive coaches and athletic directors, or if they were injured working on the job. Athletes had to sign "letters of intent" to attend specific schools and signed away ordinary freedoms after receiving athletic scholarships for the athletic work they were doing on campus. Indeed, athletes even had their government Pell Grants stripped if the money exceeded the amount generally accepted for an athletic scholarship. In short, Byers began *Unsportsmanlike Conduct* opposing[18] "the neo-plantation belief that the enormous proceeds from college games belong to the overseers (the administrators) and supervisors (coaches). The plantation workers performing in the arena may receive only those benefits authorized by the overseers." Byers's slavery-inflected diatribe against the system was correct in many ways. Greater freedom for athletes gained in the twenty-first century moved in the direction that he proposed years earlier. His book lives on decades after it was written as a testimony for athletes' rights.

UNSPORTSMANLIKE CONDUCT AND THE NCAA SANITY CODE

With the possible exception of dealing with television's impact on college football, the enforcement of NCAA eligibility rules dominated Byers's world. He was associated with the NCAA in the middle to late 1940s, when the faculty representatives who ran the NCAA were determined to keep athletics amateur. In 1946, just before Byers left the United Press as a sportswriter to take his first position in the NCAA, the NCAA faculty representatives met for an important Conference of Conferences. Leaders of twenty conferences met in Chicago to see if the NCAA could not only pass national legislation to uphold the rules of amateurism but begin effectively enforcing this legislation. The faculty representatives were strongly in favor of reform measures to control the recruiting and payment of athletes. What came out of the Conference of Conferences was initially called the "Purity Code" and was later renamed the "Sanity Code." As noted earlier, the Sanity Code consisted of a statement opposing off-campus recruiting of athletes, who would be admitted to college on the same basis as other students. The code mandated that athletes would be amateur and that financial support would be limited to need-based tuition and incidental fees, paid for only by an approved agency.[19] Once the NCAA delegates passed the Sanity Code nearly unanimously, NCAA president Karl Leib of Iowa declared that the principles would mean that all institutions could "conform or get out."[20] Twenty-six-year-old Byers was at this meeting, but he and the NCAA had to wait a year before an official vote would place the Sanity Code into the constitution.

Byers was on the side of the majority who favored the Sanity Code's tuition-only payments based on financial need, considered a tenet of amateurism. Some schools, however, particularly Southern schools in the football-dominated Southeastern Conference, wanted athlete payments to include not only tuition but room, board, and books—a full scholarship, as a number of schools had been providing since the 1930s.[21] While the majority of faculty representatives favored need-based aid, many institutions and conferences strongly preferred paying the expenses of their athletic performers based not on financial need but on athletic ability. This system would be similar to academic scholarships, which were based on academic ability rather than financial need—achievement-oriented criteria. The vote to place the Sanity Code into the NCAA constitution was nearly unanimous. But the actions of athletic departments at individual institutions were not. Many schools violated the need-based provision. When an enforcement committee called for a vote to oust the violating schools, the proposed punishment did not receive the necessary two-thirds vote. The Sanity Code died because of the lack of the will to enforce it.

In his memoir, Byers called the defeat of the Sanity Code one of the three or four most important decisions in NCAA history. For his entire adult life, Byers favored amateurism, and he believed the Sanity Code facilitated amateurism because the athlete might get his tuition paid, but this payment was based on financial need, not athletic prowess. As he said in his *Unsportsmanlike Conduct*, he considered amateurs to be "patriots, not mercenaries," believing that "students playing solely for the honor and joy of it would be good for the country's future."[22] Ironically, as a seventeen-year-old, Byers went to Rice University in Houston intending to get a football scholarship, but the coach, Jimmy Kitts, who had previously beaten the University of Colorado with the great Byron "Whizzer" White in the Cotton Bowl, denied him. After reading Byers's press clippings of his experience as an all-Kansas City center and linebacker, Kitts said that Byers's small feet indicated that he would not get any bigger and refused to give him a scholarship.[23] At this stage of his life, Byers would have accepted an athletic scholarship if it had been offered. When Byers's Saul to Paul, "road to Damascus" conversion occurred is not known, but by the time he was asked to be executive director of the NCAA, he had accepted the myth of amateurism, along with many of the leaders of college athletics.[24]

Within a half-dozen years of the failure to prosecute errant schools under the Sanity Code, the NCAA decided to allow full scholarships including tuition, room, board, books, incidental fees, and $15 per month "laundry" money. The athletic scholarship, Byers believed, only intensified the problem of athletes being paid to participate in athletics. He wondered, would tax officials and advocates for workers' compensation consider athletes to be workers? Would they therefore tax athletes and bring injured athletes under workers' compensation laws?[25] To prevent this, Byers and the NCAA would have to produce language that would make athletes appear to be both amateur and part of the educational system. Due to the longevity of his leadership, Byers was frequently in the position to protect the NCAA from harm, often recognizing problems before others in positions of authority did.

Because the new athletic scholarships were, as Byers said, "perilously close to employment contracts," he and other NCAA officials ensured that the NCAA constitution made it clear that the athletes were "amateurs" and that the financial aid was going to college students under sound academic standards.[26] Byers, in his book, explained how his made-up term "student-athlete" came about in the 1950s.[27] The term developed out of the effort to convince government officials and others that athletes were students first and athletes second. Here was a major success for Byers in denying athletes' rights to financial benefits. When he retired, Byers finally admitted that he had been working for the athletic "plantation owners." Athletic administrators became wealthy while players experienced diminished returns. Their "laundry money" was taken away, and the number of hours of work expected of them increased dramatically. Byers wrote in *Unsportsmanlike Conduct*, "Collegiate amateurism is not a moral issue; it is an economic camouflage for monopoly practice."[28] The NCAA and big-time colleges led by coaches and administrators under presidential cover were the monopolists, making the money and gaining the benefits produced by television revenue and gate receipts at the expense of workers. Meanwhile, the working athletes drew spectators.

If Byers opposed the payment of players and favored restriction on athletes when the Sanity Code was passed in the late 1940s, four decades later he called for athlete freedom. Before he retired, he would often repeat the 1957 mantra that an "athlete's picture may not be associated with a commercial product in such a way as to imply endorsement, nor may he receive remuneration."[29] However, shortly before he began writing *Unsportsmanlike Conduct*, Byers declared support for allowing athletes to sell their own names, by, for example, endorsing products. This was three decades before a US Supreme Court did away with that form of amateurism in the *NCAA v. Shawne Alston* case in 2021. Two years before retirement, Byers spoke to the NCAA Council and Executive Committee, suggesting that because colleges were exploiting the talent of athletes, "the athletes deserved the same access to the free market as the coaches enjoyed."[30] Hearing this, the council and committee stared at Byers in disbelief. Byers was likely taking notes for his forthcoming book as he addressed NCAA leaders, including college presidents, faculty representatives, coaches, and athletic directors. They were not appreciative.

Byers was attacking the arcane amateurism of the traditional NCAA and calling for athletes to be as free as other college students. These freedoms included earning income by working, transferring to another institution without penalty, and unshackling themselves from the five-hundred-page NCAA Manual that was intended primarily to control athletes in the name of amateurism. Byers eventually argued against the usual justification for these rules. The pages and pages of rules, Byers argued, "were not there to enhance competition" by leveling the playing field but rather "to enforce a modern economic order." This, he clearly stated, is the "plantation mentality resurrected and blessed by today's campus executives." Officials, from the presidents down the power ladder, were engaging in "pedantic tautology" by declaring that "players may not receive money, except what we give them, because they must remain amateur under NCAA rules."[31] Byers had changed his mind. Free the athletes who were once controlled by his and the NCAA's failed Sanity Code.

UNSPORTSMANLIKE CONDUCT AND ENFORCEMENT

"Enforcement is the bedrock upon which the NCAA's edifice is based," Byers wrote as he pondered his thirty-six-year career leading the NCAA.[32] This, he claimed, was true for the fledgling NCAA in a cramped Chicago hotel room and for the behemoth multi-million-dollar institution in Kansas City the NCAA had become by the time of his retirement. Byers supported the punishment when the University of Kentucky and its basketball players were vilified by a New York City district attorney for taking bribes in 1951. Enforcement as the bedrock was equally evident in 1987 when Southern Methodist University received another "death penalty" for paying thousands of dollars to its football players. A major difference in these cases, however, was that in 1951 conferences were the major punishers of wrongdoing, whereas in 1987, after three decades of Byers's rule, the NCAA was the principal enforcer. With its bulging financial pockets and growing staff of enforcement personnel, the NCAA conducted most of the investigations of the growing number of violations in these later years. Byers became the focal point of the individuals and institutions who believed they had been unjustly wronged by the NCAA.

Byers claimed in *Unsportsmanlike Conduct* that he was given two tasks when he became executive director—keep sports clean and generate money. The latter, he said, was "enormously successful," while the former was "barely adequate."[33] If barely adequate meant that the NCAA had eliminated or slowed down violations of its many policies, it was a misnomer. As income from televised football and men's basketball grew exponentially, violations far exceeded the increased number of investigators Byers hired with the increased NCAA wealth. Previously, responsibility for enforcement of rules relating to recruitment and payment of players had been the task of conference commissioners. Following World War II and the rapid growth of intercollegiate athletics, violations of recruiting and amateurism standards grew across the nation. Still, conference commissioners, not the NCAA, enforced the rules. These commissioners sometimes found their positions jeopardized when they had to punish the institutions that hired them.[34] In other words, as Byers noted, "investigate a power conference team and you jeopardize your job."[35] What to do? Let the NCAA do the punishing of offenders.

The basic task of enforcement therefore moved from conferences to the NCAA at about the same time that the NCAA voted to allow full athletic scholarships in the 1950s. The first NCAA case was the "death penalty" case involving Kentucky basketball, but in that case the NCAA essentially agreed with the SEC's earlier decision to ban Kentucky from conference competition. In a few years, when seven-foot Wilt Chamberlain received a "free" car from representatives of the University of Kansas to play basketball, the NCAA was unable to stick the charge until after he left school to play professionally. (Ironically, while Chamberlain left school with a new Oldsmobile 98, the head of NCAA enforcement, David Berst, rode in a similar Olds 98, furnished free of charge by the same auto agency that provided Chamberlain's.[36]) Byers was probably correct when he wrote in *Unsportsmanlike Conduct* that "only a national organization, insulated from local and regional power politics—the NCAA, to be precise—had even a faint hope of doing the enforcement job."[37] He took the brunt of the blame from those punished, justly or unjustly.[38] Byers did not excuse himself from condemnation even when he dropped out as head of the NCAA Infractions Committee that he led in the 1950s. While outsiders criticized Byers, NCAA officials such as president of the NCAA, Alabama's Bernie Moore, praised him. Two years after taking office, Byers was complimented as the NCAA's "indefatigable and able Executive Director" for the "thorough and tactful manner in which he has directed all investigations."[39]

One investigation, though, stands out as a critique of the enforcement policy—the Jerry Tarkanian case at the University of Nevada, Las Vegas. From page 1 of his 1995 book, Byers could not get Coach Tarkanian's twenty-one-year conflict and multiple lawsuits out of his mind. He concluded that Tarkanian "still looks like the winner to me." Maybe this was because, after two decades, Tarkanian was paid $2.5 million by the NCAA to close a case Tarkanian filed against the NCAA for economic damages incurred when the NCAA attempted to suspend the coach.[40] Byers had already retired, written his book, and was living on his Kansas ranch when Tarkanian and the NCAA agreed in 1998 to abandon two decades of invective. Each side was released from all legal claims, while Tarkanian was paid millions.

If nothing else, the Tarkanian case embarrassed the NCAA, causing the organization to consider changes in its enforcement due process policy. One must remember that the NCAA won the original Tarkanian case in 1988, when the US Supreme Court ruled that the NCAA was not a state entity and did not have to follow due process as set out by the Fourteenth Amendment. Nevertheless, the congressional hearings and proposed bills over the years had convinced NCAA officials that additional due process rules were needed for fairness and to better reflect national standards. Byers never admitted that the NCAA enforcement rules were less than fair to individuals and institutions. "Jerry Tarkanian received more due process in the NCAA proceedings," Byers told readers in his book, "than most citizens experience in their affairs."[41] Wrong, according to NCAA officials, who eventually changed its due process procedures to align with the US Constitution's Fifth and Fourteenth Amendments. Though Byers changed his attitude toward many NCAA policies, he never gave up criticizing Jerry Tarkanian for his ultimate out-of-court settlement win over Byers and the NCAA. He condemned Tarkanian at the beginning of the book for getting around enforcement, and he continued criticizing him at the end of his memoir.[42] He may even have muttered something negative about Tarkanian on his death bed.

UNSPORTSMANLIKE CONDUCT AND ANTITRUST ACTION

While Byers called his success in enforcement mediocre, his success in antitrust action should be considered a success, except for one faux pas: his inability to work with the football powers in the College Football Association to develop a NCAA TV plan that was satisfactory to CFA members. As a result, two CFA schools, Oklahoma and Georgia, backed by CFA money, brought a lawsuit against the NCAA for its illegal action in the TV monopoly of big-time football. "It was television," Byers stated, "that converted winning college coaches into entertainment celebrities and conveyed their views to millions. . . . As television broke into living color and reached full bloom, it enshrined the Power Coach and made him the controlling force in deciding the college's policies."[43] In reality, winning coaches were "enshrined" before the popularity of radio and television, and even before Byers was born. These included such famous athletic figures as Walter Camp, Pop Warner, and Knute Rockne, but there were many more after the advent of television. Still, Byers wasn't far off target on celebrity; his negative feeling about celebrity coaches kept him from working effectively with the coach-run CFA.

Byers's sometimes negative comments about power coaches did not endear him to individuals and institutions that were often in positions of influence within the NCAA. Well before the CFA was founded to get more money from big-time football television contracts, Byers criticized football coaches. In 1969, during the Vietnam War, with increased inflation affecting the cost of football, Byers opposed the American Football Coaches Association (AFCA) for advocating costly expenditures. The AFCA pressured the NCAA to allow unlimited substitutions, more specialists, bigger squads, more coaches, and added transportation costs from "two-platoon" football. Byers editorialized in the *NCAA News* that "College football does not belong exclusively to the coaches . . . the ruling aristocracy of winning coaches."[44] This editorial resulted in a blistering letter from the president of the AFCA, Paul Dietzel, condemning the "unwarranted . . . and unsubstantiated public attack" by the head of the NCAA. Byers responded that the AFCA would be more constructive if the coaches would advance ideas to "reduce football costs instead of repeated allegiance to two-platoon football and vows to do in anyone who thinks to the contrary."[45] It is no wonder that the power football coaches questioned Byers and NCAA policies in the future.

The influence of power coaches erupted in the mid-1970s when the CFA was founded because of the antagonism of football coaches and administrators to the idea within the NCAA that revenue from televised football should be divided more evenly among all divisions of the NCAA. Byers's legal counsel, George Gangwere, cautioned the NCAA chief as early as 1975 that TV "revenue sharing would . . . magnify the likelihood of legal attack against the [NCAA] Plan in the future."[46] Gangwere also knew that the NCAA was likely a monopoly, but he and Byers tended "to ignore the *anti-trust laws*."[47]

Only at the end of his career did Byers consider the impact of the NCAA's monopoly on the workers, athletes. Rereading famed writer Paul Gallico's *Farewell to Sport* (1938), Byers came across Gallico's claim that amateurism was the last stronghold of hypocrisy, probably second only to the prohibition of alcohol. Gallico wrote during the Great Depression that it didn't take much imagination to visualize "an athletic governing body as a monopolistic organization operating an air-tight racket of supplying cheap athletic labor." By the time he wrote *Unsportsmanlike Conduct,* Byers was in concert with Gallico's chapter titled, "Amateurs? There Ain't None."[48] After years of fighting government action and lawsuits to preserve the NCAA's monopoly on football telecasts, Byers came to believe that "prosecutors and the courts . . . should use antitrust laws to break up the collegiate cartel." One should not forget that Byers was in the driver's seat when he used the monopoly to enrich individuals, institutions, conferences, and the NCAA in the 1950s and the decades following. Was Byers the hypocrite that so many have claimed, or was he the biblical Saul who became Saint Paul on the road to Damascus?

UNSPORTSMANLIKE CONDUCT AND TREATMENT OF WOMEN AND MINORITIES

Midway through Byers's tenure at the NCAA, two groups hitherto basically unnoticed became prominent in intercollegiate athletics: women and

African Americans. Until the mid-1960s and into the 1970s, most officials of the NCAA didn't give a damn about either group. This perspective reflected an American society that traditionally placed women and minorities far down on the priority list. This was true for Walter Byers, born in 1922 in a segregated Kansas City. With Byers's father working in real estate, Byers experienced a segregated upbringing in which a major street, ten-mile-long Troost Avenue, divided Kansas City into Black and white sections.[49] Given Byers's childhood, it is not surprising that for the first two decades he administered the NCAA, Byers appointed no Blacks within an NCAA administration that had no African American officers. Ron Stratten was the first Black enforcement officer, taking the position in 1975, twenty-four years after Byers became executive director. That was a half-dozen years before the NCAA elected its first Black president, James Frank of Lincoln University in Missouri. Stratten was hired during the civil rights movement, when the NCAA was being criticized for not giving Black colleges regional and national television exposure in football and earlier had been criticized for not allowing Black college participation in the NCAA basketball tourney. Critics at this time said that NCAA stood for "No Colored Athletes Allowed."[50]

Byers did not apologize for the NCAA's belated action to bring African Americans into the mainstream of college athletics. He told the readers of his memoir that the Black athletic problem "was a sensitive issue that we preferred not to discuss in public." He did say that he tried, unsuccessfully, to gain accommodations for teams in his segregated Kansas City during the 1950s.[51] There is little evidence that Byers fought hard for the rights of Black people in athletics or for Black teams to enter the mainstream. Byers made some questionable comments as NCAA director. It is difficult to know whether he was intending to be racist or if he was merely criticizing basketball coach Jerry Tarkanian, for he so intensely disliked Tarkanian. Regardless, Byers called the Black playing style of Tarkanian's basketball players "ghetto run-and-shoot basketball" and said it showed little defense, discipline, and coaching.[52] In football TV negotiations, Byers was involved in Black colleges getting only one national telecast, for a game between Grambling College and Morgan State in 1971, with a media rating much lower than others on TV that year.[53] This resulted in the NCAA not favoring future Black college football telecasts, and a charge of discrimination resulted. The Federal Communications Commission, however, disagreed, stating that it was not true that "exclusion of regional and national television exposure and revenue is racially motivated."[54] Byers may not have pushed for racial equality, but there is no strong evidence to uphold noted sportswriter Robert Lipsyte's caustic comments upon Byers's death. Byers was the "architect," Lipsyte stated, "of a corrupt, commercialized, sexist and racist football system."[55] If that criticism has any truth, the problems are more the result of Byers carrying out the will of the white-controlled NCAA than indulging his own agenda.

Not only was Byers born into a segregationist Kansas City, Missouri, society but he was raised in a state that had rejected women's suffrage eight times by the early twentieth century.[56] This perspective likely influenced him from birth. He was not a liberal in his judgments about women's sport any more than he was about African American participation in sport. He was in the conservative mainstream relative to girls' and women's sports. The year he was born, the Kansas State High School Activities Association banned basketball as a sport for females.[57] Specifically, leading women physical educators nationally were opposed to competitive sport for girls and women. As Mabel Lee, a physical educator at the University of Nebraska pointed out in 1923, a "large majority" of women physical educators have been opposed to intercollegiate athletics "for years and are still opposed to it."[58] This position on women's physical education persisted for decades.[59] Byers likely paid little attention to the lack of competition for girls and women as he grew up. As a United Press reporter in the 1940s, he wrote little about it. Once, he followed Babe Didrikson around a golf course and admired her athleticism, but he didn't follow the progress of the first women's national intercollegiate tournament, golf, before or after he became NCAA executive director.[60] And, he generally did not follow women's sports, such as the All-American Girls Professional Baseball League (1943–54). When most college women began competition in the 1960s, Byers did not even know who was running the women's intercollegiate national golf championship, first organized in 1941.[61]

Byers was naïve about women's sport until Title IX of the Education Amendments Act of 1972 passed, calling for equality in education for women. Prior to Title IX, men were consuming about 99 percent of all athletic expenditures, with the attitude, according to Byers, that "We generate the wealth; we come first."[62] Byers did not think that women should be given financial backing to provide for intercollegiate athletics unless they earned it by working for it as the men had for generations. He fought against women getting equal facilities, accommodations, equipment, coaching—equal treatment—unless they earned it through hard work, not because the government stated that there should be equal treatment.[63] Like many political conservatives, Byers favored self-help, not government help, and he strongly favored eliminating major income producers, football and men's basketball, from any formula to provide equal expenditure for men's and women's sports under Title IX.[64]

Early in the mid-1960s, Byers told women's physical education leader Katherine Ley of SUNY Cortland that women's physical education teachers should not control women's athletics. Women's athletics should be controlled by institutions, like the NCAA, not by individuals who had a professional membership organization such as the Division for Girls and Women's Sports (DGWS). The DGWS was an individual membership group of women physical educators.[65] His work at the NCAA convinced Byers that to allow control by a coaches' association or athletic directors' association would lead to major problems in athletics. Athletics needed to be controlled by the institutions of higher education, such as those found in the NCAA. Many women, though, believed that Byers and the NCAA were only interested in taking over women's athletics in service to their fight against the Amateur Athletic Union for control of amateur sports.[66] In his memoir, Byers stated that the NCAA "tried to work out a peaceful settlement" with the leaders of the Association for Intercollegiate Athletics for Women (AIAW).[67] What he did not say was that he and the NCAA were unwilling to concede equality unless it was done on the commercialized and professionalized model of the men. Only after the AIAW went bankrupt and lost its antitrust lawsuit against the NCAA in 1984 did the NCAA commercial model become ascendant for women. Byers, in the end, won the victory for control of women's sport.

In *Unsportsmanlike Conduct,* Byers justified his leadership in college sport as doing for intercollegiate athletics what the leaders of sport at individual institutions and in conferences directed him to do. Or, as he once noted in a US Senate hearing, he simply tried to "implement the will of the organization."[68] Whether it was the control of women's sports or working out television contracts, he did this extremely effectively to the satisfaction of the majority of leading individuals and institutions comprising the NCAA. This was true even when his administrative decisions went against his own personal views, as when he allowed full athletic scholarships based on athletic talent rather than on financial need, or when he abandoned maintaining academic standards for athletes after the NCAA voted to do away with the 1.600 grand point average requirement.

Byers was a complicated individual who kept many of his opinions and personal life isolated from his administrative duties at the NCAA. He was a loner and a workaholic. According to his second wife, Betty, Byers "didn't have a buddy. He's a loner, definitely a loner. He is very happy with his own company."[69] He obviously had some difficulties in his personal life, demonstrated by his three unsuccessful marriages and his deteriorating relations with his children later in life, when he dispossessed his daughter for not living up to his standards in running his beloved ranch. His skill at administering an organization that grew from fewer than four hundred institutions when he took office to over one thousand when he retired is confirmed by his longevity and by those who worked under him. Though praised by some, he had his flaws. For thirty-six years, he helped keep an increasingly wealthy organization functioning and fused its disparate parts together well enough to last into the future. His 1995 *Unsportsmanlike Conduct* is part of the incongruity that helps tell the story of the NCAA.

EPILOGUE

In the opening of my introduction, I wrote about a lawsuit in which Walter Byers, the former executive director of the NCAA, was sued by his attorney daughter, Ellen Byers Bouton. She claimed that her father disinherited her from his ranch in Kansas when it appeared she was careless in preventing a water pipe on his ranch from freezing, jeopardizing his beef herd. At first glance, one might assume that this decision by Byers had little to do with his previous administration of the NCAA. Yet this event two decades after he retired indicates something about Byers, the man, and how he helped run the NCAA for over three decades. "The impression of carelessness," according to a longtime executive under Byers, "was to be avoided at all costs." David Pickle wrote this about his admired NCAA boss when, in 1968, Byers assailed those working under him for sloppy work. "If you don't like the way this is working," Byers told seven assistants at a NCAA convention, "don't let the door knob hit you in the ass on your way out."[1] Four decades later, the door was swinging, and his daughter was soon off the ranch without an inheritance.[2]

The door knob eventually hit both the NCAA and Walter Byers. They were careless with the meaning of amateurism under US legislation. In the wake of World War II, the NCAA's commercialism and professionalism increased at the national level, which led to state and federal inquiries into how the NCAA was run. Ultimately, lawsuits, including the 2021 *Shawn Alston v. NCAA* case, came crashing down on the NCAA, reducing the power of the organization that had existed since the Byers era.[3] Until then, athletes accessing the intellectual property rights to monetize their own names, images, and likenesses was forbidden by the NCAA under its amateur policies. The NCAA ruling on intellectual property rights began in the Byers era and lasted well into the twenty-first century. Then came the downfall of the traditional NCAA attitude about amateurism, control of athletes through *in loco parentis*, and questionable due process in the enforcement of penalties. The playacting or hypocritical amateur rules for athletes surrendered in legal cases as never before.

The Shawne Alston case affected me and several other historians because our work played a role in dismantling amateurism and legally helping to free athletes from the grip of the NCAA. Historians of sport can take solace in the Alston case, which demonstrates that their research and writing can affect important aspects of sport. In December 2020, just before the COVID-19 pandemic, I was completing a book on the myth of intercollegiate athletic amateurism.[4] I wrote to the chief counsel of the Shawn Alston case, attorney Jeffrey Kessler, that he might find supportive material in the page proofs of my book for the impending Alston case, which was to come before the US Supreme Court in the spring of 2021. Kessler asked me if I would write an *amici curiae* (an *amicus*, or friend of the court, brief) for the Supreme Court justices to read before the case was tried.[5] The brief was based on the historical record since 1852, emphasizing that intercollegiate athletics were never amateur and noting a number of examples of the payment of athletes in one form or another.[6] I asked five historians to join me in the effort: Taylor Branch of Baltimore; Richard Crepeau of the University of Central Florida; Sarah Fields of the University of Colorado, Denver; Jay Smith of the University of North Carolina, Chapel Hill; and John Thelin of the University of Kentucky. All five agreed. With the effective assistance of a member of the US Supreme Court Bar, Erik Jaffee, the *amicus* brief was submitted. Supreme Court Justice Neil Gorsuch liberally quoted factual material from the brief in the first five pages of the Supreme Court's 9–0 decision against the NCAA. The historical *amicus* brief also won an award when the document was cited by the Education Law Association as the Steinhilber Outstanding Brief of the Year. Attorney Kessler wrote me, "History can make a difference."[7]

How did the *Shawn Alston v. NCAA* case affect Walter Byers's NCAA? Nearly four decades have passed since the NCAA lost the control of football telecasting in the US Supreme Court's 1984 antitrust decision, three years before Byers retired. Since then, there has been an increasing number of cases against the NCAA, many having to do with NCAA violations of amateur rules. Of particular importance was the *Ed O'Bannon v. NCAA* case, in which the NCAA was found guilty of violating its amateur rules in the sale of electronic games based on the images and likenesses of NCAA athletes.[8] Unpaid athletes generating billions in revenue was not only unfair on the face of it but was a violation of antitrust legislation dating back to the nineteenth century, before the NCAA was born. Walter Byers discussed the unfairness toward athletes in his 1995 book, *Unsportsmanlike Conduct*, but he still clung to the concept of amateurism well into the twenty-first century. In a 2007 lawsuit deposition, Byers stated, "Amateurism is something to be defended."[9] The O'Bannon and Alston lawsuits showed that collegiate amateurism was in the midst of dying.

The concurring Supreme Court opinion of Justice Brett Kavanaugh in the Alston case was likely more important than the written decision of Justice Neil Gorsuch. Kavanaugh suggested that, in future cases related to collegiate amateurism, the NCAA would be found to violate antitrust laws. "The NCAA's business model would be flatly illegal in almost any other industry in America," he wrote, and athlete "price-fixing labor is price-fixing labor." The false argument of the NCAA, Kavanaugh pointed out, was that declining to pay athletes is because "athletes are not paid" is a circular argument, unbecoming of an educationally oriented institution.[10] In future court cases, one can assume, Kavanaugh's conclusions will be given much weight. Long after Byers retired from the NCAA, the twenty-first century NCAA promotion of amateur athletics is delusional, unrealistic, and unjust.

Walter Byers was a loser historically in promoting amateurism for college athletes, but he was a major winner in producing money for institutions, conferences, and the NCAA. He came to the NCAA at the right time, and he used his many administrative abilities to help produce great wealth from televising major collegiate sporting events. His administration came at the wrong time for continuing to exploit athletes through the passage of amateur legislation and for lacking due process in carrying out the enforcement of amateur infractions. It may be that in a free enterprise system under which American men's intercollegiate athletics have always existed—and women's athletics more recently—amateur athletics cannot easily exist.[11]

The exploitation of athletes for the benefit of coaches, administrators, presidents, institutions, conferences, and the NCAA was never adequately addressed by those in power in athletics. Only in a court of law was this exploitation partially addressed, over the protestations of those who were the exploiters. The role of Walter Byers and the NCAA in promoting the growth of intercollegiate athletics has been clearly shown, but at the same time the playacting or hypocrisy of Byers's NCAA in the post–World War II era of amateur athletes has been unmasked. Judging the success and failure of Walter Byers's years of NCAA rule remains difficult and dependent upon what qualities are being judged. The legacy of Walter Byers as long-time executive director of the NCAA is still unclear. If one focuses on the financial side, the NCAA and Byers profited greatly as the NCAA became a billion-dollar-a-year industry. In turn, it helped to create a number of millionaire coaches, athletic administrators, and even college presidents, who rode the coattails of the celebrity coaches and administrators. If one judges the legacy by unpaid "slaves" under NCAA control, both the NCAA and Byers should be condemned for their treatment of athletes as Southern plantation owners have been judged.

When assessing Byers and the NCAA, historians are given the opportunity to bring out the ambiguity and complexity of humanity. There is light and dark among all individuals and institutions. Byers and the NCAA were little different than one of America's greatest heroes and noted antiheroes, Thomas Jefferson. The writer of the Declaration of Independence gave us the "self-evident" truth that "all men are created equal" while he kept slaves and was the father of six children with his slave, Sally Hemings.[12] While it has taken two centuries for the villain in Jefferson to be brought to light, the reign of Walter Byers at the NCAA is only a few decades behind us. The lasting impact of Walter Byers on the NCAA is still an enigma, a conundrum for future historians to unpack.

NOTES

Preface

1. For a lengthy account of the 1905 football crisis, see John S. Watterson, "Football's Longest Season: The Fall of 1905" and "Football in Crisis, 1905 to 1906," in *College Football: History, Spectacle, Controversy* (Baltimore: Johns Hopkins Univ. Press, 2000), 64–98.

2. For birth, impact, and death of the "Sanity Code," see Ronald A. Smith, "National Athletic Scholarship Failure: The Sanity Code," in *The Myth of the Amateur: A History of College Athletic Scholarships* (Austin: Univ. of Texas Press, 2021), 98–108.

3. For federal action and the AAU, see Joseph M. Turrini's "The Federal Government and the Amateur Sports Act: From Mediation to Legislation, 1969–1978," in *The End of Amateurism in American Track and Field* (Urbana: Univ. of Illinois Press, 2010), 136–48.

4. Carl L. Reisner, "Tackling Intercollegiate Athletics: An Antitrust Analysis," *Yale Law Review* 87, no. 3 (January 1978): 655–79.

5. *National Collegiate Athletic Association v. Alston et al.*, Certiorari to the United States Court of Appeals for the Ninth Circuit, Supreme Court of the United States, No. 20-512, June 21, 2021; and *Robert Geathers v. NCAA* and *Hamlin v. NCAA* lawsuits, Court of Common Pleas in South Carolina, County of Darlington, for the First Judicial Circuit, Civil Action, No. 2019-CP-00516.

Introduction

1. "Rice Owls School History," SportsReference.com (website), accessed September 30, 2020, https://www.sports-reference-com/cfb/schools/rice/index.html.

2. As an example, Byers assailed top administrators in his NCAA for "sloppy work" during the 1968 NCAA conference. He told them, "If you don't like the way this is working, don't let the door knob hit you in the ass on the way out." David Pickle,

"Working with Byers," NCAA *Champion*, Winter 2009, accessed March 13, 2021, https://www.ncaa.org/static/champion/working-with-byers.

3. There were charges that Byers's son, who had earlier been asked by Byers to help run the ranch, had mismanaged the property and embezzled from his father. Marianne M. Jennings, *Real Estate Law* (Boston: Cengage, 2017), 347.

4. "Professor Byers has Left Washburn Law to Help Take Care of Her Father's Family Business," accessed March 5, 2021, https://www.washburnlaw.edu.

5. The temperature in Kansas dropped from 50 degrees to below zero Fahrenheit from December 14, 2008, to December 17, 2008. See Weather Underground (website), accessed December 1, 2020, https://www.wunderground.com/calendar/us/ks/manhattan.

6. *Bouton v. Byers*, No. 109025 (Court of Appeals of Kansas, decided March 14, 2014), FindLaw (website), accessed December 1, 2020, https://caselaw.findlaw.com/ks-court-of-appeals/1660266.html.

7. Byers sold all but ten acres of the ranch in 2011 for $1.2 million and signed a trust that upon his death his assets would be distributed to charitable foundations to provide college scholarships. Bouton was disinherited. *Bouton v. Byers.*

8. Joe Nocera, "The Man Who Built the N.C.A.A.," *New York Times*, May 30, 2015, p. A19.

9. The manuscript was published, after attempts to have it published by a visible commercial press, by the Univ. of Michigan Press as *Unsportsmanlike Conduct: Exploiting College Athletes*, in 1995. Byers told me that the commercial presses wanted him to make the book even more sensational, something I thought he had already done. I wrote for the book flap, "A wonderful book. It will be read well into the twenty-first century." After three decades, I agree on both levels.

10. See my letter to the Univ. of Illinois Press about Byers's manuscript indicating that I had read his manuscript in 1990. I told the director of Illinois Press, Richard Wentworth, that "Byers has wonderful insight into the problems of college sports today." I also sent one page of my six-page Michigan review. Ronald A. Smith to Richard L. Wentworth, Champaign, IL, October 5, 1993, in author's possession.

11. "NCAA Constitution and Bylaws," *Proceedings of the Intercollegiate Athletic Association of the United States* [NCAA in 1910], December 29, 1906, pp. 33–36. Article VIII of the constitution began, "The Colleges and Universities enrolled in this Association severally agree to take control of student athletic sports . . . ," 31.

12. *Proceedings of the Intercollegiate Athletic Association of the United States* [NCAA], December 29, 1906, pp. 8, 10, 28; and December 28, 1907, pp. 6, 11, 23, 24, 40.

13. Luther Gulick gave a lengthy talk at the 1907 NCAA convention titled "Amateurism." As a Progressive and a promoter of Muscular Morality and amateurism, he said that football "cannot stand or fall because of the number of knees sprained or the number of hearts dilated or even the number of lives lost—because lives are lost in a far larger way and with far more direful results through social and moral demoralization. . . ." *Proceedings of the Intercollegiate Athletic Association of the United States* [NCAA], December 28, 1907, pp. 40–46, esp. 40.

14. *Proceedings of the Intercollegiate Athletic Association of the United States* [NCAA], December 29, 1906, pp. 33–36.

15. As quoted by Greg Echlin, "Walter Byers Legacy Virtually Ignored at NCAA Office," KCUR, August 28, 2012, KCUR website, accessed June 9, 2022, https://www.kcur.org/sports/2012-08-28/walter-byers-legacy-virtually-ignored-at-ncaa-office.

Chapter 1

1. A. B. Hart, "Evils of Organized Athletics in American Colleges," *Current History* 31 (December 1929): 558. Hart received his PhD from the Univ. of Freiburg in German, became a distinguished Harvard professor for forty-three years, and was president of both the American Historical Association and the American Political Science Association, in addition to being the Harvard dissertation advisor of the famed W. E. B. Du Bois. He also loved sports.

2. At the first meeting of the NCAA, on December 28, 1905, it was resolved that "the conference recommend that the academic authorities of the country hold themselves as ultimately responsible for the conduct of athletics within their own respective institutions," "*Springfield* [MA] *Republican*, December 29, 1905, p. 3. See also Palmer E. Pierce, NCAA President, to President E. A. Alderman, Univ. of Virginia, 19 November 1906, VI, Box 4, Folder 34, President Alderman Papers, Univ. of Virginia Archives; and Intercollegiate Athletic Association of the United States, *Proceedings* [later NCAA *Proceedings*], 1906, pp. 31, 34; and 1909, p. 34.

3. Intercollegiate Athletic Association of the United States, *Proceedings*, 1906–1908, *passim*.

4. *New York Times*, December 14, 1935, p. 20; and NCAA *Proceedings*, January 10, 1948, pp. 188–96.

5. NCAA *Proceedings*, January 10, 1948, p. 188. Emphasis added.

6. The NCAA's H. C. Willett of the Univ. of Southern California noted, a half year before the end of World War II, that air travel would cost less and allow athletes to be away less from class. *NCAA Proceedings*, January 12, 1945, p. 150.

7. Jack F. Sheehan and Louis Honig, *The Games of California and Stanford* (San Francisco: Commercial Publishing Company, 1900), 88; and Robin Lester, *Stagg's University: The Rise, Decline, and Fall of Big-Time Football at Chicago* (Urbana: Univ. of Illinois Press, 1995), 28–30.

8. "Hesburgh: From Trains to Planes," Department of Athletics, Univ. of Notre Dame (website), accessed September 7, 2021, https://125.nd.edu/moments/hesburgh-from-trains-to-planes.

9. Ava Wallace, "Before There Was U-Conn, the Wayland Baptist Queens Ruled the Basketball Court," *Washington Post*, March 27, 2018, accessed September 7, 2021, https://washingtonpost.com/sports/colleges/before-there-was-u-conn.

10. "Sports, Early Diet of Radio, Nourish Television, *Business Week*, June 29, 1946, p. 18; and Ed Papazin, *Medium Rare: The Evolutionary Worship and Impact of Commercial Television* (New York: Media Dynamics, 1989), 1.

11. For greater detail, see Ronald A. Smith, "Notre Dame Chooses Commercial TV" and "Penn Challenges the NCAA and the Ivy League," in *Play-by-Play: Radio, Television, and Big-Time College Sport* (Baltimore: Johns Hopkins Univ. Press, 2001), 61–78.

12. "Byers Airs TV Stand of NCAA," *Chicago Daily Tribune*, April 20, 1951, p. C1. Tom Hamilton and "Tug" Wilson, NCAA Secretary-Treasurer of the NCAA, were in Washington, DC, conferring with Justice Department officials about concerns for limiting TV.

13. "Television in Education, Report of Educational Television Programs Institute, April 1952," Folder "Television 1951–July 1955," President Holt Papers, Univ. of Tennessee Archives; and *New York Times*, November 14, 1952, p. L29.

14. For an expanded version, see Smith, "The NCAA Experimental Year," in *Play-by-Play*, 72–78.

15. Walter Byers memorandum re: WGN-TV, July 29, 1949, #141-84-5, Ohio State Univ. Archives.

16. *NCAA Proceedings*, December 30, 1939, p. 117. Some can claim that the NCAA lost money on its first national basketball championship, for the report of the NCAA treasurer showed expenses of $2,573 for the basketball tournament (see p. 116).

17. Chad Carlson, *Making March Madness: The Early Years of the NCAA, NIT, and College Basketball Championships, 1922–1951* (Fayetteville: Univ. of Arkansas Press, 2017), 217, 228.

18. *NCAA Proceedings*, January 13, 1951, p. 241. His superior, Kenneth "Tug" Wilson, was paid $2,500 as secretary-treasurer of the NCAA. The total NCAA operating expense for 1950 was $105,000, with tournament receipts accounting for about $70,000 of the budget. Tug Wilson was originally hired as commissioner of the Big Ten for $15,000 with a six-year contract in 1945.

19. *NCAA Proceedings*, January 9, 1948, pp. 118–38.

20. *NCAA Proceedings*, January 9, 1948, p. 128, 136.

21. Eastern College Athletic Conference Minutes, December 17, 1947, p. 64, ECAC Offices.

22. *New York Times*, August 27, 1947, p. 27; and *Chicago Daily Tribune*, August 27, 1947, p. 27. Byers only received the position after Bill Reed turned down a similar position to become administrative assistant to Senator Homer Ferguson of Michigan.

23. For a fuller account of TV networks and expansion, see Smith, *Play-by-Play*, 54–61.

24. "Television Policy of the Big 10 Conference, 18 April 1950," 9/3-1/20, Folder "Television, 1947–50," Director of Athletics Papers, Ohio State Univ. Archives.

25. Keith Dunnavant, *The Fifty-Year Seduction: How Television Manipulated College Football, From the Birth of the Modern NCAA to the Creation of the BCS* (New York: St. Martin's Press, 2004). See chap. 2, "In His Image."

26. Stanley Cohen, *The Game They Played* (New York: Carroll & Graf, 2001); Albert J. Figone, "Gambling and College Basketball: The Scandal of 1951," *Journal of Sport History* 16 (Spring 1989): 44–61; James Blackwell, *On Brave Old Army Team: The Cheating Scandal that Rocked the Nation, West Point, 1951* (Navato, CA: Presidio, 1996); Ronald A. Smith, "The William and Mary Athletic Scandal of 1951: Governance and the Battle for Academic and Athletic Integrity," *Journal of Sport History* 34 (Fall 2007):

353–73; "Caught by the Camera," *Life Magazine* 31 (November 5, 1951): 121–34; and *New York Times*, October 22, 1951, p. 28.

27. *NCAA Proceedings*, January 8, 1953, pp. 121–23.

28. Quoted in Joseph N. Crowley, *In the Arena: The NCAA's First Century* (Indianapolis: NCAA, 2006), 84.

29. *NCAA Proceedings*, January 9, 1953, p. 270.

30. President Cloide Brehm, seventeen-page transcript of "Meeting with Administrative Group," January 20, 1955, Box 2, Folder "Employment of Bowden Wyatt," President Brehm Papers, Univ. of Tennessee Archives.

31. Kevin Edds, "Football's Founding Fathers: Today's College Game Shaped by UVA," *University of Virginia Magazine*, Fall 2011, accessed June 14, 2022, https://uvamagazine.org/articles/footballs_founding_fathers; and *John S. Watterson, College Football: History, Spectacle, Controversy* (Baltimore: Johns Hopkins Univ. Press, 2000), 209–18.

32. Walter Byers, *Unsportsmanlike Conduct: Exploiting College Athletes* (Ann Arbor: Univ. of Michigan Press, 1995), 60–61.

33. Donald K. Brazeal, "NCAA Staffers Get No-Interest Loans," *Washington Post*, November 19, 1985, accessed September 21, 2020, https://www.washingtonpost.com/archive/politics/1985/11/19/ncaa; "Executive Director Discusses Media Reports on Loan Programs," *NCAA News* 22, no. 45 (December 18, 1985): 13–24; and "NCAA Gave Execs Sweetheart Loans," *Chicago Tribune*, November 20, 1985, p. C2. At the time, Byers's salary was $78,450.

34. Byers, *Unsportsmanlike Conduct*, 68.

35. Lynn St. John Report, "Second District Report," *NCAA Proceedings*, December 29, 1939, pp. 34–35.

36. *NCAA Proceedings*, January 11, 1957, pp. 293–98.

37. Virgil M. Hancher to President E. B. Fred, Wisconsin and other Big Ten presidents, March 19, 1957, Box 274, Folder "Ath. Scholarships," Series 4/16/1, E. B. Fred General Correspondence File, 1956–57, Univ. of Wisconsin Archives.

38. Later, Byers wrote "A Personal Viewpoint: Assault on Amateurism," *NCAA News* 6, no. 4 (April 1969): 2. Byers stated that the NCAA should not yield to "some harried administrators, a few win-conscious coaches and the professionals themselves who have no regard or respect for amateur principles." In the 2000s, Byers noted that "aid not tied to need led to 'pay for play.'" *Amicus* Brief, "Alston v. NCAA and Five Conferences," Case3:cv-01011-EDL (United States District Court North District of California March 5, 2014), p. 40.

39. *NCAA Proceedings*, January 6, 1954, pp. 300–301. Under a strict interpretation, I would have been made ineligible for Northwestern's basketball and baseball teams in the mid-1950s for selling football programs at NU, a privilege given only to athletes.

40. NCAA *Proceedings*, January 9, 1957, p. 208.

41. *NCAA Proceedings*, January 7, 1958, p. 5 of Constitution. The NCAA's opposition paying of athletes for the "names, likenesses, and images" was finally overturned in the

celebrated case of *O'Bannon v. NCAA*, 802 F3d, 1049, Nos. 14-16601, 14-17068 (9th Cir. 2015).

42. *NCAA Proceedings*, January 9, 1959, p. 251.

Chapter 2

1. President Thurston Davies of Colorado College did refer to "student athletes" without the hyphen in a 1946 address to the NCAA, stating, "If we are to have student athletes. . . ." President Thurston J. Davies, Address to NCAA, *NCAA Proceedings*, January 9, 1946, p. 118.

2. W. E. Page, *Collector of Internal Revenue v. Regents of the University System of Georgia*, U.S. Circuit Court of Appeals, Fifth Circuit, No. 8466, "Brief for the Appellee" (1935), Georgia Tech Archives. It was claimed that athletic contests are an "integral part of the program of public education."

3. "Review of Football Tax by Supreme Court Seen," *New York Times*, January 10, 1937, p. 72.

4. R. O. Baumbach, Chair, NCAA Tax Campaign, to state chairmen of NCAA Tax Campaign, 3 April 1954, Folder "Unprocessed Ath. Dept. Papers on Fed. Admissions Tax—NCAA," Univ. of Alabama Archives.

5. John D. Colombo, "The NCAA, Tax Exemption and College Athletics," *Illinois Public Law Research Papers*, No. 08-08, 2010, SSRN (website), accessed June 22, 2022, https://ssrn.com/abstract=1336727.

6. "Internal Revenue Code of 1954," Report of the Committee on Finance, United States Senate to Accompany H. R. 8300, a Bill to Revise the Internal Revenue Laws of the United States, 83d Congress, 2d Session, Rep. No. 1622 (June 18, 1954). As late as 1974, the Internal Revenue Service concluded that television revenue from football and basketball "is not subject to the tax imposed under section 511" of the tax code. "Internal Revenue Service National Office Technical Advice Memorandum Regarding Tax Payer NCAA," Filed at NCAA, April 11, 1974, in Walter Byers Papers, Vol. CXIX, Folder "Legal: 1/77–6/77," NCAA Headquarters.

7. John S. Haller, "Industrial Accidents—Worker Compensation Laws and the Medical Response," *Western Journal of Medicine* 148 (March 1988): 341–48.

8. For a lengthy account of the 1905 football crisis, see John S. Watterson, "Football's Longest Season: The Fall of 1905" and "Football in Crisis, 1905 to 1906," in *College Football: History, Spectacle, Controversy* (Baltimore: Johns Hopkins Univ. Press, 2000), 64–98.

9. Gregory P. Guyton, "A Brief History of Workers' Compensation," *Iowa Orthopaedic Journal* 19 (1999): 106–10, accessed July 18, 2019, https://www.ncbi.nim.nih.gov/pmc/articles/PMC1999620.

10. *NCAA Proceedings*, December 28, 1916, p. 118.

11. *University of Denver v. Nemeth*, 257 P.2d 423 (1953), No. 16945 (Supreme Court of Colorado April 20, 1953).

12. Byers notes the importance of the Dennison case in *Unsportsmanlike Conduct,* 69–70.

13. Article III, Principles for the Conduct of Intercollegiate Athletics, "Constitution of the National Collegiate Athletic Association," *NCAA Proceedings*, January 11, 1956, Appendix, pp. 3–6.

14. I found a previous use of the term "student athlete" by the president of Colorado College, Thurston J. Davies, when, at the NCAA conference in 1946, he stated, "Institutions can set up systems of scholarship awards which will enable them to have their teams composed of student athletes." *NCAA Proceedings*, January 9, 1946, p. 119.

15. *NCAA Proceedings*, January 13, 1973, p. 123; Byers, *Unsportsmanlike Conduct,* 164; Crowley, *In the Arena*, 92. Four-year athletic scholarships became one-year renewable contracts in 1973. The change was voted on with no discussion. It was said to be a cost-cutting measure but was done in actuality to give coaches greater control of athletes during the turmoil of the Vietnam War and civil rights disturbances.

16. Article III, Principles for the Conduct of Intercollegiate Athletics, "Constitution of the National Collegiate Athletic Association," *NCAA Proceedings*, January 11, 1956, Appendix, pp. 3–6

17. Byers, *Unsportsmanlike Conduct,* 74–75.

18. John C. Weistart and Cym H. Lowell, *The Law of Sports* (Indianapolis: Bobbs-Merrill, 1979), 13–14.

19. *University of Denver v. Nemeth.*

20. From the "Principle of Educational Objective," *NCAA Proceedings*, January 9, 1959, p. 251.

21. *NCAA v. Shawne Alston,* Nos. 20-512 and 20-520 on Writs of Certiorari to the United States Court of Appeals for the Ninth Circuit (Supreme Court of the United States June 21, 2021).

22. "NCAA Constitution," December 14, 2021, passed on January 20, 2022, accessed on June 23, 2022, https://www.ncaaorg.s3.amazonaws.com/governance/ncaa/constitution/NCAAGov_Constitution121421.pdf. While not one use of the word "amateur" was found in the new constitution, the Byers phrase "student-athletes" was used fifty-three times in the twenty-page document, including four times in the opening paragraph.

23. President Robert F. Ray and Secretary-Treasurer Everett D. Barnes to faculty representatives and athletic directors, December 21, 1964, Unorganized Walter Byers Papers, Folder "Workman Compensation," NCAA Headquarters; and *Van Horn v. Industrial Acc. Com,* 219 Cal.App.2d 457 (1963), 33 Cal. Rptr.169, Docket No. 27105 (Court of Appeals of California, Second District, Division One, August 21, 1963). To me, hearing the word "student-athlete" grates my sensitivities nearly as much as hearing such terms as "red man" applied to Native Americans or "nigger" to African Americans, before it became probably the most offensive word in English.

24. *Fred Rensing v. Indiana State University Board of Trustees,* 444, N.E.2nd 1170 (1983) (Supreme Court of Indiana, February 9, 1983); and Ray Yasser, "Are Scholarship

Athletes at Big-Time Programs Really University Employees?—You Bet They Are!" *National Black Law Journal* 9, no. 1 (1984): 65–78.

25. Allen L. Sack, "*Counterfeit Amateurs: An Athlete's Journey Through the Sixties to the Age of Academic Capitalism* (University Park: Penn State Univ. Press, 2008), 115.

26. Byers, *Unsportsmanlike Conduct*, 276.

27. *Waldrop v. Texas Employers Insurance Association*, No. 03-98-00053-CV (Court of Appeals of Texas, Austin, decided June 15, 2000).

28. Joe Drape, "College Football: A Question of Responsibility: Injured Player's Case Could Shake Up N.C.A.A.," *New York Times*, October 15, 1997, C1.

29. *Berger v. NCAA*, United States Court of Appeals, No. 16-1588 (7th Cir. 2016, decided December 5, 2016).

30. Judge David Hamilton Concurring Opinion, *Berger v. NCAA*.

31. Daily Tar Heel Staff, "The Daily Tar Heel Will No Longer Use the Term 'Student Athlete,'" *Daily Tar Heel*, August 9, 2020, accessed September 13, 2020, https://www.dailytarheel.com/article/2020/08/student-athlete-term. I have been writing about college athletics for over a half-century and to my knowledge have not used the term "student-athlete" (except in quotes) in any of my twelve books on sports. No one should use the term, including US Supreme Court justice Neil Gorsuch in a 9-0 decision against the NCAA in the summer of 2021. He should be criticized for using the term forty-three times in a thirty-five-page decision.

32. Taylor Branch, email message to author, March 8, 2021.

33. "Statement of Edward R. Garvey Before the Senate Judiciary Committee," March 17, 1983, Box 18, "College Football Association," President Davison Papers, Univ. of Georgia Archives.

34. Ernie Chambers, "A Nebraska Legislator's Proposal: Pay the Players," *New York Times*, February 22, 1981, p. S2.

35. Walter Byers to Martin Massengale, February 3, 1984, Box 218, Folder "Athletics 1984–85," Chancellor's Central Files, Univ. of Nebraska Archives.

36. Byers to Massengale, February 8, 1984, and M. Massengale to Walter Byers, February 8, 1984, both in Box 218, Folder "Athletics 1984–85," Chancellor's Central Files, Univ. of Nebraska Archives.

37. Nebraska governor Orr vetoed another bill pushed by Ernie Chambers in 1988. It called for Nebraska football players to receive money as stipends. *Omaha World-Herald*, April 16, 1988, p. 14.

38. Keith A. Haskins, "Pay for Play: Should Scholarship Athletes Be Included Within State Compensation Systems?" *Loyola Los Angeles Entertainment Law Review* 12 (1992): 441–75.

Chapter 3

1. For an accurate history of the NFL, see Richard Crepeau, *NFL Football: A History of America's New National Pastime* (Urbana: Univ. of Illinois Press, 2020), esp. chap. 1, "The First Pros."

2. "Eight Notre Dame Players Confess," *New York Times*, January 31, 1922, p. 24; "College Stars Hired When Town Attempts to Clean Out Another," *Anaconda Standard*, January 29, 1922, p. 15; and Bob Braunwart and Bob Carroll, "The Taylorville Scandal," *Coffin Corner* 2, no. 6 (1980), accessed July 10, 2020, https://profootballresearchers.org/coffin-corner80s/02/06/034.pdf.

3. Robert E. Gay, "A History of the American Football Coaches Association" (PhD diss., Univ. of North Carolina, Chapel Hill, 1971), 36–38, 41. Major Charles Daly, former player at Harvard and West Point, was at West Point when he began inquiry about coaches meeting after the 1920 season. The first "official" meeting was December 7, 1921, in New York City's Astor Hotel.

4. *NCAA Proceedings*, December 29, 1921, p. 43, 45.

5. "Eight Notre Dame Players Confess," *New York Times*, January 31, 1922, p. 24.

6. Winton U. Solberg, *Creating the Big Ten: Courage Corruption, and Commercialism* (Urbana: Univ. of Illinois Press, 2018), 86–108.

7. John M. Carroll, *Red Grange and the Rise of Modern Football* (Urbana: Univ. of Illinois Press, 1999), 77–106.

8. *NCAA Proceedings*, January 9, 1948, p. 70.

9. David M. Nelson, *Anatomy of a Game: Football, the Rules, and the Men Who Made the Game* (Newark: Univ. of Delaware Press, 1994), 298; and Byers, *Unsportsmanlike Conduct*, 99.

10. "Resolution of NCAA Council" (1952), Box 4, Folder "Correspondence 1953," Fritz Crisler Papers, Michigan Historical Collection, Bentley Historical Library, Univ. of Michigan (hereafter cited as Crisler Papers).

11. Walter Byers to Will Grimsley, Associated Press, January 28, 1953, Box 4, Folder "Correspondence 1953," Crisler Papers.

12. Walter Byers, "A Personal Viewpoint: Football Feudalism," *NCAA News* 6, no. 1 (January 1969): 2.

13. Paul F. Dietzel to Walter Byers, *NCAA News* 6, no. 2 (February 1969): 2.

14. Walter Byers, "A Personal Viewpoint: Assault on Amateurism," *NCAA News* 6, no. 4 (April 1969): 2. When Dietzel coached at Louisiana State Univ. in 1958, he won a national championship with the help of the so-called "Chinese Bandits," a third team, mostly of underclassmen, who came in only on defense.

15. College Football Association Minutes, June 16, 1978, Box 19, Folder "CFA, June 16–18, 1978," President Davison Papers, Univ. of Georgia Archives.

16. Tex Maule, "The Best Football Game Ever Played," *Sports Illustrated*, January 5, 1959, 8–12; and Roone Arledge, *Roone: A Memoir* (New York: Harper Collins, 2004), 29.

17. *New York Times*, November 14, 1959, p. 15; and "Background Information on Football TV Legislation," Memo, ca. March 3, 1964, Box "TV: Legislation, 1965–1968," Folder "Television: Legislation 1964," Walter Byers Papers, NCAA Headquarters. The act also applied to antitrust exemptions for professional basketball, baseball, and hockey.

18. Walter Byers telegram to fifteen Senators, February 14, 1964, Box "Television: Legislation, 1965–1968," Folder "Television: Legislation 1964," Walter Byers Papers, NCAA Headquarters.

19. "Recommended NCAA Football Television Plan for 1955," March 11, 1955, Box 2, Folder "Television & Athletics," President Brehm Papers, Univ. of Tennessee Archives. The recommendation read: "Friday night, Saturday night, and Holidays (except Thanks[giving] may be telecast if not violating appearance rule."

20. Walter Byers to William Reed, June 25, 1964, Folder "T.V.," Unorganized Walter Byers Papers, NCAA Headquarters.

21. Harold Keith to Walter Byers, May 18, 1965, Folder "Pro-College Relations, Walter Byers Papers, NCAA Headquarters.

22. Robert C. Edwards to Walter Byers, January 6, 1965, Folder "Pro-College Relations," Walter Byers Papers, NCAA Headquarters.

23. Gordon S. White Jr., "N.C.A.A. Plans to Take Action on Premature Football Signings," *New York Times*, January 4, 1965, p. 41.

24. Walter Byers to NCAA Legislative Committee, June 5, 1965, Folder "T.V.," Unorganized Walter Byers Papers, NCAA Headquarters.

25. "Rozelle Sees Flaw in Specter Antitrust Bill," *NCAA News* 20, no. 22 (June 1, 1983): 12; "Statement of Edward R. Garvey, Executive Director of the NFL Players Association Before the Senate Judiciary Committee, March 17, 1983, Box 18, "College Football Association," President Davison Papers, Univ. of Georgia Archives; and memorandum from Chuck Neinas to CFA Membership, March 14, 1983, Box 18, "College Football Association," President Davison Papers, Univ. of Georgia Archives.

26. "Byers Criticizes NFL for Its Position on Supplemental Draft," *NCAA News* 24, no. 30 (September 2, 1987): 2.

27. Arledge, *Roone*, 86.

28. Byers, *Unsportsmanlike Conduct*, 107.

29. "N.C.A.A. Group Set to Weigh TV Data," *New York Times*, December 15, 1951, p. 172; and Jack Falla, *NCAA: The Voice of College Sports* (Mission, KS: NCAA, 1981), 104.

30. Arledge, *Roone*; and Travis Vogan, "The 'Almost Broadcasting Company' and the Birth of ABC Sports," in *ABC Sports: The Rise and Fall of Network Sports Television* (Berkeley: Univ. of California Press, 2018).

31. *NCAA v. Board of Regents of the University of Oklahoma*, 468 U.S. 85 (1984).

32. Marc Gunther, *The House that Roone Built: The Inside Story of ABC News* (Boston: Little, Brown, 1994) 8–29; and Jim Spence, *Up Close and Personal: The Inside Story of Network Television Sports* (New York: Atheneum, 1988), 51–91. See also, Ronald A. Smith, "Roone Arledge and the Influence of ABC-TV" in *Play-by-Play*, 102–13.

33. Much of this is revealed in the minutes of the NCAA Negotiations Committee for Television Rights of the Division I Basketball Tournament, Telephone Conference, November 7, 1968, Box "TV Comm 1978," Folder "TV Comm 1979, Jan–Feb," Walter Byers Papers, NCAA Headquarters.

34. NCAA Television Committee Minutes, April 4, 1967, NCAA Headquarters.

35. Walter Byers to William Flynn, NCAA television chairman, November 7, 1968, Vol. XLVII, Folder "TV: General 9/68–12/68," Walter Byers Papers, NCAA Headquarters.

36. Walter Byers to Roone Arledge, March 13, 1971, Vol. CXLIX, Folder "TV: Football, 1/71–6/71, Walter Byers Papers, NCAA Headquarters.

37. Byers, *Unsportsmanlike Conduct*, 266.

38. Spence, *Up Close and Personal*, 132.

39. As late as 2019, there were comments about New Yorkers being "often stereotyped as being self-important and acting like the world revolves around them." Michael Kranz, "10 of the Biggest Cultural Differences Between the Midwest and the East Coast," *Business Insider*, August 7, 2019, accessed July 28, 2021, https://www.businessinsider.com/differences-between-midwest-and-east-coast-2019-8.

40. NCAA Television Committee Minutes, May 4, 1966, NCAA Headquarters.

41. "TV Committee's Straw Votes, March 11–12, 1969," clipping, Vol. XLVII, Folder "TV: General 1/69–4/69," Walter Byers Papers, NCAA Headquarters.

42. Walter Byers to Roone Arledge, June 6, 1969, Box "TV: Leg., 1965–68," Folder "TV: General 5/60–6/69, Walter Byers Papers, NCAA Headquarters.

43. Charles Stanford, ABC Vice President, to George Gangwere, NCAA Counsel, August 13, 1981, Box "TV Contracts, 1981–82," Folder "TV Contracts, 1981–82," Walter Byers Papers, NCAA Headquarters.

44. NCAA Television Committee Minutes, July 1, 1963, December 17, 1963, March 10, 1966, all at NCAA Headquarters.

45. For a more in-depth discussion of TV announcers, see Smith, "Television Announcer's Role in Football Promotion," *Play-by-Play*, 122–33.

46. Forest Evashevski to Walter Byers, September 5, 1971, Vol. CI, Folder "TV: Football, 10/71–12/71," Walter Byers Papers, NCAA Headquarters.

47. It is generally recognized that the pre-Romans on the Italian peninsula, the Etruscans, developed metal trumpets, which were further developed by Roman militarists.

48. Professor Richard Crepeau of the Univ. of Central Florida emailed me that the Baltimore Colts had a marching band, founded in 1947, and that the Boston Redskins (later Washington) had a band in the 1930s. Crepeau, email message to author, March 17, 2023.

49. NCAA Television Committee Minutes, February 1, 1967, NCAA Headquarters.

50. "NCAA Asks Stadium Ban on Steelers," *Pittsburgh Post-Gazette*, February 20, 1958, p. 1. Professional football had used college stadiums several times from the 1950s through the 1970s, including stadiums at Arizona State, Boston College, Boston Univ., Clemson, Harvard, Miami, Minnesota, Tulane, Vanderbilt, Washington, and Yale.

51. *Chicago Tribune*, April 21, 1970, p. C1; July 22, 1970, p. D1; August 12, 1970, p. E1; September 28, 1970, p. C1; March 9, 1971, p. B1; "Michigan Still No to Bears—Canham," March 17, 1971, p. C1; and "Byers' Letter Put Pressure on Big 10," March 28, 1971, p. B3.

52. R. Kenneth Fairman, Princeton athletic director, to Carroll H. Cook, ABC Sports, 3 April 1970, Vol. CXLIX, Folder "TV: Football, 1/70–6/70," Walter Byers Papers, NCAA Headquarters.

53. "Eagles Pro Football Team to Play 1958 Home Games in Penn's Franklin Field," *New York Times*, January 21, 1958, p. 39.

54. *Chicago Tribune*, March 17, 1971, p. C1.

55. "History of the Pro Football Hall of Fame," Pro Football Hall of Fame (website), accessed July 20, 2022, https://www.profootballhof.com/visit/hall-of-fame-history/.

56. "History of the National Football Foundation," National Football Foundation (website), accessed July 19, 2022, https://footballfoundation.org/sports/2018/7/26/history.aspx.

57. "Ground Breaking for Football Hall of Fame Building," *New York Times*, October 16, 1967, p. 214; and *Wikipedia*, "College Football Hall of Fame," last edited August 21, 2024, 02:24 (UTC), https://en.wikipedia.org/wiki/College_Football_Hall_of_Fame.

58. Tom Hamilton, "Tentative Proposal to Athletic Directors for National Football Foundation," April 26, 1971, Vol. CXLIX, Folder "TV: Football, 1/71–6/71," Walter Byers Papers, NCAA Headquarters.

59. The Kings Island Hall closed in 1992. A new site in South Bend, Indiana, opened in 1995 and closed in 2012 because of lack of attendance. The hall reappeared in Atlanta in 2014 under new chairman Archie Manning, former college and professional quarterback.

60. William Flynn, Boston College athletic director, to Walter Byers, January 20, 1983; and Byers to Richard Kazmaier, president of the National Football Foundation and Hall of Fame, February 7, 1983, both in Box "FV, FB, 1986," Folder "TV, FB, 1/83–6/83," Walter Byers Papers, NCAA Headquarters.

61. Quoted by Gordon S. White Jr., "Penn State-Nebraska the Classic Opener," *New York Times*, August 29, 1983, p. C9.

62. "History of the National Football Foundation.".

63. Arledge, *Roone*, 86.

Chapter 4

1. For an understanding of the Cold War and the impact on sport, two volumes are worthy of perusing: Kevin B. Witherspoon and Toby C. Rider, eds., *Defending the American Way of Life: Sport, Culture, and the Cold War (*Fayetteville: Univ. of Arkansas Press, 2018); and Toby C. Rider, *Cold War Games: Propaganda, the Olympics, and U.S. Foreign Policy* (Urbana: Univ. of Illinois Press, 2016).

2. *NCAA Proceedings*, January 11, 1961, pp. 151–54.

3. *NCAA Proceedings*, January 7, 1959, pp. 142–44.

4. Anthony Moretti, "New York Times Coverage of the Soviet Union's Entrance into the Olympic Games," *Sport History Review* 38 (2007): 55–72; and Allen Guttmann, "The Cold War and the Olympics," *International Journal* 43, no. 4 (Autumn 1988): 557–58.

5. As quoted in Neil Amdur, "Officials Decry Idea of Olympic Boycott," *New York Times*, January 6, 1980, p. S1.

6. Stephen R. Wenn, "A Suitable Policy of Neutrality? FDR and the Question of American Participation in the 1936 Olympics," *International Journal of History of Sport* 8, no. 3 (1991): 319–35; and Thomas M. Hunt, "Countering the Soviet Threat in the Olympic Medals Race: The Amateur Sports Act of 1978 and American Athletics Policy Reform," *International Journal of History of Sport* 24, no. 6 (2007): 796–818.

7. Walter Byers to Roone Arledge, December 19, 1977, Box "TV Comm. 1978," Folder "TV Comm. 1978," Walter Byers Papers, NCAA Headquarters.

8. Roone Arledge to Walter Byers, January 13, 1978, Vol. CXLIV, Folder "TV, ABC, 1979," Walter Byers Papers, NCAA Headquarters; and Byers, *Unsportsmanlike Conduct*, 140–41. Byers later commented that "We were after exposure and Nielsen ratings for college football: I was as competitive and combative as a football coach."

9. Michael Oriard, *Bowled Over: Big-Time College Football from the Sixties to the BCS Era* (Chapel Hill: Univ. of North Carolina Press, 2009), 46.

10. "A Turning Point: Six Stories from the Dow Chemical Protests on Campus," Univ. of Wisconsin-Madison (website), accessed August 25, 2022, https://1967.wisc.edu/.

11. Walter Byers, "A Personal Viewpoint: Phony Plebiscites," *NCAA News* 6, no. 9 (October 1969): 15.

12. William J. Thompson, "Remembering the Rise and Fall of Spiro Agnew," *Baltimore Sun*, November 8, 2018, accessed August 25, 2022, https://www.baltimoresun.com/2018/11/08/remembering-the-rise-and-fall-of-spiro-agnew/.

13. Walter Byers, "A Personal Viewpoint: Freedom Fighters," *NCAA News* 7, no. 4 (April 1970): 2.

14. NCAA Television Committee Minutes, September 1–2, 1970, NCAA Headquarters; and Walter Byers to Forest Evashevski, NCAA TV Committee, 22 January 1970, NCAA Headquarters.

15. George H. Gangwere, NCAA Counsel, to Walter Byers, December 9, 1969, Box "TV: Leg., 1965–68," Folder "TV: General 7/69–8/69, Walter Byers Papers, NCAA Headquarters.

16. Stan Frankle, ABC Sports, to Walter Byers, October 8, 1970, Vol. CXLIII, Folder "TV, ABC, 1970," Walter Byers Papers, NCAA Headquarters.

17. Media clipping, *Variety*, July 7, 1971, Vol. CXLIII, Folder "TV, ABC, 1971," Walter Byers Papers, NCAA Headquarters.

18. Media clipping, *Variety*, July 7, 1971, Byers Papers.

19. See, for instance, Jerry Izenberg, *How Many Miles to Camelot? The All-American Sport Myth* (New York: Rinehart and Winston, 1972), 184.

20. Byers, *Unsportsmanlike Conduct*, 155.

21. Carlson, *Making March Madness*, 302.

22. For a lengthy account, see Lane Demas, "'A Fist That Was Very Much Intentional': Postwar Football in the Midwest and the 1951 Johnny Bright Scandal," in *Integrating the Gridiron: Black Civil Rights and American College Football* (New Brunswick, NJ: Rutgers Univ. Press, 2010), 49–71.

23. *NCAA Proceedings*, January 10, 1952, p. 39.

24. "Drake Quits Missouri Valley Conference: Action Grows Out of Injury to John Bright," *Chicago Daily Tribune*, November 18, 1951, p. C1.

25. "Why Are They Afraid?" *Chicago Defender*, November 10, 1951, p. 10.

26. Milton S. Katz and John B. McLendon Jr., *Breaking Through: The NAIA and the Integration of Intercollegiate Athletics in Post-World War II America* (Overland Park, KS: privately printed, 1988), 12–13, 39–46.

27. Milton S. Katz, *Breaking Through: John B. McLendon, Basketball Legend and Civil Rights Pioneer* (Fayetteville: Univ. of Arkansas Press, 2007), 65–83; and Katz and McLendon, *Breaking Through*, 12–13.

28. Katz, *Breaking Through*, 69.

29. Kevin F. Gotham, "Building the Troost Wall: School Segregation, Blockbusting, and the Racial Transitions of the Southeast Area," in *Race, Real Estate, and Uneven Development: The Kansas City Experience, 1900–2010*, 2nd ed. (Albany: State Univ. of New York Press, 2014), 95–123.

30. *NCAA Proceedings*, February 7, 1954, p. 108.

31. No action on Mack Greene's request was recorded in the next two meetings of the NCAA in the 1954 and 1955 *NCAA Proceedings*.

32. Byers, *Unsportsmanlike Conduct*.

33. Ron Gomez with Beryl Shipley, *Slam Dunked: The NCAA's Shameful Reaction to Athletic Integration in the Deep South* (Bloomington, IN: Wordclay, 2008), 36–37.

34. Gomez, *Slam Dunked*, 192–202.

35. Frank Deford, "Shipley Integrates USL," *Sports Illustrated*, October 11, 1976.

36. Gomez, *Slam Dunked*, 53–60.

37. Byers, *Unsportsmanlike Conduct*, 153; and Martin Duberman, *Paul Robeson: A Biography* (New York: Alfred A. Knopf, 1989).

38. Walter Byers, "A Personal Viewpoint: Soaring Seventies," *NCAA News* 7, no. 1 (January 1970): 2.

39. "Vietnam War Casualties by Race, Ethnicity and National Origin," American War Library (website), accessed September 17, 2022, https://americanwarlibrary.com/vietnam/vwc10.htm.

40. Crowley, *In the Arena*, 188–89.

41. Gordon S. White Jr., "Investigator for N.C.A.A. Under Fire," *New York Times*, November 8, 1977, p. 52.

42. Michael R. Lemov, *John Moss: People's Warrior* (Lanham, MD: Farleigh Dickenson Univ. Press, 2011), 73–95; and "Historical Highlights: The Freedom of Information Act, July 4, 1966," History, Art, and Archives, United States House of Representatives (website), accessed September 19, 2022, https://history.house.gov/HistoricalHighlight/Detail/15032443727.

43. *NCAA Enforcement Program: Hearings Before the Subcommittee on Oversight and Investigations, Committee on Interstate and Foreign Relations, House of Representatives, Ninety-fifth Congress, Second Session, April 18, 1978* (Washington, DC: US Government Printing Office, 1978), 598, 603.

44. President C. Peter Magrath, Univ. of Minnesota, to NCAA News Editor, 8 December 1976, *NCAA News* 4, no. 1 (January 15, 1977): 11; *NCAA Enforcement Program: Hearings*, 1325; and David Ridpath Testimony, *Due Process and the NCAA: Hearings Before the Subcommittee on the Constitution of the Committee on the Judiciary, House of Representatives, One Hundred Eighth Congress, Second Session, September 14, 2004* (Washington, DC: US Government Printing Office, 2004).

45. Barry Lorge, "Congressional Probe Eyes Alleged NCAA Abuses," *Washington Post*, December 11, 1977.

46. President C. Peter Magrath, Univ. of Minnesota, to NCAA News Editor, December 8, 1976, *NCAA News* 4, no. 1 (January 15, 1977): 11; "Memorandum, Case

No. 443, University of Nevada, Las Vegas," December 10, 1976; *NCAA Enforcement Program: Part 2, Hearings Before the Subcommittee on Oversight and Investigations of the Committee on Interstate and Foreign Commerce, House of Representatives, Ninety-Fifth Congress, Second Session, February 17 and 28; March 13 and 14; April 17 and 18; June 9; September 27 and 28; and October 4, 1978*; Beryl Shipley to Walter Byers, 4 January 1968, quoted in Gomez, *Slam Dunked*, 53–60; and *NCAA Enforcement Program: Hearings Before the House of Representatives, Subcommittee on Oversight and Investigations, Committee on Interstate and Foreign Relations, 18 April 1978.*

Chapter 5

1. *Harper's Weekly*, 1879, reproduced by John A. Lucas and Ronald A. Smith, *Saga of American Sport* (Philadelphia: Lea & Febiger, 1978), 275.

2. Diane Euston and Tim Reidy, "Dissecting the Troost Divide and Racial Segregation in Kansas City," *The Telegraph*, June 30, 2020, accessed September 19, 2021, https://martincitytelegraph.com/2020/06/30/dissecting-the-troost-divide-and-racial-segregation-in-kansas-city/; Kevin F. Gotham, "Building the Troost Wall: School Segregation, Blockbusting, and the Racial Transition of the Southeast Area," in *Race, Real Estate, and Uneven Development*, 95–123; and Van William Hutchinson, "Greater Kansas City and the Urban Crisis, 1830–1968" (PhD diss., Kansas State Univ., 2013), 134.

3. Roy Wilkins, *Standing Fast: The Autobiography of Roy Wilkins* (New York: Viking Press, 1982), 60, 84.

4. "Report of the President of Harvard College, 1897–1898," 16–17, Harvard Univ. Archives.

5. *Proceedings of the Intercollegiate Athletic Association of the United States* [NCAA], December 29, 1906, p. 33.

6. *Proceedings*, 34–36.

7. For a lengthy discussion of the Sanity Code, see Ronald A. Smith, "The NCAA and the Sanity Code: A National Reform Gone Wrong," in *Pay for Play*, 88–99.

8. Byers, *Unsportsmanlike Conduct*, 68.

9. Tim Cohane, "Let's Take the Hypocrisy Out of College Football," *Look*, December 1950, pp. 72–80.

10. Virgil M. Hancher to John A. Hannah, Michigan State president and other Big Ten presidents, athletic directors, and conference commissioner, February 11, 1957, Box 274, "Folder "Athletic Scholarships," Series 4/16/1, President E. B. Fred General Correspondence File, 1956–57, Univ. of Wisconsin Archives.

11. Byers, *Unsportsmanlike Conduct*, 338–39.

12. NCAA *Proceedings*, January 7, 1959, pp. 156–59.

13. NCAA *Proceedings*, January 7, 1959, p. 159.

14. The ACC's institutions were Clemson, Duke, Maryland, North Carolina, North Carolina State, South Carolina, Virginia, and Wake Forest.

15. Judy Nelson, "History of the ACC—Atlantic Coast Conference," Sports Team History (website), accessed September 22, 2022, https://sportsteamhistory.com

/history-of-the-acc-atlantic-coast-conference/; and Gerald Gurney, Donna A. Lopiano, and Andrew Zimbalist, *Unwinding Madness: What Went Wrong with College Sports and How to Fix It* (Washington, DC: Brookings Institution Press, 2017), 34.

16. NCAA *Proceedings*, January 7, 1963, p. 212.

17. Dan Coval and Carol A. Barr, "The Ties That Bind: Presidential Involvement with the Development of NCAA Division I Initial Eligibility Legislation," *Journal of Higher Education* 72 (July–August 2001): 414–52; and Robert F. Goheen to President Everett D. Barnes, NCAA, April 13, 1966, Series # 4, Box 1, Folder "Athletic Association," O. C. Aderhold Papers, Univ. of Georgia Archives.

18. Dan Jenkins, "It's One Point Six Pick Up Sticks," *Sports Illustrated*, March 21, 1966, pp. 33–34.

19. James H. Weaver to Walter Byers, March 30, 1967, Folder "Basketball," Unorganized Walter Byers Papers, NCAA Headquarters.

20. By 1970 there were, however, three Black Heisman trophy winners: Ernie Davis of Syracuse (1961), Mike Garrett of the Univ. of Southern California (1965), and O. J. Simpson of the Univ. of Southern California (1968). For a fuller account of Blacks in college sport, see David Wiggins, *Out of the Shadows: A Biographical History of African American Athletes* (Fayetteville: Univ. of Arkansas Press, 2008); *More Than a Game: A History of the African American Experience in Sport* (Lanham, MD: Roman & Littlefield, 2018); and "The Year of Awakening: Black Athletes, Racial Unrest, and the Civil rights Movement of 1968," and "The Future of College Athletics Is at Stake: Black Athletes and Racial Turmoil on Three Predominantly White University Campuses, 1968–1972," in David K. Wiggins, *Glory Bound: Black Athletes in a White America* (Syracuse, NY: Syracuse Univ. Press, 1997), 104–51.

21. David Squires, "In the 1960s, Michigan State Truly Helped Integrate College Football: The Spartans Won the 1966 National Championship with Black QB Jimmy Raye II," *Andscape* 6 (November 2019), accessed November 6, 2022, https://andscape.com/features/in-the-1960s-michigan-state-truly-helped-integrate-college-football/.

22. Quoted in Jenkins, "It's One Point Six Pick up Sticks," 33–34. See also Walter Byers statement in the NCAA First Media Seminar, January 24–26, 1966, Unorganized Walter Byers Papers, NCAA Headquarters.

23. Walter Byers to Carl E. Erickson, Kent State Univ. athletic director, 23 February 1966, Folder "AAHPER," Unorganized Walter Byers Papers, NCAA Headquarters.

24. Walter Byers to chairmen of Rules and Tournament Committee, 5 March 1966, Folder "1.6 Eligibility," Unorganized Walter Byers Papers, NCAA Headquarters.

25. "A. M. 'Tonto' Coleman address excerpts," Folder "Pro-College Relations," Unorganized Walter Byers Papers, NCAA Headquarters.

26. Affirmative action for college admission based on race was in existence until the US Supreme Court ruled it unconstitutional under the Fourteenth Amendment on June 29, 2023.

27. Charles Morgan Jr., Southern Regional Office, American Civil Liberties Union, to Harold Howe II, Commission of Education, Washington, DC, May 22, 1966, Series # 4, Box 1, Folder "Athletic Association," O. C. Aderhold Papers, Univ. of Georgia Archives.

28. NCAA *Proceedings*, January 13, 1973, pp. 146–47; James V. Koch, "A Troubled Cartel: The NCAA," *Law and Contemporary Problems* 18 (Winter 1973): 135–50, discusses two cases against the NCAA and its 1.600 rule, *Curtis v. NCAA* and *Parish v. NCAA*. See esp. p. 141.

29. Walter Byers Comments, *NCAA First Media Seminar*, January 24–26, 1966, p. 19, NCAA Headquarters: Byers, "A Personal Viewpoint: The Ironical Contradiction," *NCAA News* 5, no. 8 (September 1968): 2; and Byers "A Personal Viewpoint: Economic Morality," *NCAA News* 5, no. 11 (November 1968): 3.

30. Walter Byers, "A Personal Viewpoint: Signs of the Times," *NCAA News* 5, no. 10 (November 1970): 2.

31. Byers, *Unsportsmanlike Conduct*, 165, 167.

32. NCAA *Proceedings*, January 13, 1973, p. 149.

33. Vincent J. Dooley, "Response to Subjects Raised During Jan Kemp vs. Leroy Ervin—Virginia Trotter Court Case," January 31, 1986, Box "1968–70s," Ralph Beaird Papers, Univ. of Georgia Archives.

34. The Recount, "How Magic Johnson and Larry Bird's Rivalry Shook the NBA," *Yahoo!sports*, March 26, 2022, accessed October 24, 2022, https://www.yahoo.com/news/magic-johnson-larry-bird-rivalry-130000438.html.

35. For a lengthy discussion, see Smith, "Lowly Standards: Chaos in the Sports Yards," *Pay for Play*, 121–31.

36. Peter Golenbock, *Personal Fouls* (New York: Carroll & Graf, 1989), 5.

37. Brandon Robinson, "Golden State Warrior Player Goes from NBA to Crack House," *Heavy*, March 31, 2019, accessed October 20, 2022, heavy.com/ports/2019/03/golden-state-warriors-chris-washington.

38. Laura B. Randolph, "Dexter Manley's Incredible Story: How Did I Get Through School When I Couldn't Read?" *Ebony* 44, no. 12 (October 1989): 102–6.

39. *Kevin Ross v. Creighton University*, 957 F2d 410 (7th Cir. 1992).

40. Joe Paterno to John Oswald, "Athletic Candidates Submitted to J. W. Oswald for 1980 Admissions," Box 10290, Folder "Athletics Relating to Academics, Admission, Policies, Etc. 1979–1982-1," President Oswald Papers, Penn State Univ. Archives; and Ronald A. Smith, *Wounded Lions: Joe Paterno, Jerry Sandusky, and the Crises in Penn State Athletics* (Urbana: Univ. of Illinois Press, 2016) 106–8.

41. NCAA *Proceedings*, January 11, 1983, p. 104.

42. NCAA *Proceedings*, January 11, 1983, p. 110.

43. NCAA *Proceedings*, January 11, 1983, p. 104.

44. Paterno told NCAA delegates that Proposition 48 "is not a race problem. For 15 years we have had a race problem. We have raped a generation-and-a-half of young black athletes. We have taken kids and sold them on bouncing a ball and running with the football. . . . [academically] what we have now is not good enough. . . . If you want to go to a quality school and you want to compete, you are going to have to start to read a book; you are going to have to write, you are going to have to do things that you are not comfortable with. . . . They will take the challenge [of Proposition 48.]" NCAA *Proceedings*, January 11, 1983, pp. 115–17.

45. NCAA *Proceedings*, January 11, 1983, p. 124 and A-35. Joseph N. Crowley states that the vote was passed by a 52 percent majority, but there is no evidence for this vote in the *Proceedings*. See Crowley, *In the Arena*, 117.

46. Walter Byers, "A Personal Viewpoint: The Ironical Contradiction," *NCAA News* 5, no. 8 (September 1968): 2.

47. Robert Atwell to ACE Committee on Division One Intercollegiate Athletics, 10 March 1983, Box "Special Convention," Folder "Select Committee on American Concern in Higher Education," Walter Byers Papers, NCAA Archives.

48. Two important volumes with documented research on the divide between academic values and college athletics, for both men and women, are James L. Shulman and William G. Bowen, *The Game of Life: College Sports and Educational Values* (Princeton, NJ: Princeton Univ. Press, 2001); and William G. Bowen and Sarah A. Levin, *Reclaiming the Game: College Sports and Educational Values* (Princeton, NJ: Princeton Univ. Press, 2003).

49. Hugh C. Willett and Kenneth L. Wilson, "Byers Is Not 'National Commissioner,' Memo to NCAA Members," October 15, 1951, Box 4, Folder "NCAA 1951," President's Papers—1951, Univ. of Virginia Archives.

Chapter 6

1. "History," National Association of Commissions for Women (website), accessed November 2, 2021, https://www.nacw.org/history.html.

2. "Title IX, Education Amendments of 1972," Office of the Assistant Secretary for Administration and Management, United States Department of Labor (website), accessed January 1, 2016, https://www.dol.gov/agencies/oasam/centers-offices/civil-rights-center/statutes/title-ix.

3. Or, as Gladys Palmer wrote in 1940, shortly before Ohio State's "national" golf tournament took place: "A few individuals are opposed to all forms of [women's] intercollegiate athletics." "Girls Athletics," Acc. 84/94, 9/3-5a/8, Folder "Athletics: Girls: 1940s," Unprocessed Women's Athletics Papers, Ohio State Univ. Archives.

4. Ina E. Gittings, "Why Cramp Competition?" *Journal of Health and Physical Education* (January 1931): 54.

5. American women in Olympic swimming did better. Doris Duke Cromwell, heiress of the Duke tobacco money, contributed a half-million dollars to the American Olympic Committee to promote women's swimming. Ellen W. Gerber et al., *The American Woman in Sport* (Reading, MA: Addison-Wesley, 1974), 162–63.

6. NCAA *Proceedings*, January 11, 1961, pp. 251–54.

7. Less than a year after Sputnik was launched as the first artificial satellite around the Earth, the federal government passed the National Defense Education Act on September 2, 1958. Led by President Dwight Eisenhower, the NDEA poured millions of dollars into higher education, particularly in science and technology. I was a recipient of a NDEA Fellowship to fund my PhD program at the Univ. of Wisconsin. History, as a category to fund, was added to NDEA priorities in 1964. Arthur Trace's popular book

What Ivan Knows that Johnny Doesn't (New York: Random House, 1961) was a product of the Cold War and Soviet leadership.

8. NCAA *Proceedings*, January 12, 1962, p. 205.

9. NCAA *Proceedings*, April 25, 1963, p. 132; August 12, 1963, p. 144; and January 6, 1963, pp. 189, 197–99. It turns out that the United States Olympic Development Committee underwrote the women's institute in Oklahoma. See Ying Wushanley, *Playing Nice and Losing: The Struggle for Control of Women's Intercollegiate Athletics, 1960–2000* (Syracuse, NY: Syracuse Univ. Press, 2004), 34.

10. A particularly strong study of the AAU-NCAA fight over amateurism is Joseph M. Turrini, *The End of Amateurism in American Track and Field* (Urbana: Univ. of Illinois Press, 2010), esp. 18–30, 63–84, and 136–48.

11. For an analysis of the AAU-NCAA conflict influencing women's athletics see Wushanley, "The Impact of the AAU-NCAA Power Struggle on Women's Athletics" in *Playing Nice and Losing*, 29–32.

12. NCAA *Proceedings*, January 6, 1964, pp. 203–5.

13. NCAA *Proceedings*, January 6, 1964, p. 208; and January 11, 1967, p. 122.

14. "Ladies Locked Out as NCAA Remains Strictly for Men," *NCAA News*, 1, No. 2 (May 1964), 1.

15. Katherine Ley, "Increasing Opportunities for Girls' Sports," Box "Women's Athletics," Folder "Vol. LI," Walter Byers Papers, NCAA Archives.

16. Women physical educators for decades refused to use the term "athletics" as a pejorative term associated with men's athletics. "Recreation" was often used along with "sport."

17. Wushanley, *Playing Nice and Losing*, 37.

18. Walter Byers to E. Wayne Cooley, Executive Secretary, Iowa Girls' High School Athletic Union, November 24, 1965, Folder "Women's Athletics," Unorganized Walter Byers Papers, NCAA Headquarters.

19. Charles Neinas to Roswell Merrick, AAHPER, 22 December 1966, quoted in Virginia Hunt, "Governance of Women's Intercollegiate Athletics: An Historical Perspective" (EdD, Univ. of North Carolina at Greensboro, 1976), 187.

20. Walter Byers to Joel Eaves, Univ. of Georgia athletic director, February 7, 1966, Folder "Women's Athletics," Unorganized Walter Byers Papers, NCAA Headquarters. The tripartite committee was discontinued after the 1966 golf tourney and taken over by the DGWS. The tourney took place at Ohio State until 1952, then moved to the Univ. of North Carolina at Greensboro, then to Illinois Wesleyan. It was almost dropped in 1966 for lack of a site.

21. Walter Byers to Donald N. Boydston, Southern Illinois Univ.; Carl E. Erickson, Kent State; Katherine Ley, SUNY Cortland; Ernest McCoy, Penn State; Elizabeth McCue, Duke; Peter F. Newell, California, Berkeley; and Dean Trevor, Knox, July 25, 1967, Box LI, Folder "Women's Athletics," Walter Byers Papers, NCAA Archives. Ernie McCoy chaired the committee.

22. Walter Byers to Clifford Fagan, National Federation of State High School Athletic Association executive secretary, April 11, 1967, Box XXXIX, Folder

"HFSCHSAA 4/66–12/67," Walter Byers Papers, NCAA Archives; and Dale E. Plyley, "The AIAW vs. the NCAA: A Struggle for Power to Govern Women's Athletics in American Institutions of Higher Education, 1972–1974" (master's thesis, Univ. of Western Ontario, 1997), 53–54.

23. Walter Byers to Katherine Ley, October 26, 1967, quoted in Hunt, "Governance of Women's Intercollegiate Athletics," 190.

24. Joan S. Hult, "The Story of Women's Athletics: Manipulating a Dream, 1890–1985," in *Women and Sport: Interdisciplinary Perspectives*, ed. D. Margaret Costa and Sharon R. Guthrie (Champaign, IL: Human Kinetics, 1994), 93; and Susan K. Cahn, *Coming on Strong: Gender and Sexuality in Twentieth-Century Women's Sport* (New York: Free Press, 1994), 249.

25. Agnes R. Wayman, "Women's Athletics—All Uses—No Abuses," *American Physical Education Review* 29 (November 1924): 517.

26. For a controversial interpretation of women's control over college women athletes, see Ronald A. Smith's "Women's Control of American College Sport: The Good of Those Who Played or an Exploitation by Those Who Controlled?" *Sport History Review* 20, no. 1 (May 1998): 103–20.

27. Walter Byers, memorandum to NCAA Executive Committee and Council, February 26, 1971, Box "Title IX, 1970–1980," Folder "Correspondence to Member Institutions," Walter Byers Papers, NCAA Archives.

28. Walter Byers to Elizabeth Hoyt, February 2, 1971, quoted in Virginia Hunt "Governance of Women's Intercollegiate Athletics," 195.

29. Women's athletics may have philosophically been "student-centered," but Virginia Hunt clearly noted in her well-researched 1976 doctoral dissertation on the governance of women's intercollegiate athletics that "the CIAW did not have any provision for student representation." See her "Governance of Women's Intercollegiate Athletics," 269. When the AIAW took over, there was a provision for student representation, but it did not amount to much. Still, it was more than the NCAA, which had no provision for student representation, offered at that time. One can conjecture that if women's athletics had had significant input from the athletes, there would have been major intercollegiate athletics for women well before the DGWS, CIAW, or AIAW came into existence. Women physical educators wanted control and continually opposed major participation by athletes. For a lengthy study of this phenomenon, see Smith, "Women's Control of American College Sport," 103–20.

30. Joan S. Hult, "The Legacy of AIAW," in *A Century of Women's Basketball: From Frailty to Final Four, ed.* Joan S. Hult and Mariana Trekell (Reston, VA: National Association for Girls and Women's Sports, 1991), 295–97.

31. Linda Estes to Leotus Morrison, AIAW president-elect, 11 December 1973, Box 418, AIAW Papers, Univ. of Maryland Archives. As quoted from Ying Wu's introduction to his doctoral dissertation manuscript. Ying Wu, "The Demise of the AIAW and Women's Control of Intercollegiate Athletics for Women: The Sex-Separate Policy in the Reality of the NCAA, Cold War, and Title IX" (Ph.D. dissertation, Penn State University, 1997).

32. Linda Estes to Leotus Morrison, 11 December 1973, Box 418, AIAW Papers, Univ. of Maryland Archives, as quoted in Wushanley, *Playing Nice and Losing*, 81.

33. Walter Byers to Selected Representatives of the NCAA, May 17 and May 30, 1975, Folder "Athletic Office #2, 1974–75," David Mathews Papers, Univ. of Alabama Archives.

34. As quoted in Wushanley, *Playing Nice and Losing*, 87.

35. Walter Byers, "Title IX Memorandum," May 17, 1975, Box "CIV," Folder "H.E.E. (Title IX)," Walter Byers Papers, NCAA Archives.

36. NCAA *Proceedings*, January 15, 1976, pp. 80–90. Even the AIAW's Lu Magnusson of Penn State agreed that "It is highly improbably that most presidents are going to want to deal with two groups with different rules." As quoted in Hunt, "Governance of Women's Intercollegiate Athletics," 250.

37. Arthur J. Bergstrom, "Financial Growth of the NCAA," April 1977, revised March 1981, Box "NCAA History," Walter Byers Papers, NCAA Archives; and NCAA Annual Reports, 1975–76, pp. 186–87.

38. Christine H. B. Grant, "Recapturing the Vision," *Journal of Physical Education, Recreation and Dance* (March 1989): 45; and Wushanley, *Playing Nice and Losing*, 118.

39. NCAA *Proceedings*, January 10, 1979, p. 165.

40. Of the top tournament finishers in the AIAW basketball tourney in 1981, all participated in the 1982 NCAA-sponsored tourney.

41. Nancy Scannell, "AIAW Sees NCAA Plan as 'Threat,'" *Washington Post*, January 9, 1980, clipping in Box "Women's Athletics, 1/80—WSB Problems," Folder "Women's Athletics," Walter Byers Papers, NCAA Archives.

42. Walter Byers to Wanda and Paul Brechler, Denver, 1 February 1980, Box "Women's Athletics, 1/80—WSB Problems," Folder "Women's Athletics," Walter Byers Papers, NCAA Archives.

43. Donna A. Lopiano, "How Can AIAW Most Effectively Serve You?" March 29, 1980, AIAW Region 2 Delegate Assembly, Gatlinburg, Tennessee, Box "Women's Athletics, 1/80, WSB Problems," Folder "Women's Athletics," Walter Byers Papers, NCAA Archives. Ruth Berkey, a former AIAW leader who lost the election for president of the AIAW and the NCAA's new coordinator for women's championships, criticized Polivy: "The NCAA uses legal counsel only as legal counsel. It is not involved in the day-to-day operations of the NCAA, and it does not attend meetings of the Council, Executive Committee or the Convention except as invited to discuss legal issues." See Ruth Berkey, Interview, ca. November 1980, Box "Women's Athletics, 6/80–12/80," Folder "Ruth Berkey," Walter Byers Papers, NCAA Archives.

44. "Transcript of the Meeting of AIAW and NCAA Representatives," April 30, 1981, Box "AIAW," Folder "1981," Walter Byers Papers, NCAA Archives.

45. *AIAW v. NCAA*, Civil Action File No. 81-2473 (United States District Court for the District of Columbia October 9, 1981).

46. *AIAW v. NCAA*, p. 6.

47. *Proceedings of the Intercollegiate Athletic Association of the United States* [NCAA], December 29, 1906, p. 11.

48. For well-researched studies about the early NCAA, see John S. Watterson, "Football's Longest Season: The Fall of 1905" and "Football in Crisis, 1905 to 1906," in *College Football: History, Spectacle, Controversy* (Baltimore: Johns Hopkins Univ. Press, 2000), 64–98; and Ronald A. Smith, "Brutality, Ethics, and the Creation of the NCAA," in *Sports and Freedom: The Rise of Big-Time College Athletics* (New York: Oxford Univ. Press, 1988), 191–208.

49. Wushanley, *Playing Nice and Losing*, 146–49.

50. Walter Byers to John Toner, NCAA president, May 22, 1984, Box "CLXVII," Folder "AIAW, 1984," Walter Byers Papers, NCAA Archives; and "D.C. Court Rejects Pleas by AIAW,' *NCAA News* 21, no. 21 (May 1984): 1.

Chapter 7

1. Byers, *Unsportsmanlike Conduct*, 141. The quote was related to his TV negotiations, but it could easily be applied to his combat with the AAU.

2. Charles P. Sawyer, "Amateur Track and Field Athletics," *Scribner's Magazine* 7 (June 1890): 775–82; and Richard Wettan and Joe Willis, "The Effect of New York's Elite Athletic Clubs on American Amateur Athletic Governance, 1870–1915," 1975, accessed October 28, 2022, files.eric.ed.gov/fulltext/ED110429.pdf.

3. *Spirit of the Times*, September 15, 1888, p. 288, and December 29, 1888, p. 838.

4. Robert Korsgaard, "A History of the Amateur Athletic Union of the United States" (EdD diss., Teachers College, Columbia Univ., 1952), 89; and Arnold Flath, *A History of Relations Between the National Collegiate Athletic Association and the Amateur Athletic Union of the United States, 1905–1963* (Champaign, IL: Stipes Publishing, 1964).

5. Korsgaard, "History of the Amateur Athletic Union," 207.

6. Howard P. Chudacoff has a strong article about the AAU-NCAA conflict, but he is incorrect in stating that the feud commenced after the NCAA began sponsoring the NCAA track and field championship in 1921. The feud between colleges and the AAU began more than three decades earlier. See Chudacoff, "AAU v. NCAA: The Bitter Feud That Altered the Structure of American Amateur Sports," *Journal of Sport History* 40, no. 1 (Spring 2021): 50–65, esp. 52. Pierre de Coubertin is cited by NCAA president Everett Barnes in 1965 in *The Controversy in Administration of Track and Field Events in the United States: Hearings Before the Committee on Commerce, United States Senate, Eighty-Ninth Congress, First Session . . .* (Washington, DC: US Government Printing Office, 1965), see esp. testimony from August 25, 1965, p. 395.

7. Amateur Athletic Union Annual Minutes, November 18, 1907; and John A. Lucas, "The Hegemonic Rule of the American Amateur Athletic Union, 1888–1914: James Edward Sullivan as Prime Mover," in *Lucas: Teacher, Sport Historian, and One Who Lived His Life Earnestly* (Lemont, PA, and Berlin, Germany: Eifrig Publishing, 2009), 218–38.

8. *NCAA Proceedings*, December 27, 1911, p. 10.

9. Mark Dyreson, *Making the Team: Sport, Culture, and the Olympic Experiment* (Urbana: Univ. of Illinois Press, 1998), 135.

10. The famed Howard J. Savage and Carnegie Foundation for the Advancement of Teaching report, *American College Athletics* (New York: Carnegie Foundation for the

Advancement of Teaching, 1929), 218–23, discusses the conflict between the AAU and the NCAA. See also *The Final Report of the President's Commission on Olympic Sports* (Washington, DC: US Government Printing Office, 1977), 396–98.

11. Joseph M. Turrini, *The End of Amateurism in American Track and Field* (Urbana: Univ. of Illinois Press, 2010), 18–20.

12. Newton Fuessle, "America's Boss-Ridden Athletics," *Outlook*, April 19, 1922, pp. 642–45.

13. *New York Times*, November 18, 1926, p. 18.

14. Turrini, *The End of Amateurism*, 64.

15. Jack Whittaker, quoted by Red Smith, "The Amateurs Are All Upstairs," *New York Times*, November 10, 1975, p. 60.

16. Big Eight Conference members to Marcus Plant, telegram, 2 March 1967, Box "3," Folder "NCAA-AAU Corr.," Marcus L. Plant Papers, Bentley Historical Library, Univ. of Michigan; and Bob Timmons, "The NCAA: Who Protects Student-Athletes? A Proposal for a Student-Athletes' Bill of Rights," June 25, 2002, accessed November 2, 2022, bobtimmons.net/billofrights.pdf.

17. "Trackmen Feuding with A.A.U. Name Werner Executive Chief," *New York Times*, September 4, 1962, p. 68.

18. "Vote Terminates Long Agreement," *New York Times*, April 27, 1960, p. 45.

19. *New York Times*, August 10, 1962, p. 31; September 4, 1962, p. 68; and September 20, 1962, p. 43. Even before the federations were officially organized, Byers stated that the NCAA would protect its members when the AAU threatened athletes with suspension if the AAU did not sanction particular NCAA contests.

20. NCAA Executive Committee Minutes, September 13, 1965, CXLIX, Folder "TV: Football, 1/71–6/71," Walter Byers Papers, NCAA Headquarters. The amount of money from football telecasts going to other parts of the NCAA would eventually cause football schools to protest the money being spent on such activities as women's sports and postgraduate scholarships.

21. Chudacoff, "AAU v. NCAA," 53.

22. Frank Litsky, "Byers Wages Hard Fight for Equality in Sports," *New York Times*, November 24, 1963, p. 110. The other seven Olympic sports were aquatics, track and field, bobsledding, boxing, judo, luge, weight lifting, and wrestling.

23. Arthur Daley, "Advance Toward Anarchy," *New York Times*, June 5, 1963, p. 64.

24. Litsky, "Byers Wages Hard Fight," 110.

25. Walter Byers to William Reed, Big Ten commissioner, October 12, 1964, Folder "T.V.," Unorganized Walter Byers Papers, NCAA Headquarters.

26. *Final Report of the President's Commission in Olympic Sports*, 399. For greater clarification on the Cold War and athletic competition with the USSR, see Toby C. Rider and Kevin Witherspoon, eds., *Defending the American Way of Life: Sport, Culture, and the Cold War* (Fayetteville: Univ. of Arkansas Press, 2018), 4–5 and *passim*; Thomas M. Hunt, "Countering the Soviet Threat in the Olympic Medals Race: The Amateur Sports Act of 1978 and American Athletics Policy Reform," *International Journal of History of Sport* 24 (2007): 796–818; and Allen Guttmann, "The Cold War and the Olympics," *International Journal: Canada's Journal of Global Analysis* 43, no. 4 (Autumn 1988): 554–68.

27. *Controversy in Administration of Track and Field Events in the United States: Hearings*, 381, 383, 385.

28. Jerry Izenberg, *How Many Miles to Camelot? The All-American Myth* (New York: Holt, Rinehard and Winston, 1972), 42–46.

29. The Maccabiah Games were started by Jews in 1932 to connect Jews around the world who had often been denied access to athletic competitions. The games were named after Judah Maccabee, who successfully defended Jews in the second century BCE during the Greek-Roman era.

30. Walter Byers to President Gaylord P. Harnwell, Univ. of Pennsylvania, July 11, 1969, quoted in 91 Cong. Rec. H3987 (daily ed. Feb. 18, 1970). The international banning of Jack Langer gained far more recognition than a national case in which another basketball player, Oregon State's Gary Freeman, returned to playing in an alumni game at his high school in 1969. The NCAA banned him. See "The Letter and the Spirit," *Sports Illustrated*, September 15, 1969, accessed November 2, 2022, https://vault.si.com/vault/1969/09/15/scorecard.

31. Gordon S. White Jr., "Ruling to Extend to All Eli Sport," *New York Times*, January 16, 1970, accessed September 16, 1970, https://www.nytimes.com/1970/01/16/archives/ruling-to-extend-to-all-eli-sports-penalty-stems-from-yales.html. Jack Langer provided a timeline of events in his controversy. "Statement of Jack Langer," March 19, 1973, in *Protection of College Athletes: Hearings Before the Special Subcommittee on Education of the Committee on Education and Labor, House of Representatives, Ninety-Third Congress, First Session on H.R. 5623 and H.R. 5624* (Washington, DC: US Government Printing Office, 1973), 115.

32. Delaney Kipputh, Yale athletic director, to Speaker of the US House of Representatives, quoted in 91 Cong. Rec. H3986 (daily ed. Feb. 18, 1970).

33. March 5, 19, 26, 27, 28, 29, and April 2, 1973, *Protection of College Athletes.*

34. Laurence Chalip, "The Future Past of the American Sports Act: Developing American Sport," *Journal of Coaching Education* 4, no. 2 (August 2011): 23; and Neil Amdur, "Olympic Group: Tower of Babel," *New York Times*, November 5, 1972, accessed November 1, 2022, https://www.nytimes.com/1972/11/05/archives/olympic-group-tower-of-babel-too-many-committees-and-leaders-plague.html.

35. Walter Byers, "USOC Must Be Reformed from Outside—Byers," *NCAA News* 12, no. 17 (December 1, 1975): 8; and Jack Falla, *The NCAA: The Voice of College Sports* (Mission, KS: NCAA, 1981), 91.

36. March 5, 1973, *Protection of College Athletes*, 18.

37. "Statement of Jack Langer," March 19, 1973, in *Protection of College Athletes*, 116–17.

38. Walter Byers to James Scott, Marquette Univ. athletic director, as quoted in the *Hartford Courant*, February 24, 1973, in "Statement of Thomas C. Hansen, Assistant Executive Director, NCAA," March 19, 1973, *Protection of College Athletes*, 61.

39. Meredith Hindley, "How the GI Bill Became Law in Spite of Some Veterans' Groups," *Humanities* 35, no. 4 (July/August 2014), accessed November 9, 2022, https://www.neh.gov/humanities/2014/julyaugust/feature/how-the-gi-bill-became-law-in

-spite-some-veterans-groups; and W. Gardner Selby, "Lawrence O'Donnell Says Critics Called the Original GI Bill Welfare," *Politifact*, February 17, 2012, accessed November 9, 2022, https://www.politifact.com/factchecks/2012/feb/17/lawrence-odonnell/lawrence-odonnell-says-critics-called-original-gi-/.

40. Suzanne Mettler, *Soldier to Citizens: The G.I. Bill and the Making of the Greatest Generation* (New York: Oxford Univ. Press, 2005), 21–22.

41. Handwritten note, ca. November–December. 1951, Box 1, Folder "De-Emphasis of Football—Sundry," President Brehm Papers, Univ. of Tennessee Archives.

42. President John J. Cavanaugh to Walter Byers, June 11, 1952, Box 94, Vice President Theodore Hesburgh Files, UPHS; and Notre Dame press release, June 13, 1952, Box 3, Folder "Athletics: NCAA, TV," Theodore Hesburgh Papers, UVHS, both at Univ. of Notre Dame Archives.

43. Steve Cady, "N.C.A.A. Responds to Critics," *New York Times*, April 9, 1976, p. 66.

44. Walter Byers to Senator Mike Gravel, August 23, 1972, Vol. CXVI, Folder "Legal: 10/72–12/72," NCAA Headquarters. See an insightful article by Nevada Cooke and Robert K. Barney, "'Preserving The American Way,': Gerald R. Ford, the President's Commission on Olympic Sports, and the Fight Against State-Funded Sport in America," in *Defending American Way of Life: Sport, Culture, and the Cold War*, ed. Toby C. Rider and Kevin B. Witherspoon (Fayetteville: Univ. of Arkansas Press, 2018), 67–82.

45. *Congressional Record-Senate*, September 27, 1972, Vol. CXVI, Folder "Legal: 10/72–12/72"; and Vol. CXVII, Part 25, Proceedings and Debates of the 92nd, Second Session, pp. 32432–48, both in Walter Byers Papers, NCAA Headquarters.

46. Byers, through NCAA Counsel Philip Brown, wanted to terminate the AAU and USOC "destructive monopoly rights." Philip Brown to Senator Gravel, January 10, 1973, Vol. CXVI, Folder "Legal: 1/73–7/73," Walter Byers Papers, NCAA Headquarters.

47. Gordon S. White Jr., "NCAA is Scored for Olympic Act," *New York Times*, January 12, 1973, p. 27. The athletic director's name was not mentioned.

48. "U.S. President's Commission on Olympic Sports Records, 1975–77," Collection Finding Aid, Gerald R. Ford Presidential Library and Museum, accessed November 1, 2022, https://www.fordlibrarymuseum.gov/digital-research-room/finding-aids/us-presidents-commission-olympic-sports-records-1975-77.

49. "S2036 Concern NCAA," *NCAA News*, November 15, 1977, p. 4; and Amateur Sports Act of 1978, S.2727 (95th): Amateur Sports Act, November 8, 1978. Two effective articles are James A. R. Nafzinger, "The Amateur Sports Act of 1978," *BYU Law Review* 47 (1983): 47–99; and Thomas M. Hunt, "Countering the Soviet Threat in the Olympic Medals Race: The Amateur Sports Act of 1978 and American Athletics Policy Reform," *International Journal of History of Sport* 24 (2007): 796–818. Because of AAU mismanagement, it failed to control any international sport, including its two favored sports, track and field and gymnastics.

50. "Athlete Aid Bill Gains," *New York Times*, May 9, 1978, p. 45; and Chudacoff, "AAU v. NCAA," 61.

51. Byers, *Unsportmanlike Conduct*, 270.

Chapter 8

1. Smith, *Sports and Freedom*, 219–20.

2. The other colleges meeting on December 8, 1905, were Fordham, Lafayette, Rutgers, Syracuse, and Wesleyan. In an 8-5 vote, the small college dominated group voted not to ban football but to reform it.

3. Intercollegiate Athletic Association of the United States [NCAA] *Proceedings*, December 29, 1906.

4. Intercollegiate Athletic Association of the United States [NCAA] *Proceedings*, December 29, 1906, pp. 29, 33.

5. Intercollegiate Athletic Association of the United States [NCAA] *Proceedings*, December 28, 1907, p. 2; and NCAA *Proceedings*, December 28, 1915, p. 44.

6. Probably the fullest discussion of the 1905–1906 football crisis, rule changes, and the amalgamation of the two rules committees is Roger R. Tamte, *Walter Camp and the Creation of American Football* (Urbana: Univ. of Illinois Press, 2018), 223–62. See also, Smith, "Brutality, Ethics, and the Creation of the NCAA," in *Sports and Freedom*, 191–208.

7. Ronald A. Smith, "Far More than Commercialism: Stadium Building from Harvard's Innovations to Stanford's 'Dirt Bowl,' *International Journal of the History of Sport* 25, no. 11 (September 2008): 1453–74; and Alva W. Stewart, *College Football Stadiums: An Illustrated Guide to NCAA Division 1-A* (Jefferson, NC: McFarland, 2000), *passim*.

8. President William L. Bryan, Indiana Univ., to President L. D. Coffman, Univ. of Minnesota, 3 March 1931; and John L. Griffith, Big Ten commissioner, memorandum to Big Ten presidents, faculty representatives, and athletic directors, March 25, 1931, both in Box 5, Folder 125, President's Papers, Univ. of Minnesota Archives.

9. Savage et al., *American College Athletics*. Henry S. Pritchett, president of the Carnegie Foundation, knew the results of the study before it began, stating, "[When athletics] are allowed to dominate the intellectual life of the college they become abuses." *New York Times*, March 30, 1925, p. 6.

10. NCAA *Proceedings*, December 28, 1939, pp. 24–25.

11. W. B. Owens, "President's Address," NCAA *Proceedings*, December 29 ,1939, pp. 94–101, esp. 101.

12. NCAA *Proceedings*, December 29, 1939, p. 121.

13. That year, 1939, Ohio State, which stated that it did not give scholarships to athletes, complained bitterly that Southern schools, with full scholarships legislated, were siphoning off athletes, with ten outstanding Ohio football players of fifteen attending Southern universities. "Second District Report," NCAA *Proceedings*, December 29, 1939, pp. 34–35.

14. NCAA *Proceedings*, January 12, 1945, p. 104; and January 9, 1946, pp. 68, 91, 158–59.

15. NCAA *Proceedings*, January 8, 1947, pp. 173–75.

16. President H. L. Donavan, Univ. of Kentucky, to President Rufus C. Harris,

Tulane, 6 August 1947, Box 1, Folder "NCAA 1937–50," President Rufus C. Harris Papers, Tulane Univ. Archives.

17. NCAA *Proceedings,* January 10, 1948, pp. 188–89.

18. NCAA *Proceedings,* January 13, 1950, p. 131.

19. NCAA *Proceedings,* January 13, 1950, pp. 143–44. A faculty member and a recognized leader of physical education in America but who did little research was Harry A. Scott of Columbia Univ. Scott was asked to speak to the NCAA in 1955 and summed up his views in a lengthy talk, "NCAA—Athletic Programs of Smaller Institutions." He gave a history of small colleges trying to preserve educational goals and amateurism in the wake of commercialized, big-time athletics. His strong biases reflected those of many others who were "muscular moralists" and "knew" that the values of small college athletics tied to the values of physical education programs without any verification by scientific studies. They effectively stated, though falsely, that the Ancient Greeks gave us the concept of amateurism. See NCAA *Proceedings,* January 6, 1955, pp. 227–35.

20. Byers, *Unsportsmanlike Conduct,* 53; and NCAA *Proceedings,* January 14, 1950, p. 207.

21. "Jordon Defends Sports Before the College Heads at Capitol," *New York Times,* December 13, 1951, p. 47.

22. NCAA *Proceedings,* January 11, 1951, p. 209.

23. NCAA *Proceedings,* January 7, 1954, p. 206.

24. "N.C.A.A. Drafts Plan to Prevent Monopoly of Football Television by a Small Group," *New York Times,* March 11, 1952, p. 30. The big-time committee individuals were faculty representatives Jeff Coleman of Alabama and Willis Hunter of USC, and commissioners Reeves Peters of the Big Seven, E. L. Romney of the Mountain States, Howard Grubbs of the Southwestern, and Kenneth "Tug" Wilson of the Big Ten.

25. NCAA *Proceedings,* January 11, 1952, p. 214.

26. NCAA *Proceedings,* January 7, 1954, p. 235. A NCAA study in 1952 showed that smaller colleges were hurt more financially by television than the larger colleges. "The Effects of Television on College Football Attendance, Report No. 3," April 22, 1952, Series # 5/21/7, Box 1, Univ. of Wisconsin Archives.

27. For a lengthy discussion of the regional challenge to NCAA's national policy, see Smith, *Play-by-Play,* 85–92.

28. Prof. N. W. Dougherty, Univ. of Tennessee faculty representative, to Tennessee president C. E. Brehm, March 15, 1955, Box 20, Folder 7, Dougherty Collection, Univ. of Tennessee Archives.

29. NCAA *Proceedings,* January 6, 1972, p. 36.

30. NCAA Television Committee Minutes, April 1–2, 1963, NCAA Headquarters. Byers was consistent—earlier that year in a TV Committee meeting, he noted that "stimulus should in some way be given to promotion of the excellent football played by College Division members not by subsidy but by other methods. He expressed the opinion that major colleges should accept their responsibility for the game of football and should find respectable means of repaying their debt to college football." NCAA Television Committee Minutes, February 25–26, 1963, NCAA Headquarters.

31. Carlson, *Making March Madness*, 67–69; and "History of the NAIA," September 9, 2005, accessed December 16, 2022, https://www.naia.org/general/2005-06/releases/20050909kbmpt?.

32. Kurt E. Kemper, *Before March Madness: The Wars for the Soul of College Basketball* (Urbana: Univ. of Illinois Press, 2020), 121.

33. *New York Times*, January 12, 1956, p. 31.

34. Wushanley, *Playing Nice and Losing*, 26.

35. "Opinions Out Loud," *NCAA News* 14, no. 3 (March 1, 1977): 2.

36. "Championship Transportation Guarantee 100%," *NCAA News* 14, no. 10 (October 15, 1977): 1.

37. *NCAA-AAU Dispute: Hearings Before the Committee on Commerce, United States Senate, Eighty-Ninth Congress, First Session, August 16–20, 20, 22, 24–27, 1965*, Serial No. 89-40, Warren G. Magnusson, Washington, Chair (Washington, DC: US Government Printing Office, 1965), 461–62.

38. Kemper, *Before March Madness*, 62–65, 110–16, 126–29; and Carlson, *Making March Madness*, 67–77.

39. NCAA *Proceedings*, January 11, 1973, p. 56–57. The committee was composed of Stan Marshall of the College Committee; Ed Sherman from Muskingum College; Dick Bowers from South Florida; Claude Gilstrap, Univ. of Texas, Arlington; Ed Czekaj, Penn State Univ.; Bob James ACC commissioner; and David Shank, Univ. of Oklahoma.

40. NCAA *Proceedings*, January 11, 1973, pp. 56, 103.

41. NCAA *1st Special Convention Proceedings*, August 6, 1973, p. 23.

42. NCAA *1st Special Convention Proceedings*, August 7, 1973, pp. A8–9.

43. "Television Contributions to NCAA Division II and Division III," November 13, 1974, Vol. XLIV, Folder "TV, ABC, 1974, Walter Byers Papers, NCAA Headquarters.

44. "Resume: Excerpts from NCAA Documents and Related Papers Concerning Guaranteed Appearances. . . ." included in J. O. Coppedge, TV Committee, to Chief Executive Officers of Member Institutions of Southern Conference, April 13, 1978, Box "TV Comm., 1978," Folder "TV Comm., 1978," Walter Byers Papers, NCAA Headquarters.

45. Quoted in NCAA Television Committee Minutes, June 2–3, 1975, p. 4, NCAA Headquarters.

46. NCAA *Proceedings*, January 9, 1974, p. 226.

47. Robert C. James, ACC commissioner, to Walter Byers, September 5, 1975, Vol. CLI, Folder "TV: Football, 1975," Walter Byers Papers, NCAA Headquarters.

48. Byers to Horn, August 18, 1976, Box "TV Committee," Folder "TV Committee 1976," Walter Byers Papers, NCAA Headquarters.

49. Stephen Horn to Walter Byers, August 28, 1975, Box "TV Comm. 1972," Folder "TV Comm. 1976," Walter Byers Papers, NCAA Headquarters.

50. Byers to John Fuzak, NCAA president, August 7, 1975, Vol. 151, Folder "TV: Football, 1975," Walter Byers Papers, NCAA Headquarters.

51. NCAA *Proceedings*, January 14, 1976, pp. 43–48.

52. "Resume: Excerpts from NCAA Documents," Box "TV Comm., 1978," Folder "TV Comm., 1978," Walter Byers Papers, NCAA Headquarters.

53. "Report of CFA Television Study Committee," May 22, 1980, Box 74, Folder 13, President Banowsky Papers, Univ. of Oklahoma Archives.

54. Quoted in "College Football Association Minutes, June 16–17, 1978, Box 19, Folder "CFA, June 16–18, 1978," President Davison Papers, Univ. of Georgia Archives.

55. Two pages of handwritten notes by Byers, July 1978, Volume CXIX, Folder "Legal, 1978," Walter Byers Papers, NCAA Headquarters.

56. *Goldfarb v. Virginia State Bar*, 421 U.S. 773 (1975); and Carl L. Reisner, "Tackling Intercollegiate Athletics: An Antitrust Analysis," *Yale Law Review* 77 (January 1978): 658.

57. Daniel G. Gibbens, Oklahoma faculty rep, memorandum to President William Banowsky, Univ. of Oklahoma, September 10, 1981, Box 119, Folder 33, President Banowsky Papers, Univ. of Oklahoma Archives.

Chapter 9

1. Byers, *Unsportsmanlike Conduct*, 254.

2. For lengthy treatments of the NCAA as a violator of antitrust legislation, see Brian L. Porto, *The Supreme Court and the NCAA* (Ann Arbor: Univ. of Michigan Press, 2012); Arthur A. Fleisher III, Brian L. Goff, and Robert D. Tollison, *The National Collegiate Athletic Association: A Study of Cartel Behavior* (Chicago: Univ. of Chicago Press, 1992); Paul R. Lawrence, *Unsportsmanlike Conduct: The National Collegiate Athletic Association and the Business of College Sport* (Westport, CT: Praeger, 1987); Taylor Branch, *The Cartel: Inside the Rise and Imminent Fall of the NCAA* (San Francisco: Byliner, 2011); and Joe Nocera and Ben Strauss, *Indentured: The Inside Story of the Rebellion Against the NCAA* (New York: Penguin Random House, 2016).

3. Walter Byers to Richard F. Pfizenmayer, NCAA legal counsel, Washington, DC, 2 November 1977, Vol. 119, Folder "Legal: 7/77–12/77," Walter Byers Papers, NCAA Archives.

4. Minutes of the Special Meeting of Chief Executive Officers, Faculty Representatives, and Athletic Directors of the Big Eight Conference, September 2, 1981, Central Administration, President's Office, Series I, Box 171, Folder 1, "Big Eight Conference 1981–82," Univ. of Colorado Archives.

5. Minutes of the Special Meeting, September 2, 1981, Univ. of Colorado Archives; and John Underwood, "When the Rebellious CFA Signed a Deal with NBC, . . ." *Sports Illustrated* 21 (September 1981), accessed May 28, 2021, https://vault.si.com/vault/1981/09/21-to-do-over/. Of the reorganization forced by the Big Eight, a Furman Univ. vice-president wrote, "Their ploy was a bluff, and it worked." Francis W. Bonner to James Frank, September 10, 1981, Box "Special Convention," Folder "Special Convention, 1981," Walter Byers Papers, NCAA Headquarters.

6. Walter Byers, memorandum to NCAA Council, September 25, 1981, Box "TV Communications," Folder "TV, FB, 1982, Walter Byers Papers, NCAA Headquarters; and "Official Notice and Program of the 4th Special Convention of the National Collegiate Athletic Association," December 3–4, 1981, NCAA Headquarters.

7. James Frank and John Toner, memorandum to chief executive officers, faculty athletic representatives, directors of athletics, and primary women athletic administrators of NCAA member institutions, September 18, 1981, Box "Special Convention," Folder "Special Convention, 1981," Walter Byers Papers, NCAA Headquarters.

8. NCAA *Special Convention Proceedings*, December 4, 1981, p. 77, 81; and Byers, *Unsportsmanlike Conduct*, 276–77.

9. NCAA *Special Convention Proceedings*, December 4, 1981, p. 61.

10. Gordon S. White Jr., "Demotion by N.C.A.A. Irks Ivy League," *New York Times*, January 17, 1982, p. S4. Only Dartmouth and Yale would qualify for big-time football designation. Larry Albus, memorandum to athletic directors and faculty representatives, 28 October 1981, Box "Special Convention," Folder "Special Convention, 1981," Walter Byers Papers, NCAA Headquarters.

11. Byers, *Unsportsmanlike Conduc*t, 276.

12. NCAA *Proceedings*, January 13, 1982, pp. A30–31.

13. The CFA vote was thirty-three for, twenty against, and eight abstentions. Ronald M. Brown, Univ. of Texas vice president, to President Peter F. Flawn, Texas, August 24, 1981, Box "TV Negotiations, 1981," Folder "TV Negotiations," Walter Byers Papers, NCAA Headquarters. Don Canham, Michigan athletic director, believed that small colleges were hurt the most from the Oklahoma lawsuit. Don B. Canham with Larry Paladino, *From the Inside: A Half-Century of Michigan Athletics* (Ann Arbor, MI: Olympia Sports Press, 1996), 256.

14. Mary H. Tolbert and D. Kent Meyers, "The Lasting Impact of NCAA v. Bd. of Regents of the University of Oklahoma: The Football Fan Wins" *Oklahoma Bar Journal* (October 2018), accessed January 4, 2023, https://www.okbar.org/barjournal/oct2018/obj8926tolbertmeyers/.

15. Carl L. Reisner, "Tackling Intercollegiate Athletics: An Antitrust Analysis," *Yale Law Review* 77, no. 3 (January 1978): 658; and Walter Byers to Philip Brown and George Gangwere, NCAA legal counsel, February 21, 1978, Box "Legal Vol. 119," Folder, "Legal, 1978," Walter Byers Papers, NCAA Headquarters.

16. Gangwere to Byers, September 29, 1976, Vol. 118, Folder "Legal: 6/76–12/76"; and January 3, 1979, Vol. 153, Folder "TV: Negotiations Committee, 1979," both in Walter Byers Papers, NCAA Headquarters.

17. "Declaration of Judgement and Permanent Injunction," *University of Oklahoma and University of Georgia v. NCAA*, September 14, 1982, Box 18, Folder "College Football Association," President Davison Papers, Univ. of Georgia Archives.

18. United States Court of Appeals 10th Circuit No. 8202148, filed May 12, 1983, Box 156, Folder 7, President Banowsky Paper, Univ. of Oklahoma Archives.

19. Sheldon Elliot Steinbach, ACE general counsel, to ACE Executive Committee, 15 August 1983, Box "U. of OK & U. of GA v. NCAA," Ralph Beaird Papers, Univ. of Georgia Archives; and "Brief of the American Council on Education, as Amicus Curiae, in Support of the Petition for Certiorari," October 1983, Box 156, Folder 7, President Banowsky Papers, Univ. of Oklahoma Archives (hereafter cited as Banowsky Papers).

20. "Brief of the American Council on Education, as Amicus Curiae," Banowsky Papers.

21. The ACE had constructed five committees on Division I athletics in early 1983: (1) Division One Reorganization, (2) Recruiting and Enforcement, (3) Television, (4) NCAA Governance, and (5) Academic Standards. Five prominent university presidents were made chairs of the committees. Robert Atwell, ACE executive vice president, to ACE Committee on Division One Intercollegiate Athletics, March 10, 1983, Box "Special Convention," Folder "Select Committee on American Concerns in Higher Education," Walter Byers Papers, NCAA Headquarters.

22. Robert Atwell, ACE executive vice president, to ACE Committee on Division Intercollegiate Athletics, March 10, 1983; J. W. Peltason, ACE, to Byers, April 19, 1983; and Byers to John L. Toner, Univ. of Connecticut athletic director, May 13, 1983, all in Box "Special Convention," Folder "Select Committee on Athletic Concerns in Education," Walter Byers Papers, NCAA Headquarters; Charles M. Neinas to Andy Coats, Univ. of Oklahoma counsel, April 26, 1983, and Sheldon Elliot Steinbach, ACE general counsel, to ACE Executive Committee, August 25, 1983, both in Box "U. of OK & U. of GA v. NCAA," Ralph Beaird Papers, Univ of Georgia Archives.

23. Eric A. Seiken, "The NCAA and the Courts: College Football on Television," in *Sport and the Law: Major Legal Cases*, ed. Charles E. Quirk (New York: Garland, 1996), 56–62.

24. Even more quoted by the NCAA in numerous cases was John Paul Stevens, in *NCAA v. Board of Regents of University of Oklahoma*, 468 U.S. 85 (1984), 120: "The NCAA plays a critical role in the maintenance of a revered tradition of amateurism in college sports." This dictum (judges' comments having little to do with resolving the case) of a Supreme Court justice became the principal justification of NCAA amateurism until the unanimous 9-0 decision in the *NCAA v. Shawne Alston* case in 2021 removed "amateurism" as a justification for NCAA's actions in most court cases. Amateurism was no longer a "revered tradition," and the term "amateurism" was removed from its constitution shortly thereafter.

25. Seiken, "The NCAA and the Courts," 56–62.

26. Walter Byers to Donald B. Canham, October 30, 1985, Box "TV, FB, 1986," Folder "TV, FB, 1985," Walter Byers Papers, NCAA Headquarters.

27. Joe Nocera, "The Man Who Built the N.C.A.A.," *New York Times*, May 30, 2015, p. A19. For Walter Byers's views on TV, money, the Supreme Court, and the CFA, see his *Unsportsmanlike Conduct*, 253–96.

28. Charles E. Young, mailgram to President William Banowsky, Oklahoma, and fourteen other Division I presidents, November 6, 1984, Box 156, Folder 5, President Banowsky Papers, Univ. of Oklahoma Archives.

29. Gordon S. White Jr., "Colleges May Find TV's Golden Egg is Tarnished," *New York Times*, August 26, 1984, p. S9.

30. Don Canham to selected athletic directors, November 29, 1984, Box 219, Folder "Athletics 1984–85," Chancellor's Central Files, Univ. of Nebraska Archives.

31. "Old College Try," *New York Times*, September 10, 1985, p. B13.

32. Charles Neinas to President Fred Davison, Univ. of Georgia, and Dan Gibbons, Univ. of Oklahoma, February 27, 1985, Box 18, Folder "CFA," President Davison Papers, Univ. of Georgia Archives.

33. Byers to Donald B. Canham, Michigan athletic director, October 30, 1985, Box "TV: Football, 1986," Folder "TV, Football, 1985," Walter Byers Papers, NCAA Headquarters.

34. As quoted in Ritchie T. Thomas, NCAA legal counsel, to Thomas C. Hansen, NCAA assistant executive director, November 8, 1977, Vol. 152, Folder "TV Football, 7/77–12/77," Walter Byers Papers, NCAA Headquarters.

35. "Taking Away the N.C.A.A.'s Ball," *Time Magazine*, July 9, 1984, p. 77.

36. Neinas to President Fred Davison, Univ. of Georgia, and Dan Gibbens, Univ. of Oklahoma, February 27, 1985, Box 18, Folder "CFA," President Davison Papers, Univ. of Georgia Archives.

37. Byers to Donald B. Canham, Michigan, October 30, 1985, Box "TV: Football, 1986," Folder "TV, Football, 1985," Walter Byers Papers, NCAA Headquarters.

38. Andrew Begnato, "College Football: Money for Academic Scholarships Real Reason for Irish TV Deal," *Chicago Tribune*, February 18, 1990, p. 9.

39. William F. Reid, "We're Notre Dame and You're Not," *Sports Illustrated*, February 19, 1990, pp. 56–60.

40. Walter Byers to W. Hallock, PAC-10 commissioner, March 21, 1985, Box "TV, FB, 1986," Folder "TV, FB, 1985," Walter Byers Papers, NCAA Headquarters.

Chapter 10

1. Walter Byers, memorandum to Big Ten Conference athletic directors, July 29, 1949, 141-84-5, Ohio State Univ. Archives.

2. Jay Langhammer, "Luisetti, Angelo Joseph 'Hank,'" in *Biographical Dictionary of American Sports: Basketball and Other Indoor Sports*, ed. David L. Porter (Westport, CT: Greenwood Press, 1989), 187–88.

3. *New York Times*, March 17, 1938, p. 24. Byron "Whizzer" White, the star football player and soon to be Rhodes Scholar, played for the losers, Colorado. He subsequently became a Supreme Court justice, nominated by President John F. Kennedy; was selected for the top NCAA Teddy Roosevelt Award; and eventually favored amateurism over antitrust sentiment in the NCAA loss against Oklahoma in the 1984 Supreme Court 7-2 verdict.

4. Larry Fox, *Illustrated History of Basketball* (New York: Grosset & Dunlap, 1974), 61–67; and Robert W. Peterson, *Cages to Jump Shots: Pro Basketball's Early Years* (New York: Oxford Univ. Press, 1990), 108–10.

5. NCAA *Proceedings*, January 9, 1953, pp. 289, 299–300.

6. William Uricchio, "Television as History: Representations of German Television Broadcasting, 1935–1944," in *Framing the Past: The Historiography of German Cinema and Television*, ed. Bruce A. Murray and Christopher J. Wickham (Carbondale: Southern Illinois Univ. Press, 1992), 193.

7. Mike Lopresti, "March Madness: How 1968's Game of the Century Forever Shaped Basketball History," *NCAA.com*, March 31, 2016, accessed January 17, 2023, https://www.ncaa.com/news/basketball-men/article/2016-03-31/march-madness-how-1968s-game-century-forever-shaped.

8. NCAA *Proceedings*, January 9, 1953, pp. 299–300.

9. "NABC Recognizes Iba, Byers," *NCAA News* 6, no. 4 (April 1969): 1.

10. President Harold Dodds, Princeton, to President Harold Stassen, Univ. of Pennsylvania, June 12, 1951, Box "54," Folder "Intercollegiate Athletics, TV-7," Papers of the President, Univ. of Pennsylvania Archives; and *Time Magazine*, June 18, 1951, p. 69.

11. Theodore Hesburgh, Notre Dame, to Leslie Arries, Du Mont Network, April 8, 1950, UVHS, Box 3, Folder "TV-September 1949, # 2," President Hesburgh Papers, Univ. of Notre Dame Archives.

12. President Harold E. Stassen, Univ. of Pennsylvania, to William DuBarry, Francis Murray, and Kurt Peiser, Univ. of Pennsylvania, May 29, 1951, Box 53, Folder "Intercollegiate Athletics, TV, #2," Papers of the Office of the President, 1950–55, Univ. of Pennsylvania Archives.

13. NCAA President Hugh Willett, telegram to President Stassen, Penn, June 12, 1951, Box 54, Folder "Intercollegiate Athletics, TV-7," Papers of the Office of the President, Univ. of Pennsylvania Archives.

14. NCAA *Proceedings*, January 8, 1953, pp. 122–23; Charles Rosen, *Scandals of '51* (New York: Holt, Rinehart, & Winston, 1978), 20–21, 42–43, 215; and Russell Rice, *Kentucky Basketball's Big Blue Machine* (Huntsville, AL: Strode Publishers, 1976), 111, 217, 227.

15. *New York Times*, April 30, 1952, p. 1.

16. Arthur A. Fleisher III, Brian L. Goff, and Robert D. Tollison, *The National Collegiate Athletic Association: A Study in Cartel Behavior* (Chicago: Univ. of Chicago Press, 1992), 53–54; and Crowley, *In the Arena*, 101. The Fleisher book lists all NCAA network contracts during the Byers era.

17. For a lengthy discussion, see Smith, *Play-by-Play*, 72–102.

18. The vote for the 1952 TV contract was 163-8, Byers's first year on the TV Committee with Robert Hale of Yale as chair and Asa Bushnell of the Eastern College Athletic Conference as TV director. "New N.C.A.A. TV Group to Open Meeting Today," *Chicago Daily Tribune*, February 9, 1952, p. B2.

19. The TV Committee had an exhausting discussion on these issues more than a decade after it first controlled football telecasts. NCAA Television Committee Minutes, June 29–30, July 1, 1963, NCAA Headquarters.

20. Quoted in Jack McCallum, "In the Kingdom of the Solitary Man: Reticent, Reclusive Walter Byers, . . ." *Sports Illustrated*, October 6, 1986, accessed September 27, 2020, https://vault.si.com/vault/1986/10/06/in-the-kingdom-of-the-solitary-man-reticent-reclusive-walter-byers-the-executive-director-of-the-national-collegiate-athletic-association-will-retire-in-1988-but-as-byers-begins-to-relinquish-his-35-year-long-grip-on-the-ncaa-h.

21. Don B. Canham with Larry Paladino, *From the Inside: A Half-Century of Michigan Athletics* (Ann Arbor, MI: Olympia Sports Press, 1996), 205.

22. Arledge, *Roone*, 104–5.

23. Quoted in William O. Johnson Jr., *Super Spectator and the Electric Lilliputians* (Boston: Little, Brown, 1971), 159–60.

24. Beano Cook to NCAA Comrades at the NCAA, ca. 10 June 1969, Box "TV: Legislation, 1965–68," Folder "General 5/69–6/69," Walter Byers Papers, NCAA Headquarters.

25. For a list of NCAA network contracts, see Fleisher, *National Collegiate Athletic Association*, 53.

26. Byers, *Unsportsmanlike Conduct*, 266.

27. Spence, *Up Close and Personal*, 130–32; and Byers, *Unsportsmanlike Conduct*, 267.

28. *New York Herald*, August 10, 1852, p. 2; and Charles F. Livermore, "The First Harvard-Yale Boat Race," *Harvard Graduates' Magazine* 2 (December 1893), 226.

29. Henry B. Needham, "The College Athlete," *McClure's Magazine* 25 (June 1905), 115–16, 124.

30. "Beer Advertising – Western Conference Football Programs, 1935," Box 21, Folder "Papers 1935 December 1," Univ. of Michigan Board in Control of Intercollegiate Athletics, Michigan Historical Collections, Bentley Historical Library, Univ. of Michigan; and Joseph Petritz, Notre Dame Sports Publicity Director, to Joe Hasel, Blue Network, NBC, New York City, November 11, 1942, UVOC, Box 6, Folder 57, "Radio Broadcasts, Football, 1942," Vice President's Records, 1934–46, Univ. of Notre Dame Archives.

31. "Contract Between Notre Dame and Television Productions, Inc., September 1948," UVMR, Box 4, Folder "TV," Vice President John Murphy Papers, Univ. of Notre Dame Archives; President Harold E. Stassen, Univ. of Pennsylvania, draft of letter to President Hugh C. Willet, NCAA, November 6, 1952, Box 54, Folder "Intercollegiate Athletics, TV-15," Papers of the Office of the President, Univ. of Pennsylvania Archives; and "Excerpt from the 1951 Football Broadcasting Policy of the University of Notre Dame," Box 88, Folder "Football 1951," President Cross Papers, Univ. of Oklahoma Archives.

32. "Recommended NCAA Football Television Plan for 1968 and 1969," Vol. 48, Folder "TV: General 8/67–9/69," Walter Byers Papers, NCAA Headquarters.

33. Marcus Plant, NCAA President, to Walter Byers, 4 September 1968, Vol. 47, Folder "TV: General 9/68–12/68," Walter Byers Papers, NCAA Headquarters.

34. "Hamm's Beer 1970s TV Commercial. Quite Possibly the Best Beer Commercial Ever Produced," Reddit, accessed April 3, 2024, https://www.reddit.com/r/videos/comments/b9t5td/hamms_beer_1970s_tv_commercial_quite_possibly_the/.

35. NCAA Television Committee Minutes, June 29–30, 1967, NCAA Headquarters.

36. Walter Byers to Asa Bushnell, August 12, 1968, Vol. 47, Folder "TV: General 9/68–12/68," Walter Byers Papers, NCAA Headquarters.

37. NCAA Television Committee Minutes, September 1–2, 1970, NCAA Headquarters.

38. Robert C. Edwards to Bill McLellan, April 24, 1978, Box 19, Folder "CFA-3," President Davison Papers, Univ. of Georgia Archives.

39. Byers, *Unsportsmanlike Conduct, passim.*

Chapter 11

1. For understanding the 1951 basketball scandal, see Albert J. Figone, *Cheating the Spread: Gamblers, Point Shavers, and Game Fixers in College Football and Basketball* (Urbana: Univ. of Illinois Press, 2012); Stanley Cohen, *The Game They Played* (New

York: Carroll & Graf, 2001); Charles Rosen, *Scandals of '51: How the Gamblers Almost Killed College Basketball* (New York: Holt, Rinehart & Winston, 1978); and Charles Rosen, *The Wizard of Odds: How Jack Molinas Almost Destroyed the Game of Basketball* (New York: Seven Stories Press, 2001).

2. Humbert S. Neli, "Adolph Rupp, The Kentucky Wildcats, and the Basketball Scandal of 1951," *Register of the Kentucky Historical Society* 84, no. 1 (Winter 1986): 51–75.

3. Byers, *Unsportsmanlike Conduct*, 60–61.

4. William McCarter, NCAA *Proceedings*, January 8, 1954, p. 267.

5. "Trust in Government: 1958–2015," *Pew Research Center*, November 23, 2015, accessed February 11, 2023, https://www.pewresearch.org/politics/2015/11/23/1-trust-in-government-1958-2015/. See, for instance, Karl Marlantes, "Vietnam: The War That Killed Trust," *New York Times*, January 7, 2017, accessed February 11, 2023, https://www.nytimes.com/2017/01/07/opinion/sunday/vietnam-the-war-that-killed-trust.html.

6. *Washington Post*, September 17, 1976, p. D4.

7. *Regents of University of Minnesota v. National Collegiate Athletic Association*, 560 F.2d 352 (8th Cir. 1977).

8. NCAA Special Convention *Proceedings*, June 20, 1985, pp. 69–71, A9–A10.

9. For a summary of due process problems, see *Due Process and the NCAA: Hearings*, paragraph 27. An important article on NCAA monopoly did not deal directly with enforcement of NCAA rules, but it did note due process of the NCAA and could have forewarned the NCAA about providing appropriate due process to institutions and individuals. See Carl Reisner's "Tackling Intercollegiate Athletics: An Antitrust Analysis," *Yale Law Review* 87, no. 3 (January 1978): 655–79. Reisner specifically notes questionable antitrust areas: (1) athletes' compensation, (2) number of coaches allowed, (3) NCAA TV plan, and (4) NCAA enforcement programs. See esp. pp. 676–78. Walter Byers was well aware of this article from its origin in 1978. See Byer to Philip Brown and George Gangwere, counsels to NCAA, February 21, 1978, Vol. 109, Folder "Legal, 1978," Walter Byers Papers, NCAA Headquarters.

10. *NCAA Enforcement Program: Hearings*, 446.

11. See legal and financial problems: Byers to Alan J. Chapman, NCAA president, October 14, 1974; and Ted C. Tow, NCAA, to NCAA cabinet, October 1, 1974, both in Vol. CXVII, Folder "Legal: 1974"; and Byers to Marcus L. Plant, Univ. of Michigan; and Charley Scott, Univ. of Alabama, to J. Neils Thompson, NCAA president, February 3, 1977, both in Vol. CXIX, Folder "Legal: 1/77–6/77," all in Walter Byers Papers, NCAA Headquarters.

12. Walter Byers to Marcus L. Plant, Univ. of Michigan lawyer, January 4, 1977, Vol. CXIX, Folder "Legal: 1/77–6/77," Walter Byers Papers, NCAA Headquarters.

13. *Regents of University of Minnesota v. National Collegiate Athletic Association*; and John W. Johnson, "Minnesota Gopher Basketball: Problems on the Court and in the Courts," in *Sports and the Law: Major Legal Cases*, ed. Charles E. Quirk (New York: Garland Publishing, 1996).

14. Walter Byers, "Legal Obfuscations," *NCAA News* 13, no. 15 (November 15, 1976), 2.

15. For a fine analysis of Tarkanian and the NCAA, see Brian L. Porto, "Hunting the

Shark" and "Taming the Shark" in *Supreme Court and the NCAA*, 100–26, 127–50. Much of this chapter is based on his research. See also, Don Yaeger, "Shooting at the Shark," in *Undue Process: The NCAA's Injustice for All* (Champaign, IL: Sagamore Publishing, 1991), 195–236.

16. Crowley, *In the Arena*, 167.

17. *NCAA Enforcement Program: Hearings*, 599–607; Jim Trotter, "Wright Speaks on Due Process Question," *NCAA News* 15, no. 8 (June 1, 1978): 7; Gordon White Jr., "N.C.A.A. Charges Untrue Tarkanian Tells Hearing," *New York Times*, June 10, 1978, p. 16; Gary Roberts Prepared Statement, *Due Process and the NCAA: Hearings*, 21–22; Yaeger, *Undue Process*, 249–70; and Nocera and Strauss, *Indentured*, chap. 1, "The Turncoat."

18. Quoted in "Aidan M. McCormack, "Seeking Procedural Due Process in NCAA Infractions Procedures," *Marquette Sports Law Review* 2, no. 2 (Spring 1992), 275.

19. David A. Savage, "Tarkanian Loses in Supreme Court," *Los Angeles Times*, December 13, 1988, accessed February 27, 2023, https://www.latimes.com/archives/la-xpm-1988-12-13-sp-226-story.html.

20. Robin J. Green, "Does the NCAA Play Fair: A Due Process Analysis of NCAA Enforcement Regulations," *Duke Law Journal* 42, no. 3 (1992): 110–11; Alison Muscatine, "NCAA Urged to Modify Inquires," *Washington Post*, October 29, 1991, accessed February 20, 2023, https://www. washingtonpost.com/archive/sports/1991/10/29/ncaa-urged-to-modify-inquires; and Porto, *Supreme Court and the NCAA*, 145–46.

21. William C. Friday and Theodore M. Hesburgh, co-chairs, *Keeping Faith with the Student-Athlete: A New Model for Intercollegiate Athletics, Report of the Knight Foundation: Commission on Intercollegiate Athletics* (Miami, FL: John S. and James L. Knight Foundation, 1991), 20.

22. Byers, *Unsportsmanlike Conduct*, 130.

23. Byers was likely correct when he noted that having the Tarkanian case tried in Nevada state court was a home court advantage for Tarkanian. Byers, *Unsportsmanlike Conduct*, 212–13.

24. "Tarkanian Gets Settlement from the NCAA," *Chicago Tribune*, April 3, 1998, p. B2; *New York Times*, April 2, 1998, p. C6; and Porto, *Supreme Court and the NCAA*, 158.

25. See, for instance, *Adrian Arrington et al. v. NCAA*, Case No. 11-cv-06356, Document E#25 (United States District Court Northern District of Illinois Eastern District November 21, 2011); *Corman v. NCAA*, No. 1 M.D. 2013 (Commonwealth Court of Pennsylvania October 15, 2014); and *Sheely Family v. NCAA* et al., Case No. 380569 (Circuit Court for Montgomery County, MD, August 22, 2013).

26. "After 26 Years, It's Case Closed," *Washington Post*, April 3, 1998, accessed February 22, 2023, https://www.washingtonpost.com/archive/sports/1998/04/03/after-26-years-its-case-closed/7ccbcfc9-1dc6-4c2a-883a-df95ace7dac1/.

27. Later in life, Walter Byers could not forgive his daughter for allowing the water on his cattle ranch to freeze in an unexpected deep freeze in mid-December 2008. As a result, he disinherited his daughter to the ranch. *Bouton v. Byers*.

28. "After 26 Years, It's Case Closed," *Washington Post.*

29. Byers, *Unsportsmanlike Conduct*, 1–2, 216.

30. By the time of Jeremy Bloom, the International Olympic Committee had already taken the term "amateurism" out of its constitution. The NCAA, by contrast, continued its myth of the amateur.

31. Jeremy Bloom Testimony, *Due Process and the NCAA: Hearing*, 82.

32. Byers, *Unsportsmanlike Conduct*, 216.

Chapter 12

1. For early college athletics, see Smith, *Sports and Freedom.*

2. NCAA *Proceedings*, December 29, 1921, pp. 52, 106.

3. NCAA *Proceedings*, December 28, 1922, p. 52.

4. *New York Times*, April 12, 1924, p. 13; and April 28, 1924, p. 12.

5. NCAA Proceedings, December 29, 1920, p. 85; and *Official Handbook of the Intercollegiate Association of Amateur Athletes of America, 1924* (New York: American Sports Publishing Company, 1924), 95. For a harsh critique of NCAA football lacking concern for athletes and head concussions, see Ronald A. Smith, "The NCAA, Concussions, and the Treatment of Athletes: Historical Revelations from 1905 to 2022," part of the *Robert Geathers v. NCAA* lawsuit in 2024.

6. The NCAA Presidents' Commission Special Convention in 1987, which took place during Byers's last year as executive director and looked at major issues in college athletics, produced 269 pages of *Proceedings* but never once were athletes' health and safety concerns, including brain injuries and concussions, noted. The NCAA did not pass a Concussion Management Plan until 2010, and even then the organization did not make it mandatory.

7. Martin Kane, "The End of College Boxing," *Sports Illustrated*, April 25, 1960, accessed August 27, 2023, https://vault.si.com/vault/1960/04/25/the-end-of-college-boxing.

8. Frank J. Lubin, interview by George A. Hodak on the 1936 Olympic basketball games, May 1988, Olympian Oral History, LA84 Foundation, accessed March 1, 2023, https://digital.la84.org/digital/collection/p17103coll11/id/217. The United States won 19-8, though good play was nearly impossible and the basketball was waterlogged. A fine history of Olympic basketball is found in Carson Cunningham, "American Hoops: The History of the United States Olympic Basketball from Berlin to Barcelona" (PhD diss., Purdue Univ., 2006), 19–50; and Cunningham, *American Hoops* (Lincoln: Univ. of Nebraska Press, 2010), 1–28.

9. As quoted by Falla, *NCAA*, 186.

10. *Controversy in Administration of Track and Field Events in the United States: Hearings*, 367.

11. The NCAA recorded a profit of $42.54, but a NCAA Timeline by NCAA's Arthur Bergstrom notes a net loss of $2,531. NCAA *Proceedings*, December 31, 1939, p. 111, and

December 29, 1940, p. 51; and Arthur W. Bergstrom, "Financial Growth of the NCAA, Timeline," April 1977, revised March 1981, Box "NCAA-History," Walter Byers Papers, NCAA Archives.

12. NCAA *Proceedings*, December 31, 1940, p. 166, and January 13, 1945, p. 24.

13. Byers was honored by the National Association of Basketball Coaches in 1969 at the annual March Madness tourney as the "individual who has made an outstanding contribution to the game of basketball." This honor was given only two months after the college-dominated Football Coaches Association condemned Byers for his attack on the power-hungry big-time football coaches in the *NCAA News*. "NABC Recognizes Iba, Byers," *NCAA News* 6, no. 1 (April 1969): 1.

14. NCAA *Proceedings*, January 10, 1948, p. 201.

15. NCAA *Proceedings*, January 12, 1951, pp. 244–47.

16. NCAA *Proceedings*, January 9, 1953, pp. 298–300.

17. NCAA *Proceedings*, January 13, 1951, p. 241.

18. Walter Byers, memorandum to Big Ten Conference Athletic Directors, July 29, 1949, File 141-84-5, Ohio State Univ. Archives.

19. NCAA *Proceedings*, January 13, 1951, pp. 239, 241–42. NCAA basketball tournament receipts in 1949 were far in excess of the other seven NCAA tournaments in 1949.

20. *Controversy in Administration of Track and Field Events in the United States: Hearings*, 367.

21. Theodore Hesburgh to Henry Little, executive VP Campbell-Ewald Company, 8 May 1950, VIHS, Box 3, Folder "TV Sept. 1949 # 2," Theodore Hesburgh Papers, Univ. of Notre Dame Archives.

22. *NCAA Proceedings*, January 11, 1951, pp. 101–2.

23. NCAA *Proceedings*, January 7, 1954, p. 120; J. Samuel Walker and Randy Roberts, *The Road to Madness: How the 1973–1974 Season Transformed College Basketball* (Chapel Hill: Univ. of North Carolina Press, 2016), 80–81; and *Byers, Unsportsmanlike Conduct*, 131–32.

24. For a fuller discussion, see Ronald A. Smith, "Sport and the New Medium of Television," in *Play-by-Play*, 47–54.

25. NCAA *Proceedings*, January 7, 1955, p. 322; William Hyland, Sports Network Inc., to Walter Byers, 27 May 1968, Vol. XLVII, Folder "TV: General 5/68–8/68," Walter Byers Papers, NCAA Headquarters; "1954 NCAA Tournament: Bracket, Scores, Stats, Records," NCAA.com, May 26, 2020, accessed March 14, 2023, https://www.ncaa.com/news/basketball-men/article/2020-05-26/1954-ncaa-tournament-bracket-scores-stats-records; "May Settle TV Plan at NCAA Meet," *Chicago Tribune*, March 17, 1954, p. B3; and Kyle Kensing, "Made-for-TV: The Evolution of March Madness Basketball Broadcasting," Awful Announcing (website), March 14, 2022, accessed March 14, 2022, https://awfulannouncing.com/ncaa/made-for-tv-the-evolution-of-march-madness-and-basketball-broadcasting.html.

26. "MSU vs. Loyola 1963—The Game of Change," *Mississippi State Univ. Scholars Junction*, undated, accessed March 14, 2023, https://scholarsjunction.msstate.edu/ua-msu-loyola-1963/. Primary sources are noted to allow MSU's basketball team to travel North.

27. "UH Stuns Mighty UCLA, 71-69," *Houston Chronicle*, January 21, 1968, Section 6, p. 1.

28. William Hyland, VP Sports Network, to Walter Byers, May 27, 1968, Vol. XLVII, Folder "TV: General 5/68–8/68," Walter Byers Papers, NCAA Headquarters. J. Samuel Walker states that the figure was $150,000 in his "March Went Mad Gradually and Inadvertently," *American Historian*, Organization of American Historians (website), ca. 2016, accessed March 16, 2023, https://www.oah.org/tah/extras/march-went-mad-gradually-and-inadvertently/.

29. Walker, "March Went Mad."

30. "Financial Analysis of National Collegiate Division I Men's Basketball Championship," Box "TV Negotiations, 1983, Folder "TV Negotiations, 1983, Folder "1980–1987 Basketball Television Contracts"; and "TV, Other Sports 1982–1985," Folder "1982–87," all in Walter Byers Papers, NCAA Headquarters.

31. Forest Evashevski to Walter Byers, 5 September 1971, Vol. "CL." Folder "TV: Football, 10/71–12/71," Walter Byers Papers, NCAA Headquarters.

32. Byers to Evashevski, November 3, 1971, Vol. "CL," Folder "TV: Football, 10/71–12/71," Walter Byers Papers, NCAA Headquarters.

33. NCAA Television Committee Minutes, February 7, 1974, Vol. CLIII, Folder "TV: Negotiations Committee, 1974, Walter Byers Papers, NCAA Headquarters.

34. "Report on Basketball Television Questionnaire," April 30, 1974, Box "TV Committee 1972," Folder "TV Committee 1974," Walter Byers Papers, NCAA Headquarters.

35. *Goldfarb v. Virginia State Bar.*

36. NCAA Negotiations Committee for Television Rights of the Division I Basketball Tournament Minutes, January 6, 1979, NCAA Headquarters.

37. *New York Times*, February 26, 1939, p. 10; and Orrin E. Dunlap Jr., *The Future of Television* (New York: Harper & Brothers, 1942), 1, 5.

38. *Daily Pennsylvanian*, October 7, 1940, p. 1.

39. Walter Byers, "Stuhldreher Says Goodbye to Championship," *Daily Iowan*, November 8, 1942, p. 4.

40. Byers, *Unsportsmanlike Conduct*, 85; and "The Original Site of Toots Shor's Restaurant," plaque, Flickr (website), accessed August 18, 2021, https://flickr.com/photos/wallyg/5899801603. Toots Shor was noted for accommodating celebrities such as Joe DiMaggio, Marilyn Monroe, Frank Sinatra, and Howard Cosell.

41. *Daily Worker*, May 5, 1945, quoted in Irwin Silber, *The Story of Lester Rodney, The Communist Who Helped Break the Color Line in American Sports* (Philadelphia: Temple Univ. Press, 2003). The best book on baseball integration is Jules Tygiel's *Baseball's Great Experiment (New York: Oxford Univ. Press, 1983).* He notes that Chandler was a Southern Democrat from Kentucky, a Confederate whose grandfather rode in the cavalry during the Civil War, and offered the closest thing to support for the desegregation of baseball, "endorsement by abstinence" (82).

42. *New York Times*, August 27, 1947, p. 127; "Big Nine Names Walter Byers Publicity Chief," *Chicago Daily Tribune*, August 27, 1947, p. 27; and Smith, *Play-by-Play*, 50–61, 216–17.

43. "Round Table Meetings: Television," NCAA *Proceedings*, January 9, 1948, pp. 118–38, esp. 125, 128.

44. Twenty-five-year-old Byers replaced the first executive secretary of the NCAA in 1947, when Bill Reed took a position as assistant to Senator Homer Ferguson of Michigan. NCAA *Proceedings*, January 10, 1948, p. 181.

45. Ronald A. Smith, "George Gipp, Knute Rockne, and the Post-Mortem Faux Pas," in *Replays, Rivalries, and Rumbles: The Most Iconic Moments in American Sports*, ed. Steven Gietschier (Urbana: Univ. of Illinois Press, 2017), 33–41, esp. 35.

46. E. F. McDonald Jr., Zenith Radio Corporation president, to Albert Chandler, baseball commissioner, September 28, 1950, UVHS, Box 3, Folder "TV-Sept. 1949, # 3, President Hesburgh Papers, Univ. of Notre Dame Archives. Notre Dame officials were receiving documents on the value of TV from a variety of sources.

47. Theodore Hesburgh to Joseph McConnell, president of NBC, April 8, 1950, UVHS, Box 3, Folder "TV-Sept 1949 # 2," President Hesburgh Papers, Univ. of Notre Dame Archives.

48. NCAA *Proceedings*, January 13, 1950, p. 122.

49. Hesburgh to Leslie Arries, April 8, 1950, VIHS, Box 3, Folder "TV-September 1949 # 2," President Hesburgh Papers, Univ. of Notre Dame Archives.

50. Edward Prell, "Byers Airs TV Stand of NCAA," *Chicago Daily Tribune*, April 20, 1951, p. C2.

51. "New N.C.A.A. TV Group to Open Meeting Today," *Chicago Daily Tribune*, February 9, 1952, p. B2; and Jack Falla, *The NCAA: The Voice of College Sports* (Mission, KS: NCAA, 1981), 104. Others on the committee, however, represented big-time schools—Jeff Coleman of Alabama, W. O. Hunter of Southern California, Reaves Peters of the Big Seven Conference, E. L. Romney of the Mountain States conference, and K. L. "Tug" Wilson of the Big Ten.

Chapter 13

1. Four volumes on the early history of college football are Parke H. Davis, *Football the American Intercollegiate Game* (New York: Charles Scribner's Sons, 1911); John S. Watterson, *College Football: History, Spectacle, Controversy* (Baltimore: Johns Hopkins Univ. Press, 2000); Smith, *Sports and Freedom*; and Guy M. Lewis, "The American Intercollegiate Football Spectacle, 1869–1917" (PhD diss., Univ. of Maryland, 1964).

2. L. H. Baker, *Football: Facts and Figures* (New York: Farrar & Rinehart, 1945), 639–43; Davis, *Football*, 69–70; and "Unofficial Major College Football National Championship" in "Report to the Special Committee to Study a Division IA Football Championship," May 9, 1994, pp. B163–77. The 1994 report notes twenty-four possible methods of selecting a national football champion, with twelve existing when the report was issued.

3. Lester, *Stagg's University*, 28–30.

4. Jack F. Sheehan and Louis Honig, *The Games of California and Stanford* (San Francisco: Commercial Publishing Company, 1900), 88.

5. Morgan Owen, "The History of the Tournament of Roses," *Pasadena Weekly*, January 2, 2023, accessed April 21, 2023, https://www.pasadenaweekly.com/news/the-history-of-the-tournament-of-roses/article_2dd5e054-8878-11ed-9f0d-3f3ab7445993.html.

6. William Thomas, San Francisco, telegrams to Harvard president A. Lawrence Lowell, November 19 and 26, 1919, Folder 16, President Lowell Papers, 1919–22, Harvard Univ. Archives.

7. *Cambridge to Pasadena and Return* (1920 report, Cambridge Harvard Varsity Club, 1994), 46.

8. Dr. William H. Barrow, Stanford director of physical education, to Stanford president Ray Lyman Wilbur, August 18, 1922, SC64A, Box 54, Folder 14, President Wilbur Papers, Stanford Univ. Special Collection.

9. President Ray Lyman Wilbur, Stanford, to Glenn S. Warner, Los Angeles, January 28, 1922, SC64A, Box 51, Folder 13; and Wilbur to Dr. W. H. Barrow, Concord, MA, May 27, 1922, Folder 14, both in President Wilbur Papers, Stanford Univ. Special Collection.

10. Smith, *Wounded Lions*, 19.

11. Marc Tracy, "Alabama Win in 1926 Rose Bowl Put Southern Stamp on College Football," *New York Times*, December 27, 2016, accessed May 2, 2023, https://www.nytimes.com/2016/12/27/sports/ncaafootball/alabama-crimson-tide-washington-huskies.html.

12. Suzanne Rau Wolf, *The University of Alabama* (Tuscaloosa: Univ. of Alabama Press, 1983), 148.

13. "Standards of Athletic Eligibility as Endorsed by the National Association of State Universities, November 11, 1935," II, Box 4, Folder "Athletics," President Newcomb Papers, Univ. of Virginia Archives.

14. G. Norlin to Professor Marshall, Univ. of Utah, November 19, 1937, Central Administration, President's Office I-29-1, Univ. of Colorado Archives.

15. William Bingham to President James B. Conant, Harvard, January 6, 1937, Box 2, Folder "Athletic Board of Review," President Conant Papers, 1936–37, Harvard Univ. Archives.

16. "Net Receipts and Bonuses of all Five Rose Bowl Games [1926–1938]," Folder "Athletics—Contracts," Unprocessed Athletic Department Papers, Univ. of Alabama Archives; and Walter J. Greenleaf, *College Salaries, 1936*, Bulletin 1937, No. 9, United States Department of the Interior (Washington, DC: US Government Printing Office, 1937), 5, 23.

17. *Washington Post*, December 9, 1941, p. 26.

18. D. W. Brogan, *The American Character* (New York: A. A. Knopf, 1944), 143.

19. Harvard Athletic Committee Minutes, November 6, 1937, Harvard Univ. Archives. The new president of the Univ. of Minnesota, Justin L. Morrill, was "disappointed that our group [Big Ten] has seen fit to succumb to the bowl craze." *New York Times*, January 8, 1947, p. 30.

20. L. W. St. John, Ohio State athletic director, to Big Ten faculty representatives, August 31, 1940, Box 2, Folder 29, President Franklyn Snyder Papers, Northwestern Univ. Archives.

21. "Big Ten and Coast Agree on Rose Bowl Contract," *New York Times*, June 17, 1951, p. S3.

22. W. B. Owens to Ralph Aigler, Univ. of Michigan faculty representative, October

6, 1938, Box 2, Folder "Western Conference, 38–39," Senate Athletic Committee Chair and Faculty Representatives File, 1907–1968, Univ. of Illinois Archives; and *New York Times*, June 17, 1951, p. S3.

23. L. W. St John to Big Ten faculty representatives, August 31, 1940, Box 2, Folder 29, President Franklyn Snyder Papers, Northwestern Univ. Archives.

24. In 1907, when the will of Anna T. Jeans offered Swarthmore College her estate worth more than the entire college, President Joseph Swain asked twenty-five college presidents if he should accept the endowment, which would only come to Swarthmore if all intercollegiate athletics at Swarthmore were abandoned. President Northrop advised Swain, "Money talks, as it always does, and I for my part would accept it." Swain did not. *The Last Will and Codicils of Anna T. Jeans, Deceased* (Philadelphia: J. B. Lippincott, 1907), 9, in Anna T. Jeanes, 1822–1907 File, Swarthmore College Library; and "Summary of the Opinions of College and University Presidents," *Swarthmore College Bulletin* 5 (December 1907), 10–23.

25. Clayton Sedgwick Cooper, "Concerning Athletics," *Why Go to College* (New York: Century Company, 1912), 32.

26. Byers, *Unsportsmanlike Conduct*, 138.

27. Harvard's twenty-six-year-old football coach in 1905 was paid nearly as much as was the president, Charles W. Eliot, who had presided over Harvard since 1869. Harvard Athletic Committee Minutes, February 17, 1905, Harvard Univ. Archives; and "Athletics," *Harvard Graduates' Magazine* 13 (June 1905), 630–31, 682.

28. NCAA *Proceedings*, January 10, 1961, p. 246.

29. NCAA Television Committee Minutes, June 29–30 and July 1, 1963, and June 9–10, 1964, NCAA Headquarters.

30. Falla, *NCAA*, 197.

31. NCAA Television Committee Minutes, January 9–10, 1966, NCAA Headquarters.

32. Earle Edwards to Walter Byers, November 28, 1966; and Charles Neinas, assistant NCAA executive director, to Walter Byers, December 14, 1966, both in Folder "Football Bowls," Walter Byers Papers, NCAA Headquarters.

33. "Attention: NBC-TV Sales," November 1, 1968, Vol. XLVII, Folder "TV: General 9/68–12/68, Walter Byes Papers, NCAA Headquarters.

34. Walter Byers to Committee for National Collegiate Football Championship, July 21, 1967, Folder "Football Championships Big-Time," Walter Byers Papers, NCAA Headquarters.

35. NCAA Television Committee Minutes, October 11–12, 1967, NCAA Headquarters.

36. NCAA Television Committee Minutes, January 31 and February 1, 1967, NCAA Headquarters.

37. NCAA Television Committee Minutes, March 11–12, 1969, Box "TV: Leg., 1965–68," Walter Byers Papers, NCAA Headquarters.

38. Jesse M. Brill, MTS president, to Walter Byers, March 23, 1971; and "Like Your Seats? TV Quiz Game," *Long Island Press*, January 8, 1971, both in Vol. CL, Folder "TV: Football 7/71–9/71," Walter Byers Papers, NCAA Headquarters.

39. Asa S. Bushnell to James H. Decker, NCAA TV Committee, May 10, 1971, Vol. CL, Folder "TV: Football, 7/71–9/71, Walter Byers Papers, NCAA Headquarters.

40. Roone Arledge to Walter Byers, July 16, 1971, Vol. CL, Folder ""TV: Football, 7/71–9/71," and Charles Neinas memorandum to Walter Byers, October 21, 1971, Folder "TV: Football, 10/71–12/71," both in Walter Byers Papers, NCAA Headquarters.

41. Roone Arledge to Walter Byers, July 21, 1971, Vol. CL, Folder "TV: Football, 7/71–9/71," Walter Byers Papers, NCAA Headquarters.

42. *Washington Post*, January 15, 1975, p. D1.

43. Jim Brock to CEOs, faculty representatives, athletic directors, and football coaches of Division IA, June 19, 1984, Box 218, Folder "Athletics, 1984–85," Chancellors' Central Files, Univ. of Nebraska Archives. Brock noted the previous NCAA playoff proposals of 1971, 1975, and 1979.

44. College Football Association Minutes, June 2–3, 1979, Box 19, Folder "CFA-2," President Davison Papers, Univ. of Georgia Archives.

45. Charles M. Neinas, CFA executive director, memorandum to College Football Association Board of Directors, February 19, 1980, Box 19, Folder "CFA-2," President Davison Papers, Univ. of Georgia Archives.

46. "Byers Reviews Issues in Athletics," *NCAA News* 24, no. 24 (June 10, 1987), 1, 10.

47. Charles M. Neinas to CFA Television Committee, December 5, 1984, Box 218, Folder "Athletics 1984-85," Chancellor's Central Files, Univ. of Nebraska Archives.

48. Bob Devaney to Chancellor Martin A. Massengale, Univ. of Nebraska, Box 218, Folder "Athletics 1984–85," Chancellors' Central Files, Univ. of Nebraska Archives.

49. Gordon S. White Jr., "NCAA Opposes Playoff," *New York Times*, January 9, 1987, p. A23; and Peter Alfano, "The Future Is Now for Fiesta Committee," *New York Times*, January 2, 1987, p. A22.

50. "NCAA Rejects I-A Football Playoffs," *New York Times*, January 13, 1988, p. B11.

51. *Chronicle of Higher Education*, June 14, 1989, p. A32.

52. *Report to the NCAA Special Committee to Study a Division I-A Football Championship* (Overland Park, KS: NCAA, May 6, 1994).

53. *Report to the NCAA Special Committee*, A-11.

54. *Report to the NCAA Special Committee*, A-9.

55. *Report to the NCAA Special Committee*, B-45.

56. Dan Wetzel, Josh Peter, and Jeff Passan, *Death to the BCS* (New York: Gotham Books, 2011), 1.

57. Wetzel, Peter, and Passan, *Death to the BCS*, 96–97, 101–2.

58. Byers, *Unsportsmanlike Conduct*, 359.

Chapter 14

1. Ronald A. Smith to Pamela Friedman, Univ. of Michigan Press, January 28, 1995, in author's possession.

2. Joe Nocera, "Two Adversaries Who Made N.C.A.A. Their Battleground," *New York Times*, December 26, 2015, p. D1.

3. Tim Sullivan, "Analysis—Byers' Book Attacks System He Created," *Seattle Times*, September 24, 1995, accessed March 30, 2023, https://archive.seattletimes.com/archive/?date=19950924&slug=2143227.

4. Rick Telander, "The Tainted Legacy of NCAA President Walter Byers," *Chicago Sun Times*, May 29, 2015, accessed March 28, 2023, https://chicago.suntimes.com/sports/2015/5/29/18597986/the-tainted-legacy-of-ncaa-president-walter-byers.

5. "Faculty Representatives Round Table," NCAA *Proceedings*, January 6, 1954, pp. 267, 176, and January 8, 1953, p. 116; "Enforcement History," *New York Times*, March 23, 1982, p. D26; and Walter Byers to A. B. Moore, Univ. of Alabama, December 16, 1953, "Walter Byers Corres. 1953," Unprocessed Athletic Department Papers, Univ. of Alabama Archives.

6. "Report of the Secretary-Treasurer," NCAA *Proceedings*, January 10, 1948, p. 181.

7. *NCAA Proceedings*, January 13, 1951, p. 241.

8. Edward Press, "Byers Airs TV Stand of NCAA," *Chicago Daily Tribune*, April 26, 1951, p C1.

9. *NCAA Proceedings*, January 13, 1951, p. 235.

10. Falla, *NCAA*, 219.

11. As quoted by William C. Rhoden, "The Vision of a Flawed Leader Still Shapes the N.C.A. A.," *New York Times*, May 31, 2015, p. SP4.

12. "Byers Plans Book About College Sports," *NCAA News* 24, no. 34 (October 5, 1987), 6. Byers told reporter Jack McCallum in the fall of 1986 that he would possibly write a book. McCallum, "In the Kingdom of the Solitary Man." Byers originally was to be assisted in the writing by J. Patrick Wright of Gross Pointe, Michigan, author of John Delorean's biography *On a Clear Day You Can See General Motors* (1979). Instead, Charles Hammer, a newspaper journalist from Kansas City, helped with the writing.

13. Byers complained in 1977 that "the NCAA's success in the courts does not appear to have discouraged further litigation." Byers to Marcus L. Plant, Univ. of Michigan, January 4, 1977, Vol. XIX, Folder "Legal: 1/77–6/77," Walter Byers Papers, NCAA Archives.

14. "Association to Honor Byers at Convention," *NCAA News* 24, no. 36 (October 19, 1987): 1.

15. McCallum, "In the Kingdom of the Solitary Man."

16. Walter Byers, "Opinions Out Loud," *NCAA News* 24, no. 24 (June 10, 1987): 14.

17. Drake Witham and Douglas Lederman, "Walter Byers's About-face," *Chronicle of Higher Education* 42, no. 3 (September 15, 1995): A39.

18. Byers, *Unsportsmanlike Conduct*, 2–3.

19. NCAA *Proceedings*, January 8, 1947, pp. 77–87.

20. *New York Times*, January 9, 1947, p. 30.

21. For a fuller account, see Ronald A. Smith, "National Athletic Scholarship Failure: The Sanity Code," in *The Myth of the Amateur: A History of College Athletic Scholarships* (Austin: Univ. of Texas Press, 2021), 98–108.

22. Byers, *Unsportsmanlike Conduct*, 65.

23. Byers, *Unsportsmanlike Conduct*, 66.

24. I have written an entire book on the amateur myth entitled *The Myth of the Amateur: A History of College Athletic Scholarships.*

25. Byers wrote in 1995 that "Workmen's compensation. . . would make all athletics income vulnerable to income tax." Byers, *Unsportsmanlike Conduct*, 378.

26. Byers, *Unsportsmanlike Conduct*, 75.

27. For a lengthy discussion, see Smith, "Taxation, Workers' Compensation, and the 'Student-Athlete,'" in *Myth of the Amateur*, 147–59.

28. Byers, *Unsportsmanlike Conduct*, 376.

29. NCAA *Proceedings*, January 6, 1957, p. 140.

30. Byers, *Unsportsmanlike Conduct*, 13, 390–91. Endorsing products was promoted in Byers's "Memorandum No. 5" to NCAA officers and division vice presidents, on March 22, 1985. See Byers, *Unsportsmanlike Conduct*, 16n8.

31. Byers, *Unsportsmanlike Conduct*, 390.

32. Byers, *Unsportsmanlike Conduct*, 132.

33. Byers, *Unsportsmanlike Conduct*, 5.

34. Byers explained the process in "Enforcement Under Attack," in *Unsportsmanlike Conduct*, 111–33.

35. Byers, *Unsportsmanlike Conduct*, 118.

36. Byers, *Unsportsmanlike Conduct*, 128.

37. Byers, *Unsportsmanlike Conduct*, 125–28.

38. "Colleges Penalized by N.C.A.A. Raise Protest Against Rulings," *New York Times*, November 15, 1956, p. 46.

39. NCAA *Proceedings*, January 6, 1954, pp. 151, 153.

40. For a lengthy and insightful discussion, see Brian L. Porto, "What Process is Due? The Implications of the *NCAA v. Tarkanian*," in *Supreme Court and the NCAA*, 151–77.

41. Byers, *Unsportsmanlike Conduct*, 210.

42. Byers, *Unsportsmanlike Conduct*, 1, 306–9, 377.

43. Byers, *Unsportsmanlike Conduct*, 133.

44. Walter Byers, "A Personal Viewpoint. . . Football Feudalism," *NCAA News* 6, no. 1 (January 1969), 2.

45. Paul F. Dietzel, AFCA president, to Walter Byers, *NCAA News* 6, no. 2 (February 1969): 2; and Walter Byers, "A Personal Viewpoint: Assault on Amateurism," *NCAA News* 6, no.4 (April 1969), 2.

46. George H. Gangwere to Walter Byers, August 8, 1975, Vol. CLI, Folder "TV: Football, 1975," Walter Byers Papers, NCAA Headquarters.

47. George Gangwere to Walter Byers, January 3, 1979, Vol. CLIII, Folder "TV: Negotiations Committee, 1979," Walter Byers Papers, NCAA Headquarters.

48. Paul Gallico, *Farewell to Sport* (1938; repr., Lincoln: Univ. of Nebraska Press, 2008), 108.

49. Kevin Fox Gotham, *Race, Real Estate, and Uneven Development: The Kansas City Experience, 1900–2010, 2nd ed.* (Albany: State Univ. of New York Press, 2014), 95–123.

50. Carlson, *Making March Madness*, 302.

51. Byers, *Unsportsmanlike Conduct*, 155.

52. As quoted by Joe Nocera in "Two Adversaries who Made the N.C.A.A. Their Battleground," *New York Times*, December 26, 2015, p. D1.

53. Richie T. Thomas, NCAA legal counsel, to Thomas C. Hansen, NCAA assistant executive director, November 8, 1977, Vol. CLII, Folder "TV: Football 7/77–12/77, Walter Byers Papers, NCAA Headquarters.

54. "Response of the National Collegiate Athletic Association Before the Federal Communications Commission," draft submitted to Walter Byers for his approval on October 17, 1975; and Jan West to Philip Brown, Cox, Langford, and Brown, 29 October 1975, both in Vol. CXVIII, Folder "Legal: 1975," Walter Byers Papers, NCAA Headquarters.

55. Robert Lipsyte, "The Latest Craze on Campus: Learning to Do the McNamara," *New York Times*, September 15, 1995, p. B13.

56. Brian Burnes, "Kansas City's Long Road to Women's Suffrage," *Flatland* (website), October 8, 2020, accessed November 21, 2021, https://flatlandkc.org/news-issues/kansas-citys-long-road-to-womens-suffrage/.

57. "Women's Basketball," *Kansapedia*, Kansas Historical Society, accessed April 15, 2023, https://www.kshs.org/kansapedia/women-s-basketball/12243.

58. Mabel Lee, "The Case For and Against Intercollegiate Athletics for Women and the Situation as It Stands Today," *Mind and Body* 30 (November 1923), 255. The opposition continued, and in April 1941 the National Association of Directors of Physical Education for College Women condemned the Ohio State women physical educators for sponsoring a national golf tournament for women. The NADPECW stated, "We consider a national tournament inadvisable [and] do not approve a national [tournament] organized" for varsity competition. As quoted in Virginia Hunt, "Governance of Women's Intercollegiate Athletics: An Historical Perspective" (EdD diss., Univ. of North Carolina at Greensboro, 1976), 19.

59. Ronald A. Smith, "Women's Control of American College Sport: The Good Those Who Played or an Exploitation by Those Who Controlled?" *Sport History Review* 29, no. 1 (May 1998): 103–20.

60. Byers, *Unsportsmanlike Conduct*, 241.

61. Walter Byers to Joel Eaves, Univ. of Georgia athletic director, 1 February 1966, Box "Vol. LI," Folder "Women's Athletics," Walter Byers Papers, NCAA Archives.

62. Byers, *Unsportsmanlike Conduct*, 242.

63. Crowley, *In the Arena*, 196.

64. Walter Byers to Senator John Tower, June 6, 1974, Box "Title IX, 1970–1980," Folder "Correspondence to Member Institutions," Walter Byers Papers, NCAA Archives; Wushanley, *Playing Nice and Losing*, 87; and Crowley, *In the Arena*, 196.

65. Walter Byers to Katherine Ley, October 26, 1967, in Hunt, "Governance of Women's Intercollegiate Athletics," 190.

66. Hunt, "Governance of Women's Intercollegiate Athletics," 193–94.

67. Byers, *Unsportsmanlike Conduct*, 243.

68. *Controversy in Administration of Track and Field Events in the United States: Hearings*, 367.

69. As quoted in McCallum, "In the Kingdom of the Solitary Man."

Epilogue

1. David Pickle, "Working with Byers," *Champion Magazine*, Winter 2009, accessed March 13, 2021, https://www.ncaa.org/static/champion/working-with-byers. Pickle commented that Byers "was demanding, but usually reasonable."

2. A solid case summary of *Bouton v. Byers* is found in Marianne M. Jennings, *Real Estate Law* (Boston: Cengage, 2017), 347–50.

3. *NCAA v. Shawne Alston*; John T. Holden, Marc Edelman, and Michael McCann, "A Short Treatise on College-Athlete Name, Image, and Likeness Rights: How America Regulates College Sports' New Economic Frontier," *Georgia Law Review* 57, no. 1 (November 18, 2022), accessed April 3, 2024, https://digitalcommons.law.uga.edu/glr/vol57/iss1/2/.

4. Smith, *Myth of the Amateur.*

5. Jeffrey Kessler, email to Ronald A. Smith, December 28, 2020; and Ronald A. Smith, emails to Jeffrey L. Kessler, December 28, 2020, December 29, 2020, and December 30, 2020. In my original email to Kessler, I quoted Walter Byers from his address in 1994: "The management of intercollegiate athletics stays in place, committed to an outmoded code of amateurism. . . . I predict that the amateur code now based on a foregone philosophy and held in place for sheer economic purposes will not long stand the test of the law." See Walter Byers, "Overseers, Not Athletes, Reap Benefits," *NCAA News*, June 15, 1994, p. 4.

6. "Brief of Historians *Amici Curiae* Supporting the Respondent," *NCAA v. Shawne Alston.*

7. Jeffrey L. Kessler, email to Ronald A. Smith, July 21, 2021.

8. *O'Bannon v. NCAA; Electronic Arts; and Collegiate Licensing*, Nos. 14-16601, D.C. No. 4:09-cv-03329-cw (US Court of Appeals for the Ninth Circuit).

9. Deposition of Walter Byers, Volume 1, *Jason White et al. v. NCAA*, Case No. CV06-0999, BBG (MANx) (United States District Court, Central District of California, Western Division, July 24, 2007), p. 55.

10. Justice Brett Kavanaugh Concurring, *NCAA v. Shawne Alston.*

11. I have previously written about the failure of amateurism in America in Ronald A. Smith, "Amateur College Sport: An Untenable Concept in a Free and Open Society," in *Sports and Freedom*, 165–74; and "Amateurism Then and Now" in *Myth of the Amateur*, 9–18.

12. Appendix H: Sally Hemings and Her Children, Report of the Research Committee on Thomas Jefferson and Sally Hemings, Thomas Jefferson Foundation, January 2000, Monticello (website), accessed September 4, 2024, https://www.monticello.org/thomas-jefferson/jefferson-slavery/thomas-jefferson-and-sally-hemings-a-brief-account/research-report-on-jefferson-and-hemings/appendix-h-sally-hemings-and-her-children/; "Thomas Jefferson's Education: Alan Taylor on the Trouble Origins of 'Mr. Jefferson's University,'" Interview, November 6, 2019, Library of America (website), accessed April 4, 2024, https://www.loa.org/news-and-views/1566-thomas-jeffersons-education-alan-taylor-on-the-troubled-origins-of-mr-jeffersons-university/; and Alan Taylor, *Thomas Jefferson's Education* (New York: W. W. Norton, 2019).

CHRONOLOGY

August 3, 1852

The first US intercollegiate contest, a Harvard v. Yale crew meet, is contested.

November 30, 1876

The first "national" championship takes place in college football, Yale v. Princeton.

October 9, 1905

President Theodore Roosevelt brings athletic leaders from Harvard, Yale, and Princeton to the White House to attempt to raise football ethics and safety rules.

December 8, 1905

Chancellor Henry MacCracken conference, precursor to the NCAA, is held.

December 28, 1905

The NCAA is created to form new football rules, to uphold amateurism, and to place men's athletics under faculty control.

December 29, 1906

The NCAA Bylaws provide "Home Rule," with each institution or conference to create its own rules to govern athletics.

January 1913

The NCAA Executive Committee discusses "whether it is feasible and advisable to appoint a field secretary for the Association."

October 23, 1920

Intercollegiate Boxing Association is formed with NCAA rules requiring a medical doctor, unlike football, to be in attendance at each meeting.

June 16-17, 1921

The first NCAA-sponsored tournament, track and field, is contested with sixty-two schools at the University of Chicago.

November 27, 1921

Taylorville and Carlinville, Illinois towns, hire Illinois and Notre Dame players and threaten college amateur football.

December 27, 1921

The American Football Coaches Association is created to save amateur college football from professionals.

March 13, 1922

Walter Byers is born in segregated Kansas City, Missouri.

April 19, 1922

The *Federal Baseball Club of Baltimore v. National League* lawsuit is argued that baseball is not commerce under the Sherman Antitrust Act of 1890.

July 29, 1922

Major John Griffith is appointed commissioner of the Big Ten Conference to maintain amateurism.

March 24, 1924

The first Intercollegiate Boxing Tournament is held at Penn State.

April 11–12, 1924

The NCAA swimming championships are first contested at the Naval Academy.

November 22, 1925

Harold "Red" Grange signs with agent, Charles Pyle, to play football with the Chicago Bears, leading to major debate about colleges and amateurism.

March 30–31, 1928

The NCAA first conducts wrestling championships at Iowa State.

December 13, 1935

The Southeastern Conference votes 11–1 to allow full athletic scholarships.

March 11, 1937

The first national championship in basketball is held in Kansas City by the soon-to-be-named National Intercollegiate Basketball Association.

August 6, 1937

The NCAA creates a "College Committee" to serve the small colleges.

February 1938

The New York Metropolitan Basketball Writers Association announces the start of an intercollegiate invitation tourney, National Invitational Tournament.

April 16, 1938
The NCAA holds the first gymnastics championship at the University of Chicago.

Spring 1938
Walter Byers graduates from segregated Westport High School, Kansas City and is an all-city center and linebacker in football.

July 4–9, 1938
The NCAA holds the first tennis championships.

Fall 1938
Walter Byers attends segregated and tuition-free Rice University, but he is considered too small for the football team at 5'9".

November 22, 1938
The NCAA cross country championships are conducted at Michigan State.

March 27, 1939
The first NCAA basketball championship is held at Northwestern University.

June 6, 1939
John Griffith, Big Ten Commissioner, believes the "Conference had outlived its usefulness as a law enforcing agency."

June 24–29, 1939
The NCAA men's golf championship is first conducted.

Fall 1939
Walter Byers transfers to the University of Iowa, majoring in English and minoring in journalism, enlisting in the army before graduation.

December 27, 1939
The NCAA Small College Committee considers a strict code for recruiting and subsidization.

October 5, 1940
The University of Pennsylvania begins regular football telecasts.

December 6, 1940
The Big Ten is told "There is no rule barring women."

March 29, 1941
The first NCAA fencing championship is held at Ohio State.

June 29–30, 1941
Ohio State University hosts the first college women championship, a golf contest.

November 1, 1942
Walter Byers does some staff writing on football for the *Daily Iowan*.

1943
Walter Byers begins working for United Press in St. Louis, Missouri.

March 12, 1944
The first integrated Southern basketball contest is played between John McLendon's Black North Carolina College and the white Duke Medical School.

March 28, 1944
The NCAA basketball tournament nets $26,029 in Madison Square Garden.

June 22, 1944
The GI Bill of Rights becomes law, enabling war veterans to be eligible for college tuition and living expenses challenging NCAA amateurism.

January 9, 1946
The NCAA Executive Committee recommends a new office for "publicity and statistical service."

January 9, 1946
Clarence Houston, an NCAA Council member, notes the importance of the NCAA basketball tourney to the financial stability of the NCAA.

March 5, 1946
Britain's Winston Churchill announces the "Iron Curtin," a Cold War term.

July 22-23, 1946
An NCAA Conference on Conferences drafts principles to govern athletics that led to the 1948 Sanity Code for limited recruitment and payment of athletes.

March 1947
The NCAA basketball tourney grosses $61,000 and the boxing tourney, $9,000.

August 26, 1947
Walter Byers is appointed director of the Big Ten service bureau and executive assistant of the NCAA by Kenneth "Tug" Wilson, NCAA Secretary-Treasurer.

January 9, 1948
An NCAA Round Table discussion takes place regarding the adverse effect television may have on football.

January 10, 1948
The NCAA creates a Constitutional Compliance Committee of three members to ensure that the Sanity Code is being complied with.

January 10, 1948
Walter Byers is praised by NCAA Secretary-Treasurer Tug Wilson.

July 26, 1948
President Truman desegregates the military by Executive Order 9981.

October 10, 1948
Walter Byers, working for NCAA's Tug Wilson, asks if the Small College Committee might have a more detailed position on the NCAA Sanity Code.

July 29, 1949
Walter Byers is involved in Big Ten football highlight films and TV.

1949–1950
Walter Byers's salary as NCAA Executive Assistant is $4,218.

April 1950
Ernest Nemeth is injured in spring football and becomes the first workers' compensation case.

June 15, 1950
Walter Byers, publicity chair for the NCAA baseball tournament in Omaha, is congratulated for making the tourney a financial success.

January 14, 1950
The NCAA lacks a two-thirds vote to expel seven violators of the Sanity Code, effectively killing the Code.

January 14, 1950
The NCAA appoints the first television committee to study the problem of television's negative effect on football gate receipts.

January 13, 1951
The NCAA defeats the Sanity Code 130–60, voting to eliminate national controls on athletic scholarships.

January 13, 1951
The NCAA mandates national TV control and declares a moratorium on live football television for 1951.

August 28, 1951
Walter Byers is chosen as NCAA Executive Director by the NCAA Executive Committee and Council.

October 1, 1951
Walter Byers, age 29, begins as executive director of the NCAA, clearly noted as not a "National Commissioner," with a salary of $11,000.

October 1, 1951
The NCAA budget is $170,000 when Byers is Executive Director and $79 million when he retires in 1987. Membership grows from 381 institutions to 1,003.

ca. 1951
The NCAA is advised not to seek an antitrust exemption for TV policy.

October 15, 1951
NCAA President Hugh Willett declares that Walter Byers is not a "national commissioner," such as the organized baseball's commissioner.

October 20, 1951
A white Oklahoma State lineman breaks the jaw of African American star at Drake, Johnny Bright, causing a major racial incident and ignored by the NCAA.

January 11, 1952

NCAA passes a limited football TV schedule with Byers as an important TV committee member.

January 12, 1952

The NCAA votes "to legislate through bylaws or by resolution . . . any subjects of general concern to the members in the administration of intercollegiate athletics."

March 1952

The National Association of Intercollegiate Basketball becomes the NAIA with the addition of golf, tennis, and track competitions.

March 1952

The NCAA basketball tournament, moving from eight teams to sixteen, brings in over three times as much gate income for the NCAA as the football TV contract.

April 18, 1952

The NCAA Membership Committee creates a "Subcommittee on Infractions," chaired by ex officio Walter Byers.

June 6, 1952

The NCAA signs a $1.14 million TV deal for the 1952 football season with 18 percent of the proceeds going to the NCAA office, not the 60 percent first proposed.

July 1952

The NCAA officially implements an enforcement policy following the failure of the Sanity Code enforcement of 1948.

July 23, 1952

The NCAA office is moved from Chicago to Kansas City.

Summer 1952

The USSR enters the Olympics and becomes a Cold War issue.

September 1, 1952

The inaugural NCAA group insurance plan enrolls 121 member institutions to provide catastrophe medical coverage for athletes.

September 1, 1952

The NCAA Case Report No. 1 by the Subcommittee on Infractions against the University of Kentucky is filed by Walter Byers.

October 14, 1952

The NCAA Council recommends a one-year "death" penalty for the University of Kentucky for paying players and playing ineligible players.

November 14, 1952

The Federal Communications Commission sets aside 242 education TV channels for a proposed 48-state Educational Television Network on coaxial cable.

January 9, 1953

The NCAA votes 122–1 to recommend a boycott of Kentucky basketball and declare Kentucky ineligible for the NCAA basketball tourney.

January 9, 1953

The two-platoon football system is eliminated, but not for long.

February 17, 1953

Walter Byers suggests separate national basketball championships for separate classes of NCAA members to compete with the NAIA.

March 1953

The NCAA basketball tourney net receipts are $160,000 of total NCAA income of $207,000. Football TV receipts are not part of the general budget.

April 1953

The Wilfred Crowley Committee first meets to examine small college concerns.

April 10, 1953

Walter Byers believes it is time to attempt to get Congress to exempt college athletic tickets from federal taxation.

October 9, 1953

Walter Byers notes that taking grants away from students is not consistent with NCAA policy.

January 1954

Louisiana State University AD James Corbett proposes that college football telecast revenues be evenly divided among all NCAA. It is not adopted.

January 7, 1954

The NCAA rewrites its Principle of Amateurism so that "athletic skill for pay in any form does not meet this definition of an amateur."

January 7, 1954

The Big Ten and Pacific Coast Conferences threaten to sign a separate TV contract to have more national and regional appearances. It is defeated.

January 8, 1954

The NCAA creates a small college office of Vice-President-at-Large.

January 9, 1954

The NCAA seeks elimination of the Federal Admission Tax of 20 percent.

February 18, 1954

The 1952 NCAA Subcommittee of the Membership Committee is made a committee on infractions with Walter Byers as chair reporting to the NCAA Council.

March 31, 1954
The Federal Excise Tax on college sports admissions is eliminated.

May 17, 1954
The Supreme Court in *Brown v. Board of Education* votes 9–0 to deny "separate but equal" schools based on race.

January 7, 1955
The mention of the word "athlete" is found four times and "student-athlete" zero times in the NCAA Constitution and Bylaws, but "student-athlete" appears twenty-five times by 1956.

September 24, 1955
The death of Ray Dennison in a Colorado football accident and worker's compensation triggers Walter Byers to come up with the name "student-athlete."

January 10, 1956
The NCAA approves the first College Division basketball championship.

January 10, 1956
The NCAA treasurer reports that the NCAA is reasonably stable financially.

January 10, 1956
Walter Byers notes amateur violations in Nova Scotia League summer baseball.

January 11, 1956
In the first four years Walter Byers is Executive Director, there are seventy-seven investigations of bylaw violations and twenty-five institutions are found guilty.

January 11, 1956
The NCAA votes to allow full athletic scholarships on a national level.

April 29, 1956
Arthur Bergstrom is hired as the first NCAA enforcement officer.

January 11, 1957
The NCAA defines athletic scholarships as four-year grants to include tuition, fees, room, board, and $15 a month for incidentals ("laundry").

January 11, 1957
Government GI Bill grants are used in determining the maximum amount of financial aid athletes may receive.

March 23, 1957
The first NCAA College Division basketball championship is held in Evansville, Indiana.

October 4, 1957
The USSR launches the Sputnik satellite, leading America in a space contest.

June 6, 1958

Walter Byers of the NCAA and Donald Hall of the AAU meet to attempt a coalition to run amateur track and field. It fails.

August 26, 1958

The International Amateur Athletic Federation (IAAF) condemns US college athletic scholarships as not being amateur.

December 28, 1958

The Baltimore Colts defeat the New York Giants in the "Greatest Game Ever Played," symbolizing the rise of pro-football, feared by the NCAA.

January 7, 1959

Rixford Snyder of Stanford University argues before the NCAA that the use of high school GPA and the SAT scores are the best predictors of academic success.

January 8, 1959

The NCAA votes 150–0 to "retain a clear line of demarcation between college athletics and professional sports."

March 1960

The National Association of Basketball Coaches helps form the Basketball Federation of the United States in opposition to the mismanagement of the AAU.

March 14, 1960

ABC wins the football TV contract, outwitting CBS with its low bid.

April 27, 1960

The NCAA withdraws from the NCAA-AAU Articles of Alliance.

January 11, 1961

Admiral Thomas Hamilton's cold war talks about Soviet dominance of the Olympics and the need for women's competitive athletics in colleges.

January 11, 1961

The NCAA abolishes its boxing championship.

April 12, 1961

The USSR's Yuri Gagarin becomes the first person to orbit the earth.

September 30, 1961

Congress passes legislation exempting pro-football from antitrust law but prohibiting pro-football from telecasting on Friday evenings and Saturdays.

December 8, 1961

The Big Ten votes 6–4 to allow full athletic scholarships.

January 13, 1962

Following the creation of a Basketball Federation of the US to bypass the AAU, the NCAA supports federations in basketball, gymnastics, and track and field.

July 24, 1962

The United States Track and Field Federation is formed with NCAA backing.

April 2, 1963

Walter Byers advocates increased appearances for those institutions that have not been on football telecasts.

April 25, 1963

The NCAA Council grants $9,500 to underwrite the cost of a National Institute for Girls' Sport.

May 7, 1963

Walter Byers rules that an athlete deciding not to engage in athletics, "by itself, is not proper grounds for [having] his grant-in-aid removed."

June 26, 1963

Walter Byers asks if an athletic scholarship can be permitted "without contravening the principle of the amateur rule."

December 1963

The first football playoffs begin with the College Division contests.

February 14, 1964

Walter Byers telegraphs fifteen US Senators protesting pro-football's plan to telecast on Friday nights.

March 3, 1964

Rep. Emanuel Celler notes that the NFL has canceled its plans to televise Friday night football games.

April 19, 1964

The NCAA creates a Special Committee on Women's Sports, helping to define the role of the NCAA in women's sports.

July 2, 1964

The Civil Rights Act of 1964 is passed to prevent racial discrimination.

Fall 1964

The NCAA permits unlimited substitutions in football, allowing college football to better compete with the National Football League.

December 21, 1964

The Van Horn workers' compensation case raises questions about employment of athletes and asks institutions to review athletic scholarship wording.

January 9, 1965

Walter Byers opposes increased commercialization of football telecasts, but the TV Committee votes 9–0 to allow two extra minutes of advertising.

January 12, 1965

The NCAA passes the 1.600 grade point average prediction for freshmen to receive an athletic scholarship and be eligible for athletic participation.

January 13, 1965

Walter Byers opposes one-year athletic scholarships.

March 17, 1965

Walter Byers loses in the TV Committee to allow teams that have never been on TV to contract on their own for live Saturday or Thanksgiving Day games.

August 19, 1965

The US Senate holds hearings on the NCAA-AAU dispute over track and field administration.

August 25, 1965

Walter Byers and the NCAA TV Committee vote unanimously to request NBC to turn its cameras away from political demonstrations (such as civil rights).

September 20, 1965

The US Congress establishes Sports Arbitration Board for the AAU-NCAA fight.

January 9, 1966

Roone Arledge of ABC-TV campaigns for an 8-team NCAA football playoff.

January 24, 1966

Walter Byers tells the media that air travel and television changed the role of the NCAA.

March 21, 1966

Walter Byers justifies the 1.600 GPA in a *Sports Illustrated* article.

April 23, 1966

The NCAA establishes the Theodore Roosevelt Award with Dwight Eisenhower receiving the award at the 1967 convention.

June 1966

The Division for Girls' and Women's Sports (DGWS) appoints a Commission on Intercollegiate Sports for Women (CISW and soon to be CIA[Athletics]W).

July 13, 1966

The NCAA decides to hire a full-time investigator, Warren Brown.

Fall 1966

The admittance of Black people on the University of Southwestern Louisiana basketball team leads racist actions against Coach Beryl Shipley and due process questions.

November 2, 1966

Walter Byers calls for a playoff in big-time football as in other sports.

January 1967

A Sports Arbitration Board is appointed by Vice President Hubert Humphrey.

January 11, 1967

The NCAA passes a vote 214–13 to allow athletic scholarships to be taken away if the athlete "voluntarily renders himself ineligible for intercollegiate competition."

January 11, 1967

GI Bill of Rights payments will not be computed in financial aid packages.

April 3, 1967

Walter Byers is concerned that pro-football's four divisions and playoffs in December will overshadow college football telecasts.

June 30, 1967

Walter Byers loses a vote to ban cigarette TV advertising 2–8 by the television committee.

October 11, 1967

The NCAA Television Committee votes unanimously to not place basketball in the football TV contract.

October 24, 1967

The NCAA appoints a committee to study the feasibility of providing for women's intercollegiate athletics.

December 7, 1967

The Commission on Intercollegiate Athletics for Women is officially formed to govern college women's sport and conduct championships.

1968

Walter Byers inherits the Seven Cross Ranch in Pottawatomie County, Kansas.

January 1968

Women's sport leaders ask the NCAA not to be involved in women's programs.

January 8, 1968

The NCAA announces that it is appointing a committee to study the feasibility "for supervision and administration of women's intercollegiate athletics."

January 10, 1968

The NCAA votes 163–160 to allow freshman eligibility for all sports except football and basketball.

September 1968

Walter Byers's first lengthy editorial favors the 1.600 GPA rule that should "assure academic integrity for the races and maintain athletic equality for the races. . . ."

September 1968

Walter Byers opposes a double-standard admissions for "disadvantaged students," while accepting the banning of "separate but equal" from the 1954 Supreme Court decision.

November 1968

Walter Byers argues against Keynes-oriented economists who favor a 2 percent inflation rate as best for economic growth.

November 1968

Walter Byers opposes athletic dorms, for he claims that "separate but equal" went out with the *Brown v. Board of Education* ruling in 1954.

November 7, 1968

Walter Byers states the possibility of prime time *Monday Night Football* by ABC that "a good movie will do better."

January 1969

Walter Byers opposes the "aristocracy of winning coaches, free substitution, and two-platoon football."

January 1969

Walter Byers condemns some football coaches: "College football does not belong exclusively to the coaches."

January 8, 1969

The NCAA passes legislation 167–79 to terminate athletic scholarships for disobeying athletic or institutional policy, probably to stop athlete protests to the Vietnam War or civil rights movement.

February 1969

Paul Dietzel, head of the American Football Coaches Association, chastises Walter Byers for his "unwarranted and flimsy attacks" on football coaches.

March 1969

Walter Byers is honored by the National Association of Basketball Coaches.

March 11, 1969

The Television Committee straw votes 9–2 for a big-time football playoff.

August 12, 1969

Walter Byers writes that "ABC has no real or imagined rights to the playoff games" if a playoff becomes possible.

December 1969

The *NCAA News* condemns "Communist-oriented, revolutionary groups," undermining intercollegiate athletics.

January 14, 1970

The number of football games is increased from 10 to 11.

September 2, 1970

The NCAA TV Committee votes 9–0–2 to allow unrestricted beer ads.

January 13, 1971

Freshman eligibility, except for basketball and football, is approved.

March 12, 1971
A $15 million single-game playoff for a national champion football team is proposed by Management Television System.

July 15, 1971
Walter Byers dismisses the proposal for a Division I football single-game championship.

August 1971
An NCAA Reorganization Committee is appointed. It recommends three Divisions, I, II, and III, and it is opposed by the NCAA Council.

October 12, 1971
Walter Byers, discussing the AIAW-NCAA relationships, states that athletic control must be by institutional membership, not by a professional organization.

November 3, 1971
Walter Byers favors a national basketball TV and football package.

January 7, 1972
Joanne Thorpe of Southern Illinois University speaks to the NCAA opposing the "divine right of the NCAA" to regulate women's sports.

January 8, 1972
The NCAA votes to allow freshman eligibility for football and basketball.

February 20, 1972
Walter Byers advocates reasonable controls on football, limiting financial aid and recruiting restraints.

June 1, 1972
The AIAW becomes the official organization for college women's sports.

June 23, 1972
Title IX of the Education Amendments Act of 1972 passes Congress, banning gender discrimination in federally supported educational programs.

August 23, 1972
Walter Byers recommends to Senator Mike Gravel that the US Olympic Committee be reorganized to control amateur sport, becoming more democratic.

January 11, 1973
The NCAA repeals its 1.600 grade point average for athletic participation, one of Walter Byers "most painful experiences."

January 11, 1973
The NCAA passes, with a show of hands and no debate, a one-year scholarship to replace a four-year scholarship since 1956, legalizing the "freshman tryout."

January 17, 1973
The *Kellmeyer v. NEA* lawsuit allows women's athletic scholarships.

January 25, 1973
The NCAA sets up a Special Committee on Reorganization for restructuring.

March 1, 1973
Walter Byers challenges the AAU-sponsored US basketball tour to Russia.

March 1, 1973
A proposed NCAA basketball TV plan is dropped.

March 15, 1973
The first female to compete against men in an NCAA championship event is Dacia Schileru of Wayne State University in diving.

March 25, 1973
Walter Byers suggests that an antitrust exemption would need to be obtained to ensure the legality of an NCAA regular-season basketball TV package.

August 4, 1973
The NCAA gives the University of Southwestern Louisiana the "death penalty" for violating its amateur rules for recruiting and retention of athletes.

August 6–7, 1973
The NCAA holds its first Special Convention, creating the traditional three Divisions, I, II, and III.

December 26, 1973
Walter Byers incorporates his Seven Cross Ranch near Emmett, Kansas.

March 1, 1974
The NCAA announces that two athletes, without votes, have been placed on an NCAA committee, the first time in sixty-eight years of existence.

August 8, 1974
Walter Byers is advised by counsel that antitrust laws will not likely be used against the NCAA because it is not considered a commercial institution.

October 14, 1974
Walter Byers calls for universities to discourage questionable lawsuits by athletes.

October 26, 1974
Kent Waldrop of Texas Christian is paralyzed in a football game against Alabama. The case is not settled for nearly three decades.

January 1975
The NCAA backs the Senator John Tower amendment to Title IX to eliminate revenue-generating football and basketball from the law.

January 3, 1975
Walter Byers pushes for NCAA to offer championships for women's sports

as the NCAA is vulnerable to legal action if women are not given equal opportunities.

January 14, 1975
Walter Byers endorses a Division I football championship playoff but believes a substantial majority oppose a playoff.

June 7, 1975
The NCAA asks Congress to exempt Title IX from being athletically enforced.

June 16, 1975
Goldfarb v. Virginia State Bar places college athletics in jeopardy relative to future antitrust action.

June 19, 1975
President Gerald Ford creates the President's Commission on Olympic Sports to confront the "declining performance by the U. S. in the Olympic games."

June 29, 1975
Walter Byers asks Ruth Berkey of Occidental College to join the NCAA as its leader for women's sports.

July 21, 1975
An NCAA "letter of inquiry" to the University of Minnesota relative to three basketball players violating amateur rules leads to problems of due process.

August 1975
Don Canham of Michigan opposes President Steven Horn's "Robinhood" plan to divide football television money as "socialism."

September 24, 1975
Walter Byers meets with a joint AIAW-NCAA committee to make recommendations to the NCAA on possible NCAA championships for women.

October 1975
Ron Stratton, NCAA investigator, is charged with misrepresenting himself as a federal agent when investigating Oklahoma State violations in football.

October 6, 1975
Walter Byers cites the US Constitution's 14th Amendment, equal protection, and whether the NCAA eligibility rules apply to both men and women.

October 6, 1975
Walter Byers is reappointed to the important US Track and Field Federation Committee, fighting the AAU control of amateur sport.

October 15, 1975
Seven major conferences and independents discuss reorganizing the NCAA to meet the needs of big-time football and its TV contract. This

group, minus the Big Ten and the Pac-10, becomes the College Football Association on July 6, 1976.

November 21, 1975

The law firm of George Gangwere, NCAA Counsel, gives the legal opinion that the NCAA should legally, under Title IX and the Fourteenth Amendment of equal protection, offer championship opportunities to college women.

1976-1977

The NCAA hires Ken Rappoport to write a book on the history of the NCAA basketball tournament, the NCAA's first history book.

1976-1977

The NCAA receives over twice as much money from its basketball tournament than from its football TV contract.

January 14, 1976

Walter Byers indicates that the NCAA is compelled by Title IX and the 14th Amendment of the US Constitution (equal protection clause) to offer championships for both men and women.

January 15, 1976

Counsels for the NCAA, George Gangwere and Philip Brown, tell the convention that equal protections of the law under the 14th Amendment requires women's and men's athletics to operate under the same policy—Walter Byers's position.

January 15, 1976

NCAA Council believes that the Department of Health, Education, and Welfare overreaches its authority in the application of Title IX to athletics.

January 15, 1976

The NCAA notes that the lawsuits against it are placing a financial burden on the NCAA, even though nearly every case is won by the NCAA.

February 26, 1976

The formal NCAA investigation of Coach Jerry Tarkanian and the University of Nevada, Las Vegas begins.

April 8, 1976

Walter Byers reacts to the Presidents Commission on Olympic Sport with concern that federal intervention in sport may be "a socialistic kind of central board."

April 8, 1976

Walter Byers states that Americans in the Olympics "should play their pros with our pros."

April 19, 1976

Walter Byers is told by NCAA Counsel that it is against the law for the non-profit NCAA to form a political action committee to support political candidates.

April 21, 1976

The CFA drafts criteria for Division I membership.

June 16, 1976

The CFA's first annual meeting is held with sixty institutions.

July 1976

The total NCAA legal fees from September 1, 1971–August 31, 1976, is $1,689,288, reaching an all-time high of $537,442 for 1975–76, mostly trial expense.

July 15, 1976

The NCAA's interpretation of amateurism includes the prohibition of NILs, such as photographs, T-shirts, and playing cards.

September 1976

The NCAA agrees to pay 80 percent of transportation costs to teams and individual medal winners at NCAA championships.

September 14, 1976

The NCAA TV Committee writes to Chuck Neinas, the Big Eight Conference Commissioner, that he should consider resigning from the Committee for trying to influence appearances on TV for the Big Eight.

September 17, 1976

The *Washington Post* announces that the NCAA has won 29 of 30 cases from 1971 through September 1976.

September 27, 1976

The *Hennessey v. NCAA* case finds that limiting the number of coaches, like limiting the number of scholarships, is reasonable under antitrust law.

September 29, 1976

Walter Byers is warned by counsel that the Hennessey case "may serve to encourage other anti-trust cases."

September 29, 1976

NCAA Counsel, George Gangwere, warns Walter Byers that antitrust cases may ensue for the NCAA following the *Goldfarb v. Virginia State Bar* case for tax-free institutions in 1975.

October 22, 1976

The University of Minnesota takes the NCAA to court over three basketball players punished by the NCAA without due process.

November 15, 1976

Walter Byers criticizes athlete property rights found in the *Behagen v. NCAA* case at the University of Minnesota.

November 26, 1976

The Pittsburgh–Penn State Friday night football telecast is protested by the National Federation of High School Sports, similar to opposing Friday night NFL games.

December 20, 1976

The College Football Association is officially formed. The CFA advocates criteria for Division I football membership: stadium for 30,000, average home attendance of 20,000 over past three years, and 70 percent of games with Division I members.

January 11, 1977

All three NCAA Divisions table a motion to divide football into two, Division I and Division IA (exiting the Ivy League) for legislative and competitive purposes.

January 13, 1977

Walter Byers warns the NCAA to reorganize, giving power to big-time institutions, or it "may lead to a strong College Football Association" and NCAA destruction.

January 15, 1977

The NCAA limits BEOG (Pell Grants) to allow no more than the cost of a scholarship. The rest of the money would go to the athletic department.

February 1977

Walter Byers and the NCAA begin a product licensing program to sell T-shirts with Artex Manufacturing Company of Overland Park, Kansas.

February 28, 1977

Tony Smith of the University of Nevada, Las Vegas challenges the NCAA rule that prohibits Pell Grant (BEOG) recipients from receiving their full grants.

March 23, 1977

Kevin Newall and Stanley Whitaker legally challenge the NCAA for prohibiting Pell Grant recipients from receiving their full grants.

May 15, 1977

The NCAA merchandizing policy with CITC Industries in NYC from 1976 proves successful in selling shoes and other goods through Montgomery Wards.

May 19, 1977

The University of Minnesota sues the NCAA for not providing due process to three basketball players before declaring them ineligible.

June 9, 1977

Walter Byers negotiates with ABC's Roone Arledge, sets NCAA apart, and sets precedent for empowering big-time institutions.

September 8, 1977
Jerry Tarkanian sues the NCAA for lack of due process.

September 28, 1977
Walter Byers warns that college athletes "do have a property interest protected by the due process clause."

October 1977
The US Court of Appeals for the Eighth Circuit reverses the District Court's decision and allows three University of Minnesota basketball players to participate.

November 2, 1977
Walter Byers foresees the NCAA being "blind-sided with antitrust charges" in the future, following a planned NCAA basketball TV program.

November 17, 1977
Walter Byers informs the House of Representatives Subcommittee on Oversight and Investigations that the Committee on Infractions does not violate due process.

November 19, 1977
Walter Byers is criticized for opposing the telecasting of Egypt's Anwar Sadat visit to Israel, interrupting the Ohio State-Michigan football game.

December 7, 1977
Larry Gillard of Mississippi State football is made ineligible by paying for clothing at one-third off price.

December 15, 1977
Walter Byers argues that the NCAA did not violate due process in the Jerry Tarkanian case.

January 1978
The influential Carl Reisner *Yale Law Review* article, "Tackling Intercollegiate Athletics: An Antitrust Analysis," is published.

January 9, 1978
Walter Byers states again that the NCAA director and staff exists to "execute policy, not to formulate it."

January 9, 1978
The attempt by the CFA to create a separate Division IA loses 77–74. Division IA is created in the Summer 1978 with 105 schools.

January 23, 1978
Walter Byers charges ABC-TV with bribing institutions in the past to move games for the financial advantage of ABC.

Feb. 27-Oct. 1978
US House of Representatives Hearings are held, questioning the NCAA's enforcement policies relative to Coach Jerry Tarkanian and others.

April 24, 1978
The NCAA survey of Division I, II, and III relative to the NCAA holding championships for women is overwhelmingly defeated 131–40 for Division I.

April 24, 1978
Clemson President Robert Edwards charges the NCAA and Byers with being more interested in football TV and basketball tourney money than the welfare of athletes.

May 25, 1978
Representative John Moss, chair of the House Subcommittee on Oversight and Investigations, charges the NCAA with "intimidating, impeding or punishing any witness who appears before this committee."

May 28, 1978
Walter Byers receives an honorary Doctor of Humanities degree at Springfield College.

June 1, 1978
The NCAA (and Walter Byers) is criticized in Congress for ignoring "due process, is arbitrary and vindictive, and lacks a proper separation of function between its investigative staff and the infractions committee that judges the cases."

July 1978
Walter Byers notes that the NCAA must "limit appearances on TV to restrain TV aristocracy" and "what we do here must stand as a pattern elsewhere."

July 27, 1978
The NCAA notes that the state of Ohio and Warner Cable Corporation withdrew their antitrust television plan lawsuit against the NCAA.

September 15, 1978
Walter Byers rails against the "threat of dependency, red tape, burdensome requirements and unintended side effects" in fighting Title IX enforcement.

September 28, 1978
Walter Byers and others testify before the House Commerce Subcommittee on Oversight and Investigation about NCAA enforcement policy.

November 8, 1978
The passage of the Amateur Sports Act of 1978 essentially destroys the power of the AAU to control amateur sport in America.

November 9, 1978
Walter Byers receives a $75,000 interest-free loan from the NCAA to pay for a home in Mission Hills, Kansas.

January 3, 1979

NCAA Counsel George Gangware advises the NCAA TV Negotiations Committee not to pursue an in-season NCAA basketball TV plan.

January 6, 1979

The NCAA TV Committee abandons a plan to combine basketball tournament and in-season basketball package.

January 8, 1979

President William Davis of the University of New Mexico lectures Walter Byers and the NCAA not to oppose Title IX because it is a lost cause.

January 14, 1979

Walter Byers changes his mind on a football playoff, indicating that there are too many pressures on big-time football.

February 2, 1979

Walter Byers suggests a "limited exemption from the antitrust law" might be successful for pooling the television income of college athletics.

March 1979

The NCAA signs a two-year TV agreement with ESPN.

March 26, 1979

Michigan State with Magic Johnson and Indiana State with Larry Bird meet in the highest ever TV rated NCAA basketball finals—a viewership of 24.1.

July 13, 1979

Walter Byers's intimidation of the University of Nevada, Las Vegas for not firing Coach Jerry Tarkanian is questioned by a US congressional committee and by a member of the NCAA infractions committee.

July 13, 1979

The NCAA and its investigative staff will no longer be supervised by the NCAA Committee on Infractions, a due process decision.

August 15, 1979

The NCAA Council votes that the views held in the *NCAA News* "may not always represent the views of the membership" and should be thus noted.

August 16, 1979

The NCAA Council opposes having athletes represented in NCAA affairs and having student questionnaires on issues.

December 5, 1979

Walter Byers opposes the "sex-dictated quota system" on athletic scholarships of the Title IX HEW policy guidelines.

December 7, 1979

Larry Gillard is ruled NCAA ineligible for purchasing clothing at a one-third discount.

December 1979
The NCAA reports $15 million income, Division I championships accounts for over $8 million, football TV over $2 million, and surplus over $1.1 million.

1980
Walter Byers bad-mouths New Yorkers, telling NBC's Art Watson, "We'll fake these outlanders right out of their boots."

1980
The AIAW begins losing membership as the NCAA championships begin.

January 6, 1980
Walter Byers supports President Carter's withdrawal from the 1980 Moscow Olympics "as a national response to an unacceptable aggression."

January 7–9, 1980
The NCAA establishes women's championships in five sports.

January 9, 1980
Walter Byers states that women playing in the NCAA tournaments must participate under NCAA rules.

January 10, 1980
Walter Byers, who opposed beer sales, justifies TV beer sales by the NCAA in part because "the economics of television dictate some beer usage."

February 15, 1980
Charles Neinas, former NCAA executive, is chosen Executive Director of the CFA at a salary of $65,000.

May 6, 1980
Walter Byers states, "There is room for both the A.I.A.W. and the N.C.A.A., and I personally hope the A.I.A.W. continues to exist."

May 26, 1980
Seaver Peters, Athletic Director at Dartmouth and NCAA leader, recommends a cabinet position for the new coordinator for women's championships.

June 23, 1980
A new organization in opposition to the AIAW, Collegiate Women Athletic Administrators and led by Barbara Hedges of the University of Southern California, is favorable toward NCAA women's championships.

August 8, 1980
Ruth Berkey is announced as the NCAA Director of Women's Championships, coming from Occidental College as athletic director for men's and women's athletics.

August 11, 1980
The Committee on Safeguards and Medical Aspects of Sport recommends the hiring of a director of research and an athletic injury surveillance system.

ca. November 1980

Ruth Berkey, NCAA Coordinator for Women's Championships is opposed to "separate but equal" for women's athletics.

November 5, 1980

The NCAA Council votes unanimously to recommend adoption of the proposed governance plan that includes women's athletics in the NCAA.

December 4, 1980

AIAW President Christine Grant praises the AIAW for giving some "speaking privileges" (not "voting") to women athletes while the NCAA continues to give athletes almost no power within the NCAA.

December 22, 1980

To exacerbate AIAW-NCAA complications, the American Council on Education suggests returning to athlete aid based on financial need.

January 13, 1981

The NCAA women's governance plan is approved, establishing women's athletic championships effective 1981–82.

January 14, 1981

The NCAA elects its first Black president, James Frank of Lincoln University.

January 23, 1981

The AIAW Delegate Assembly votes 280–40 urging the NCAA to postpone any plans to offer women's championships until after a mutually agreed unified governance structure for men's and women's sports is negotiated.

March 20, 1981

Walter Byers walks out of NBC negotiation meeting, accusing NBC of bad faith.

April 30, 1981

Walter Byers refuses to attend an AIAW-NCAA meeting in which AIAW members claim "absolutely, totally committed on a joint, equal basis."

May 13, 1981

The US Supreme Court turns down a challenge to NCAA limits on athletic scholarships and the Pell Grant (EOP) giving athletes more than the NCAA limit.

July 1981

Walter Byers's TV negotiating skills with ABC are clearly shown.

July 6, 1981

Linda Estes, University of New Mexico AD and antagonist to the AIAW leadership, suggests to Walter Byers to not fight Title IX because it would lose some women's support of NCAA's championship efforts for women's sport.

September 2, 1981

Walter Byers proposes that "football television policies should be determined by the institutions that conduct intercollegiate football programs."

September 2, 1981

The Big Eight Conference threatens to leave the NCAA over differing TV contract proposals of the CFA and the NCAA.

September 8, 1981

The University of Oklahoma sues the NCAA, claiming television is an institutional property right, and that the contract violates the Sherman Antitrust Act.

September 25, 1981

Walter Byers states that restructuring NCAA Divisions "is a separate and more important issue than television" control.

September 27, 1981

Walter Byers sees the need to react to Allen Sack's Center for Athletes Rights and Education that will "have to be dealt with in some fashion. . . ."

October 9, 1981

The Association for Intercollegiate Athletics for Women sues the NCAA for antitrust violations in taking over women's athletics.

October 12, 1981

The CFA backs the University of Oklahoma in its antitrust suit against the NCAA by paying legal fees.

November 30, 1981

NCAA legal counsel states that the NCAA "has no obligation to bargain collectively" with athletes.

Fall 1981

The first women's NCAA championships are contested.

December 3–4, 1981

The CFA's demand for a greater share of TV money creates a Special Convention, limiting the number of Division I schools.

December 4, 1981

The CFA call for a Division IV to better control big-time football is defeated at the Special Convention.

December 4, 1981

NCAA leadership prohibits the question of television property rights from being discussed at the Special Convention.

December 4, 1981

The Special Convention places limits on the number of institutions in Division I football, allowing the 61 CFA institutions greater power.

January 9, 1982

Judith R. Hollard, UCLA's Athletic Director for Women and former AIAW president, testifies against the AIAW on holding national championships.

January 12, 1982

Walter Byers praises NCAA national championships for women.

January 13, 1982

The NCAA votes down the property rights proposal that would have prevented the NCAA from penalizing CFA institutions for exercising their property rights.

March 10, 1982

Following successful football TV negotiations, Wiles Hallock, Commissioner of the PAC-10, compliments and calls Walter Byers a "benevolent despot."

April 26, 1982

Walter Byers calls beer and wine TV ads as "economic realities."

May 24, 1982

Walter Byers testifies at the AIAW lawsuit against the NCAA that men and women compete in the same telecasting market based on supply and demand.

June 30, 1982

The Association for Intercollegiate Athletics for Women ceases operations.

September 27, 1982

Walter Byers, concerned about the TV monopoly case, asks if the IRS will tax football TV revenue, and whether union membership and workers' compensation will come available to athletes.

November 18, 1982

A draft resolution by the NCAA seeks an antitrust exemption for its football television plan if it loses its appeal in the CFA lawsuit.

December 3, 1982

The CFA opposes the possible NCAA antitrust exemption from Congress.

January 11, 1983

The NCAA passes Proposition 48 dictating academic standards for freshmen.

January 17, 1983

Walter Byers denies knowledge of racial problems associated with Proposition 48 and its reliance on academic test scores for participation.

January 31, 1983

Big Ten and Pac 10 presidents oppose antitrust exemption for the NCAA TV Policy, something favored by the CFA.

February 21, 1983

The College Football Association charges that Byers and the NCAA are using delay tactics, preventing CFA and Big Ten-Pac 10 TV contract signings.

February 28, 1983

The court in *AIAW v. NCAA* rules that the NCAA is not a monopolist of women's sport and is not involved in "smothering competition."

March 2, 1983

Senator Arlen Spector introduces antitrust legislation to prohibit professional football from signing college athletes with remaining eligibility.

March 10, 1983

Robert Atwell from the American Council on Education reports that an antitrust exemption may have negative effects on other areas of higher education.

March 17, 1983

Edward Garvey, Executive Director of the NFL Players Association, gives congressional testimony that universities should require four-year scholarships.

April 26, 1983

Charles Neinas reports for the CFA that the Big Ten and Pac 10 are opposed to the CFA TV plan and would back the NCAA plan.

June 1, 1983

The signing of Herschel Walker to a United States Football League contract brings action in Congress to prevent signings of active college football players.

October 1983

The American Council on Education's amicus brief to the US Supreme Court favors a rule of reason, not a per se analysis of the NCAA TV antitrust case.

January 11, 1984

The NCAA Presidents Commission, devised to empower presidents, is approved.

February 3, 1984

Walter Byers, following the Rensing workers' compensation case, notes the NCAA is attempting to provide catastrophic injury insurance to protect athletes.

February 28, 1984

The *Grove City v. Bell* decision removes the applicability of Title IX in athletic programs not receiving federal grants.

May 22, 1984

Ruth Bader Ginsburg and two other appeals court judges affirm the 1983 decision rejecting the AIAW's claims of antitrust laws were violated by the NCAA.

June 27, 1984

The US Supreme Court in *NCAA v. University of Oklahoma* votes 7–2 to ban the NCAA's TV football policy as a violation of the Sherman Antitrust Act of 1890.

June 27, 1984

The US Supreme Court, for the first time, rules that amateur sports violate antitrust laws.

July 27, 1984

NCAA members return to Home Rule relative to TV contracts.

July 31, 1984

Justice Bryon White's minority decision indicates that college athletics should uphold amateur principles and has strong future implications.

September 10, 1984

Walter Byers, after losing the football TV case, concedes "it is unrealistic for the colleges to limit benefits to college athletes in a dollar-oriented sports culture."

September 23, 1984

Walter Byers calls for an "Open Division," like the Olympics, for big-time athletics, with money going to athletes who risk their bodies.

October 22, 1984

Walter Byers reveals that 10–15 percent of Division I programs have "deliberate transgressors" of NCAA rules brought by transcontinental travel and television.

October 29, 1984

Walter Byers believes that "presidents are going to have to be part of the effort to save [college sports]."

Winter 1985

James Koch writes a well-reasoned article on the NCAA as a cartel, setting a maximum price paid to athletes and fixing prices for outputs.

January 14, 1985

The NCAA states that each Division I member shall strive "to finance its athletics Program . . . from revenues generated by the program itself."

February 25, 1985

NCAA lawyers propose an antitrust exemption for NCAA TV rights.

February 25, 1985

Walter Byers states, "the tyranny of the lowest common denominator as it affects the competitive balance of major-college football and basketball . . . must be denied."

March 12, 1985

Walter Byers probes ways to seek an antitrust exemption for FB television.

March 13, 1985

Michigan's Don Canhan, friend of Walter Byers, is quoted: "The most discriminated against single group of people I know is the college athlete."

March 21, 1985

After the NCAA football telecasting defeat, Byers writes that the "pyrrhic victory" of the CFA "worked against the financial interests of their clients."

March 22, 1985

Walter Byers advocates allowing athletes to endorse products and have the proceeds placed in the athletes' trust funds.

March 1985

The NCAA's March Madness basketball tourney revenue is over $37 million, creating 75 percent of the NCAA annual budget.

August 14, 1985

The Southern Methodist University payment of players scandal case of 1985 is presented to the NCAA Council.

August 15, 1985

The NCAA notes that 19 of 74 athlete eligibility cases involve the promotion of commercial products, later known as NILs.

September 1, 1985

This is the date a "death" penalty is possible for major violations of NCAA policy.

October 30, 1995

Walter Byers tells Michigan AD Donald Canham he doesn't "understand what we did for football television that was so bad. . . ."

December 9, 1985

Walter Byers says that "it is unjustified" for coaches to receive shoe contracts.

December 18, 1985

Walter Byers denies that the real estate loans to administrators from the NCAA were wrong and that it is done to keep good employees with the NCAA.

1986

Walter Byers is given a four-year contract extension to 1992.

January 13, 1986

The NCAA drug-testing program is approved.

February 3, 1986

Walter Byers believes that it is a "propitious time" to seek an antitrust exemption for telecasting NCAA football.

February 26, 1986

Walter Byers believes that the NCAA Presidents Commission is a great success.

March 7, 1986

NCAA officials are considering another attempt at seeking an antitrust exemption for an NCAA football television plan.

May 23, 1986
Walter Byers does not believe that an "anti-trust exemption would be achieved regardless of who undertook the task."

June 3, 1986
Wilford Bailey, NCAA Secretary-Treasurer, believes that an antitrust exemption "must be our long range goal" but not at the present time.

September 3, 1986
Walter Byers indicates that he will retire in the next two years.

September 13, 1986
Walter Byers opposes additional compensation for athletic scholarships.

September 13, 1986
Walter Byers praises the NCAA Presidents Commission, for "their commitment is firm; the goals they have set are attainable."

October 6, 1986
Walter Byers suggests that an open division, like the Olympics, without amateur rules, be developed in the NCAA to develop world-class athletes.

January 9, 1987
The NCAA Committee on Women's Athletics is created with twelve members, four men, four women, and four unallocated, one woman had to be a varsity letter winner.

June 9, 1987
A search committee member believes the new NCAA Executive Director "will be much more publicly visible than Walter."

June 10, 1987
Walter Byers discusses recruiting: "We cannot live with the proposition that adults make a deal with a youngster, who then has to lie for four or five years to maintain his eligibility."

July 1, 1987
Walter Byers does not believe that financial cuts in minor sports will be unfair to Black people and women.

October 1, 1987
Richard Schultz succeeds Walter Byers as NCAA Executive Director.

October 19, 1987
Walter Byers receives a special NCAA award, allowing for a one-year moratorium on giving its annual Teddy Award.

December 23, 1987
The NCAA challenges the Tarkanian case, stating that the NCAA is not a state actor—eventually losing in the US Supreme Court.

1988
The NCAA establishes the Walter Byers Postgraduate Scholarship Program.

January 6, 1988

It is announced that Walter Byers will receive a special NCAA Service Award.

March 22, 1988

The Civil Rights Restoration Act becomes law over President Reagan's veto, overriding the *Grove City v. Bell* decision of 1984 on Title IX and athletics.

October 24, 1988

The NCAA Council, after eight decades, approves an athlete advisory committee, with no voting rights, to advise NCAA officials on issues such as drug testing, financial aid, and freshman eligibility.

December 12, 1988

The US Supreme Court rules 5–4 that the NCAA is not a state actor and did not violate Coach Tarkanian's due process and therefore could discipline him.

January 8, 1989

The NCAA creates the Student-Athlete Advisory Committee for the first time.

September 27, 1989

The Knight Foundation Commission on Intercollegiate Athletics is formed to help reform college athletics.

November 22, 1989

The NCAA and CBS sign a $1 billion basketball TV agreement for 1991-1997.

February 5, 1990

Notre Dame breaks its contract with the CFA by signing a $38 million contract with NBC for national telecasts.

February 26, 1990

The NCAA new headquarters are in Overland Park, Kansas.

December 20, 1990

Stanford women athletes sue the NCAA for invasion of privacy in requiring drug testing.

December 23, 1990

Walter Byers says the NCAA is weakened by "caving in to the threat of a lawsuit" in negotiating the end of the 13-year Jerry Tarkanian case.

January 2, 1991

Walter Byers does not believe that the NCAA presidential reform convention is one of the most important in the past two or three decades.

January 10, 1991

Judith Sweet of San Diego State is the first woman elected NCAA president.

March 19, 1991

The Knight Foundation Commission on Intercollegiate Athletics issues its report, "One-Plus-Three," on intercollegiate athletic reform.

July 25, 1991

Rep. Tom McMillen introduces the Collegiate Athletics Reform Act that would grant the NCAA post-season competition antitrust exemption. It does not pass.

October 28, 1991

The Rex Lee Special Committee to Review the NCAA Enforcement and Infractions Process gives its recommendations for due process reform.

December 6, 1991

The *Banks v. NCAA* case charges the NCAA for violations of antitrust laws for banning Banks from competition following his failed bid at the NFL draft.

January 10, 1992

The NCAA Council approves recommendations from the Special Committee to review the NCAA Enforcement and Infractions Process.

November 5, 1993

Cedrick Dempsey of the University of Arizona succeeds Richard Schultz as NCAA Executive Director.

June 1, 1994

Walter Byers gives a speech at the Greater Kansas City Sports Commission Awards Banquet and says that the NCAA amateur code will not last legal tests.

June 15, 1994

Walter Byers complains of the "neoplantation mentality that exists . . . in the conference offices and in the NCAA—that the rewards belong to the overseers, and the supervisors and what trickles down after that can go to the athletes."

June 15, 1994

Walter Byers: "I predict that the amateur code now . . . and held in place for sheer economic purposes will not long stand the test of the law."

January 2, 1995

Walter Byers's book, *Unsportsmanlike Conduct: Exploiting College Athletes*, is published by the University of Michigan Press.

January 2, 1995

Walter Byers argues: "Athletes should be entitled to the freedoms of other students . . . work opportunities, . . . transfer, . . . , and use their names . . . for financial gain."

January 2, 1995
Walter Byers states that "losing the 1.600 rule [1973] was one of the most painful experiences in the 22 years I had then served as executive director."

January 2, 1995
Walter Byer proclaims that "Collegiate amateurism is not a moral issue, it is an economic camouflage for monopoly practice."

January 13, 1997
The NCAA approves a new federated governance structure with university president leadership.

July 27, 1999
The NCAA moves into its Indianapolis office.

June 2000
Cedric Dempsey, NCAA President, opposes athletes as employees and a $2,000 stipend, favoring a special assistance fund and the academic enhancement fund.

January 1, 2003
Myles Brand of Indiana University succeeds Cedric Dempsey as NCAA president and becomes the first university president to head the NCAA.

September 14, 2004
Jeremy Bloom, Olympic skier and gold medal winner, testifies before Congress against the NCAA for taking away his right to participate in Colorado football.

March 2005
Ellen Byers Bouton claims, after giving up her law school professorship to help Walter Byers, that he verbally bequeathed his ranch to her to follow his death.

August 3, 2007
Walter Byers, well into his 80s, still believes in amateurism, that scholarships are "pay for play" and opposes a one-year athletic scholarship as a "one-year tryout."

December 14, 2008
An unusual cold spell in Kansas contributes to the Byers's ranch water system freezing, imperiling the livestock, and Ellen Byers Bouton is accused by Walter Byers of allowing this to happen.

September 16, 2009
President Myles Brand dies of cancer, and James Isch is named interim president.

April 27, 2010
Mark Emmert, President of the University of Washington, is named NCAA president, taking over on October 5, 2010.

December 8, 2011

Walter Byers's daughter, Ellen Bouton, files suit against Byers for reneging on his promise to leave property to her for her helping to run Byers's ranch.

March 14, 2014

Walter Byers's lawsuit by his daughter, Ellen, over rights to Byers's ranch is remanded to the District Court by the Court of Appeals in Kansas.

August 18, 2014

Judge Wilken, in the *O'Bannon* case decision to profit athletes from electronic games, uses the Byers's 1955 coined term "student-athlete" 253 times in ninety-nine pages.

May 26, 2015

Walter Byers dies at his ranch near Emmett, Kansas.

May 6, 2016

Beach volleyball becomes the 90th NCAA championship.

March 6, 2019

In *Bouton v. Byers*, Byers's daughter is still claiming legal rights to Walter Byers's ranch, four years after his death.

November 17, 2019

The Byers' Seven Cross Ranch is dissolved as a Kansas for-profit corporation.

March 2020

The NCAA creates a COVID-19 advisory panel, and on March 12, 2020, the men's and women's basketball championships are canceled.

September 18, 2020

Wisconsin Chancellor Rebecca Blank suggests an antitrust exemption to prevent athletes from being paid and becoming university employees.

June 21, 2021

Justice Neil Gorsuch delivers the 9–0 US Supreme Court decision in the *NCAA v. Shawne Alston* case, allowing names, images, and likenesses payments to athletes.

June 30, 2021

The NCAA announces that athletes are free to profit from NIL opportunities, finally agreeing with Walter Byers desires in the 1990s.

January 20, 2022

The NCAA annual convention approves the new NCAA Constitution that includes one non-voting athlete. There is no mention of amateurism.

March 1, 2023

Charlie Baker, Governor of Massachusetts, becomes NCAA president, following the failed administration of Mark Emmert.

May 24, 2024

The NCAA announces that Power Five athletic conferences agree to allow athletes to receive pay directly from universities, about $20 million per year each.

January 20, 2025

The first 12-team national championship in big-time football is contested in Atlanta, Georgia.

INDEX

www.ingramcontent.com/pod-product-compliance
Lightning Source LLC
Chambersburg PA
CBHW071855090426
42811CB00004B/621

* 9 7 8 1 6 2 1 9 0 9 4 9 1 *